Reframing Humans in Information Systems Development

T0189344

Computer Supported Cooperative Work

For other titles published in this series, go to
http://www.springer.com/series/2861

Hannakaisa Isomäki · Samuli Pekkola
Editors

Reframing Humans in Information Systems Development

 Springer

Editors
Hannakaisa Isomäki
University of Jyväskylä
Department of Mathematical Information
Technology
Computer Science Teacher Education
Mattilanniemi 2
40014 Jyväskylä
Finland
hannakaisa.isomaki@jyu.fi

Samuli Pekkola
Tampere University of Technology
Department of Business Information
Management and Logistics
33101 Tampere
Finland
samuli.pekkola@tut.fi

ISBN 978-1-4471-2601-0   ISBN 978-1-84996-347-3 (eBook)
DOI 10.1007/978-1-84996-347-3
Springer London Dordrecht Heidelberg New York

British Library Cataloguing in Publication Data
A catalogue record for this book is available from the British Library

Printed on acid-free paper

Springer is part of Springer Science+Business Media (www.springer.com)

Preface

This book aims to provide a thorough examination of the dimensions of end-users in ISD. The need for a diverse and profound introduction of methods and approaches regarding the users and information systems development was made evident by both the minitrack "End-Users in Information Systems Development: Theories, Applications and Implications" run by the editors in HICSS conferences in 2005 and 2006 and the Information Systems Journal special issue on "User – the great unknown" with Juhani Iivari. It is also obvious that the detached tradition of human-centred ISD creates problems in terms of accurate sources of information when trying to understand the multifaceted nature of the area. At present, it is important to aim for a solid view of human-centred ISD.

This book provides a comprehensive view to different human-centered ISD methods and approaches and will benefit IS researchers, practitioners and students. The representatives of the fields of Human–Computer Interaction (HCI) and Computer Supported Collaborative Work (CSCW) are most likely to be interested in our approach. For this reason, we do not offer only a theoretical handbook or a collection of practical experiences, but both of them as well as some critical discussions of utilization the methods in ISD and their implications with some interconnecting commentary viewpoints. As the title of the book: "Reframing Humans in Information Systems" illustrates, we aim to provide a novel and accurate viewpoint to the understanding of the user in ISD. Our aim is to reframe the phenomenon by connecting scientific constructs produced within information systems science that has recently provided a plethora of multidisciplinary user views without explicitly defining clear constructs that serve the IS field in particular.

We have divided the book in three thematic areas that are interwoven in ISD. First, human systems analysis focuses on understanding the user as human beings instead of utilizing a task- or role-related view. Second, methodology section studies ISD methods and how humans are involved there. Third, we include articles that consider humans as the users of a certain system in the practices of everyday life.

By presenting such variety of viewpoints, we hope to convince the reader of acknowledging and perhaps even understanding the user holistically. This kind of reframing of humans in ISD will be emphasized if and when more user-friendly systems are designed and developed. Therefore, we dedicate this book to the users of future information systems: Hopefully you personally will not have to suffer from incompatible, illogical, unusable, impractical, irritating, stressful, time-consuming, resource-demanding, unsafe, graceless or complicated systems that support your objectives poorly. We have enough of those in current organizations.

Acknowledgements

Editing a book is not just a job for a person or two. First, we would like to thank Springer London for this possibility and their help. Our thanks go to Natasha Harding, Helen Desmond, Rebecca Mowat and Beverley Ford. Second, it has been a pleasure to work with Juhani Iivari on earlier occasions. It has definitely been interesting and educating to cooperate with you. Also big thanks to him and Netta Iivari, and Liam Bannon for their commentary chapters. Fourth, thanks to the reviewers (hopefully we didn't forget anyone): Karen Baker, Liam Bannon, Jeanette Blomberg, Francesca Costabile, Marikka Heikkilä, Jon Hindmarsh, Birgit Krogstie, Rikard Lindgren, Sabine Matook, Preben Holst Mogensen, Bjørn Erik Munkvold, Anja Mursu, Antti Pirhonen, Tero Päivärinta, Tarja Tiainen, Virpi Tuunainen, and Susan Wyche. Finally, we would like to thank our families for endurance with spouses always hands-on on a computer and minds in literary spheres.

Jyväskylä and Tampere, Finland, April 15 2010
Editors

Contents

Chapter 1
Introduction: Reframing Humans and Information Systems

Hannakaisa Isomäki and Samuli Pekkola

1.1 Introduction

Recent development of information and communication technologies (ICT) provides information systems (IS) designers with new potentialities to build systems for various purposes. The ongoing digital convergence refers to and discloses new views on the interactive reconfiguration of technological and social arrangements on a large scale in the contemporary society (Tilson et al. 2009). In addition to work-related activities, people use new technologies for increasingly diverse purposes, for example organizing their domestic affairs, for finding information and e-services, and for staying in touch with their friends and relatives (Lyytinen and Yoo 2002; Sørensen and Yoo 2005; Iivari et al. 2010). Different uses of IS can be classified to range from automation, support and mediation to informing, entertaining, artisticizing and accompanying (Iivari 2007). In addition to these seven "traditional" archetypes of IT applications, the emergence of ubiquitous computing and wearable computers supported by wireless technologies and distributed interfaces facilitates the design of innovative new applications for users. For example the notion of ambient intelligence foresees a future where technologies embed themselves and disappear into the fabrics of everyday life. This shift introduces new possibilities for IS to fulfil more and more everyday functions, and enhance their value and worth to the user. All this development emphasizes user-friendliness, user empowerment and support for human interactions, encompassing a number of dimensions: technical, economical and social (Vuojärvi et al. 2010). All this means that there is a growing need of know-how regarding IS as constructed for mediating and supporting

H. Isomäki (✉)
Department of Mathematical Information Technology, University of Jyväskylä, Jyväskylä
FI-40014, Finland
e-mail: hannakaisa.isomaki@jyu.fi

S. Pekkola
Department of Business Information Management and Logistics, Tampere University
of Technology, Tampere 33101, Finland
e-mail: samuli.pekkola@tut.fi

H. Isomäki and S. Pekkola (eds.), *Reframing Humans in Information*
Systems Development, Computer Supported Cooperative Work 201,
DOI 10.1007/978-1-84996-347-3_1, © Springer-Verlag London Limited 2011

users' needs, purposes, and experiences, as is often the case in approaches known as human-centered information systems development (ISD).

Users, their conceptualization and involvement in ISD has been a topical issue for decades. Traditionally, the perspectives of human-centered ISD are discussed from several different viewpoints: participatory design and other user-oriented approaches consider how end users can participate[1] or be more involved in IS design; ethnomethodological approaches offer tools for capturing requirements and understanding work processes, cognitive engineering aims at the implementation of systems that effectively support adaptive perception-based behavior, while some other scholars aim at understanding IS as social systems, among many other perspectives. These viewpoints have been implemented to advance both user-friendliness and user empowerment in IS during the distinctive activities of ISD (Iivari et al. 2004): (1) mutual alignment of IT artifacts and the organizational and social context in which the artifact is to be used; (2) identifying and specifying the needs of people who are assumed to use the system (user requirements construction); (3) the organizational implementation; and (4) the evaluation/assessment of these artifacts and related changes. User involvement is crucial for successful accomplishment of these activities. Users usually are the best experts on the local work practices to be aligned with and to be supported by an IS. Users also are the final "implementers" of the system, and the evaluation of the system without any attention to authentic user-oriented criteria, such as perceived usefulness, perceived ease of use, perceived usability, and user satisfaction, is seriously limited (Iivari et al. 2010).

Although there have been numerous studies on understanding the user and capturing the requirements, already since the 1960s (Iivari 1991), it is evident that the user largely remains unknown when the studies are examined in detail. In most traditional technology-oriented IS development methods (Avison and Fitzgerald 2002) the user is often seen only as an insubstantial user of a technology, not a social-psychological actor in a particular setting (Isomäki 2002). Even when recognized, the role of the user as a human actor is often reduced to that of a static entity (Lindsay 2003), a source of individual task productivity (Isomäki 2007) or reflecting the IS designers' own images and interests (Woolgar 1991; Akrich 1995). Furthermore, the view of the 'social' is still limited in most IS development methods and approaches. It is seen either as non-interpretive communicative interaction resting on individualistic cognitive models, or as straightforward, joint performance of certain organizational tasks (c.f. Lamb and Kling 2003). Under the circumstances, the users are considered as mere faceless objects for who the systems are designed. This is due to the tenuous connections between IS development methods and user involvement (Iivari and Iivari 2010; Isomäki and Pekkola 2005). This implies an unclear connection between the development methods and means for user involvement. In fact, it is not clear how user involvement should be integrated with systems development but there is a gap between ISD methods and user involvement (Markus and Mao 2004; Pekkola et al. 2006).

---

[1] There is a difference between user participation and user involvement in ISD. User participation often refers to the users' conscious activies in ISD while user involvement may be passive or active (Barki and Hartwick 1994). User participation is consequently one mode of user involvement.

The situation is awkward for IS researchers and practitioners embracing a user-oriented approach in their work as an accurate view on the human-centred issues is missing. Practitioners suffer the situation as appropriate methods are not available. Researchers, on the other hand, aim at bridging the gap but have not been successful so far. Particularly this becomes problematic for IS discipline at large, since without such accurate view the discipline will not evolve effectively, as different approaches never meet. This prohibits both effective development of IS that meet users' needs and the theory development in the field.

Today the need to understand the user comprehensively has increased (Avison and Fitzgerald 2003). This has put demands on increasing the IS designers' awareness and perception of the user in general. This is of utmost importance as the designers' intellectual frameworks, first, determine the operationalisation of human-centeredness within a certain ISD methodology or approach (e.g. Checkland 1981), and second, are of practical relevance in that the designers' views of users are mediated to practice through the use of ISD methodologies, methods, techniques, and tools (Iivari 1991). Consequently in this book, we try to increase both researchers' and practitioners' understanding on the user. For this we will first present a historical review of different features of human-centeredness in ISD in order to set a context for the area and to comprehend the progress to the current situation that necessitates the consolidation of ISD and human–computer interaction (HCI). Second, different approaches to the user are presented in the form of chapters by different authors active in the field. In this way, a holistic picture of the nuances of human-centeredness in systems development and the changes in the interpretation of users during the evolution of various ISD approaches are drawn.

1.2   Nuances of Human-Centeredness in ISD

As depicted above, taking end-users into account in ISD has been pursued by developing different methodologies and approaches for ISD, with the aid of administrative actions and training (Iivari and Iivari 2010; Isomäki and Pekkola 2005; Zhang et al. 2005; Pekkola et al. 2006). Nevertheless, or should we say therefore, the issue is still very important. As the field of users and ISD is dispersed, the there is evidently a need for an accurate picture of how the users should be studied or considered in the ISD, or what should their role be there (Iivari et al. 2010).

In this book we will ask how the awareness on user-centered ISD approaches can be increased. As argued earlier, the requirements for IS designers to understand contemporary users and their needs are increasing in various contexts within contemporary IS research and practice. Correspondingly the trajectories of different ideas concerning ISD approaches are ever-increasingly geared towards a deeper understanding of the human user of computerised IS. To illustrate this, in the following we will present a brief overview of the most significant strategies or ideas aiming at human-centred ISD since the 1950s. Figure 1.1 displays different methodologies and approaches, and the relations of transitions of ideological ideas and perspectives from one to another (Isomäki and Pekkola 2005).

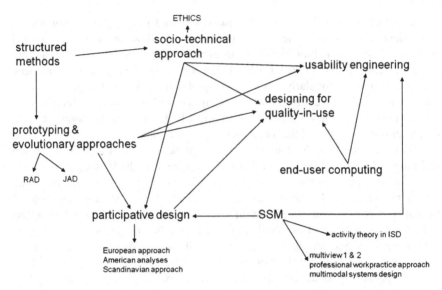

Fig. 1.1 Accommodation and trajectories of different ideas concerning IS development methodologies and approaches

An increased understanding human characteristics and behaviour can thus be seen to influence various contexts within contemporary IS research and practice. We attempt this by distinguishing relations and the transitions of ideological ideas and perspectives between different approaches (Fig. 1.1). For example, participative design approaches often incorporate prototyping or other evolutionary methods. Also, those approaches usually study both social and technical systems from the organisation cultural viewpoint. Correspondingly, the soft systems methodology origins from socio-cultural studies but its ideas on cultural analysis in a certain context have been utilised both in participative design approaches and in usability engineering. However, despite of these shared roots, often only a part of the fundamental philosophical background and paradigms are incorporated. A user oriented method, as any ISD method, is tailored to a context according to the practical needs of its users, as demonstrated by Päivärinta et al. (2010) through an analysis of deployments of an ISD method. This means that individual methods are misused as their epistemological bases are often ignored. The same applies with human-centred methods, as for example, many participatory methods origin themselves from trade-unionist movement in Scandinavia in the 1070s. This background of increasing work place democracy has then been neglected as practical needs to *understand* the user have overridden the brave attempts to *increase his or her abilities to influence the work practices.*

The comparison between our approach Iivari et al. framework of ISD methods (Iivari et al. 2001) depicts a typical ISD methodology approach; usually the methods do not explicitly focus on humans but technologies instead (see also Iivari and Iivari 2010). If the methods focus on the user, the approach is commonly managerial or organisational, i.e. the user is seen as a target subject that is going to use the system as specified by managers or designers. Similar kinds of biased approaches to user have been recognized elsewhere. Koskinen et al. (2005) found out that the majority of articles in an IS forum focus on users as the users of an application only. Understanding the user in a context or a culture, their interaction, and their communication are not of anybody's interest. Often IS designers are intellectually more oriented towards designing IS for objectified, streamlined organisational processes consisting of external work tasks set by management rather than concentrating on human-centred design issues (Isomäki 2007; Gross and Pekkola 2010, in this book). However, as already the early studies on CSCW point out, this is a completely insufficient approach – users always find out different ways to (mis) use the system in another way than specified in the design (Pekkola 2003; Robinson 1993; Schmidt and Bannon 1992). On a way to IS designers' increased awareness on the user and his or her behaviour in a certain context for which the system is designed, it is important to explicitly list out the approaches and their position towards the user. Iivari and Iivari (2010) summarised the generic perceptions on the user in ISD as user focus, work-centeredness, user participation, and system personalization. However, they did not portray these dimensions in contrast to different methods. We take a more detailed approach and try to accomplish this in Table 1.1.

Nowadays the evolution of ISD methodologies has geared towards human-centredness, as asked by Avison and Fitzgerald (2003). Yet it is still common that the user-oriented methods are not connected with ISD processes. The methods increase designers' understanding about the user, but they do not implicitly and unambiguously provide guidelines to combine that information with the systems development process (c.f. Pekkola et al. 2006; Zhang et al 2005; Iivari and Iivari 2010). Why it is so? Following the structuration theoretical approach to conceptualise ISD discipline (Päivärinta and Pekkola 2003), we argue there is a lack of information exchange between the communities studying the workplaces and attempting to make design suggestions for the systems designers and the community developing ISD methods. Socially oriented human-centred methods, that are common in the former community, are not known well enough by the latter community – and vice versa; technical process-oriented ISD methods are not know or practically acknowledged by the former community, that is a community focusing on human computer interaction (HCI). This separation of different communities is actually evident also within the HCI discipline: there are at least three communities (cognitive psychology-origins, social-psychology origin, and organisational science origins) each having their own paradigms, questions of interest and publication forums (Grudin 2006). Thus, we argue that in order to build adequate user-friendly information systems, it is essential not only to understand the technology development, of which is usually not a problem for an ISD expert, but also to understand the human-being intended to use the system, which, respectively if usually not a problem for a HCI expert. This means that we have to step outside our conventional comfort zones, and try to understand the multifaceted nature of humans in information systems development context.

Table 1.1 User-centeredness in different ISD approaches

User view—Methodology	User perception in ISD process	User role in organisation information processing	Behavioural features in ISD
Structured methods	User is consulted only about the inputs and outputs of the system.	An 'object' whose task is to be supported.	Not considered
Prototyping and evolutionary approaches	An evaluator of the design decisions.	Task is considered through professional role in the organisation.	User performs certain tasks.
The socio-technical approach	ISD process is divided into two separate systems, social and technical, that are supposed to be integrated (only) at the end.	The needs for organisational information processing are considered comprehensively consisting of both individual and organisational points of views.	In principle, the user is considered as a psychological, emotional and social actor. However, the human-centred issues might be overlooked.
Soft systems methodology	ISD process as a whole is disregarded. SSM emphasises only the early (analysis) phase of the development.	Organisational performance is dealt through social norms and power relations.	User is considered as a social, cultural and political actor.
End-user computing	ISD process as a whole is disregarded. EUC focuses on the utilisation of the system.	Organisational issues are omitted, individual users' preferences are emphasised.	User is regarded as a computer expert.
Participative design	The connection between ISD process and PD methodologies is weak.	Scandinavian approach attempts to combine user's information utilisation to organisational objectives. In European and American approaches, user role is weaker and only consultative.	User is domain expert that performs certain task.
Users in agile development	Close customer-designer cooperation is seen essential.	The needs for organisational information processing are considered from individual points of views.	User is seen as a narrative and collaborating actor.
Human–computer interaction in ISD	Process models are many, but their use in practice is questionable.	Individual users are emphasised in terms of their own information processing functions.	User is seen as a cognitive and collaborating actor. New concept of user experience still open.

1.3 Reframing Humans in Information Systems Development

The tradition of human-centered ISD incorporates numerous different methods and approaches with varying perceptions of users. The evolution leading to this situation parallels with the earlier evolution of telephone. In the words of Grudin (2006):

> Management of telephony (like computing) in a large organization involved planning, acquisition, policy, and personnel decisions. Telephone (computer) operators were nondiscretionary, hands-on users. Ergonomic effort was devoted to reducing the time spent handling calls (computer operation). Some callers (computer users), in contrast, were initially discretionary users who had alternative channels for communication (work). Managers delegated calls (computer use) to secretaries. (Grudin 2006, p. 418)

This long quote illustrates multifaceted uses of telephone and computer. It also highlights the diversity of the users and of their tasks. The significant observation here is the distinction between discretionary and mandatory uses. The evolution of technology (telephone or computer) evidently changes the practices, policies, planning, and decision making – and the stakeholders involved. Consequently it is understandable, although not necessarily acceptable, that each developer group focuses on their own area: management on issues that improve management or profitability, technology developers on technological issues, and users on the use related items. Yet in practice, as it is now known, the areas are tightly interwoven. In other words, the development of user-friendly systems (telephone) was diverted to multiple directions.

In order to divert and delineate this kind of fragmented field, a solid view and understanding of essential features in contemporary ISD is needed. Consequently we propose an approach that reduces the detached viewpoints by concentrating on the essence of the current human-centred ISD: human system analysis, methodologies and practices. These views are evident when the ISD is subdivided into its components. First, in order to understand the users and the use situation comprehensively, human system analysis needs to be performed. Second, to construct or develop appropriate technical systems, specified or drafted through human systems analysis, some kind of ISD methodology, no matter whether used wilfully or purposefully is needed. Third, following the old argument by Nurminen and Forsman (1994) that ISD begins only after the system is introduced into the organisation, some kind of post-implementation evaluation is needed. This can be done to learn from past mistakes, to reveal new requirements for the next version, or simply to assist the systems introduction. In other words, practices are on focus.

By dividing this book into three distinct but closely connected views we aim at avoiding the pitfalls of separating IS into separate systems. This has been seen as the weakness of the socio-technical approach for instance. If the social part of the whole system is detached, the system becomes solely technical. Accordingly, the pitfall in the use of human-centred ISD methods (i.e. ETHICS) is that the technical design objectives are the primary concern and the social objectives are neglected (Nurminen 1988). Also Ehn and Löwgren (1997) criticised the early socio-technical approach for not being truly participative or democratic, but being managerialist. Pain et al. (1993) argued that the early approaches take too simplistic a view of job satisfaction, skill and the impact of technology. Despite these criticisms, socio-technical approach is still significant in relation to the humanisation of IS as it addresses IS as social systems and makes a serious attempt to offer means for building bonds between the social and technical aspects. Under the circumstances, the socio-technical approach broadened IS research and practice intellectually and gave rise to new delineations where information systems are perceived as technical systems with social implications, or oppositely, IS are social systems but which are only technically implemented (Hirschheim et al. 1995).

Consequently our thematic division to three views of contemporary ISD forms a structure for this book. By so doing we hope it is possible to concentrate on the focal areas of ISD that aims to provide users IS that they prefer to use, developing the theory of human-centred ISD, and increasing general awareness of the multi-faceted perspectives that need to be combined.

The contents of the book are structured around three distinct but intertwining ISD themes which incorporate papers which disclose necessary views on understanding the 'object system' of ISD in terms of human activity, methodology and practice.

1.3.1   Human System Analysis

The human-centred ISD process has yielded a move from an exclusively rationalistic and objective perspective to the inclusion of interpretive social and subjective aspects, with the emphasis on the process factors of ISD (Smith 1997). For instance extreme programming and agile methods have lately become popular in order to avoid different kinds of mistakes and problems, including the lack of user involvement (Abrahamsson 2001). To increase user involvement, the utilization of design-by-doing approach, where mock-ups and prototypes are applied and developed has been quite common as traditional, formal systems development techniques are found to be too abstract (e.g., Pain et al. 1993). They are thus perceived as inappropriate tools for communication between IS experts and users. However, the conceptualizations of end-users, their representatives, or their representations within the process of ISD vary a lot. Nowadays ISD methods often concentrate on investigating users through user profiles, generalized human factors, or fictive users (c.f. Iivari and Iivari 2010). However, in developing human-centered IS it is necessary to conceptualize users also in terms of their inherent and learned human qualities. This means that users need to be understood in terms of the nature of the human beings instead of utilizing task- or role-related view. That is to say, humans should be conceptualised according to the fundamental constituents of people rather than in terms of different instrumental tasks and purposes which people accomplish with the aid of IS. Abovementioned issues are discussed in the following papers.

Heba El-Sayed, Anita Greenhill and Chris Westrup discuss a transition from the traditional distinctions of IS developer/user or technology/user towards investigation of how technologies become significant in social life in their article *"On the emergence of techno-religious spaces"*. In particular, they show how attempts to regulate social activity through technologies appear to remain incomplete aspirations. Their case does not fit to the ordinary work or leisure but focus on how technologies are being used to mediate religious practices for Muslims. This illustration discloses how technologies are being adopted and adapted in daily practice where users and technologies mingle agency in often unexpected ways.

A holistic view is pursued by Andrew Basden in his paper *"Towards lifeworld-oriented information systems development"*. He argues that many methodologies and academic discussions of ISD take often an approach that focuses on certain aspects of human users while overlooking the others, and that a more lifeworld-oriented approach would be beneficial. In his model, the lifeworld of the IS developer is revealed as four interwoven multi-aspectual human activities those help distinguish diverse issues while retaining a holistic perspective on humans in ISD.

In paper *"A power perspective for understanding the business client – systems developer relationship"* Bruce Rowlands takes a more traditional view in discussing the social relations between developers and business clients in terms of influence of ISD methods. His findings are distinctive in that they illustrate how the business client or the user is able to exercise power over systems developers through the enactment of organizational structures and routine operating procedures embedded within an ISD method.

The social view of users is complemented by a HCI-oriented paper *"A semiotic analysis of interactions between end users and information systems"* by Sheng-Cheng Huang and Randolph G. Bias. They propose a conceptual model of human–computer interaction. The model is based on a semiotic triangle which analyses three key issues in ISD, namely the representational issue, the user diversity issue and the usability feedback issue. This semiotic model is enriched by a discussion of a neuroergonomic approach of usability.

Results from an empirical study investigating IS designers' perceptions of users during the process of ISD is illustrated in paper *Information Systems Development as an Intellectual Process: Designers' Perceptions of Users* by Hannakaisa Isomäki. Contrary to the prevailing methodology centered approach, this study regards ISD as knowledge work. ISD is an intellectual and personal process which takes its form and consequences by the conceptions of the actors of the process. The results show that IS designers' perceptions of users are versatile. They associate humanlike cognitive characteristics with technology, recognise forms of learning, and give credit to emotional coping.

1.3.2 Methodology

The emphasis on work situations has been brought forward in different ISD methodologies that often draw on ethnography. For instance, end-users may be perceived through practice-oriented application of ethnography where the users are studied as members of a professional culture. This approach aims at extracting the actions, goals of actions and the values that animate them from a 'stream of behaviour', which is seen as interconnected acts within a task. By iteratively sampling the end-users' actions and confirming their interpretations with the future users, a model of the situation is built for the subsequent design of the IS. The advantage on ethnography is that it facilitates the capturing of tacit knowledge inherited in human activity. However, the ethnography-based approaches are often criticized for micromanagement of the research and development situation, and detachment from the whole (organisational) information system – especially within large corporations. Consequently it becomes important for novel approaches to specify how to conceptualize and represent work, and how to introduce change in work as a part of ISD. This would take the focus away from sheer work processes and work flows which underemphasise the role of users. In this section novel and innovative views of methodologies in ISD are discussed in terms of user involvement.

In their paper *"Participatory design in information systems development"*, Keld Bødker, Finn Kensing and Jesper Simonsen provide new ideas on participatory design. They introduce concepts from architecture and insist on genuine participation of humans. Their ISD domain is the traditional work context with complex organizational structure, diverse professional groups and workplace cultures, and established ways of working that are challenged by new IS projects. The authors develop a new ISD method referred to as MUST which incorporates principles for genuine user participation and a coherent view for change. In order to take the method in practice, they also discuss issues about bringing it to IS practitioners.

A transition towards a theoretical discussion is offered by Dirk Hovorka and Matt Germonprez. Their paper *"Reflecting, tinkering and tailoring: Implications for theories of information systems design"* challenges the current structural specifications and guidelines for design theory and claim they fall short of creating theories that account for the end-users' reflections, tinkering and subsequent tailoring of IS in a process of so-called secondary design conducted by the users. The authors offer a view on the issues of "unexpected consequences" of IS usage.

The role of end-user is maintained in Anders I Mørch's paper "Evolutionary application development: Tools to make tools and boundary crossing." He argues that end-user development is about empowering users to develop computer applications in order to better democratize the design process of professional IS development. He also states that end-user developers create new applications from high-level building blocks and adapt existing applications to new needs.

Juhani Iivari and Netta Iivari's article "Design Science Research for User-Centeredness" analyses three aforementioned articles and provides some reflections of how those issues are seen from information systems tradition. They first use their framework (see Iivari and Iivari 2010) to examine user-centredness. Second similar analysis from the design science research perspective is performed. In their conclusions Iivari and Iivari provide justifiable criticism of each article. Yet the criticism origins from a certain ISD tradition while the papers represent other traditions. Consequently this should be seen as sabre-rattling between different communities, which, however, provides eye-opening views to the same topic.

Similarly, Liam Bannon, in his article "20 years a-growing": Revisiting From Human Factors to Human Actors", examines the same papers. While Iivari and Iivari are critical, Bannon's approach is more supportive revealing a human activity-centred view of computing. Technology is seen both as a tool and a medium. Bannon's approach focuses on understanding human activity, in all its guises, in order to provide useful and pertinent observations on human action in the world. In this approach the user perspective is highlighted by examining how they accomplish their goals. While technology may play an important role in these human activities, often the use of the technology is as an intrinsic mediating influencing instead of being the goal of the activity.

1.3.3   Practice

The nature of co-operation between the users and developers is often seen as crucial. User participation should be authentic and full, aiming at enhancing workplace skills rather than degrading or rationalizing them. Also, IS are often studied and designed from an organizational viewpoint – how they support organizational activities and processes – rather than how they support individual users' preferences and actions. This undermines, even ignores individual perspectives which can be seen through examples of monitoring or prohibiting web browsing or email for personal issues at work. However, IS are not used by organizations but individuals acting in organizations. End users are doing their job, and using information systems for their tasks. IS should be therefore designed and developed also from individual viewpoints, not only from the organizational needs. In this section different views of perceiving end-users within the process of ISD are depicted in terms of both indirect and surrogate representation as well as direct involvement. The viewpoints in these papers offer also insights to ISD practice.

Tom Gross and Samuli Pekkola in their paper "*Three levels of failure: Analysing a workflow management system*" report on a case study of the introduction of a workflow management for travel management in a higher education organisation. They identify and reflect on issues concerning the changes of the processes induced by the system, concerning the functionality of the specific system used, and concerning the usability of the system used. These issues, when combined with socio-technical perspective, provide an easily usable checklist for systems designers. The case study also points out a need for holistic view that goes beyond separate scientific communities when developing systems for organisational settings by proposing several issues for future research.

In her paper "*When and how do we become a 'user'?*" Katarina Lindblad-Gidlund also aims at making both theoretical and practical contributions to ISD. She analyses different design positions from the viewpoints of users and of other people involved in ISD by drawing on Feenberg's notions of dominant and subordinate subject positions. This way her analysis gives a detailed view of one of the most dehumanising pitfalls of ISD – the process of instrumentalisation that often occurs during systems design.

Bo Andersson and Stefan Henningsson deal with the questions arising from the proposition that mobile IS use has distinctive characteristics compared to traditional IS use. Their paper, titled as *"Use of mobile IS: new requirements for the IS development process"* aims to develop a framework for capturing aspects of mobile IS use during the phases of analysis and design in ISD.

In their paper *"Reframing online shopping through innovative and organic user-oriented design"* Anita Greenhill and Gordon Fletcher analyse the design of online shops. Their examples consist of careful in-depth socio-cultural analysis of Web2.0 based online shopping sites referred to as blogshops. They frame design ideas to IS designers in terms of contemporary polymorphic and interactive design practices that yield the structure, form and functionality of blogshop applications that contribute to utilisation of blogging systems in a way that extends users personal and financial capacity to obtain goods.

Finally, Hilary Berger in her paper *"User involvement and team working in system development practice"* approaches the issue of user involvement in agile development with a specific team culture. Her paper is full of insights based on both theoretical view and practical experience of how the inherent social nature of an organization adversely affected by the key characteristics of the agile approach utilised in a bureaucratic environment.

Altogether, these papers provide analyses, methods and practices on human-centred IS and their design. These contributions offer new views that not only challenge but also develop the traditional notions of human-centred ISD. The ideas are interesting, inspiring and offer means to involve users to the development of new IS. We hope that you will both find useful and enjoy the reframing presented in this book.

References

Abrahamsson, P. 2001. Rethinking the concept of commitment in software process improvement. *Scandinavian journal of Information Systems*, 13, 69–98.

Akrich, M. 1995. User representations: Practices, methods and sociology. In Rip, A., Misa, T.J. and Schot, J. (Eds.) *Managing technology in society. The approach of constructive technology assessment*. London: Pinter Publishers, 167–184.

Avison, D. & Fitzgerald, G. 2002. *Information systems development: Methodologies, techniques and tools*, Second Edition, London: McGraw Hill.

Avison, D. & Fitzgerald, G. 2003. Where now for development methodologies? *Communications of the ACM*, 46, 78–82.

Barki, H. & Hartwick, J. 1994. Measuring user participation, user involvement, and user attitude. *MIS Quarterly*, 18(1), pp. 59–82.

Checkland, P. 1981. *Systems thinking, systems practice*. Chichester: Wiley.

Ehn, P. & Löwgren, J. 1997. Design for quality-in-use: Human–computer interaction meets information systems development. In: Helander, M., Landauer, T.K. and P. Prabhu (Eds.) *Handbook of human–computer interaction*. Amsterdam: Elsevier, 299–313.

Gross, T. & Pekkola, S. 2010. Three levels of failure: Analysing a workflow management system. In *this book*, chapter 12.

Grudin, J. 2006. Human factors, CHI, and MIS. In: P. Zhang and D. Galletta (Eds.) *Human–computer interaction and management information systems: Foundations*. New York: M.E. Sharpe, 402–421.

Hirschheim, R., Klein, H.K. & Lyytinen, K. 1995. *Information systems development and data modeling. Conceptual and philosophical foundations.* Cambridge: Cambridge University Press.

Iivari, J. 1991. A Paradigmatic analysis of contemporary schools of IS development. *European Journal of Information Systems,* 1(4), 249–272.

Iivari, J. 2007. Paradigmatic analysis of information systems as a design science. *Scandinavian Journal of Information Systems,* 19, 39–63.

Iivari, J., Hirschheim, R. & H.K. Klein. 2001. A dynamic framework for classifying information systems development methodologies and approaches. *Journal of Management Information Systems,* 17(3), pp. 179–218.

Iivari, J., Hirschheim, R.A. & Klein, H.K. 2004. Towards a distinctive body of knowledge for information systems experts: Coding ISD process knowledge in two IS journals. *Information Systems Journal,* 14, 313–342.

Iivari, J. & Iivari, N. 2010. Varieties of user-centredness: an analysis of four systems development methods. *Information Systems Journal* (forthcoming).

Iivari, J., Isomäki, H. & Pekkola, S. 2010. The user – the great unknown of systems development: Reasons, forms, challenges, experiences and intellectual contributions of user involvement. *Information Systems Journal,* 20(2), 109–117.

Isomäki, H. & Pekkola. S. 2005. Nuances of human-centredness in information systems development. *Hawaii International Conference on System Sciences HICSS-38.* Big Island, Hawaii: IEEE Press.

Isomäki, H. 2002. *The prevailing conceptions of the human being in information systems development: Systems designers' reflections.* Computer Science Department, University of Tampere, Finland, Ph.D. Thesis, June 2002.

Isomäki, H. 2007. Different levels of information systems designers' forms of thought and potential for human-centred design. *International Journal of Technology Human Interaction,* 31, 30–48.

Koskinen, M., Liimatainen, K. & Pekkola, S. 2005. Human orientation in Scandinavian IS research as it appears in SJIS. In: Hustad, E., Munkvold, B.E., Rolland, K. and Flak, L.S. (Eds.) *Proceedings of the 28th Information Systems Research Seminar in Scandinavia (IRIS'28).* Kristiansand, Norway August 6–9 2005. Agder University College, Department of Information Systems, CD-ROM.

Lamb, R. & Kling. R. 2003. Reconceptualizing users as social actors in information systems research. *MIS Quarterly,* 27(2), 197–229.

Lindsay, C. 2003. From the shadows: Users as designers, producers, marketers, distributors, and technical support. In: Oudshoorn, N. and Pinch, T. (Eds.) *How users matter: The co-construction of users and technology.* Cambridge, MA: MIT Press.

Lyytinen, K. & Yoo, Y. 2002. Issues and challenges in Ubiquitous computing. *Communications of the ACM,* 45 (12), 63–65.

Markus, M.L. & Mao, J.-Y. 2004. Participation in development and implementation – updating an old, tired concept for today's IS contexts. *Journal of the Association for Information Systems,* 5, 11–12, 514–544.

Nurminen, M. I. & Forsman, U. 1994. Reversed quality life cycle model. In: Bradley, G.E. and Hendrick H.W. (Eds.) *Human factors in organizational design and management IV.* Amsterdam: Elsevier, 393–398.

Nurminen, M.I. 1988. *People or computers: Three ways of looking at information systems.* Lund: Studentlitteratur.

Pain, D., Owen, J., Franklin, I. & Green, E. 1993. Human-centred systems design: A review of trends within the broader systems development context. In: Green, E., Owen, J. and Pain, D. (Eds.) *Gendered by design? Information technology and office systems.* London: Taylor & Francis.

Päivärinta, T. & Pekkola, S. 2003. Structurational approach to studying research and practice of information systems development. In: *The JAIS sponsored theory development workshop* (after ICIS 2003). Seattle, WA, USA, December 14–17, 2003.

Päivärinta, T., Sein, M.K. & Peltola, T. 2010. From ideals towards practice: Paradigmatic mismatches and drifts in method deployment. *Information Systems Journal*, 20(5), 481–516.

Pekkola, S. 2003. Designed for unanticipated use: Common artefacts as design principle for CSCW applications. In: Pendergast, M., Schmidt, K., Simone, C. and Tremaine M. (Eds.) *Proceedings of the 2003 International ACM SIGGROUP Conference on Supporting Group Work (GROUP'03)*. Sanibel Island, FL: ACM Press, November 9–12, 2003, pp. 359–368.

Pekkola, S., Kaarilahti, N. & Pohjola P. 2006. Towards formalised end-user participation in information systems development process: Bridging the gap between participatory design and ISD methodologies. In: *2006 Participatory Design Conference (PDC 2006)*. Trento, Italy: ACM Press, August 1–5, 2006, pp. 21–30.

Robinson, M. 1993. Design for unanticipated use... In: de Michelis, G., Simone, C., and Schmidt, K. (Eds.) *Proceedings of the Third European Conference on Computer Supported cooperative Work (ECSCW'93)*. Kluwer, New York, 1993. pp. 187–202.

Schmidt, K. & Bannon, L. 1992. Taking CSCW seriously: Supporting articulation work. *Computer Supported Cooperative Work*, 1, 1–2, 7–40.

Smith, A. 1997. *Human computer factors: A study of users and information systems*. London: McGraw-Hill.

Sørensen, C. & Yoo, Y. 2005. Socio-technical studies of mobility and ubiquity. In *Proceedings of IFIP WG 8.2*, Cleveland, OH, USA, Springer, 1–13.

Tilson, D., Lyytinen, K. & Sørensen, C. 2009. Desperately seeking the Infrastructure in IS Research: Conceptualization of "Digital Convergence" as the co-evolution of social and technical infrastructures. In: Isomäki, H., Häkkinen, P. and Viteli, J. (Eds.) *Future educational technologies*. Reports of Information Technology Research Institute 20/2009. Jyväskylä: University of Jyväskylä Printing House.

Vuojärvi, H., Isomäki, H. & Hynes, D. 2010. Domestication of a laptop on a wireless university campus: A case study. *Australasian Journal of Educational Technology*, 26(2), 250–267.

Woolgar, S. 1991. Configuring the user: The case of usability trials. In: Law, J. (Ed.) *A sociology of monsters: Essays on power, technology and domination*. London: Routledge.

Zhang, P., Carey, J., Te'eni, D. & Tremaine, M. 2005. Integrating human–computer interaction development into the systems development life cycle: A methodology. *Communications of the Association for Information Systems*, 15, 512–543.

Part I
Human Systems Analysis

Chapter 2
On the Emergence of Techno-Religious Spaces: Implications for Design and End Users

Heba El-Sayed, Anita Greenhill, and Chris Westrup

2.1 Introduction

The developer/user or technology/user dichotomy has long been an important feature in thinking about information systems (IS) development and IS use (for example: Greenbaum and Kyng 1991; Lamb and Kling 2003; He and King 2008). Calls to reframe our understanding of the user of technologies are timely and invite us to rethink some well worn issues. One is the mediation of social preoccupations through technologies. Here the move is away from the frame of a dyad of developer and user towards investigation of how technologies become significant in social life and how attempts to regulate social activity through technologies appear to remain incomplete aspirations.

A key argument of this chapter is that attempts to frame or reframe those who use ICT applications, described as users, social actors, humans, always remains *incomplete* due to impossibility of defining activity which is on-going and continually susceptible to being redefined in changing relationships. This relational view does not deny the importance of attempting holistic understandings, but points to the impossibility of complete and final descriptions of humans as users of technologies. The key to this argument is that we need to pay particular attention to how technologies are being adopted and adapted in daily practice where users and technologies mingle agency in often unexpected ways.

To illustrate this argument we choose an example that does not fit the categories of work or leisure and focus on how technologies are being used to mediate religious practices for Muslims. Muslims are utilising technology to assist with their religious requirements that is, to pray five times a day, at specific times, and in a specific direction. Technologies are being utilised because these specific prayer times and locations may change on a daily basis. To gauge an understanding of end user application of technology we argue that it is neither enough to simply consider end user

H. El-Sayed (✉), A. Greenhill, and C. Westrup
Manchester Business School, University of Manchester, Booth Street West,
Manchester M15 6PB, UK
e-mail: Chris.westrup@mbs.ac.uk; A.Greenhill@manchester.ac.uk;
Heba.F.El-Sayed@manchester.ac.uk

H. Isomäki and S. Pekkola (eds.), *Reframing Humans in Information*
Systems Development, Computer Supported Cooperative Work 201,
DOI 10.1007/978-1-84996-347-3_2, © Springer-Verlag London Limited 2011

functionality nor end user usage in relation to the technology alone, but that iterative practices and a breadth of social, technical, cultural concerns must also be recognised in the use of information systems. This chapter suggests that there are some important implications for IS development in broadening understandings and attempts to re-frame the user. We propose that an increasing presence of *multiple* technologies providing solutions engages a range of behaviours from unthinking acceptance of one particular technological solution to critical appraisals of the sources of legitimacy of competing technological 'solutions'. These techno-religious spaces (Kong 2001) reframe notions of what it means to be designers or users and show how such conceptions are enacted in a contested arena in which competing technological solutions and cultural preoccupations interact in often highly innovative ways.

The chapter begins by discussing issues of framing and reframing of people in information systems development which are then explored developing the idea of spaces and techno-religious spaces in particular to rethink how the notion of people can be addressed in information systems development.

2.2   Framing and Reframing the Human

In 1992 a particularly lively debate arose in science and technologies studies on the distribution of agency between humans and machines (see Collins and Yearley 1992; Callon and Latour 1992). Collins and Yearley defended the conventional view that agency is asymmetrically distributed. We can attribute agency and intentionality to people while neither can be directly attributed to machines that achieve agency through design and lack intentionality. As a well known sociologist joked at the end of a recent discussion on this topic, 'hands up those who believe in agency for machines'. Then looking around, said 'humans one, machines nil' as only people responded (Molotch 2009). Callon and Latour took a different line and proposed that human and machine agency were similar and, using a semiotic definition, attributed agency to any 'actant' who is recognised as a source of agency. In this analysis agency is performed by humans, nonhumans and combinations of both. For example, writing and sending an email involves humans and also machines. Humans are both doing *more* than directing the computer as they usually are engaged in several things at once. Humans are also doing *less* than directing the computer as their interaction and prose style are shaped by the technology. Machines too have agency in their capacity to (somehow) direct the visible text to a place accessible by specific individuals. But, the most striking feature is that we can recognise a hybridity of human and technology that enable and frame action which would be impossible otherwise. Two consequences for our discussion flow from Callon and Latour's proposal. First, we cannot know what the agency of machines or humans are going to be in advance. Hence, we must look closely at how technologies and people act and how agency is distributed between them. Secondly, it is to be expected that technologies and people will operate together to produce agency, just as I am doing now typing this document on (with) a laptop.

What does rethinking agency in this way imply for debates about designers and users in information systems development? Our attention moves from design practice itself, no matter how nuanced, to how technologies are appropriated in use.[1] The term user remains in wide circulation. Useful though it is in providing a common vocabulary it is both somewhat prescriptive and vague. User implies the use of something, such as technology, and a specific type of relationship that of use with its implications of usefulness and use-value. For Marx, use-value was what something was worth, consequent on its material qualities, and was to be contrasted with the exchange-value which assigned a monetary value which may bear little relationship to its use. Identifying people as users of technology suggests a functional and a productive relationship with technologies. Equally, the term user is often opposed to the term designer in a relationship in which the designer designs the technology which the user uses (see Cooley 1999). However, the term user is also vague: in the US it has tended to refer to the manager of a specific area or function while in Europe it refers to those who are day to day operators of technologies (Westrup 1997).

Lamb and Kling (2003) also considered the term user posited a relationship of people as users of technologies when, in their experience, these 'users' often considered technologies as one aspect of their working environment. In its place they appropriate the term social actor As they put it '[a] social actor is an *organizational entity* whose interactions are simultaneously enabled and constrained by the socio-technical affiliations and environments of the firm, its members, and its industry. In short, social actors are not primarily users of ICTs.' (Lamb and Kling 2003:218 (our emphasis). This is a helpful development distinguishing people from their usage of technologies. At the same time, it restricts its definition to people in organisations, and presents us with the well known demarcation of a socio-technical split. Echoing Collins and Yearley, Lamb and Kling frame agency as human centred and asymmetrical as indicated in their preference for the term *social* actor.[2] What is missing is an appreciation of agency distributed amongst people and machines. This is more than people as users of machines – the tool metaphor – but points to an increasing use of technology, especially digital technology, as mediation in a range of social settings.

A decentring of either technology or humans as the prime focus of explanation leads to an interest in practice; how technologies and people interact and how agency arises. Pickering (1993) refers to a mangle of practice in which human and material agency is emergent and entangled together in a dialectic of resistance and accommodation. This is a posthumanist account as humans and technologies are not simply twinned together but '...that material and human agencies are mutually

---

[1] Though we have considerable sympathy with the aspirations of improving design techniques (examples include participatory design, value sensitive design, or soft systems methods (Greenbaum and Kyng 1991; Friedman et al. 2007; Checkland and Scholes 1999) a lacuna in such work is a limited interest in how technologies and users interact outside the 'laboratory' conditions of design and how users and technologies work 'in the wild' (Hutchins 1996).

[2] Lamb (2006) makes an initial and eclectic start to re-examine social actors in relation to actor networks (ibid: 9).

and emergently productive of one another.' (Pickering 1993:567) This reframing places humans as being at times parts of a temporally emergent assemblage in which agency is redefined between humans and technologies in reciprocal relations of both accommodation and resistance.

At this point perhaps it is helpful to summarise the argument. When we consider the use of information systems a call to reframe humans has potentially liberating implications. The use of information systems, we argue, does not necessarily restrict people to either a utopian enhancement of their agency or a dystopian routinisation of their capabilities as users of technologies based on a quasi deterministic design of the technology. Instead we focus on the practices of people and technologies as temporary ensembles in which agency may be continually redefined.[3] The implication is that the usage of technologies is unstable, and though designers may seek to create scripts which users must follow, unexpected workarounds or novel capabilities are to be expected (see, for example, Kline and Pinch 1996). Indeed, in organizational environments, we find that a considerable amount of managerial effort is expended identifying and stabilizing business processes. The creativity of novel human–technology assemblages has been harnessed in open source development in which users become developers and developers learn to improve design through their use of such systems. The blurring of design and use mirrors an intermingling of work and leisure (Castells 1999) and a rapid use of technologies outside workplaces.

It is possible to view much of the debate on designers, users and ICTs as still carrying assumptions about the workplace usage of these technologies (see for example Lamb and Kling 2003). The spread of technologies such as the internet to many aspects of daily life leads to diversity of engagement with technologies not simply as a pervasive electronic space but as a 'co-mingling of electronic and physical space' (Page and Phillips, 2003:73 quoted in Crang et al. 2007). These engagements are highly diverse for example: the use of ATMs, iphones, ipods, accessing the internet at home or on the move (see also Lyytinen and Yoo 2002) . Each encompasses a materiality of specific technologies and a diversity of use showing that user engagement becomes increasingly complex. A further development is the advent of Web2.0 technologies whose defining characteristic is claimed to be the move from the consumption of information by users to the creation and linking of content by multiple users (Beer and Burrows 2007; Cormode and Krishnamurthy 2008). In social networking sites (SNS) people create digital profiles of themselves whose interests and friends are intertwined with messages, photographs and video (boyd and Ellison 2007) to create active 'online' modes of interaction. Forms of usage become infused with issues of identity created and maintained though performance on SNS which have recursive effects on the identity and behaviour of people more generally. To take the example of friends, Friends in Facebook refer to a network of relationships mediated through technology but these Friends are often the same friends met in day to day life (Beer 2008). What we find is a bringing together of the technological and the social

---

[3] We restrict the argument to agency, the ability to effect action, and we do not seek to impute intentionality to machines.

or as Lash (2002:15) puts its 'forms of life become technological' (quoted in Beer 2008). The 'online' and the 'offline' of boyd and Ellison become intermingled as mediated activity through technology devices. Thus the spaces of interaction, of networking and of mediated social relations which inform discussions of Web2.0 need to be understood in terms of the materialities of these interactions and the everyday contexts in which such spaces are produced and performed. This, in turn, has repercussions on our understanding of people and technologies.

In short, recognition of mediation becoming more integral to everyday activity suggests the necessity for a holistic, as in more complete, analysis of people and their engagement with and through technologies. In particular we need to explore the interweaving of mediated and non mediated activity in everyday settings in which spaces are created for specific activities. We can expect hybridity and blurring of agency in assemblages of people and technologies in such situations and we suggest that emergent actions cannot be read off as scripted from technologies but are, in Pickering's words, akin to mangles of practice.

2.3 Techno-religious Spaces and Muslim Practices

Though we, in Europe, remain heirs to the Enlightenment, and a modernity based on an increasingly secular conception of the world, these assumptions are open to question. Globally most humans subscribe to some form of religious belief and religious practice is an important aspect of many people's day to day activity (Dawson and Cowan 2004). The historical development of technology has been credited to a religious understanding of natural world as rational and capable of manipulation (Whitehead 1970) but the relationship between technologies and religious practice remains less understood (see Noble 1997). When it comes to digital technologies Bell suggests that a focus on religious practices is an important addition to two dominant sites of user – computing interaction as either work or leisure (Bell 2006:153).

Our interest in mediated practices of identifying prayer times and prayer direction for Muslims stems from an awareness that religious traditions are not easily classified and often have generated problems which spawn innovative technologies reassigning agency amongst machines and users. For example, the western Christian tradition's concerns with the dating of Easter led to a variety of solutions culminating with the Gregorian calendar. Similarly an interest in the timing of prayers led to use of bells, the development of clocks, and the insertion of clock time in daily life (see Mumford 1934). Islamic practice of daily prayer in non Muslim countries is particularly interesting as it requires believers to find the times and direction of prayer without overt communal signs such as the call to prayer proclaimed from local mosques. Faced with these situations Muslims turn to a variety of sophisticated technologies.

Lily Kong (2001) argues that religious experience is predicated on the existence of sacred space which is often in conflict with secular space. Sacred space is itself founded on power relations of domination and subordination, inclusion and exclusion. Technologies have enabled new spaces to be created, what Kong calls techno-religious spaces, which are mediated though technologies such as television, radio, the internet and the mobile phone, and create a new politics of space. For example, Islamic software applications, in particular those incorporating the Quran, are developed in different formats: personal digital assistance (PDAs), web-assisted mobile phones, Islamic digital organizers and digital Qur'an readers; computer programs giving the prayer direction, timing and recordings of the *Adhan*; E-Jihad, Online Fatwas (Bunt 2003), and chat rooms for discussions of religious matters, are but few examples of technological developments opening up new spaces and mediating religious practices.

These spaces, as Kong indicates, remain contested. Mandaville (2007:102) proposes that new technologies lead in Islam to a further decentralisation of authority in an already decentralised structure and also to a related democratisation of authority allowing practitioners and others to reshape and construct new (re)formulations of Islamic practice. For practitioners questions arise about what technologies are to be used to create spaces for religious practice and how to negotiate (or ignore) the sometimes subtle conflicts in information and advice in the creation of techno-religious space. Put differently, users, as religious practitioners, have to make implicit or explicit choices about multiple and changing technologies which mirror decisions about how agency is to be distributed in an assemblage of user and technology.

In spite of the differences among Muslims (Sunni and Shiaa) the five pillars of Islam[4] are common to all. Praying known as *salah* is one of those pillars and is considered 'the foundation of the religion'. Muslims should make five prayers in the day and they should do them on time. The five daily praying times are set according to the movement of the sun and they are known as: *salat al fajr* which is the time from dawn to sunrise; *salat al zuhr*, the noon praying due after the sun passes its highest; *salat al asr* afternoon prayer; *salat al maghrib* sunset prayer; and *salat al isha* evening prayer. It is always preferable to offer the prayer as soon as the time arrives. Although the prayers are fixed at the same 'time' period each day – before dawn, noon, afternoon, sunset, and evening, the times (according to the clock) of these prayers varies from place to place and from day to day because of the rotation of the earth around the sun, and the various latitudes of the earth's locations.

Finding praying time is easy in Islamic countries where the public call to prayer (*adhan*) from mosques reminds people of the daily prayer times and sets the rhythm of the day for Muslims and non-Muslims alike.[5] *Adhan* is heard from mosques though in modern times loudspeakers are used to transmit it and is also broadcast

---

[4] Five pillars of Islam are the foundation of Muslim's life and they include: the declaration of faith (shahada), five prescribed daily prayers (salah), fasting during the month of Rawadan (sawm), money for the poor (zaka) and a pilgrimage to Mecca (hajj).

[5] At one extreme in a country like Saudi Arabia everything shuts down at praying time and everyone should go to mosques to pray.

in radio and TV thus making the call to prayer more prominent in daily life. In these situations *adhan* reaffirms a sense of communal inclusion founded on a sharing of time and spatial proximity even if the call is mediated by loudspeakers. Agency is deferred to the call which is accepted as being correct and legitimate.[6] This practice is, of course, one of inclusion, but it also signals exclusion and controversy can arise when Muslims are in a minority or when circumstances change. Lee (1999) gives an interesting example of how a Muslim village in Singapore which practiced *adhan* as a public call to prayer, ran into difficulties as the area was developed and occupied by non Muslims. As he puts it "...the amplified call to prayer became a source of conflict in an emerging reinterpretation of social and acoustical spaces". He pointed out how the rearrangement for prayer calls to be made via radio caused a change in conceptualization of religious place consciously is used as a means for affirming religious and cultural identity important for Islamic culture reproduction. Listening to the call to prayer on radio instead of the mosque's loudspeakers according to Lee (1999:94) 'reunites each member of the Islamic community and creates an abstract communal Islamic space without the encroachment of non-Islamic social spaces' and demonstrates how a community actively employs technology to maintain collectivity in a pluralistic society.

For Muslims living and practising Islam in non-Islamic countries or when travelling adhering to *salah* can be challenging. Different forms of technologies are mobilised and, in terms of *salah*, they range from printed prayer schedules obtained from mosques, computer programmes, and different electronic gadgets. The choice among these different technologies has important implications for Muslims' techno-religious practices. Bell (2006) highlighted how the 3G Ilkone mobile phone which explicitly caters to Islamic users incorporates a 'mosque-function' which disables the phone for a short period of time during prayer so as not to ring during that time. Bell (2006:149–150) argued that this function can be regarded as a challenge to the notion of constant connectivity and thus "...in thinking about designing for techno-spiritual practices, we might have to consider a different range of practices and priorities and conceptualization of space and location that is driven by a broader set of use patterns." Sacred spaces are supported and affirmed by technologies such as the use of calls to prayer played from internet programmes, and affirmed by the their exclusion in the case of the Ilkone mobile and its 'mosque function'.

One possibility of mediating this social preoccupation is to develop a killer app which will work everywhere at anytime. One Egyptian entrepreneur, Mr. Bhagat, made his first fortune in the 1980s designing and marketing a wristwatch in the United States of America that aimed to do just that. However the possibility of a complete mediated experience that tells the time of *salah* and points the direction of prayer is only recently become a possibility with the advent of sophisticated mobile phones with GPS positioning. Wyche et al. (2008, 2009) have developed an

---

[6] Even in these situations of physical proximity moves can be initiated to co-ordinate the calls of each mosque using technologies. Bell (2006:141) notes 'an ongoing debate about the use of Cairo's nascent wireless cloud to broadcast a single call to prayer from the city's many minaret towers' though we have been unable to find any further evidence.

interesting prototype device that combines a mobile phone and a Sun Dial programme which graphically shows a digital sun moving across the silhouette of two mosques, designed to evoke 'reflection on holy sites' (Wyche et al., 2009:57) and passing through a series of five circles each indicating the time for prayer. The use of their prototypes was found helpful by users. The digital representation evoked nostalgia for original Islamic precepts which are defined by the sun though, we might add, in a completely different manner. As one participant commented 'we are in a society where no one is watching the sun'. Another mentioned ' the phone reminded me of how I should keep track of prayer times and follow the natural progression of the sun, which I don't do , I let mechanical devices [referring to his watch and computer] to do it'. The minarets in the digital skyline were also favourably received as reminders of the Middle East and the importance of Islamic practice. This phone does not incorporate GPS so it remained restricted to Atlanta, Georgia though conceivably it could be developed into the killer app able to be used more widely. Nonetheless deferring agency to the Sun Dial may be problematic as it uses IslamicFinder to calculate the times of *salah*. This programme is widely used but has been criticised by some as being inaccurate.[7] Even if this was resolved, the use of a killer app technological solution as an unchallenged source of authority in creating legitimate techno-religious space still runs into difficulty as it is said (Islam on-line Fatwa Desk 2003) that the time of *salah*, particularly in higher latitudes, is to be decided by adherence to local practice.

Although it is preferable to carry out praying in mosques, praying can also take place at home, work, or in an open space. Wherever they are, Muslims should pray facing Ka'bah (known as *qibla*) in the city of Mecca in Saudi Arabia. Again finding out *qibla* direction in Islamic countries is easy, where inside mosques, a niche in a wall indicates the *qibla* and in public buildings and hotel rooms the *qibla* is often indicated by an arrow on the ceiling or walls. Once in non Islamic countries problems arise. For example Mohammadi et al. (2007:312) highlighted how in Australian hospitals Islamic values which Muslims incorporated into daily life are not incorporated into the provision of health care for Muslims and how " meeting the obligations of prayer within a busy care facility can be difficult and challenging. Even determining the direction of Mecca might be more difficult than usual, as few public building in Australia have signs indicating the direction of Mecca as is common practice in Islamic countries". In America an on-going debate continues on which direction to pray. If one takes a world map using the common Mercator projection then Mecca appears to be almost directly east of the US and many people pray in that direction. However, because the earth is a sphere, the most direct route to Mecca follows a great circle and points north east. The commonsense example here is that to fly the Atlantic planes go over Iceland following the great circle which appears further on a map. Others again argue that East, South, East is the correct direction as it is the shortest route if you could go point to point *through* the earth (Hamidullah 1969).

---

[7] http://www.moonsighting.com/prayer.html#fajr&isha

As Muslims seek guidance in different situations ingenuity and innovation in the interpretation of guidelines become more pronounced. At an extreme is how a Muslim is the practice in space where the temporal and spatial markers guiding practice are missing. This is a practical concern as a number of Muslims have been in space. For example in October 2007, Malaysia sent its' first astronaut into space (Fischer 2008). As the astronaut was a practicing Muslim, the Malaysian space agency provided him with advice on religious practice in the form of a guideline for performing the Islamic rites at the space station. The journey nevertheless raised several issues, for example, how would prayer time be calculated, how would the direction of prayer be determined, how to perform the required prayer motion? And most important who has the authority to provide answers to these questions and articulate the guidelines for performing Islamic rites at the outer space. Indeed, according to Fischer, two other authorities, one from Egypt and one from Guinea, have also issued Fatwas governing Islamic prayer practice in space.

The mediation of technology makes Islamic experience more decentralised, the mosques or traditional Islamic institutions are no longer the exclusive source from which the call to prayer is recited. Through technology, increasing numbers of participants are involved in what Eickelman and Anderson (2003) called an 'Islamic public sphere' where all have an authority to talk about Islam. This thereby results in the reframing of Islam's traditional and institutional authority and a move towards individualised prayer practice on the one hand and an increasing reliance on technologies to provide solutions to the problems of prayer time and direction. Individuals appear to be recast as consumers of technological products which they can pick and choose from. This is, to some extent, the democratisation of Islamic practice that Mandaville pointed to, but it is hedged by interactions with other practicing Muslims, the seeking of direction from Muslim scholars and the materiality of specific technologies. How much do they cost? how easy are they to use?; do they work and so on. Answers to these questions await further research which is currently in progress.

The cultural preoccupation of Islamic prayer practice in seeking to standardise prayer times and the direction of practice shows how religious practice and technology innovation and mediation remain strongly entwined. The arena of religious practice provides an interesting site for exploring how the relationship between technologies and being human plays out. Different modes of communications enact different forms of 'techno-religious spaces' and alter conceptions of place, space, identity and community. The implications for design are important of this shared and evolving agency distributed between people and technologies. We would like to point to two consequences for design.

First, in techno-religious practice the relationship between technologies and users is multivalent. At times it appears that people just 'use' technologies as tools to enable them to perform their religious practices, but we draw attention to the constitutive features of this engagement where technologies are central to the creation of techno-religious spaces of practice. However, this does not have to imply that these technologies are given privileged status; it seems that one technology can be replaced by others either for its increasing utility or as a preferred mode of consumption. Nor is it clear in advance as to how much authority will be accorded these technological devices. At times it seems that the calculations used in the technologies are accepted whereas at other points debate can flare up, for example, on which direction prayer should adopt and which technology is most appropriate. For designers the entwining of agency between human and machine suggests that devices and software need explicitly to enable flexibility as the use value in Marx's terms of products changes in relation to other offerings and new insights.

Second, as a consequence of the constitutive and reciprocal relationship between technologies and people, design needs to pay increased attention to how their products are made to work (see Suchman 2006) and how the scripts they design to control the actions of users are enacted in practice. To do this designers have to return to the multivalent properties of technology–user relations. Users are at once consumers of technological products and hence customers to be listened to, but the implications of a shifting agency distributed between people and machines implies that investigation of how these relations work is equally necessary and a good account of what is happening may not be consciously available to the user as customer.

2.4 Concluding Comments

Technologies change and, over the last fifty years, ICTs have become increasingly present in the social environments of the developed (and developing) world (Friedman 1992) prompting reassessments of the role of people and their relationship to ICTs. Heidegger, when faced an increasingly technological world, evinced a profound pessimism. He saw it as an aspect of nature and humans becoming treated as a standing reserve or resource; to be deployed as and when necessary, which enframes humans (Heidegger 1977). Technologies, we might say, require certain behaviours of people, which though they might be subverted, remain a relationship of control which people willingly or unwittingly engage. In contrast Heidegger posited an earlier conception of technology as one of revealing and a giving forth which enhanced humanity. In a sense Heidegger was recalling a smaller scale technology which exemplified the skill of its design and construction. Today, a Heideggerian reading of the current ubiquity of computing seems salient especially in the worlds of corporate computing (see Kallinikos 2009). Taking a different tack, Thrift (2005:7) points to 'the increasing mediatisation of everyday life as the various media become ubiquitous, ambient presences in our lives' and argues that commodities and consumer objects have become 'increasingly animated.' As we suggested earlier people in new technology environments are drawn in to become active consumers of mediated relationships in spaces that are increasingly common and commonplace. The rise of social networking sites such as Facebook or MySpace shows how people operate in a mediated and animated environment in which the differences between 'online' and 'offline' start to fold into each other as iPhones, PDAs, netbooks and computers become commonplace. If this is enframing as Heidegger might see it, it is a willing engagement and representation of identity in the spaces afforded by these technologies. Perhaps the technological mediation of religious practices, especially those of Islam and Eastern religions offer the possibility of alternative understandings of the framing of people and technologies (see Bell 2006) which, in turn, may allow us to reappraise conventional understanding.

The dyadic relationship of designer and user, so prevalent in earlier conceptions of the use of technologies, is better seen as a product of a specific set of circumstances when businesses created their own bespoke systems and their employees used them as parts of their working environment. Design has become distributed as users become consumers of technology products and their engagement with these systems is actively sought through the use of beta releases, blogs and wikis. In everyday life, at least in the developed world, a myriad of technologies and softwares are available and their usage becomes bound up with the identity of people as knowing consumers or as putative members of social groups. This interweaving of human and machine agency is on-going and emergent or, as Pickering (1993) puts it, a mangle of practice. Though this term takes up the collapsing together of agency in unexpected ways it is also a productive engagement leading to new spaces of practice. Framing and reframing humans in these processes remains a necessarily incomplete aspiration as agency becomes distributed and relational in changing, technologically mediated, and animate spaces.[8]

For Muslims the *salah*, the necessity of praying five times a day, and the *qibla*, the direction in which prayer takes place, are key elements of devout practice. Though the precept to practice in this way is universal to Muslims, how it is to be achieved is, as we have shown, an on-going problematic highly dependent on notions of time and place, but also acknowledging the legitimacy of local customs of practice. Muslims use multiple sources of authority to negotiate these complex difficulties which are called on depending on a variety of circumstances. Each scheduling of times and direction is mediated in multiple ways. Watches, televisions, radios tell the time; custom, compasses, or specific religious artefacts give the direction; and friends, type written schedules, televisions, radios, internet programmes give either lists of the times or an audible call to prayer. Their usage is a creative and sometimes eclectic activity, which is on-going as prayer times change with the sun's seasonal movement relative to the earth. Muslims and their mediated resources together create, what Kong calls, techno-religious spaces in which prayer can be performed in any corner of the earth or even in a spacecraft. These practices demonstrate that a variety of technologies can be brought together to perform intensely emotional and significant acts which belie ideas of technology as alienation and disenchantment.

This chapter proposes that the dyadic developer user conception of information systems development should now be (only) seen as a specific instance of a more complex mediation of sociality and the deployment of technologies. Even nuanced understandings of design, such as participatory design or value sensitive design,

---

[8] That is not to deny that from an epochal perspective most forms of engagement with technologies carry with them an enframing (Gestell) as Heidegger (1977:19) posited.

should recognise that agency becomes redistributed and mangled in the appropriation of technologies in use. Use becomes more than following design prescripts and is both expected to adapt and change technologies on the one hand, or, on the other, to see any particular technology as just one of multiple potential solutions to be taken up (or discarded) in use. Design becomes more distributed and less certain of its effects in environments that are increasingly mediated with technology. Put differently attempts to regulate sociality through technologies remain incomplete aspirations incapable of consummation. Whether the diversity and complexity of the unfolding usage of technologies as a mangle of practice(s) itself conceals an overarching enframing, as Heidegger might suggest, remains a spectre inviting further investigation.

References

Beer, D., (2008) Social network(ing) sites revisiting the story so far: A response to danah boyd & Nicole Ellison, *Journal of Computer-Mediated Communication*, 13(2): 516–529.

Beer, D., & Burrows, R., (2007) Sociology and, of and in Web 2.0: Some initial considerations, *Sociological Research Online*, 12(5), http://www.socresonline.org.uk/12/5/17.html.

Bell, G., (2006) No more SMS from Jesus: Ubicomp, religion and techno-spiritual practices, *UbiComp*, 4206: 141–158.

boyd, D., & Ellison, N., (2007) Social networking sites: Definition, history, and scholarship, *Journal of Computer-Mediated Communication* 13(1): 210–230.

Bunt, G., (2003) *Islam in the Digital Age, e-Jihad, Online Fatwas and Cyber Islamic Environments*, London: Pluto Press.

Callon, M., & Latour, B., (1992) "Don't Throw the Baby Out with the Bath School! A Reply to Collins and Yearley." Pp. 343–68 in *Science as Practice and Culture*, edited by A. Pickering, Chicago: University of Chicago Press.

Castells, M., (1999) *The Information Age: Economy, Society and Culture*, Oxford: Blackwell.

Checkland, P., & Scholes, J., (1999) *Soft Systems in Action*, Chichester: Wiley.

Collins, H., & Yearley, S., (1992) "Epistemological Chicken." Pp. 301–26 in *Science as Practice and Culture*, edited by A. Pickering, Chicago: University of Chicago Press.

Cooley, M., (1999) *Architect or Bee?: The Human/Technology Relationship*, Boston: South End Press.

Cormode, G., & Krishnamurthy, B., (2008) Key Differences between Web 1.0 and Web2.0, *First Monday*, 13: 6, http://firstmonday.org/htbin/cgiwrap/bin/ojs/index.php/fm/article/view/2125.

Crang, M., Crosbie, T., & Graham, S., (2007) Technology, time – space, and the remediation of neighbourhood life, *Environment and Planning A*, 39, pp. 2405–2422.

Dawson, L., & Cowan, D., (2004) *Religion online, finding faith on the internet*, New York: Routledge.

Eickelman, D., & Anderson, J., (2003) *New Media in the Muslim World: The Emerging Public Sphere*, Bloomington: Indiana University Press.

He, J., & King, W., (2008) The role of user participation in information systems development: Implications from a meta-analysis, *Journal of Management Information Systems*, 25(1): 301–331.

Hutchins, E., (1996) *Cognition in the Wild*, Boston: MIT Press.

Fischer, N., (2008) Islamic religious practice in outer space, *ISIM Review*, 22: 39.

Friedman, A. (with D. Cornford), (1992) *Computer Systems Development: History, Organization and Implementation*, London: Wiley.

Friedman, B., Kahn, P., & Borning, A., (2007) "Value Sensitive Sign and Information Systems". in *Human-Computer Interaction in Management Information Systems: Foundations*, edited by P. Zhang & D. Galletta (Eds.), New York: M.E. Sharpe.

Greenbaum, J., & Kyng,M., (1991) *Design at Work: Cooperative Design of Computer Systems*, Hillsdale, NJ: Lawrence Erlbaum.

Hamidullah, M., (1969) *Introduction to Islam.* (http://muslim-canada.org/hamidullah_all.html accessed 7th May 2009).

Heidegger, M., (1977) *The Question concerning Technology and Other Essays,* (translated by W. Lovitt), London: Harper Row.

Islam on-line Fatwa Desk (2003) Determining the times of prayer in the high latitudes, *Islamonline* www.islamonline.net/servlet/Satellite?pagename=IslamOnline-English-Ask_Scholar/FatwaE/ FatwaE&cid=111950354 accessed 9th December 2009).

Kallinikos, J., (2009) On the computational rendition of reality: Artefacts and human agency, *Organization*, 16/2: 183–202.

Kline, R., and Pinch, T., (1996) Users as Agents of Technological Change: The Social Construction of the Automobile in the Rural United States *Technology and Culture*, 37(4):763–795.

Kong, L., (2001) Religion and technology: refiguring place, space, identity and community, *Area*, 33.4: 404–413.

Lamb, R., (2006). "Alternative Paths Toward a Social Actor Concept". Pp. 4113–4123 in *Proceedings of the Twelfth Americas Conference on Information Systems*, Mexico: Acapulco.

Lamb, R. & Kling R., (2003) Reconceptualising users as social actors in information systems research, *MIS Quarterly* 27(2): 197–235.

Lash, S., (2002) *Critique of Information*, London: Sage.

Lee, T., (1999) Technology and the production of islamic space: The call to prayer in Singapore, *Ethnomusicology*, 43(1), 86–100.

Lyytinen, K., Yoo, Y., (2002) Research commentary: The next wave of nomadic computing, *Information Systems Research*, 13(4), 377–388.

Mandaville, P., (2007) Globalization and the politics of religious knowledge pluralizing authority in the muslim world, *Theory, Culture & Society*, 24(2): 101–115.

Mohammadi, N., Evans, D., & Jones, T., (2007) Muslims in Australian hospitals: The clash of cultures, *International Journal of Nursing Practices*, 13: 310–315.

Molotch, H., (2009) Personal Communication, *Materialising the Subject: phenomenological and post-ANT objects in the social sciences* CRESC, University of Manchester, Manchester, UK.

Mumford, L., (1934) *Technics and Civilization*, New York: Harcourt, Brace & Co.

Noble, D., (1997) *The Religion of Technology*, New York: Knopf, Apfred A Knopf.

Page, S., & Phillips, B., (2003) Telecommunications and urban design: representing Jersey City, *City: Analysis of Urban Trends, Culture, Theory, Policy, Action*, 7: 73–94.

Pickering, A., (1993) The mangle of practice: Agency and emergence in the sociology of science, *American Journal of Sociology*, 99: 3, 559–589.

Suchman, L., (2006) *Human-Machine Reconfigurations: Plans and Situated Actions*, Cambridge University Press, Cambridge (2nd Edition).

Thrift, N., (2005) *Knowing Capitalism*, London: Sage.

Westrup, C., (1997) "Constituting Users in Systems Development." Pp. 182–206 in *Information Systems and Qualitative Research*, edited by A. Lee, J. Liebenau & J. DeGross (eds.), London: Chapman & Hall.

Whitehead, A., (1970) *Science and the Modern World*, New York: Free Press.

Wyche, S., Caine, K., Davison, B., Arteaga M., & Grinter R., (2008) Sun Dial: Exploring Techno-spiritual design through a mobile islamic call to prayer application, *CHI 8: ACM Conference on Human Factors and Computing Systems*, Florence, Italy, April 2008.

Wyche, S., Caine, K., Davison, B., Patel, S., Arteaga M., & Grinter R., (2009) Sacred imagery in techno-spiritual design, *Proceedings of the 27th International Conference on Human Factors in Computing Systems*, MA, ACM, Boston, Massachusetts, USA.

Chapter 3
Towards Lifeworld-Oriented Information Systems Development

Andrew Basden

3.1 Introduction

Information systems (IS) fail far too often. Sometimes the IS never reaches the stage of use, because the IS development (ISD) project fails, or sometimes failure occurs once the IS is in use, in that it provides no real benefits or might even bring harm. In the latter case, ISD failed to anticipate the real needs and possible repercussions of use. How can ISD-related failures be prevented, or at least reduced in frequency?

3.1.1 Attempts to Assist ISD Success

To reduce failure rates in both the ISD process and in future use of the IS, many and varied software development methodologies have emerged, ranging from linear approaches derived from the Waterfall model (Royce 1970) through iterative approaches such as Boehm's (1988) classic spiral model to the agile methodologies of today (Beck 2000). Another attack on the problem has been to seek better data models and computer languages, from procedural to declarative languages and from database models like Chen's (1976) Entity Relationship Model and Codd's (1970) Relational Data Model, then object-oriented approaches (Booch 1991), to more recent approaches like Design Patterns (Gamma et al. 1995). Yet another attack has been to focus on defining and clarifying the business or application problem and solution, such as with Checkland's (1999) Soft Systems Methodology.

Though Soft Systems Methodology has been quite widely applied in professional practice, it has also been criticised. Bergvall-Kåreborn et al. (2004) review some of its problems in practice – such as that it tends to generate statements of the status quo rather than stimulating new insights (which was its aim). The root of this seems to be

A. Basden (✉)
Salford Business School, University of Salford, UK
e-mail: sbs@basden.demon.co.uk

H. Isomäki and S. Pekkola (eds.), *Reframing Humans in Information
Systems Development*, Computer Supported Cooperative Work 201,
DOI 10.1007/978-1-84996-347-3_3, © Springer-Verlag London Limited 2011

its grounding in phenomenology, which Hirshheim et al. (1995) and Probert (1997) criticise and argue that it results in difficulty in addressing power relations and other distortions in the communicative process during analysis, possible misuse by one group at the expense of another, and epistemological reductionism. Instead of grounding a methodology in phenomenology, Hirschheim and Klein (1994) advocate grounding ISD in the critical notion of emancipation. Problems with their proposal include that emancipation is not well defined, and that, though emancipation is one important factor in ISD, there is much in ISD that cannot be appropriately thought about in terms of emancipation.

A plethora of IS methodologies and approaches have been proposed, yet the problem of failed or inappropriate ISD and IS stubbornly remains. In 1994 Jayaratna estimated there were around 1,000 extant ISD methodologies (cited by Iivari et al. 1998), most of which are not making any impact on practice.

The IS research literature tries to make some sense of this by trying to generalise. For example, Kautz et al. (2007a) discuss 'persistent problems' in ISD, which they identify as organisation and specialisation of diversity, acquisition and negotiation of knowledge and perception and establishment of structure. They argue that neither changes in information technologies and applications, nor the move from traditional to agile techniques, have significantly changed the underlying challenging characteristics of ISD. In response to criticism, Kautz et al. (2007b) admit that they consider only a limited class of IS (websites) but there is a more serious issue here: they presuppose that diversity should be 'reduced', and that the only knowledge of interest has been "acquired" and "negotiated". Both presuppositions may be questioned: diversity might be welcomed and taken-for-granted knowledge often plays a role in actual ISD.

Iivari et al. (1998) have suggested that instead of looking at ISD methodologies (ISDMs) it is useful to abstract from these and look at ISD approaches (ISDAs), to analyse the broad types of approach in the hope of being able to engage in 'methodology engineering'. Whereas ISDMs may be evaluated according to their impact, this does not allow navigation through the "methodology jungle", and study of ISDAs, which are general types of ISDM, separates the 'essentials' from the 'accidentals'. Of five ISDAs, which they call Interactionist, Speech-Act Based, Soft Systems Methodology, Trade Unionist and Professional Work Practices, they examine the ontological, epistemological, methodological and ethical assumptions. This systematises the jungle so that new types of ISDA may be considered. While study of extant ISDMs looks backward to the past, study of ISDAs can chart a course into the future. This is the approach taken here, but this paper does not follow Iivari et al.'s approach because it is not entirely appropriate.

On the one hand, as they acknowledge, their analysis was of what has been written about ISD methodology from the point of view of IS research rather than of actual practice. It is perhaps as a result of this that they propose the following as a way ahead:

> Concrete ISDMs as instances of ISDAs have various 'sediments' in terms of methods and tools that are not necessarily essential for the ISDA. After purifying them of such inessential sediments, and abstracting them to the level of ISDAs, the generation of an integrated ISDM could take place in a much more structured and elegant way.

While some 'sediments' might be 'accidentals' others are often the very things that determine the quality of an ISDM in real-life ISD. They range from small aspects of everyday human living, such as Wenger (1998) discusses and illustrates in relation to Communities of Practice, to major issues that occupy whole fields of research, such as software engineering and data modelling. While such issues should never dominate ISD, they are nevertheless essential components of ISD, and it is surprising to find no mention of them.

The reason for this might be found in another limitation they acknowledge: they base their analysis on Burrell and Morgan's (1979) model of sociological paradigms, which sets objectivism over against subjectivism and order or consensus over against conflict. As a result, most of their discussion takes on a dualistic nature, even though they weaken it a little to allow opposing poles to coexist. The ontological discussion is about how each approach views data/information (as either descriptive or constitutive), information systems (as either social or technical), human beings (as either determined or voluntaristic), technology (as either determined or a matter of human choice) and organisations (as either structural or interactional). Epistemology is discussed in terms of being either positivist or anti-positivist (interpretivist or critical). Ethics covers the role of IS science, which is conceived of as either a means to an end or as (critical) interpretation, and the value of IS research, which takes a more pluralistic than dualistic view. The value of IS research to each approach is largely determined by what the approach deems important and meaningful; the Interactionist approach focuses on the social aspect, the Speech-Act approach on the communicational aspect, Soft Systems Methodology on problem-solving and learning, the Trades Union approach on justice for workers and their interests, and the Professional Work Practices approach on professional management. Methodology refers not to ISD methodology but to IS research methodology, and their discussion of this is also pluralistic, but merely enumerates methodologies made use of in the past.

The prevalence of dualistic views seems problematic when compared with everyday reality of ISD. For example, human beings are more than just deterministic or voluntaristic, they are self-giving or selfish, just or unjust, frugal or wasteful, friendly or hostile, and many more. That everyday experience escapes the confines of the dualisms may be seen clearly in Wenger's (1998) detailed vignettes of IS use, but the author knows of no such detailed description of the everyday experience of ISD. So he presents the following case study of his own actual experience of one ISD project.

3.1.2   A Case Study of Everyday Experience of ISD

Research in ISD (or most other fields) is permeated with a tendency to focus on certain issues at the expense of others because it is based on theories or assumptions about what is important and how the world is shaped, leaving other issues unaddressed which are deemed unimportant ('sediments'). Column 1 of Table 3.1 lists the main issues the discussion above cited. To be able to see the other issues that are important in real-life ISD we cannot presume to rely on the IS research literature as Iivari et al. (1998) did but must turn to the data of everyday experience.

Table 3.1 Comparison of issues discussed and overlooked in ISD literature

Issues addressed in ISD literature	Additional issues important in Elsie
ISD methodology: linear versus iterative, and combining both; agile approaches	Bestowing credibility on project
	Dignity of all team members
Data models: procedural versus declarative; entity-relationship versus relational versus object-oriented	Team members given space to develop expertise
Defining and clarifying business problem: hard versus soft versus critical systems thinking	Trustability: knowledge in IS will not users down even in exceptional condition
'Persistent Problems':	Saleability: attract those who would benefit but do not yet realise they might
Diversity to be reduced by organisation and specialisation	Ethical aspect overrides sales maximisation
Knowledge to be acquired and negotiated	Diversity of knowledge to be encapsulated
Structure to be perceived and established	Disclosing domain understanding by separating out problem-solving contextual knowledge
Assumptions of ISD Approaches:	Trust and mutual respect in relationships with domain experts
Data/information as descriptive versus constitutive	Maintaining dignity of all who disagree with each other
IS as technical versus social systems	'Frills': features important in everyday use but not worth reporting in academic papers
Human beings as determined versus voluntaristic	Attitude in team: willing to learn, to expend oneself on behalf of others
Technology as determining versus human choice	Users changing their minds as a source of valuable knowledge
Organisations as structural versus interactional	A listening attitude coupled with common sense, putting oneself in shoes of other
Epistemology as positivist versus anti-positivist	Criticality must be generous, not destructive
Role of IS science as end to means versus interpretation	Importance of aiming for beneficial real-life use rather than mere delivery or sale of IS
Value of IS research: to assist organisations, communication, problem-solving, justice (interests), management (professionalism)	Giving domain knowledge its due; no cutting corners
Research methodology: case studies, conceptual development, formal analysis, technical development, action research	Unexpected and indirect repercussions of use
	Build so stakeholders can discover their own ways of working
	Paradox: loss of power welcomed

For this reason, an example will be given of ISD in which this author was involved. Though some time ago (1986–1987), he still remembers very well the kinds of issues that he found important. Some of those that are seldom addressed in the IS research literature even today will be emphasised here. They are summarised in column 2 of Table 3.1. For more complete explanation than is given here, the reader is directed to Basden et al. (1995).

The author was in a team building what became known as Elsie (Brandon et al. 1988), an expert system designed to assist quantity surveyors when taking a lead in construction projects in the UK (that is, before any architect had designed the building). The type of building was offices. Elsie proved to be a 'success', a study of its use being discussed in chapter IV of Basden (2008). Part of its success was due to the involvement of the Royal Institution of Chartered Surveyors, who bestowed credibility. This is an example of an issue often ignored in ISD literature.

Elsie comprised four modules, the purpose of which was to assist the users (quantity surveyors) in setting a budget, gauging project timescale, recommending a procurement method, and assessing long-term financial performance of the building. This author was the senior knowledge engineer and acted as mentor to the others. It was important that the other team members did not feel daunted and could develop their expertise in knowledge engineering with dignity – a second oft-ignored issue.

Elsie was developed over 30 months using a combination of iterative and linear approaches and intensive engagement with a variety of stakeholders, after which it was not only useful and usable but also 'trustable' and 'saleable'. Trustable meant it would not let the user down (by giving misleading or erroneous results) even in exceptional conditions. Saleable (psychologically as well as financially) meant that Elsie was made attractive so that it would be taken up by all those – and only those – who would benefit from using it but did not yet realise they might do so (notice this has an ethical component that overrides sales maximisation). At the time, combining iterative with linear approaches, participative development, and focusing on both usefulness and usability were rare, but they now occupy the ISD literature. However, the importance of trustability and saleability of the kind meant here is still not given due attention.

During the project, the author was assigned to developing the most complex module, budget-setting. He undertook knowledge acquisition interviews with six partner-level surveyors, who acted as domain experts, to elicit expert knowledge of how they would set budgets for new office developments. This knowledge included not only that which applies to most projects but also rare exceptions. There were several issues here that are seldom discussed in the IS literature. The knowledge was highly diverse, ranging over physical aspects of foundations, building shape, movement around building, health, functional quality, provision for technology, flexibility, cultural expectations, aesthetics of materials, legal issues and so on. Much of it was not readily explainable (tacit) and was probed by separating the problem-solving and contextual knowledge from underlying understanding, however informal the latter might be (Attarwala and Basden 1985). It was important to develop and maintain close relationships with these experts, built on trust and mutual respect, because the knowledge elicited was what gave them their dignity as experts. When two experts disagreed, it was important to ensure it did not become a conflict, and especially that neither felt they had 'won' or 'lost', but use the disagreement as a valuable source of knowledge. The issues of tacit knowledge and conflict are now discussed in the IS literature, but not in the way addressed in the project.

These experts also conveyed what was needed from a user's point of view, which indicated what 'frills' (as we knowledge engineers tended to call them at the time)

would be useful – such as good, concise explanations of results, ability to override
the reasoning with one's own values for such things as the quality level or the cost
of bricks, ability to change inputs, and, crucially, ability to save current state of
model for later. The author learned that it is such frills that are important in everyday
use rather than more academically noteworthy attributes like knowledge completeness
and Bayesian probabilities. An attitude of being willing to learn was vital here,
informed by an attitude of being willing to expend oneself in giving more than is
strictly necessary, combined with a certain creativity.

The potential users would change their minds about what was wanted. Though
this was considered a problem in ISD at the time, the author believed differently:
mind-change was an opportunity to probe and explore what would be truly useful.
This came from a listening attitude coupled with employing common sense that was
both critical and generous, putting oneself in the shoes of the other, and aiming for
real-life use rather than mere delivery of an artifact.

The author was also involved in programming, developing algorithms not available
in the knowledge representation system. This was always undertaken with an awareness of wider issues, not only of the application domain, but also of being 'true' to
the nature of the reality being programmed. The author learned by experience not to
cut corners nor simplify models!

A study of Elsie in use a few years later (Castell et al. 1992) revealed many interesting findings, including that Elsie changed the way the surveyors worked in ways
that were unexpected but which were discovered by the users themselves. See chapter
IV of Basden (2008) for details. Of particularly interest, in view of the prevalence of
Foucauldian power-knowledge perspectives, was the replacement of a novice-expert
relationship with that of two partners working towards a shared goal, in which the
apparent loss of power was welcomed by both parties. Unexpected and indirect
impacts of IS use are issues still not adequately addressed in ISD literature.

3.1.3   The Need for Lifeworld-Orientated ISD (LOISD)

The Elsie case reveals a wide range of issues that could be important to the success
of ISD projects but which are seldom, if ever, given adequate attention in the ISD
research literature nor even in extant methodologies (though agile methods might
address some of them). Doubtless other experience can bring up many more.
Table 3.1 lists the Elsie issues in column 2, set against the issues mentioned in
section 3.1.1.

It may be seen that many of the issues that made Elsie ISD successful are those
found in everyday life. Many are to do with such things as attitude, which has until
now been difficult to discuss in the IS literature because very few conceptual frameworks are available within which to make sense of it.

The central question this paper addresses is: How can we ensure that everyday
issues are given the attention they deserve in both ISD research and ISD practice?

This suggests the need for a new approach rather than merely a new methodology
(in Iivari et al.'s (1998) terms, new ISDA rather than ISDM), which embodies a new

set of philosophical assumptions. This paper advocates a 'lifeworld' approach. The lifeworld may be defined loosely as that shared background knowledge on which we rely in everyday life (which includes both home and professional life and, particularly for this paper, ISD). It thus has close links with everyday activity itself, and therefore an understanding of the lifeworld might enable us to understand the 'real world' issues of ISD without treating them as mere 'sediments'.

It was noted that most of Iivari et al.'s analysis of what may be assumed is guided by a dualistic view. Everyday experience of ISD itself transcends these dualistic views and presents us with phenomena that cannot be neatly squeezed into their mould, even though, by convention, we might import them into professional ISD practice. It is not that the dualisms (such as the deterministic-voluntaristic dimension with which they view human beings) are wrong, but that they are too restrictive.

To answer the central question of this paper we must reflect of the very nature of the lifeworld and everyday experience. So section 3.2 builds up a picture of the lifeworld and everyday life by briefly reviewing what philosophers have said about the lifeworld and everyday life. The philosophy of Dooyeweerd (1955/1984) is particularly useful here. Section 3.3 applies this picture to ISD to propose 'lifeworld-orientated ISD' (LOISD). Section 3.4 concludes with discussion.

3.2   Lifeworld

It was Husserl (1954/1970) who first used the term, 'life-world', when arguing that European sciences were in crisis. Science generates 'worlds' of knowledge, such as those of mathematics, geometry, physics, psychology, sociology, but there is a considerable amount of other knowledge by which we live our everyday lives – the 'life-world'. He argued that the process of doing science necessarily presupposed the life-world, in that many things done in science were only meaningful and justified by reference to the life-world. The long-assumed 'objectivity' of science was shown to rest on intersubjective foundations.

Since then other thinkers have extended the notion of lifeworld (now spelled without hyphen) far beyond Husserl's original use, to refer to the shared knowledge that we take for granted in everyday life, and by which everyday life functions smoothly. Some have used other names, including 'natural', 'everyday', 'self-evident', 'pre-theoretical' and 'naïve' (without negative connotations); the opposite is 'theorizing' or 'theoretical'.

3.2.1   Attitudes: Lifeworld and Theorizing

The terms 'everyday' and 'lifeworld' refer not so much to situations or spheres of life as to an attitude we take to them, be they home life, work or even the activity of scientific research. In a lifeworld (or everyday, pre-theoretical, naïve) attitude we take things "as they give themselves to us" (Husserl 1954/1970, p. 156). Husserl proposed a 'principle of principles', that we should let the lifeworld present itself to us, rather than approaching it with a priori theoretical constructs, which is the theorizing or theoretical attitude. Theories can be very useful (how, is discussed below) but the danger with a theoretical attitude is that it narrows the gaze onto certain factors so that other factors or aspects are overlooked and ignored.

In ISD prior theoretical constructs may be seen expressed in the type of development methodology adopted (e.g. linear or iterative) which in turn embodies presuppositions about what is meaningful and important (e.g. control of deadlines and resources, or user participation); other things, some illustrated by the Elsie case, are ignored. The data model adopted expresses theoretical constructs about on what basis the world to be modelled can be represented in symbols (e.g. mathematical tuples if relational model is adopted). ISD research also brings prior theoretical constructs. Kautz et al. (2007a) bring the theory that all that is important may be categorised into diversity, knowledge and structure, which embody the presuppositions that diversity is to be reduced and only explicit knowledge is important. Prior theoretical constructs in Iivari et al. (1998) include the components into which ontology and ethics are divided (including information, IS, humans, technology and organisations, but not, for example, the wider world or the nature of diversity) and the issues they discuss within each (which are mainly dualistic and thus, as we have seen, limiting). Each of these constitutes a theory about what is important and, therefore, what is less important, which they call 'sediments'. Prior theoretical constructs brought to ISD practice become troublesome when adherence to the methodology or data model is rigid. Prior theories brought to bear on IS research become troublesome when they restrict what is deemed worthy of research.

A lifeworld attitude might help to avoid this danger. If we are to move towards LOISD we need to understand the nature and characteristics of the lifeworld.

How may we understand the lifeworld? If we take a theoretical attitude to understanding the lifeworld, such as approaching it with the prior constructs of psychology, sociology or a prior perspective like functionalism (as Dewey's pragmatism does) then we fail to take the lifeworld as it presents itself to us. It is preferable to take a lifeworld attitude to understanding both the lifeworld and theoretical thought.

The Dutch philosopher, Dooyeweerd (1955/1984), is one thinker who attempted this. He began his magnum opus (1955/1984) with

> If I consider reality as it is given in the naïve pre-theoretical experience, … (Vol. I, p. 3)

Pieces of his thought will be employed, along with that of others, to draw together some characteristics of everyday life and lifeworld, which differentiate a lifeworld or everyday attitude from a theorizing one. (For a systematic introduction to this little-known philosopher see Clouser (2005) or Basden (2008).)

3.2.2 Diversity of Everyday Life and Lifeworld

Dooyeweerd continued (1955/1984, I, p. 3):

> … and then confront it with a theoretical analysis through which reality appears to split up into various modal aspects, then the first thing that strikes me, is the original indissoluble

interrelation among these aspects … A indissoluble inner coherence binds the numerical to the spatial aspect, the latter to the aspect of mathematical movement, the aspect of movement to that of physical energy, which itself is the necessary basis of the aspect of organic life. The aspect of organic life has an inner connection with that of psychical feeling, the latter refers in its logical anticipation (the feeling of logical correctness or incorrectness) to the analytical-logical aspect. This in turn is connected with the historical, the linguistic, the aspect of social intercourse, the economic, the aesthetic, the jural, the moral aspects and that of faith. In this inter-modal cosmic coherence no single aspect stands by itself; every-one refers within and beyond itself to all the others.

Dooyeweerd is here suggesting three things that most immediately present themselves to us. First, there is diversity. Second, to be aware of this we "split up" reality. Third, despite being "split up" by us the diversity coheres. It is only later that he attempts to discuss the nature of the diversity, of theoretical analysis and of coherence philosophically. What was key to his approach and makes if fruitful here is that he focused first not on diversity of things or occurrences (the 'what' of reality) but on diversity of ways in which the world can be and occur (the 'how').

Dooyeweerd is not alone in drawing attention to such diversity; for example Gadamer referred to a "wealth of modes" (1977, p. 191). It has already been noted that Kautz et al. (2007a) sees diversity as a challenge for ISD. Reflecting on diversity with a lifeworld attitude involves distinguishing the aspects of what is concretely experienced. So thinkers differentiate aspects from each other, resulting in suites of aspects (or 'levels', 'strata') that range from formal ontologies (Bunge 1977; Hartmann 1952), through proposals for action types (Habermas 1986) and Maslow's (1943) famous set of needs, to informal, alliterative lists of factors to be taken into account, such as Checkland's (1999) efficiency, effectiveness, efficacy, ethicality and elegance.

The relevance to ISD is the diversity of aspects of the human activities that constitute ISD and the coherence of the ISD project. It is useful to select a suite of aspects to guide our thinking and though we could select any of the above, we will employ Dooyeweerd's suite here not only because it is more comprehensive than most others, but because Dooyeweerd provided a more penetrating analysis of diversity, 'splitting-up' and coherence than most others have done. His suite is also more directly linked to everyday experience; some of the others were devised in relation to scientific conceptualization or with specific focus. Moreover, use of some suites might denature ISD. For example, employing Maslow's (1943) suite of needs would redefine ISD as an exercise in meeting the personal needs of individuals, rather than one of producing beneficial information systems.

Dooyeweerd's list cited above, though extensively discussed, is left only loosely defined in (1955/1984), partly because he maintained:

In fact the system of the law-spheres designed by us can never lay claim to material completion. A more penetrating examination may at any time bring new modal aspects of reality to the light not yet perceived before. And the discovery of new law-spheres will always require a revision and further development of our modal analyses. (1955/1984, II, p. 556)

That Dooyeweerd sometimes called aspects "law spheres", is because of his exploration of what aspects are. Each aspect is a way in which things can be meaningful (a sphere of meaning), a mode of being, a mode of functioning, a basic kind of property, a way of relating, a way in which things make sense (rationality), a kind of normativity (good and bad), and a kind of possibility for the future; see Basden (2008) for explanation of these. In this article the terms 'sphere of meaning', 'sphere of law' and 'aspect' will be used interchangeably, depending on what is being emphasised.

According to Dooyeweerd, all things exhibit all aspects. So, as discussed later, ISD exhibits logical thought, history, language, social relationships, resources, legal issues, and so on.

3.2.3   Use of Theory in Everyday Living

If we accept Husserl's 'principle of principles', that we should not come with a priori theory, how can we make use of theory in ISD? Dooyeweerd (1955/1984, III, p. 31) argued that "Naïve experience may be deepened through … scientific knowledge, but cannot be destroyed by it." Theory may be brought in as long as it deepens without narrowing or causing undue distortion, and this is possible if we understand what lies at the root of the theoretical attitude.

Using transcendental critique, Dooyeweerd (1955/1984) argued that theoretical thinking necessarily pulls aspects apart (an extreme form of 'split up'), disrupting our view of their mutual interweaving, and Clouser (2005) explains this as high levels of abstraction of aspects away from reality, so that we focus exclusively on one aspect and study its laws without regard to its relationship with others. This generates theory, but to apply that theory requires re-integration, and that is a pre-theoretical act, presupposing human activity (lifeworld). Dooyeweerd and Clouser both argue that this grounds all theory-making in presuppositions that are religious in nature, so no theory can ever be neutral ('objective'), nor can it have any ultimate authority in itself. Because of its abstracted focus on one aspect, theoretical knowledge is likely to be inferior, not superior, to lifeworld knowledge.

There are two mitigations. One is that the aspects actually remain interwoven even when supposedly pulled apart, so we can always look for inter-aspect relationships, especially those of dependency and analogy (Basden 2008, p. 71–72). The other is what Clouser calls lower abstraction, in which we are aware of the distinctions among aspects (e.g. the beauty versus the cost of a rose) but do not abstract them away from the types of things that exhibit them.

3.2.4   Lifeworld as Background

The lifeworld attitude therefore eschews this pulling-apart of aspects. Other philosophers have thrown light on this. Heidegger (1927/1962) emphasised that the human being is immersed in the world, 'thrown' into it, and that is the lifeworld attitude, prior to splitting up reality. In everyday life we "live within" the world, so the knowledge of it that we make use of and rely on as we do so (viz. the lifeworld) must have a background character. "To live is always to live-in-certainty-of-the-world" wrote Husserl (1954/1970, p. 142); in everyday living we place reliance on our lifeworld knowledge. To Husserl, the lifeworld is intuitive knowledge, 'pregiven', taken for granted (1954/1970, p. 109). "By this taken-for-grantedness," say Schutz and Luckmann (1973, p. 3–4), who developed his thought, "we designate everything which we experience as unquestionable". It has a 'tacit dimension' (Polanyi 1967).

In a theoretical attitude, by contrast, we adopt a role of detached observers of the world, distancing ourselves from what is known, questioning what is taken for granted and trying to make aspects explicit. As a result, "The lifeworld ... dissolves ... before our eyes as soon as we try to take it up piece by piece," (Habermas, in Honneth et al. 1981, p. 16).

The challenge is to minimise such distortion and the 'dissolving' of the lifeworld even though in ISD we must sometimes "take it up piece by piece". ISD involves both splitting the world up conceptually while at the same time engaging with it. How LOISD allows these to work in harmony, abating the detachment, is discussed later.

3.2.5   Meaning and Normativity

What is it that is taken for granted? Some of our background knowledge is of relational facts (for example, that programs need testing). A considerable amount of the lifeworld, however, is meaning (for example, what is important in testing) and norms (what we conceive as good and bad testing). Husserl's main concern, a 'crisis' in the European sciences, was loss of meaning and of "norms upon which man relies" (1954/1970, p. 6–7). Habermas (1987) too acknowledged the lifeworld's meaning and normativity, though his concern was apparent loss of meaning in modern life in general.

Modern thinking has fundamental problems with meaning and normativity because Hume and Kant divorced them from existence (or process), and since that time much Western thinking has presupposed that 'facts' may be studied apart from 'values'. Ethics is relegated to something personal and optional. But the lifeworld knows nothing of the supposed divorce. Husserl sought "truths that are destined to be norms" (1954/1970, p. 303), for example "the genuine judge, true honor, true courage and justice" – though it is debated whether he found a way to them. Dooyeweerd, however, might have found a way, because he rejected the Kantian-Humean presuppositions and grounded existence in meaning and law (1955/1984, I, p. 4): to be a judge, qua judge, cannot be divorced from the normative notion of justice. However, he sharply differentiated between deep normativity, which transcends us, and norms that are concrete expressions of this, which are usually socially constructed.

3.2.6   The Social Aspect of the Lifeworld

The lifeworld is shared with others: when "thinking together, valuing, planning, acting together" (Husserl 1954/1970, p. 109), we cannot do so successfully unless what is meaningful and normative to one is so to others in largely the same way. The lifeworld has an important social aspect and a strong (though weakly-understood) link with culture and world-view.

This makes language an important issue, as stressed by Hirschheim and Klein (1994). Shared meanings enable us to understand what the other is saying, and language enables shared meanings and norms to develop. Habermas (1987) argued that this occurs when we critique the truthfulness, sincerity or appropriateness of each others' statements.

There are "highly different lifeworlds in which highly different things pass as unquestioningly self-evident" (Gadamer 1977, p. 189) – e.g. those of engineers and judges, right- and left-wingers, adults and children, IS developers, domain experts and users. A person will live in several lifeworlds (a judge may be a left-winger), and some overlap. Some encompass others, e.g. left- and right-wing are mainly within the lifeworld of the Western world-view.

As human beings function well – for example in the domain of application of an IS – they do so with a background shared understanding of what is meaningful and important. This includes knowledge and experience of many meaningful things, norms, rationalities, happenings past and present, and future possibilities, including such things as how the domain has come to weave legal, ethical, economic, social and other demands into a coherent story. A vocabulary for the domain builds up, including special connotation of common words of which the outsider might not be aware.

How can there be understanding across different lifeworlds? This question is important in cross-cultural considerations in the Internet age, as well as between developers, users and domain experts in ISD. If all lifeworld meaning is socially constructed via language, it is possible in principle for there to be two lifeworlds that have almost no meaning or normativity in common. As alluded to above, however, Dooyeweerd (1955/1984) believed socially constructed norms and meanings to be concrete expressions of more fundamental meaning and normativity that transcends humanity. It is this that makes human living possible, including social construction itself, and of which there are distinct yet interrelated spheres or aspects. These aspects, therefore, are common to all lifeworlds and they present themselves to us in the lifeworld attitude, which Dooyeweerd listed informally in his opening paragraph above. He argued that the kernel meanings of aspects can never be grasped by theoretical thought but may be grasped intuitively. If Dooyeweerd is correct, then there might be two sides to the lifeworld: kernel meanings that are intuitively graspable across cultures, and specific meanings that are socially constructed within specific cultures (Basden and Klein 2008). There are hints of this in Husserl (1954/1970, p. 144) when he differentiated "objects ... as substrates of their properties" from "manners of appearance, or manners of givenness".

3.3 Lifeworld-Oriented Information Systems Development

How, then, can we undertake, recognise or evaluate lifeworld-oriented information systems development (LOISD)? We may begin by saying that ISD is lifeworld-oriented to the extent that all relevant lifeworlds are respected and taken into account. Each lifeworld is likely to differ from others because of different background knowledge. Two main lifeworlds will be briefly considered with regard to the characteristics of the lifeworld outlined above, those of IS developer and of application domain (others could be considered in the same way).

3.3.1 The Various Lifeworlds of ISD

That in the lifeworld attitude we are closely engaged with the world draws attention to the engagements that IS developers make with their world. The everyday experience of ISD exhibits this engaged character rather than a distance that is characteristic of rational planning and legal relationships. This drives ISD towards closer engagement among team members, and between team members and those not organisationally in the team, such as users and domain experts. If the relationship between the developers and domain experts takes on this distal nature then the knowledge that is conveyed will be of poor quality, so the IS will not become 'trustable'. If the relationship between developers and users is distal then what the users really need will not become adequately known by the developers, so the IS will not become useful and 'saleable'. If inter-developer relationships are distal, such as mediated by deliverables that are signed off before being passed across to the next developer, then increased errors can be expected.

This might explain why agile development methods are providing greater productivity, lower rates of errors and greater programmer satisfaction. To the extent that it encourages such engagement, agile methods may be seen as a step towards LOISD.

From a lifeworld perspective as outlined above, ISD is usefully seen as human activity that exhibits multiple aspects. If we employ Dooyeweerd's suite of aspects as a categorization with which to approach this, then an investigation of the everyday life of ISD will find many aspects, if the case study above is not untypical. Basden (2008) did so, separating out the plethora of issues that are important in everyday ISD, finding that not only is every aspect exhibited, but that it is exhibited in several ways. ISD may be seen as a several multi-aspectual human activities interwoven with each other, each involving a different relationship, including at least:

- Orchestration of the overall ISD project; relationships within the team and with clients
- Anticipation of use of the IS and planning for it; relationships with users
- Acquiring knowledge about the domain of application; relationships with experts
- Construction of the technical artifact; relationships with the technology

The first and fourth are mainly linked to the lifeworld of the IS developers, while the second and third are linked to the lifeworld of the application domain, though they are also human activities of IS development.

3.3.2 The Lifeworld of the IS Developer

Table 3.2 gives examples of aspects of the overall ISD project. In column 1 is the name of each aspect (those in Dooyeweerd's introductory list above but some renamed), in column 2 is the kernel meaning of the aspect, so this table may be referred to for what

Table 3.2 Illustrates aspects of overall ISD project and team

Aspect	Meaning	As exemplified in ISD project	As emphasised in
Quantitative	Discrete amount	Number in team	Relational data model (tuples)
Spatial	Continuous space	Layout of team's office	–
Kinematic	Movement	People movement	–
Physical	Energy, matter	Power consumption	–
Biotic	Life functions	Health of team members	–
Sensitive	Feeling and response	Emotions in team	Reactive approaches
Analytical	Distinctness	Clarity of objectives	Linear approaches (clarity of stages)
Formative	Construction, design, goals, technique, technology	Project planning, team skills	Boehm's Spiral model; Kautz et al.'s diversity reduction; Soft Systems Methodology problem-solving
Lingual	Symbolic signification	Documentation, communication	Kautz et al.'s knowledge; Iivari et al.'s Speech-Act approach
Social	Relationships and roles	Team structure, socializing	Kautz et al.'s structure Iivari et al.'s Interactionist approach
Economic	Management of scarce resources	Budgets, deadlines, facilities, expertise	Linear methodologies; Iivari et al.'s PWP approach
Aesthetic	Harmony (as in music), humour, enjoyment	Orchestration of whole project; fun or boredom of the project	–
Juridical	Due, appropriateness	Justice to team members or otherwise; Contract with client	Hirschheim and Klein's (1994) emancipatory ISD; Iivari et al.'s Trades Union approach
Ethical	Self-giving love	Attitude of generosity or self-interest pervading team	–
Faith	Belief, vision, commitment, morale	Loyalty to project	Religious faith of members SSM's Weltanschauung?

each aspect covers. Column 3 shows is how this may be manifested in the overall ISD project. Column 4 shows the main issues emphasised by the methodologies and academic literature discussed above.

It may be seen that from the analytic aspect onwards, and possibly from the biotic, there is a difference between good and bad; these aspects are normative. Using the aspects in this way can provide methodological guidance for LOISD. Column 4 shows that each methodology or approach focuses on one or two aspects. This means each could be in danger of ignoring others unless positive action is taken to consider all aspects; this accounts for the tendency of both extant methodologies and IS research to ignore issues that might be important in everyday ISD.

Table 3.3 shows aspects of the other three human activities in ISD, starting at the analytic aspect. (Earlier aspects are largely as for the overall ISD project.)

Even though this is far from complete, this aspectual analysis paints a richer picture of ISD than is commonly seen. While some aspects are well-covered in existing approaches, many are not. That the aspects are spheres of law means that most of these entries are normative, and may be incorporated into methodological guidelines for each of the activities of LOISD. Future research could add aspectual rationality, functioning and possibility to the picture.

Such an approach must be taken with care. It would be tempting to treat the aspects as mere categories or simple norms and, though that might indeed provide

Table 3.3 Some examples of aspects of three human activities in ISD

Aspect	Anticipating Use	Knowledge acquisition	Creating the IS
Analytical	Clarifying user requirements	'Splitting up' aspects of domain	Deciding data types, classes
Formative	Imagining future use	Structuring the knowledge	Designing program architecture and structures
Lingual	Communicating with users	Communicating with experts; Drawing knowledge maps	Writing the program; Documentation
Social	Respecting users	Close relationship with experts	Pair programming, etc.
Economic	Need to understand future use early on in project	Experts give limited time	Efficiency of algorithms, data storage, etc.
Aesthetic	Appreciating how IS will fit its context of use; Ensuring it is pleasant to use	Seeing how all domain knowledge works in harmony	The fun and beauty of programs (Knuth 2001); Style of user interface, web pages.
Juridical	Ensuring appropriateness of IS to all stakeholders	Doing justice to all (diverse) domain knowledge	Not cutting corners in building the IS
Ethical	Giving priority to users' ideas	Generous attitude to experts	Doing extra work to make the IS better
Faith	Vision for why the IS will be important in use	Critical trust of experts	Commitment to getting program right

a superior methodology, it would not be full LOISD. LOISD must take account that much lifeworld knowledge is taken for granted, and thus tends not to emerge during discussion. This can plague all the ISD activities, but especially knowledge acquisition. It can be useful, therefore, to take stock from time to time, to ask ourselves "Which aspects are being over-emphasised here, and which are being ignored?" It is often the case, for example, that the economic aspect is over-emphasised while the ethical aspect of self-giving is overlooked, partly because of the assumption of competition as a high norm of business. When such a realisation occurs action can be taken to give fuller consideration the overlooked aspects.

The aspects should not be treated as simple categories, but rather as spheres or areas of meaning from the standpoints of which we can consider all the issues involved. For example, the juridical sphere of 'due' does not by itself tell us what is due to each entity with which we engage; what it does is strongly urge us to consider that, and, in conjunction with the ethical aspect, to give ourselves whole-heartedly to this consideration.

3.3.3   The Lifeworld of the Application Domain

The challenge for IS development is that in it (at least) two lifeworlds meet, those of the human activities of ISD discussed above, especially the activities of anticipating use and knowledge acquisition, and that of the domain of application. Both domain experts and users of the IS being developed are immersed in this domain. Rather than treat the lifeworlds of experts and users separately, it is useful to first examine the lifeworld of the application domain.

IS developers function best when they have internalised lifeworlds of both ISD and the domain. It is usually assumed that developers will be expert at development and will learn something of the domain, but the reverse can happen: those already functioning in the domain can themselves become the IS developers. The author had one experience of this: a world-leading corrosion expert became an IS developer when he began building his own expert systems, under the author's guidance (Hines and Basden 1986; Basden and Hines 1986). That the domain expert could become an IS developer was made possible because the expert system used, 'Savoir', was very easy to understand while also being powerful and flexible, and also because of the good relationship of respect built up between the two people, as referred to above. Arguably it should be preferable and easier for a domain expert to learn ISD than an expert developer to internalise the domain lifeworld. There has been too little discussion of the domain experts or users becoming undertaking their own ISD.

The more common way is that an expert in ISD learns something of the domain, about the structure of its knowledge from experts and how the IS should be used from potential users. All too often, what they learn is restricted to the explicit knowledge of the application, such as objectives, processes and formal organisational relationships among those operating in the domain, and too sharp a division is maintained between experts and users. In LOISD, however, the IS developer must also intuitively grasp much of the lifeworld of the domain, which is shared by both experts and users. How can this be achieved without a 30-year apprenticeship in the domain? It is possible that sufficient may be grasped to ensure reasonable quality ISD if the following pertain for the developer:

- The developer has a strong intuitive grasp of all the kernel meanings of the aspects, recognising that none can be reduced to the others in terms of their normative force or the ways they make things meaningful. If Dooyeweerd is correct, then these kernels are intuitively graspable across lifeworlds, and this can help mutual understanding with users and experts.
- The developer expects all aspects to be active in the domain, in both positive and negative ways. Table 3.4 provides examples for the later aspects, including the types of practical question that might be asked during analysis.
- It can be helpful to identify the central, 'qualifying' aspect(s) of the domain and keep seeking to understand how all in the domain links back to these. A useful way to achieve this is to ask users or experts to nominate which aspects are most important. Then knowledge acquisition spreads out to all aspects as they see fit. This is the approach of Winfield's (2000) 'Multi-aspectual Knowledge Elicitation' process (Winfield and Basden 2006).
- The developer keeps looking for aspects of the lifeworld that have not yet been fully discussed, and giving users and experts the opportunity to express whatever might be meaningful in these.

Table 3.4 How aspects can separate out what is important in domain

Aspect	What is important in domain	Useful question to ask
Analytical	Distinctions important to domain; rationalities of domain	What are the main categories?
Formative	Goals, techniques, technologies of domain	What happens in this domain? What techniques are used?
Lingual	Vocabulary and special connotations given to common words	What does this phrase mean? What types of diagram or signs are there?
Social	Social structures and relationships in domain	How is X related to Y? What institutions have authority here?
Economic	Limitations coped with in the domain	What resources is it most important to keep an eye on? How are they managed?
Aesthetic	How the domain holds together; Enjoyment of domain	How does everything hold together? What fun do you get? Tell me some jokes!
Juridical	What is appropriate and proportional in domain	What kinds of behaviour would be inappropriate? Who are the main stakeholders, and what is due to them?
Ethical	Willingness to 'go the extra mile'	What is it about life in this domain that you love?
Faith	Belief that the domain is important	What does this contribute to humanity and history (in the eyes of God)?

– The developer has an attitude of respect for how all aspects make sense and are worked out in specific ways by those living in the domain, especially the concrete norms of the domain and what is deemed important.

When expert or user are themselves the developer, most of these still apply, and can be quite useful in stimulating self-critique in relation to the status quo.

What this table tells us is that, even while the developer need not grasp the details of the domain, especially those of its science, he/she can and should grasp the overall shape the domain has in each aspect. Most knowledge acquisition or systems analysis texts emphasise the need to accurately understand the analytical and formative shape, but few extend to other aspects of its shape, from the aesthetics of the domain onwards. This table suggests that in LOISD the developer should proactively seek to understand the overall shape of the domain in every aspect.

The kinds of questions shown in the table (suitably reworded according to situation) are ones that are likely to be reasonably understandable in all cultures, because they try to express the intuitively-grasped kernel meanings of the aspects that transcend cultures.

3.4   Conclusion

This paper has proposed a new approach to IS development: lifeworld-oriented IS development (LOISD). The aim is to provide a framework for understanding real-life ISD so that all the issues that might determine its quality and success or failure can be recognised, discussed and responded to. It is suggested that not only many extant methodologies and data models but especially much academic literature on ISD can be problematic because they restrict the developer's and researcher's view so that many important issues are treated as 'sediments' to be discarded rather than given the attention they deserve. To rectify this, LOISD takes full account of the lifeworlds of IS developer, users and domain experts – the highly diverse, taken-for-granted pools of knowledge that are active in everyday life of each of these. Though a number of the characteristics of the lifeworld (discussed above) may be detected in ISD methods, they have not previously been put together in the way outlined here.

Dooyeweerd's (1955/1984) notion of aspects as distinct spheres of meaning and law has been widely used here to conceptualise the diversity of the lifeworld, making it possible to paint a richer picture than hitherto available. Doing this separates out four distinct multi-aspectual human activities that constitute ISD, each exhibiting all the aspects: conducting the overall project, anticipating use, acquiring knowledge and constructing the IS. Dooyeweerd tentatively proposed a suite of aspects, which is arguable more suited than others are to our use here because it has been carefully thought-out and philosophically grounded.

Iivari et al. (1998) show that examining philosophical assumptions can differentiate ISD approaches. Table 3.5 shows the ontological, epistemological, ethical and methodological assumptions of LOISD based on Dooyeweerd, comparing them with those of the five ISDAs mentioned in Iivari et al. See Basden (2008) for explanation of Dooyeweerd's ideas.

Table 3.5 Philosophical assumptions of LOISD based on Dooyeweerd

Assumption	As in Iivari et al. (1998)	Made by LOISD based on Dooyeweerd
View of data/ information	Descriptive or constitutive	An object of human lingual functioning, in which the whole diversity of meaning may be expressed
View of IS	Technical or social system	Human living with I.T
View of human beings	Deterministic or voluntaristic	We function in all aspects all the time and in each we experience a different kind of freedom and constraint (Dooyeweerd's discussion of the human ego is not relevant here.)
View of (information) technology	Determining us, or a matter of human choice	Technology in general opens up the potential of the formative aspect; Information technology opens up the potential of the lingual aspect; In both cases, this should be done in service of all other aspects, and we should not let it dominate us. See Basden (2010)
View of organisations	Structural or interactional	Voluntary or involuntary associations in which roles and relationships are important (Dooyeweerd 1986)
Epistemology	Positivist or anti-positivist	The human knower as part of the knowable world; multi-aspectual ways of knowing beyond the theoretical; intuition and everyday knowing; reality as friendly rather than hostile to human knowing (contra Kant); transcendental critique of theoretical thought
Role of IS science	Means-end oriented or interpretative	Disclosure of laws of lingual aspect in relation to all others
Value of IS research	To assist communicational, social, problem-solving, justice or managerial aspects	To enable technology-mediated lingual functioning to serve all aspects, including these
IS research methodology	Case studies, action research, conceptual development, technical development or formal analysis	Any of these; it is attitude that is important

Though it is not appropriate to elaborate further on the entries in this table here, it is intended that a paper will be forthcoming that does this. Two things however may be noted for further discussion. One is that though Iivari et al.'s discussion of most assumptions is dualistic, their discussion of the value of IS research is not dualistic but prefigures a Dooyeweerdian discussion; this may be because 'value' presupposes meaning and normativity, both of which are central to Dooyeweerd's notion of aspects. This suggests that Iivari et al.'s approach might be commensurate with a Dooyeweerdian one. The second is to suggest it might be important to discuss additional things about which ontological assumptions are made than those included by Iivari et al., such as the nature of the world in which IS are situated, the nature of diversity and coherence, and the long-term destiny of humanity and technology.

The notion of aspects as spheres of meaning and law that make all human (and other) functioning possible provides us with the interesting idea that the lifeworld has two sides. The fact-side lifeworld is socially-constructed knowledge of all that has occurred or exists, including social norms, and this differs between different cultural groups. By contrast, the law-side lifeworld transcends cultural groups and is constituted of the kernel meanings of the aspects, which are intuitively grasped. This offers a way in which people from different lifeworlds (such as IS developers, users, domain experts) can understand each other; a set of example questions, based on this, is offered that might assist communication between IS developers and those involved in the application domain.

LOISD might also narrow the gulf between the practice of ISD and academic discussion thereof. A lifeworld-oriented approach could provide a ground on which a number of extant debates in the ISD community can take place. For example, the debate between Kautz et al. (2007a, b) and Baskerville et al. (2007) over whether agile methods are fundamentally different from traditional ones may be conducted as follows. The difference between methods is likely to be more evident in certain of the multi-aspectual human activities than in others, especially those relating to the overall project and to creation of the IS. This might help to focus the discussion. Reference to the aspects can then help to separate out the ways in which the difference might be particularly salient, such as social (team structure), formative (planning), lingual (type of documentation) and aesthetic (fun). Then what is taken for granted in each aspect might be debated, and the cultures that have built up, differentiating between fact-side and law-side lifeworlds.

LOISD is a new idea, so it may be too early to know what its advantages and drawbacks might be, whether based on Dooyeweerd or not. It could require more effort, especially in handling a wider range of factors. Unless care is taken, ISD could become characterized by slot-filling – addressing each aspect of each ISD activity once, and then moving on to the next. That would be a travesty of LOISD, because aspects are not mere categories but are spheres of meaning that should be used to stimulate human thinking. Dooyeweerd maintained that the kernel meanings of the aspects are grasped by our intuition, which should make the aspects easy to use during the flow of thinking that characterizes ISD and other analysis. This is indeed what the author has experienced, and thinking aspectually tends to become second-nature. It is especially useful in sensitizing the analyst to what is being overlooked and to tacit knowledge.

Perhaps the biggest danger of LOISD is that its focus on shared background knowledge might lead to upholding the status quo when it should be challenged. This danger is more pronounced when most attention is given to what we called the fact-side of the lifeworld, which is background knowledge of the structures, things, histories, and socially-constructed norms of the domain and of the ISD process.

When attention is given to the law-side lifeworld, however, then new possibilities might be more readily brought to attention. This is because the aspects as spheres of law define broad types of possibility, each of which is irreducible to other types. For example, the juridical aspect tells us that 'what is due' or 'appropriate' is an important sphere of meaning to consider, leaving open the possibility that current legal structures, developed from earlier eras, hinder this and therefore should be radically changed. The use of aspects as aids to out-of-the-box thinking has yet to be properly researched.

The above might seem a rather developer-centric view of ISD, rather than user-centred. That would be a mistaken impression because 'user-centred' does not mean the developer merely responds to what the user wants. Instead, LOISD evokes a responsibility that looks outward not only to the user as such but to the user who is immersed in the domain of application, and beyond the user to the lifeworld of the domain, and even beyond that to the wider world of which it is part.

Dooyeweerd's aspects should not be seen as providing answers to the question "What should I do in LOISD?" nor even as providing questions to ask, though some examples questions have been offered above. Rather, the aspects enable us to formulate areas of discussion, and in this way to encourage free yet meaningful engagement and mutual respect between developers, users and experts. Mutual understanding might be enhanced by reference to the intuitively-grasped kernel meanings of aspects.

LOISD welcomes diversity, rather than reducing it as Kautz et al. (2007a) sought to do, and recognises importance of taken-for-granted knowledge as well as that which is 'negotiated'. Seeing LOISD as several interwoven multi-aspectual human activities, allows an holistic view in which the different factors are nevertheless clearly distinguished. LOISD can be likened to a symphony, in which all the instruments of the orchestra play their part and are essential to the whole. Bringing such orchestration to ISD is what lifeworld-oriented information systems development hopes to achieve.

References

Attarwala, F.T. & Basden, A. (1985). A methodology for constructing Expert Systems. *R&D Management*, 15(2), 141–149.

Basden, A. (2008). *Philosophical Frameworks for Understanding Information Systems*. IGI Global, Hershey, PA, USA.

Basden, A. (2010). On Using Spheres of Meaning to Define and Dignify the IS Discipline. *International Journal of Information Management*, February 2010.

Basden, A., Hines, J. G. (1986). Implications of the relation between information and knowledge in use of computers to handle corrosion knowledge. *British Corrosion Journal*, 21(3), 157–162.

Basden, A., & Klein, H.K. (2008). New research directions for data and knowledge engineering: A philosophy of language approach. *Data & Knowledge Engineering*, 67, 2, 260–285.

Basden, A., Watson, I.D., Brandon, P.S. (1995). *Client-Centred: An Approach to Knowledge Based Systems*. CLRC: Rutherford Appleton Laboratory, U.K. ISBN 0 9023 7635 7.

Baskerville, R, Pries-Heje, J., Ramesh, B. (2007). The enduring contradictions of new software development approaches. *Information Systems Journal*, 17, 241–245.

Beck, K. (2000). *Extreme programming explained: Embrace change*. Boston, MA: Addison-Wesley.

Bergvall-Kåreborn B, Mirijamdotter A, Basden A. (2004). Basic principles of SSM Modeling: An examination of CATWOE from a soft perspective. *Systemic Practice and Action Research*, 17(2), 55–73.

Boehm, B. W. (1988, May). A spiral model of software development and enhancement. *IEEE Computer*, 21(5), 61–72.

Booch, G. (1991), *Object Oriented Design, with applications*, The Benjamin/Cummings Publishing Company, Redwood City, California, USA.

Brandon, P. S., Basden, A., Hamilton, I., & Stockley, J. (1988). *Application of expert systems to quantity surveying*. London: Royal Institution of Chartered Surveyors.

Bunge, M. (1977). *Treatise on basic philosophy*, Vol. 3: Ontology 1: The furniture of the world. Boston, MA: Reidal.

Burrell, B., Morgan, G. (1979). *Sociological Paradigms and Organisational Analysis*. London: Heinemann.

Castells, A. C., Basden, A., Erdos, G., Barrows, P., & Brandon, P. S. (1992). Knowledge based systems in use: A case study. *British Computer Society Specialist Group for Knowledge Based Systems, Proceedings from Expert Systems 92 (Applications Stream)*. Swindon, England: British Computer Society.

Checkland P. (1999). Soft Systems Methodology: a 30-year retrospective. *Systems Thinking, Systems Practice – includes a 30-year retrospective*. Wiley, New York.

Chen, P.P. (1976). The entity-relationship model – towards a unified view of data. *ACM Trans Database Systems*, 1(1), 9–36.

Clouser, R. (2005). *The Myth of Religious Neutrality; An Essay on the Hidden Role of Religious Belief in Theories*. University of Notre Dame Press, Notre Dame, IN, USA.

Codd, E. A. (1970). A relational model for large shared databanks. *Communications of the ACM*, 13(6), 377–387.

Dooyeweerd, H. (1955/1984). *A New Critique of Theoretical Thought*, Vol. I–IV. 1975 edition. Paideia Press, Jordan Station, Ontario.

Dooyeweerd, H. (1986). *A Christian Theory of Social Institutions*, tr. M. Verbrugge. The Herman Dooyeweerd Foundation, La Jolla, CA, USA.

Gadamer, H-G. (1977). *Philosophical Hermeneutics*. tr. D.E. Linge. University of California Press, Los Angeles, CA, USA.

Gamma, E., Helm, R., Johnson, R., & Vlissides, J. (1995). *Design patterns: Elements of reusable object-oriented software*. Reading, MA: Addison-Wesley.

Habermas, J. (1986). *The theory of communicative action: Vol. 1. Reason and the rationalization of society* (T. McCarthy, Trans.). Cambridge, England: Polity Press.

Habermas, J. (1987). *The Theory of Communicative Action; Volume Two: The Critique of Functionalist Reason*. tr. T.McCarthy. Polity Press, Cambridge, UK.

Hartmann, N. (1952). *The new ways of ontology*. Chicago, IL: Chicago University Press.

Heidegger, M. (1927/1962). *Being and Time*. tr. J. Macquarrie, Robinson. Blackwell Publishing, Oxford, UK.

Hines, J. G., & Basden, A. (1986). Experience with use of computers to handle corrosion knowledge. *British Corrosion Journal*, 21(3), 151–156.

Hirschheim, R., & Klein, H. K. (1994). Realizing emancipatory principles in information systems development: The case for ETHICS. *MIS Quarterly*, 18(1), 85–109.

Hirschheim, R., Klein, H.K., Lyytinen, K. (1995). *Information Systems Development and Data Modelling: Conceptual and Philosophical Foundations*. Cambridge University Press, Cambridge.

Honneth, A., Knodler-Bunte, E., Windmann, A. (1981). The Dialectics of Rationalization: an interview with Jürgen Habermas. *Telos*, 49, 3–31.

Husserl, E. (1954/1970). *The Crisis of European Sciences and Transcendental Phenomenology*. Northwestern University Press, Evanston, IL, USA.

Iivari, J., Hirschheim, R., Klein, H.K. (1998), A Paradigmatic Analysis of Contemporary Schools of IS Development Approaches and Methodologies. *Information Systems Research*, 9(2), 164–193.

Kautz, K., Madson, S., Nørbjerg, J. (2007a). Persistent problems and practices in information systems development. *Information Systems Journal*, 17, 217–239.

Kautz, K., Madson, S., Nørbjerg, J. (2007b). Continuing the debate: a response to a response – persistent problems and practices in information systems development as enduring contradictions of new software development approaches. *Information Systems Journal*, 17, 247–249.

Knuth, D. (2001). *Things a computer scientist rarely talks about*. Stanford, CA: CSLI.

Maslow, A. (1943). A theory of human motivation. *Psychological Review*, 50, 370–396.

Polanyi, M. (1967). *The Tacit Dimension*. Routledge & Kegan Paul, London.

Probert, S.K. (1997). The metaphysical assumptions of the (main) soft systems methodology advocates. In Winder, R.L., Probert, S.K., Beeson, I.A. (eds) *Philosophical Aspects of Information Systems*. Taylor and Francis, London.

Royce, W.W. (1970). Managing the development of large software systems: concepts and techniques. *Proc. IEEE*, Wescon, pp. 328–339.

Schutz, A. & T. Luckmann. (1973). *Structures of the Life-World, Volume I*. Northwestern University Press, Evanston, IL, USA.

Wenger, E. (1998). *Communities of Practice*. Cambridge University Press, Cambridge.

Winfield, M. (2000). *Multi-Aspectual Knowledge Elicitation*. PhD Thesis, University of Salford, U.K.

Winfield, M.J. & Basden, A. (2006). Elicitation of highly interdisciplinary knowledge. In S. Strijbos, A. Basden (eds.) *In Search of an Integrated Vision for Technology; Interdisciplinary Studies in Information Systems*. Springer, New York, pp. 63–78.

Chapter 4
Understanding the Business Client – Systems Developer Relationship: A Power Perspective

Bruce Rowlands

4.1 Introduction

This chapter reports on field research into the relations between developers and the business client and explores the role that systems development methods can play in influencing this relationship. The findings of this field study are distinctive in that they illustrate how the business client (user) is able to exercise power over systems developers through the enactment of organisational structures and routine operating procedures embedded within a development method. The chapter also describes a scenario where developers see the systems development process as unequal and where there is a conflict of interest. Using a neglected view of power in the information systems literature, our particular focus is on applying Hardy's (1985) model of unobtrusive power to help us understand the dynamics between developers and the business client and why grievances do not exist.

The relationship between power and information systems (IS) has been extensively studied (Sillince and Mouakket 1997; Jasperson et al. 2002), but questions about the role development methods play in the distribution of power in the development of systems in organisations have largely been neglected in the literature.

Within the field of IS, information and power were considered to be synonymous (Markus 1983) and those who built business systems were viewed as the dominant partner in influencing power relationships (Markus and Bjørn-Andersen 1987; Smith 1990; Beath and Orlikowski 1994). Later research, starting with Saunders and Scammel (1986:145), challenged this view stating that "rarely does the IT department become involved in key decisions closely related to the mission of organisations". Sauer and Lau (1997) reported on a case specific to systems development, where the business client exercised its political discretion and directly determined the outcome. What made this research unusual in terms of prior literature was that the business client was able to impose their priorities demonstrating a

B. Rowlands (✉)
School of ICT, Griffith University, Brisbane, Australia
e-mail: b.rowlands@griffith.edu.au

H. Isomäki and S. Pekkola (eds.), *Reframing Humans in Information Systems Development*, Computer Supported Cooperative Work 201, DOI 10.1007/978-1-84996-347-3_4, © Springer-Verlag London Limited 2011

shift in power away from developers in the systems development process. However, research of this kind is rare and furthermore, the IS research community of late has not scrutinised the role methods play in distributing authority. In this paper we attempt such a scrutiny by examining in-depth the enactment of a development method. By examining how one method lays out the power relationship between the business client and systems developers, how it distributes resources, how systems developers respond to its prescriptions, we gain insight into how authority structures embedded within the method constrain the actions of developers.

For our research we conducted a field study of method enactment in a major Australian Bank, and applied Lamb and Kling's (2003) *user as social actor model* as a lens to analyse the case. Rowlands (2009b) found that the *user as social actor model* draws out the power concepts, but not why developers are compliant with an unequal power arrangement. Faced with this limitation, the analysis in this chapter has been strengthened by the incorporation of Hardy's (1985) model of unobtrusive power. This model allows us to understand why, in a scenario involving a conflict of interest, developers cooperate with the business client and furthermore there are no grievances and conflict does not arise.

Our research is justified based on our belief that researchers still have an incomplete understanding of how systems developers collectively use development methods in their day-to-day work, or the forces that impact on the situated use of these devices for systems development. We argue that the work that has been carried out is limited in its ability to consider the complex social and organisational context of method enactment. Most field research on the enactment of methods have neglected the messy and complex way people work and live, and the dynamics by which power and authority processes shape method enactment. We believe that more research is needed as there has been insufficient consideration of the power relations that exist in the client-developer relationship, especially when the client and developer come from the same organisation. A lack of field research on the impact of power relations precludes a full understanding of how methods are enacted. Our research addresses these limitations by continuing the discussion about the enactment of methods but with an emphasis on how systems developers' concerns and every day work practices are shaped by institutional structures, with a focus on power relations existing between the business client and systems developers.

Other IS research also features the importance of developing a holistic understanding of the working relationships between systems developers and the business client. For instance, Day (2007) developed a framework showing how the organisational setting, attitudes of individuals, social processes and outcomes affect how relationships are built. A key finding of her work is that good working relationships between the information systems organisation (IT department) and the business client will be established when their belief states are congruent or similar. Where belief states are not similar, or where there is a conflict of interest, Day (2007) also recommends a power-based perspective to understand the unequal relations that can exist between developer and client.

In this chapter, we argue that to gain a more holistic understanding of the role of the business client (or user) in the systems development process, we need to study both halves in the business client-systems developer pair. While we would expect the business client to say that 'they want results, quicker delivery of systems, and to control costs', and that 'project management is about control'; the impressions of the developer and how they view their relationship with clients would be insightful. This chapter provides such an understanding from the perspective of the systems developer.

This research has further significance in that it addresses two pressing issues in the IS community. The first is in diagnosing and bridging the relationship gap or mis-alignment between the IT organisation and the rest of the business (Peppard 2007). From their literature review, Reich and Benbasat (2000) report on two main approaches to the study of alignment: examining strategies, structure and planning in organisations; and to investigate the social dimension of actors in organisations and their understanding of each others' domain. The focus of this chapter is solely on the social dimension. The second pressing issue is in determining the role that methods play in guiding the development of software (Avison and Fitzgerald 2006). However, central to the philosophy of methods is the assertion that systems development is founded upon dialogue and agreements between developers and the business client. Despite this, little extant research has explored the role that methods can play in influencing the client-developer relationship.

Four key terms, as used in this chapter need defining. Our definition of the business client includes all those user departments who operate and interact with software systems to achieve organisational goals. The business client generally initiates the development or enhancement of systems but most importantly, funds the development of these systems. We understand systems developers within *The Bank* to include all those individuals and groups, both inside and outside *The Bank*, who 'consult' with the business client; that is, assess their needs, propose solutions, and develop software systems. This broad category of systems developer in this case study includes project leaders, systems analysts, analyst/programmers, IT managers, and the method support personnel. This chapter also uses the term method very broadly along with Fitzgerald et al. (2002) as any formally documented in-house or commercially available systems development approach. Lastly, recognising that power holds multiple meanings (Jasperson et al. 2002) a broad definition is used in which power is conceived as the ability to affect the behaviour of others. From our perspective then, to say that the business client has exercised power over systems developers means that developers behave differently from the way they would have if not for the business client.

The chapter is organised as follows. In the next section we review research relevant to the political role of methods. In the following, we explore the concept of method as an institution, and how an extrapolation of Lamb and Kling's (2003) *user as social actor* model can be used as an analytical research framework. We review recent studies of research on power in systems development, and then present Hardy's (1985) model of unobtrusive power to help us understand the dynamics between developers and the business client. The following section describes our research approach. A summary of the case findings are then presented and discussed, illustrating that the *user as social actor* model works as a framework for identifying sources of power and authority, but is silent on how power mechanisms operate. In the final section, Hardy's model of power is used to understand power mechanisms, and describes how power can be used unobtrusively to quell grievances and to prevent conflict from arising.

4.2 Research Relevant to the Political Role of Methods

A small, but growing body of research has been conducted on the specific topic of the role of methods. Fitzgerald et al. (2002) proposed a framework to understand the complex nature of systems development and how methods are enacted in practice. Included in this framework is a set of covert political roles diametrically opposed to a set of rational roles that methods may play. However, these political roles are all described from the perspective of the developer. More importantly, in their framework the role of the business client in the deployment of the method is ignored. Furthermore, it remains silent on any political role from the client's perspective.

In an early study into business users' interests in the adoption of an organisational-wide development method, Sauer and Lau (1997) reported on a case where the business client exercised its political discretion and directly determined the outcome. These findings recognised that the business client is a main source of influence on method deployment. Sauer and Lau (1997) highlighted a conflict of interest between developers and business client and the legitimacy of their dispute. Developers were portrayed as having a legitimate concern for delivering a quality product. By contrast, the business client was more interested in organisational survival, business strategy, and in seeking early system delivery at low cost. What is interesting in terms of our research focus is that due to environmental pressures, the business client was able to exert overt power over developers in that they rejected the developers' choice of a replacement development method.

In one of the first studies of the impact of organisational context involving method enactment, Nandhakumar and Avison (1999) highlighted various influences such as developers' knowledge about methods, implicit social norms, organisational form, and culture. Further studies advanced a growing argument that IT practice should be seen as more than a technical activity and as argued by Goulielmos (2004), method enactment can and should be understood as a complex social activity influenced by the organisational and institutional context in which it takes place. As noted in Aydin et al. (2005) context played an important role in their study of the adaptation of an agile systems development method. Madsen et al. (2006) conceptualised method enactment as a process of organisational innovation and portrayed their role and usefulness as a means for communication, coordination and (re)direction, rather than as a rigorous or rigid means for control. In an opposite view, Huisman and Iivari (2006) studied the difference in perception between IS managers and developers about the deployment of methods, and found that both groups saw methods as a control technology in terms of keeping to deadlines and budget yet offered no discussion of how control was achieved.

We conclude this brief review by arguing that the work that has been carried out is limited in its ability to consider the dynamics by which power and authority shapes method enactment. Further inquiry into these elements is a critical area of research for the field (Beath and Orlikowski 1994; Silva 2007).

4.3   Theoretical Background

Three literatures helped ground this research. First, we offer an overview of Lamb and Kling's (2003) *user as social actor model*; second we briefly review power frameworks used in recent IS research; and third, we review Hardy's (1985) model of unobtrusive power as a theoretical backdrop for interpreting the findings from our study.

4.3.1   User as Social Actor Model

Recognising that no studies have directly addressed the enactment of methods in the context of power between developers and the business client, attempts were made to seek a theoretical explanation within the organizational and information systems literature. We had a need for theory and an analytical framework that addressed issues of the technological artefact, the role that developers play in enacting the technology, power relations between developers and the business client, and at different levels of analysis. This was found in the seminal work of Lamb and Kling (2003) in their conceptualization of *the user as a social actor*, with its theoretical antecedents in the area of new institutional theory (Scott 2001).

Drawing on the work of Scott (2001), Lamb (2006) describes how the social actor concept has been theoretically supported by new institutionalist approaches, whereby institutions provide a framing context within which social actors make constrained choices about ICT use, particularly when they are situated in organisations. According to the *user as social actor model*, people's individual autonomy (their agency) and their behaviours are shaped by the social norms, institutional forces, and other social and physical structures that surround them. In terms of this research example, structure includes work procedures mandated by the method, the day-to-day interactions within and among project groups, and authority based on power and expertise. Given this view, systems developers can be seen as complex social actors acting in constrained ways, rather than simple "users" of the method (Lamb and Kling 2003), and where the method operates largely as a structure around which systems developers operate.

Seen as a means to explain the role that methods play in influencing the systems developer-business client relationship, the *user as social actor model* is most appropriate and was chosen for theoretical and methodological reasons. As Lamb and Kling (2003: 219) offered, "the model provides a framework for the systematic research of complex, highly contextualised ICT use in organisations, rather than the study of isolated aspects of ICT use in de-contextualised settings". We also considered the model provides an appropriate theoretical lens to examine method enactment; first, because of its emphasis on exploring the impact of institutional structures on the enactment process in organisational settings; and second, because of its focus on networked technologies in increasingly knowledge-intensive industries such as in the finance and IT industry.

The *user as social actor model* has only recently been applied to the study of information systems elsewhere: Rowlands (2009a) in a study of the institutional aspects of method use, and Ferneley and Light (2008) in a study of different user groups' appropriation of mobile and ubiquitous computing. Our research made use of the *user as social actor model* by illuminating method enactment at multiple levels: individual (systems developers as a social actors), organisational sub-system (the IT department with *The Bank*), organisation (*The Bank*), and organisational field (the finance and IT industry). The following paragraphs provide descriptions of the model in terms of the context of the case.

The *user as social actor model* involves four dimensions – interactions, identities, affiliations, and environment that characterise organisational members and their enactment context. According to Lamb (2006) *interactions* and *identities* relate organisationally situated individuals to others and to the information technologies they use to interact with and present themselves to others. The second two dimensions – *affiliations* and *environments* relate people to their organisation, and to the industries and environments of those organisations. To illuminate the context that impacts on method enactment, we provide a general description of the four interdependent social actor dimensions.

Affiliations. The affiliations represent inter and intra-organisational relationships created and supported by organisational members as a result of their day-to-day activities as part of the organisation. Systems developers work together comprising social networks. These networks exist within *The Bank* but also apply to the IT and financial industries as well, and to a wider national and international context.

Environments. The environment an organisation operates in is formed by the kind of affiliations it has formed with industry, financial institutions and its clients. A social actor view of method enactment recognises the regulated and/or institutionalised practices of *The Bank*, and other associations that circumscribe organisational action.

Interactions. Systems developers see themselves as organisational members working with others (clients, and business partners exchanging information) enacting a method (and other media such as email, telephone, web sites) in support of their interactions. Information and resources are mobilised as systems developers engage with *affiliated* organisations.

Identities. Systems developers regularly enact methods to compile and present information to various affiliates. In so doing, they create an identity for their organisation and for themselves. Systems developers are therefore defined by their avowed presentations of the self and ascribed profiles of organisation members as individuals (analyst programmer) or a collective entity (IT professional).

In terms of research approach, the *user as social actor model* was used a priori to help make sense of what occurred in the field, provided a set of sensitising constructs to be investigated, and guided our interpretation and focus. The model was used both to organise and classify the field data, but also to identify assumptions and perceptions that systems developers had of the business client.

4.3.2   Power Frameworks

In this section, we rectify the omission of discussions about power relationships between developers and the business client by showing how power applies to systems development methods.

Jasperson et al. (2002) identified a number of paradigms underlying power research and four lenses to better understand researcher's views regarding the causal structure between IT and organisational power. The four lenses (based on a modified version of Burrell and Morgan's (1979) framework of sociological paradigms) are: rational, pluralist, interpretive and radical.

This research adopts a combination of Jasperson et al.'s (2002:406) *pluralist* and *interpretive* perspectives of power. In the *pluralist* lens, actors are assumed to have different, potentially conflicting interests. This perspective defines power in terms of actors' ability to influence others' behaviours. A *pluralist* conceptualisation of power assumes that resources, possession of resources, and the resulting dependency relationship are characteristics of the social context. Unlike the *pluralist* perspective with a focus on resources, the *interpretive* perspective deals primarily with perceptions and the processes that shape them. Power is defined in terms of actors' (the business client's) ability to control and to shape the dominant interpretation of organisational events. In this perspective, 'whoever controls the dialogue, and hence the formation of subjective meaning, has the power to alter another actor's perspective, and ultimately determine outcomes' (Jasperson et al. 2002:412).

Only a few studies focus on the deployment of methods in their social and organisational contexts and the power relations existing between developers and the business client in this context. Markus and Bjørn-Anderson (1987) provide some reference of its early occurrence by providing a framework to identify different forms of exercised power to make business clients and systems developers more aware of the influence of power. Their framework presented two dimensions of context and target demarcating four types of power exercise: technical, structural, conceptual and symbolic. Their view of power was somewhat controversial because the dominant literature on power (at the time) tended to focus primarily on overt power, that is, when two parties disagree and behaviour of one of the parties is intended to influence the outcome.

Markus and Bjørn-Anderson drew on the work of Lukes (1974) to consider covert issues: looking beyond observable conflict to consider why grievances are not formulated, and why conflict does not arise. Their 'structural' and 'symbolic' exercise of power is relevant to this study as it describes the exercise of power taking place, not within a particular project, but rather over time as organisational structures and routine operating procedures offer the client formal authority over developers or foster dependence on them for resources. According to Markus and Bjørn-Anderson (1987:500) "in this structural exercise of power it is primarily the development of policies and practices that constitutes the exercise of power, ... and that structural constraints on [developers] can obviate the need for more direct [or overt] forms of power".

4.3.3 Hardy's (1985) Multi-Dimensional Model of Power

Since the publication of Markus and Bjørn-Anderson (1987) other writers have utilized and adapted Lukes (1974) three-dimensional view of power. Hardy (1985, 1996, 1998) integrated Lukes' three-dimensional view into a model which incorporates both the use of power to defeat declared and identifiable opponents, and its use to prevent resistance, known as covert or *unobtrusive power*. Unobtrusive power concerns attempts to create legitimacy and justification for certain arrangements, so that outcomes are never questioned.

Hardy's (1985) first dimension seeks to study actual behaviour in making decisions, with the locus of 'power' being presumed to reside with the victor in a decision situation that entails a conflict of interest. At this level the focus is on the use of resources and decision outcomes, and helps to explain decision outcomes as political rather than rational (Hardy and Leiba-O'Sullivan 1998). According to Horton (2003) a limitation of this view is that in studying decisions that are made, no account is made of those issues that have been ignored, or sidelined.

The second dimension addresses this limitation by revealing the ways in which some groups may dominate others in relation to non-decision making by considering the ways in which decisions are prevented from being taken on potential issues over which there is an observable conflict of interest. While an advance over the first, the second dimension is still focused on decisions whether taken or not. According to Horton (2003) it does not take account of the exercise of power through the inactivity of people, or where institutions represent an exercise of power in preventing issues from arising or being deployed.

The third dimension addresses exercises of power that prevent potential issues from arising by considering the many ways through which potential issues are kept out of politics, whether through the operation of social forces and institutional practices or through individuals' decisions. The main contribution of the third dimension, according to Horton (2003) is to move thinking about a concept of power beyond a link with conflict, and to understand how issues can be prevented from arising at all. The proposition is that the basis for things not happening may be due to power. However, validating why something did not happen is problematic. Hardy (1996) provides a solution to this problem by distinguishing between instrumental power (dimension 1 and 2 above) and symbolic or *unobtrusive* power concerned with the 'management of meaning' to prevent conflict from arising (dimension 3).

From our search of the information systems literature, Hardy's model has rarely been used in prior IS studies, with three notable exceptions: Dhillon (2004), Howcroft and Light (2006), and Howcroft and McDonald (2007). However, Hardy's model of unobtrusive power has been used extensively in the organisational and management literature

Dhillon (2004) showed the value of applying Hardy's (1985) power model when analysing a case of a failed IS implementation project in a state government department. Using a power perspective, Dhillon found that the department relied exclusively on the power of resources to bring about change to their structure, systems, people and culture, but this was not sufficient. Instead, Dhillon reported that to effect organisation change, an understanding of three power dimensions (resource, process, and meaning) is a precursor to successful implementation. Dhillon took the first three dimensions of Hardy's power model and provided examples from the case where intended outcomes in terms of systems, people and culture could have been better mobilised through the power of resources, process and meaning. Dhillon (2004: 641) concluded, almost self-evidently, that "organisational power is one of the most important variables that should be understood properly and leveraged to ensure IT implementation success", and endorsed Hardy's model with its emphasis on understanding power from multiple dimensions. Surprisingly though, Dhillon did not describe Hardy's (1985) model in any detail, or offer explanations of the three dimensions.

Howcroft and Light (2006) applied the Markus and Bjørn-Anderson (1987) framework to contemporary IS development by focusing on a longitudinal case of packaged software selection and procurement. Their analysis of the case was strengthened by the incorporation of Hardy's (1985) work on unobtrusive power. Howcroft and Light took each element of Markus and Bjørn-Anderson's (1987) framework and discussed this in relation to the specifics of software selection. The case highlighted both overt and covert power issues involved in the procurement of software and illustrated the interplay of power between senior management, IT managers, IT vendors, and end-users. Howcroft and Light (2006) did not explicitly identify who was in the more powerful position, but instead emphasised that the three types of power should not be viewed separately, and are indeed interwoven. The authors concluded that further empirical research utilizing Hardy's (1985) concept of unobtrusive power to identify ways symbolic power functions is warranted.

Howcroft and McDonald (2007) also applied Hardy's (1985) power model as 'theoretical scaffolding' when interpreting aspects of the political and social nature of IS evaluation. Howcroft and McDonald undertook an ethnography of the process of IS investment evaluation after the appraisal had taken place in a large international financial institution. Their focus was to compare experiences of observed practice with the rhetoric of company policy, and to contrast these observations with the IS evaluation literature. Howcroft and McDonald conceptualised the process of systems development, and in particular – evaluation and feasibility of projects – as a process of political and social contention. Using Hardy's model as an illuminating tool to move beyond surface explanations of IS evaluation, Howcroft and McDonald reported instances of the exercise of overt power (e.g. senior executives deliberately bypassing the evaluation process so that they could push through their own sponsored projects); and illustrated instances of the use of covert or unobtrusive power (e.g. certain dominant stakeholders engineering a situation in such a way as to endow their actions with legitimacy). Howcroft and McDonald concluded that in the field of IS research in general, and in IS evaluation in particular, there is increasing concern with the social and organisational aspects of IS, increased need for interpretivist research, and utility in applying Hardy's (1985) model of power.

We apply Hardy's (1985) multi-dimensional model of power to help us understand the dynamics between developers and the business client involving power and authority. Hardy's model is appropriate to our case as it examines both overt and unobtrusive uses of power, and offers explanations of political inactivity. That is, understanding a situation of unequal power relations, where grievances do not exist, or conflict does not arise.

4.4   Research Approach and Methods

The research approach reported on in this study is that of an interpretive case study (Walsham 1995; Klein and Myers 1999). As pointed out by Kling et al. (2005), people's interpretations of information technologies are based on prior beliefs, and the perceived new opportunities and demands it creates. How systems developers interpret a method is important because those with different interpretations will enact the method differently. Therefore, an interpretive case study was chosen to produce a subjective albeit shared (between the researcher and the interviewee) understanding of phenomena.

The research study was carried out in a large Australian bank. The banking and financial services sector was chosen because of the extremely important role that IT plays in the success of companies in this industry, and The Bank selected has extensive experience and use in practice of an in-house developed systems development method. Importantly, the banking industry is highly technical, highly competitive, highly regulated and institutionalised. The selection of the case site was based on a combination of accessibility to the company's IT managers and project members, and interestingness – in the sense that the chosen bank is one of Australia's top four banks, and its IT organisation is considered to be a leading player in providing state-of-the-art IS solutions to customers.

The sampling strategy for the interviews included a combination of purposeful and theoretical sampling. Three occupational functions within The Bank were selected for their similarities as well as their differences. Interviews were conducted with systems developers comprised of project managers, senior consultants, and consultants within the systems support, new development, and method support divisions of the IT division. A total of 30 interviews were conducted with 28 informants from different projects and at varying levels within the organisation. Two method support personnel were interviewed twice. A further tactic to ensure credibility was to submit the transcribed interview to the scrutiny of the individuals upon whom they are based, and to seek their responses to its authenticity – known as member checking (Schwandt 2001:155). In the majority of cases, each face to face interview was complemented by a follow-up email to clarify issues and to obtain supplementary information.

Further and complete descriptions of the research procedures are found in Rowlands (2008).

4.5   Analysis

Preliminary analysis of data has also been presented previously (Rowlands 2008) and due to space restrictions, are not repeated here. However in summary, the findings (1) illustrated structures of systems development embedded in the method; (2) portrayed power inequalities where systems developers are dependent on the business client; and (3) identified that the business client can be considered a method user too.

Using the *user as social actor* model and reference to Rowlands (2008), the transcripts confirmed the inherent power of the business client. The interviews confirmed that in the end it is the business client who has control over the systems development process, and bears the most responsibility for the system in terms of funding and signing off on it. Systems developers need the business client to fund the design and construction of new or enhanced systems. However, there is a dichotomy of mind-sets. From the perspective of developers, the business client is portrayed as more interested in controlling costs, monitoring deadlines and delivering projects on time; whereas the developer is more interested in building quality systems and employing their technical expertise.

The transcripts also told us that the policies and practices embedded in the method through sign-off and stage-gate funding constitutes a form of 'structural' exercise of power (Markus and Bjørn-Anderson 1987) in the form of developer dependence on the business client for important resources. While a form of overt power, this finding indicates that the constraints based around the accepted and everyday use of a method by systems developers obviates the need for more direct forms of control. Our findings also indicate that control structures embedded in the method, while not undetected by developers, remain largely un-discussed. For instance, many interviewees when asked if they discussed the relative merits of the method with other colleagues said 'they did not' as the following excerpt from a programmer illustrates:

> It's one of those things that you discuss when you're relatively new to the organisation but after that it's just accepted. You do it because it's part of the culture. You don't necessarily discuss it in a meeting or at lunch. You don't say to someone 'Awww crikey, I'm having a problem with that part of [the method], so I probably wouldn't discuss it very often.

Second, transcripts were provided indicating the environment the bank operates in greatly effects the enactment of the method. Examples of adherence to industry-wide and global work practices included: development phases being based on the traditional water-fall life-cycle, systems built complying to standards imposed by regulatory agencies such as *APRA*,[1] *The Bank* mimicking other organisations by placing the method on an intranet site, and having to conform to specifications agreed to with major technology partners. These examples illustrate a source of power emanating from other than the business client. The environment imposes on the developer a requirement to comply with industry, national and global work practices, where the enactment of the method is subject to external institutional forces.

Further transcripts illustrated how the development life-cycle, sign-off, and routine patterns of work embedded within the method create a mechanism for the business client to exert and maintain control over the systems development group. The transcripts illustrate that the business client has 'ownership' of the method and therefore has control over important aspects of systems development, and accordingly is able to exert unobtrusive power over systems developers. What has not been reported in the literature before is that through ownership and control, the business client can be considered a user of the development method too.

Developers were also reported as being dependent on the business client to validate and legitimate their contributions to the organisation. Knowing how to use the method and using the method competently constructed their *identities*, legitimised their role, and constructed perceptions that they are professional. There were multiple data points confirming that the enactment of the method legitimises their role as a systems developer in the eyes of a project manager or the business client. Hence, systems developers pursue their interests directly by invoking 'directives' prescribed by the method, while acknowledging the legitimacy of the business client.

Lamb & Kling's *user as social actor* model also enabled us to identify the source of authority and power afforded the business client, and to identify mechanisms of unmistakable power operating in *The Bank*. For example, one local source of overt power in favour of the business client is a set of development procedures (sign off, and the stage gate approval process) that have transpired over time to institutionalize their interests in structures embedded in the method. As a consequence of the method being 'virtually' owned and controlled by the business client, and the method being mandated, developers were constrained in their actions by the need to 'rationalise' their work practice – a common theme among developers is that 'we all need to use the method to speak a common language'. Another local source of overt power in favour of the business client were market pressures such as the clients' ability to outsource development work rendering the developer dependent on the client for funding; or if developed in-house, subject to unreasonable demands in terms of delivery schedules.

In illustrating how social structures shape the method enactment process, the case (Rowlands 2008) showed that structures that have developed over time – such as norms and beliefs – played an active and covert role in constraining developers in the systems development process. For instance, the method provides a repertoire of already existing institutional principles of work (e.g. conventions, work practices, common understandings, authority relationships) that developers enrol in their activities. For example, many developers held the view that the method provides a

---

[1] APRA stands for the Australian Prudential Regulatory Authority.

common language and valued standardized terms enabling communication of ideas between developers, the client, and those external to the organisation. Developers when they joined *The Bank* accepted their role in the existing order of things because they saw it as natural; and their use of the method went relatively unnoticed as it has become habitualised and part of the work culture of the organisation.

These examples show how enactment of the method over time has lead to the development of change-resistant cognitive schemas (norms and values) that are perceived as natural and legitimate by developers. Furthermore, the findings of the case demonstrated, as it is the business client who is in control, it is the values and conventions of the business client that holds legitimacy in *The Bank*. In the case we inquired into the circumstances within which systems developers used the method, and identified conditions that resulted in the subjugation of developers by the business client, leaving them with little control over the development process. We conclude that the advantages in terms of whose interests are met in the systems development process are clearly in favour of the business client.

In sum, we found that Lamb and Kling's (2003) *user as social actor* model enabled us to identify concepts of control, authority and power, but it doesn't explain how the concepts of power operate; and is silent on explanations as to why developers are compliant with an unequal power scenario. A plausible explanation of this scenario is provided by Hardy's (1985) multi-dimensional model of power summarised in Table 4.1 with examples from the case. This model explains why

Table 4.1 Hardy's (1985) multi-dimensional model of power

Model dimension and explanation	Examples from the case (Rowlands 2008)
Dimension 1: power of resources. The powerful are able to deploy key resources on which others depend, such as the control of funding. This is overt power.	The business client has the ability to procure services in-house or external to the organisation. Developers are therefore reliant on the business client for funding of projects.
Dimension 2: power of decision-making processes. Some issues can beexcluded from decision-making, and the agenda confined to 'safe' questions, with opponents side-lined. Overt power.	Developers were prevented from replacing the existing method and acquiring a new method based on new techniques and re-use of code. The client said they "couldn't understand the diagrams" and decisions were prevented from being taken, even though there was an observable conflict of subjective interest.
Dimension 3: power of managing meaning. People can be prevented from having grievances by shaping their perceptions and preferences in such a way that they accept their role in the existing order of things, because they see it as natural. This is an example of unobtrusive power.	Developers were influenced by symbolic aspects of power – the use of language and rituals in the workforce. For example, standardised terms for communication; the habitual use of the method in producing lifecycle deliverables as evidence of work performance; and the ritualistic use of "walk-through" meetings with clients to validate the 'accuracy' of design decisions and to gain their signature of approval. Developers saw this as natural and legitimate.

there is apparent cooperation with the business client, and an absence of resistance
by developers.

4.6   Discussion and Conclusion

Hardy's model (cf. Table 4.1) suggests that power can work at a number of different levels. In terms of how power is mobilized by dominant actors, on the
surface (dimensions 1 & 2), power is exercised through the mobilization of
scarce, critical resources, and through the control of decision-making processes.
At a deeper level (dimension 3), power is exercised through the managing of
meanings to create legitimacy for an issue and prevent conflict (Hardy and Leiba-
O'Sullivan 1998).

Hardy's model clarifies the conditions necessary for why opposition or conflict
does not arise. In the first dimension, developers lose out to the client by being
unable either to procure or deploy critical resources; in the second, by being unable
to secure access to the decision-making forum; and in the third, by being unaware
of political issues (Hardy and Leiba-O'Sullivan 1998). According to Lukes
(1974) and Hardy (1985) power can be used to prevent people from having grievances by shaping their perceptions and preferences in such a way that they accept
their role in the existing order of things, either because they see or imagine no
alternative to it, or because they see it as natural. In other words, to explain why
developers are accepting of their situation in relation to an unequal relationship
with the business client, we need to move our thinking to why grievances are not
formulated, why demands are not made, and why conflict does not surface. In
Hardy's third dimension of power, quiescence may be the result of the unobtrusive exercise of power.

Whereas Hardy's (1985) first two dimensions are grounded in access to material
and structural resources such as information, expertise, control of rewards, and
budgets (also known as overt power), unobtrusive power refers to the ability to
secure preferred outcomes by preventing conflict from arising. The unobtrusive
side of power revolves around attempts to create legitimacy and justification for
certain arrangements, actions and outcomes so that they are never questioned. The
essence of unobtrusive power, in this case example, is the ability of the business
client to give meaning to events and actions, and to influence the perceptions of
developers so that they either remain unaware of the political implications, or view
them in a favourable way.

The transcripts discussed in Rowlands (2008) and summarised in Table 4.1 indicated that developers are influenced by symbolic aspects of power – the use of
language, symbols and rituals in the workforce. Developers value standardized
terms for communication; the habitual use of the method in producing lifecycle
deliverables as evidence of design creativity and work performance; and the use of
"walk-through" meetings with clients to validate the 'accuracy' of design decisions
to gain their signature of approval. These meetings took on a ritualistic character in

order to convey a powerful message to developers: 'cooperate, come to us, and we will reward you'. Unobtrusively, these symbolic aspects of systems work are seen by developers as legitimate development policy. Developers do not work outside this policy because it is seen as natural, habitual, acceptable, and is contextually and culturally grounded.

Developers also comply with these work arrangements because it meets their sense of professional reality. In terms of symbolism, the method stands for something more than a 'way to build systems'. The meaning of the method comes from its context and use within the IT department. Analysis of transcripts using the *Identities* dimension of the social actor model (see Appendix) found that the method defines developers' identity as competent and legitimizes their role as professional. Unobtrusive power then is derived from symbolic sources which are brought into play to legitimize outcomes in a process called the 'management of meaning' (Hardy 1985).

Hardy (1985:396) documented a model showing the complex relationships among overt and covert aspects of power. This model has been adapted and modified to the specifics of this case by the inclusion of external power via a necessity to conform, and is presented in Fig. 4.1. Figure 4.1 (with descriptions below) illustrates that the various forms of power are interwoven and should not be viewed separately.

1. Overt power is based on the control of resources. Success depends upon bringing these resources into action through power mobilization.
2. The mobilization of overt power resources enables the business client to achieve outcomes they desire, for example control over the development process in the form of budget or resource allocations, or a decision outcome to outsource or not.
3. Unobtrusive power is derived from symbolic sources which are brought into play to legitimize outcomes in a process called the management of meaning.

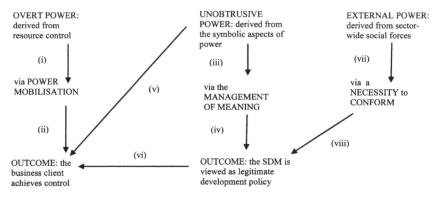

Fig. 4.1 The external, overt and unobtrusive aspects of power

4. Unobtrusive power can be used to influence sentiments with the use of mechanisms such as symbols, language, and rituals.
5. Unobtrusive power can produce outcomes directly. Factors such as 'walk-through' meetings with clients to obtain their signature of approval ensure that certain demands and challenges are never made. In this case the business client achieves outcomes by default: benefiting from a situation that favours them, rather than having to consciously manipulate it for their own needs.
6. Unobtrusive power can be consciously used by the business client to achieve outcomes. In this case the lifecycle, sign-off and routine patterns of work are used to legitimize and justify desired outcomes, producing favourable sentiments, and removing the threat of opposition – steps are taken to 'influence' developers to accept certain outcomes although they may be unaware of this.
7. External power is derived from sector-wide social and organizational requirements.
8. External sources of power are brought into play through a process of coercive isomorphism (DiMaggio and Powell 1983), or a necessity to conform. For example, in this case regulatory agencies, professional codes of practice, and industry-wide practices directly influenced *The Bank* to conform to, and have similar mandated method configurations.

In conclusion, we argue that a power perspective of method enactment brings about the identification of different elements across various levels of the organizational field that might otherwise escape analysis. As stated in the *Introduction*,

Table 4.2 Theoretical statements from the findings

1	Enactment of the method is CONTROLLED by the business client. The business client has 'ownership' of the method, controls the resources, and is able to exert OVERT power over the systems development process.
2	Enactment is POWER based. The life-cycle and sign-off process embedded within the method creates a mechanism for the business client to mobilise OVERT power and thereby maintain control over the systems development process.
3	Power is LEGITIMISED. Constraints based around the accepted and everyday use of a method by systems developers are not just a form of overt power, but can instead can be covert or UNOBTRUSIVE and institutionalised in the form of development policy as a means of LEGITIMISING power.
4	The business client manages the MEANING of the method – so that using the method is considered by developers as LEGITIMATE development policy. Therefore, the business client should be considered as a METHOD USER too, and not as an independent, arbitrary provider or withholder of cooperation in systems development.
5	Enactment of the method LEGITIMISES their role as systems developers in the eyes of the business client.
6	Developers see the systems development process as UNEQUAL. However, enactment of the method acquiesces any CONFLICT of interest in which the business client achieves their objectives (CONTROL) to the relative disadvantage of developers.
7	EXTERNAL power is derived from sector-wide social and organizational requirements in the form of mimicking, or a necessity to conform.

a lack of established theory about method enactment necessitated the generation of a number of new perspectives and empirical insights adding to the existing body of knowledge in this arena. Indeed, the findings developed in this study and summarised in Table 4.2 define seven theoretical statements or high-level propositions about the distribution of power, control and responsibility between systems developers and the business client from Hardy's multi-dimensional power perspective.

In this chapter, our theoretical contribution is threefold. The first is the adaptation of the *user as social actor model* to identify sources of authority and power. The second is the application of Hardy's unobtrusive power model to understand why developers are compliant with an unequal power scenario, and how power can be used to prevent conflict from arising. The third is in documenting the role that development methods can play in distributing power.

Finally, this chapter illustrates a case where developers see the systems development process as unequal involving a conflict of subjective interest; yet enactment of the development method acquiesces any grievance enabling the business client to achieve their objective (control) to the relative disadvantage of developers. Given the lack of studies in our discipline that integrate different dimensions of power (Jasperson et al. 2002); and insufficient consideration of the power relations that exist in the client-developer relationship, this is an appropriate contribution.

References

Avison, D. and Fitzgerald, G. (2006). *Information Systems Development: Methodologies, Techniques and Tools*, (4th ed.) McGraw Hill, London.

Aydin, M. Harmsen, F. van Slooten, K. and Stegwee, R. (2005). On the adaptation of an agile information systems development method. *Journal of Database Management*, 16(4), 24–40.

Beath, C. and Orlikowski, W. (1994). The Contradictory Structure of Systems Development Methodologies: deconstructing the IS-user relationship in Information Engineering. *Information Systems Research,* 5(4), 350–377.

Burrell, G. and Morgan, G. (1979). *Sociological Paradigms and Organizational Analysis*, Heinemann.

Day, J. (2007). Strangers on the Train: the relationship of the IT department with the rest of the business. *Information Technology & People*, 20(1), 6–31.

Dhillon, G. (2004). Dimensions of Power and IS Implementation. *Information & Management*, 41, 635–644.

DiMaggio, P. and Powell, W. (1983). The iron cage revisited: institutional isomorphism and collective rationality in organisational fields. *American Sociological Review*, 48(2), 147–160.

Ferneley, E. and Light, B. (2008). Unpacking user relations in an emerging ubiquitous computing environment: introducing the bystander. *Journal of Information Technology*, 23, 163–175.

Fitzgerald, B. Russo, N. and Stolterman, E. (2002). *Information Systems Development: Methods in Action*, McGraw Hill, Berkshire.

Goulielmos, M. (2004). Systems Development Approach: transcending methodology. *Information Systems Journal*, 14, 363–386.

Hardy, C. (1985). The Nature of Unobtrusive Power. *Journal of Management Studies*, 22(4), 384–399.

Hardy, C. (1996). Understanding Power: Bringing about Strategic Change. *British Journal of Management*, 7, S3–S16.

Hardy, C. and Leiba-O'Sullivan, S. (1998). The Power Behind Empowerment: Implications for Research and Practice, *Human Relations*, 51(4), 451–483.

Horton, K. (2003). Strategy, practice, and the dynamics of power. *Journal of Business Research*, 56, 121–126.

Howcroft, D. and Light, B. (2006). Reflections on Issues of Power in Packaged Software Selection. *Information Systems Journal*, 16, 215–235.

Howcroft, D. and McDonald, R. (2007). An Ethnographic Study of IS Investment Appraisal. *International Journal of Technology and Human Interaction*, 3(3), 69–86.

Huisman, M. and Iivari, J. (2006). Deployment of Systems Development Methodologies: Perceptual Congruence Between IS Managers and Systems Developers. *Information & Management*, 43, 29–49.

Jasperson, J. Carte, T. Saunders, C. Butler, B. Croes, H. and Zheng, W. (2002). Power and Information Technology Research: a Metatriangulation Review. *MIS Quarterly*, 26(4), 397–459.

Klein, H., & Myers, M., (1999). A Set of Principals for Conducting and Evaluating Interpretive Field Studies in Information Systems. *MIS Quarterly*, 23(1), 67–94.

Kling, R. Rosenbaum, H. and Sawyer, S. (2005). *Understanding and Communication Social Informatics: a framework for study and teaching the human contexts of ICTs*, Information Today, Medford, NJ.

Lamb, R. (2006). Alternative Paths Toward a Social Actor Concept. *Proceedings of the Twelfth Americas Conference on Information Systems,* Acapulco, Mexico, pp 4113–4123.

Lamb, R. and Kling, R. (2003). Reconceptualising Users as Social Actors in Information Systems Research. *MIS Quarterly*, 27(2), 197–235.

Lukes, S. (1974). *Power: A Radical View*, Macmillan, New York.

Madsen, S. Kautz, K. and Vidgen, R. (2006). A Framework for Understanding How a Unique and Local IS Development Method Emerges in Practice. *European Journal of Information Systems*, 15, 225–238.

Markus, M. (1983). Power, politics and MIS implementation. *Communications of the ACM*, 26(6), 430–444.

Markus, M, and Bjørn-Andersen, N. (1987). Power over users: its exercise by systems professionals. *Communications of the ACM*, 30(6), 498–504.

Nandhakumar, J. and Avison, D. (1999). The Fiction of Methodical Development: a field study of information systems development. *Information Technology & People*, 12(2), 176–191.

Peppard, J. (2007). The Conundrum of IT Management. *European Journal of Information Systems*, 16, 336–345.

Reich, B., and Benbasat, I. (2000). Factors that Influence the Social Dimension of Alignment between Business and Information Technology Objectives. *MIS Quarterly*, 24(1), 81–113.

Rowlands, B. (2008). The Enactment of Methodology: an Institutional Account of Systems Developers as Social Actors. *Scandinavian Journal of Information Systems*, 20 (2), 21–50.

Rowlands, B. (2009a). A Social Actor Understanding of the Institutional Structures at Play in Information Systems Development. *Information Technology & People*, 22 (1), 51–62.

Rowlands, B. (2009b). Exploring the Role that SDMs can Play in Influencing the Business Client – Systems Developer Relationship: an Institutional Theory Perspective. In J. Molka-Danielsen (Ed.) *Selected papers of the 32nd Information Systems Research Seminar in Scandinavia*, (pp. 41–57), Tapir Academic Press, Trondheim.

Sauer, C. and Lau, C. (1997). Trying to Adopt Systems Development Methodologies – a Case-based Exploration of Business Users' Interests. *Information Systems Journal*, 7, 255–275.

Saunders, C. and Scammel, R. (1986). Organisational Power and the Information Services Department: a re-examination. *Communications of the ACM*, 29(2), 142–147.

Schwandt, T. (2001). *Dictionary of Qualitative Inquiry*, 2nd Ed, Sage, Thousand Oaks, CA.

Scott, W. (2001). *Institutions and Organisations*, Thousand Oaks, CA, Sage.

Sillince, J. and Mouakket, S. (1997). Varieties of Political Process During Systems Development. *Information Systems Research*, 8(4), 368–397.

Silva, L. (2007). Epistemological and Theoretical Challenges for Studying Power and Politics in Information Systems. *Information Systems Journal*, 17, 165–183.

Smith, H. (1990). The User/Information Systems Relationship: a Study in Power and Attitudes. *Journal of Information Technology Management*, 1(2), 9–23.

Walsham, G. (1995). Interpretive Case Studies in IS Research: Nature and Method. *European Journal of Information Systems*, 4(2), 74–81.

Chapter 5
A Semiotic Analysis of Interactions Between End Users and Information Systems

Sheng-Cheng Huang and Randolph G. Bias

5.1 Motivation and Introduction

The study of HCI is essentially a multidisciplinary science because "it is concerned with understanding how people make use of devices and systems that incorporate or embed computation, and how such devices and systems can be more useful and usable (Carroll 2003, p. 1)." Researchers of HCI analyze and design user interfaces and new technologies. They also need to understand the tasks and work practices of people and their environments. It is by the collective knowledge of system engineering and human psychology that HCI professionals can offer better computational support to end users.

Retrospectively, HCI introduced principles of human-factors research into software engineering. As an applied science, theories and methods of cognitive science were initially brought in the process of information systems development (ISD). An early, influential example was Card et al. (1983) GOMS model (Goals, Operators, Methods and Selection rules) that emphasized the cognitive structures underlying manifest behaviors of HCI. The application of cognitive psychology in HCI research gained significant progress in human-factors modeling. However, as an emerging scientific discipline, HCI was not restricted by the doctrine of cognitive science. Many discourses involved ideas from social psychologists, anthropologists and sociologists. For example, Suchman's (2007) study of interactions between the user and the photocopier indicated that concepts and techniques of field studies, anthropology, ethnomethodology, and sociology also benefited the development of information systems that offer better HCI.

Carroll (2003) suggested that the multidisciplinarity of HCI research created a breath of working knowledge that required continually synthesizing a coherent methodological framework. The analysis of HCI between end users and information systems is often a difficult task. There is a clear need to conceptualize such a task within a framework that tends towards a more holistic view of human-centered approaches.

S.-C. Huang (✉) and R.G. Bias
School of Information, University of Texas at Austin, USA
e-mail: huangsc@mail.utexas.edu; rbias@ischool.utexas.edu

H. Isomäki and S. Pekkola (eds.), *Reframing Humans in Information Systems Development*, Computer Supported Cooperative Work 201, DOI 10.1007/978-1-84996-347-3_5, © Springer-Verlag London Limited 2011

In this chapter, we aim to (1) use semiotic principles to analyze dimensions and their relations between the end user and an information system; (2) discuss the important role of usability evaluation and its evolution in human-centered ISD; and (3) suggest a framework of HCI that integrates principles of semiotics and usability engineering.

5.2 Overview: A Semiotic Model of HCI

To model HCI, we need to analyze three parts: (1) the user, (2) the system, and (3) interactions. In comparison to the complexity of the user and the dynamics of interactions, analyzing a system is often easier. For example, the system of a chess game contains a limited number of rules (mechanisms) that are easy to understand, whereas the process and outcome of players' strategies and their interactions with the game are very hard to dissect and predict. Modeling HCI faces the same challenge of analyzing end users and their possible interactions with the system.

Many people have made efforts in analyzing end users. Hansen's (1971) first principle of user-engineering, "know thy user," marked the first milestone of user-centered approach of ISD. By acknowledging the challenge of controlling psychological and physical variables of human input such as the mapping problem in an information system, Norman (1983, 1986) used the term *cognitive engineering* "to understand the fundamental principles behind human action and performance that are relevant for the development of engineering principles of design." Noyes and Baber (1999) presented a synthesis of system theory considering the human as a part of a system that facilitates exchanges of information between human and machine. The synthesis incorporates human perceptions and reactions to machine-mediated signs as part of the information system's inputs and outputs. To achieve desired outputs in an information system where human operators exist, system designers must apply a control strategy to monitor and integrate human inputs and feedback in order to improve the overall system performance. Therefore, to control human performance requires extensive observations, analyses and knowledge of human factors in an operational environment where the dynamics of tasks and work practices of people take place.

On the other hand, the analysis of interactions often places the emphasis on the dynamics between humans and options that are given to them in the environment. This is exemplified by the dynamical modeling of system design that addresses the diversity of human inputs and feedback in a working environment (Jagacinski and Flach 2003, p. 3). Such a modeling of system design also requires a thorough understanding of end users' potential reactions and inputs to the system in order to predict consequential outcomes. This thorough understanding of possible interactions is critical because it is statistically improbable for a system design universally adoptable to the whole population due to individual differences of end users (cf., Mayhew 1999, p. 35; Nielsen 1994, p. 43; Noyes and Baber 1999, p. 19; Shneiderman 1998, pp. 18–76). Since different users might have different interactions with the system, without relevant knowledge about end users' characteristics will jeopardize the quality of user and system's performance and outcomes and cause monetary loss and, ultimately, design failure (Bias and Mayhew 2005; Nielsen 1994, pp. 2–8).

As Jagacinski and Flach (2003, p. 354) indicated, "the dynamics of human information processing are far more complex than the dynamics of … a communication channel," to effectively and efficiently analyze and understand end users and how they interact with an information system poses a greater challenge than to just analyze the system. We need a methodological or conceptual model that can help analyzing the user, the system, and their interactions in a clear way.

Semiotics (or semiology) is the analysis of signs and their use in relations to their interpreters (Chandler 2001). Using the semiotic model is helpful in understanding human information processing that has components that are difficult to distinguish. This is especially true when we need to analyze how a person performs situated actions in an environment such as an information system filled with instrumental signs. Early development of computer and information science regarded semiotics as a valuable paradigm and expected a broader implementation of it in language-based applications (Gorn 1983; Pearson and Slamecka 1983). ISDs in the past decade have proven the semiotic approach useful in the design of semantic networks, semantic indexing, information retrieval, and natural language processing (e.g., Andersen 1997; Calway 1995; Gonzalez 1997; de Souza 1993, 2005; Liu 2000a, b; Liu et al. 1998, 1999; Mai 2001; Resnik 1999; Stamper et al. 2000). Moreover, Andersen (cf. 1991, 1997), who has promoted the semiotic approach of computer system assessments, proposes that computer semiotics can be seen as the study of computer-based signs and their functions in relation with end users' inputs in an information system.

Viewing the entire universe as an extended network of signs, Charles Sanders Peirce (1839–1914) tried to find a proposition of epistemology of how meanings are created and understood through analysis of signs and their use. Peirce proposed a thesis that divided all signs into three components that form a triadic relation. Morris (1938) later designated these three components as the *semantic*, *syntactic*, and *pragmatic* dimensions of a semiotic sign. Figure 5.1 shows the Peirce-Morris model of a semiotic sign and the corresponding dimensions based on the Ogden

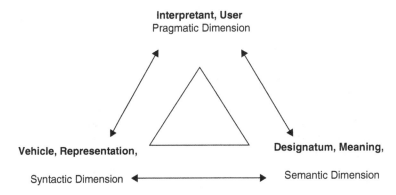

Fig. 5.1 The Peirce-Morris semiotic triangle

Triangle (cf. Johansen 1993, p. 62; Ogden and Richards 1923). The semiotic triangle illustrates three relations among the user, the representation, and the meaning of a sign. The user created such relations by establishing the connection between the act of understanding representative symbols or objects and the production of signified meanings in a communicative environment.

The approach of semiotics exemplifies a workable model that has three potential areas to be addressed if we view an information system as a complex sign that requires the end user's cognitive interpretations and behavioral interactions. The triadic concept of semiotics suggests three dimensions that characterize relations between the end user, the representational interface, and the system content, in any information system to be analyzed in human-centered ISD. We use Fig. 5.2 to illustrate the semiotic model of HCI based on the Peirce-Morris triangle.

The communication between the user and the information system is bridged by interacting with the interface and linking machine-mediated representations to the content of the system through perceptive or cognitive information processing of the user. However, such a communication between the user and the system is not easy to bridge.

Norman (1986) argued that there were often mismatches between a designer's model of the system's functionality and the end user's mental model of how to perform a task in the system. In the terms of Markman and Gentner (2001, p. 229), "A mental model is a representation of some domain or situation that supports understanding, reasoning, and prediction." The machine interface and the process of human cognition and perception, and the merging of these two "views," represent a great technical challenge of an HCI design in the ISD.

In order to establish a useful and usable information system, the communication between the user and the content of the system must overcome the interfacing and cognitive boundaries that separate the dimensions of HCI (i.e., dotted lines that indicate machine interfaces and cognition/perception barriers in Fig. 5.2). To establish effective communication between the system and the user, there are two routes to cross the boundaries between these dimensions. One is to seek the optimal

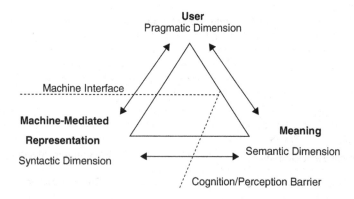

Fig. 5.2 A semiotic model of HCI

representations (interfaces) of the system for the user, and the other is to reduce the cognition and perception barriers by lowering loads of mental processes of the user. These are also the major goals of ISD.

In the next section, we will discuss how to use this semiotic model in user-system analyses to have an overview of development goals and provide an example regarding icon design.

5.3 Applications

5.3.1 Applying the Semiotic Model in User-System Analyses

By using semiotic principles to dissect HCI into three dimensions, we can establish a model that incorporates many well-established approaches of human-centered ISD. These approaches include end-user analysis, user experience research, and usability evaluation that can improve system functionality and reduce loads of user cognition for the design of HCI.

For example, using tools of entity-relationship diagram (ERD) developed by Chen (1976), Fig. 5.3 illustrates a conceptual model by applying semiotic concepts as a graphical notation that reflects relations between end users and the information system. Such a graphical notation can help us understand variables that might affect HCI of the information system. This will also allow a system designer to gain an overview of relations between entities (i.e., the user, the interface, and the context of the information system) and each entity's attributes or variables (e.g. end users' individual differences such as cultural influences and level of education).

Analyses of users, representations, and contents of the system each represent pragmatic, syntactic, and semantic dimensions of the semiotic model of HCI. Different end users will have individual differences (variables of human diversity that bring effects to the information system use) including factors such as age, gender, language, literacy and technical skills. Representations of the system such as the interface or operation panels will have different attributes like mapping, formation, and layouts. In addition, different types of artifacts, formats of data, records, and codes are also vehicles of system-mediated information that are used in communication between end users and the system. Interpretations, ideas, responses, feedback and contents of the system that are generated by the users will depend on contents and meanings that are constructed during the dynamics of user-system interactions.

These three entities of the system are often connected by optional many-to-many relations with the exception between the user and the content of the system, where all meanings must be created by end users although any user might have meaningless or no interaction with the system at all. Although many representations can refer to many contents, a representation does not necessarily have inherent meanings and an abstract meaning cannot always have a concrete representation. End users will create

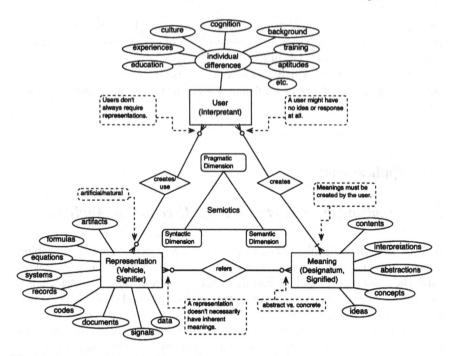

Fig. 5.3 An entity-relationship diagram of user-system analysis

or use representations, but not all of them require the presence of a certain element
of the interface (e.g., a color-blinded user will ignore certain displays of hues).

Although the overall scope might seem overwhelming given there are so many
variables and relations to be considered in Fig. 5.3, the semiotic model presents
three key issues to be addressed in HCI design:

1. *The representational issue*: Representations (e.g., designs of interfaces or visual
   elements) are not to be equalized to the context of an information system that
   depends on meaningful interactions between end users and the system. Fairthorne
   (1954, p. 69) argued that "information is an attribute of the receiver's knowledge
   and interpretation of the signal, not of the sender's, nor some omniscient observer's,
   nor of the signal itself." Therefore, the meaningfulness of the system content
   does not only depend on representations of the system, but also relies on how
   end users perceive and interpret the system.
2. *The user diversity issue*: The context of an information system is determined by
   the end user in "the processes and effects of the production and reproduction,
   reception and circulation of meaning in communication (Hodge and Kress 1988,
   p. 261)." Different users with varieties of individual differences will bring diverse
   human factors to the information system and influence system inputs and outputs.
   It is critical to control and monitor such diversity. This issue reflects challenges
   of user modeling in HCI that focus on cognitive modeling, learning, and problem

solving of end users, which has led to form the paradigm of user-centered system development and researches of human context in information systems (cf. Carroll 1997; Koskinen et al. 2003).

3. *The usability feedback issue*: Human feedback is an essential and critical element that controls performance and usability of a dynamical system (Jagacinski and Flach 2003). The ISD is not a linear design process. It often requires iterative development of constant prototyping and evaluation throughout the lifecycle to ensure the quality and performance of products (cf., Bias and Mayhew 2005; Mayhew 1999). Being aware of this issue is to pay homage to usability engineering of HCI and to broaden the empirical scope of design with user testing. Such user participations in the design lifecycle of ISD will provide essential feedback to improve usability of an information system (Nielsen 1994).

Addressing the above three issues are critical because we need to bridge semiotic dimensions of HCI in order to achieve effective and efficient user-system interactions. The first issue makes a clear distinction between representations and contents of the system. In a computer-mediated communication (CMC) environment, machine-mediated information is a representation of the system designer's modeling of system content, encoded to communicate with end users to achieve a planned or expected interaction or outcome. For example, a website's page layouts, font variants, menu items, icon images, media features, and pattern styles are syntactic combinations of the contents. These design elements can use intuitive metaphors or be standardized to achieve optimized representations of the information system. However, an information system designer must not assume that all end users interpret the representations identically because the first and the second issue both indicate that the diversity of human implications can generate end-user perceptions dissimilar from the system designer's objectives. Again, in Norman's (1986) term, a mismatch between the designer's system model and the user's mental model can easily occur. Therefore, according to the third issue, integrating end-user feedback to refine the system design is critical and beneficial in reducing the user's uncertainty so that the system effectiveness and efficiency can be enhanced correspondingly.

Being aware of these HCI dimensions and the three issues to be addressed can help system designers having a better overview of design challenges and consequently avoiding overlooking a certain area in the process of ISD. To further stress the importance of such awareness, we will use icon design as an example to discuss these three issues that are suggested by the semiotic model of HCI.

5.3.2 Applying Semiotic Analyses in Icon Design: An Example

A distinctive feature in modern graphical user interfaces (GUIs) is the extensive use of icons to visualize the content of an information system. Designing well-communicative icons for a GUI that facilitates better HCI is vital in the process of ISD.

An icon is a small symbol that functions as a pictogram representing a program (such as a visual shortcut of a command), file, directory (such as a folder), or device (such as a hard disk or floppy) on computer displays (Horton 1994). Modern GUIs often use icons to provide alternative visual representations of a certain concept, object, activity, place or event by illustration instead of offering plain text descriptions or text-based labels in the computing environment. Iconic representations have become popular since the first graphical interface was developed at Xerox PARC in 1979 and later embraced by mainstream software developers such as Microsoft and Apple (Caplin 2001, p. 20).

Creating good icons that are cognitively intuitive and instrumental to users is a highly specialized skill that requires both artistic talent and an understanding of usability concepts. A GUI icon is a graphical sign that is designed with a specific purpose to convey some fact about the software in use to the user (Barr 2003). Because icons are signs, we can apply semiotic analyses on them and discuss *the representational issue*, *the user diversity issue*, and *the usability feedback issue* of icon design.

The representational issue of icon design is related to the fact that there are many visual variables (i.e., orientation, metaphorical diversity, relative position, size, color, resolution, and labeling) that can make an iconic representation of the same item or concept different from each other (Fig. 5.4). Many studies have reported the effects of these variables that influenced outcomes and performance of user-system interactions. For example, Kamba et al.'s (1996) study on widget arrangement and Wang et al.'s (2006) study on visual information piles show that careful optimization of icons and text is a critical factor to use small screen space more efficiently to present information content for user interactions. Moyes (1994) found that the position of an icon was more important than the shape of an icon to the user to recognize it in a GUI menu. Everett and Byrne's (2004) study identified effects of icon spacing that might change users' visual search strategy. Chu et al. (1999) suggested that 5 × 5 mm is the smallest size that an icon can be recognized

Fig. 5.4 Representational variables of an icon design

with details of its graphical elements. Nine hues and 4-bit color scale are recommended as maximum colors to be used in an icon for the best outcome (Kurniawan 2000). In addition, for an individual icon to be physically distinctive based on the rules of human visual acuity and contract sensitivity, Kurniawan (2000) suggested that the minimum size of the finest detail cannot be less than 0.873 mm, which sets the limitation of an icon's resolution.

Although many effects of visual variables of an icon have been identified, the representational issue of icon design is not a simple question of good or bad manipulations of visual presentations. Specifically, as in Fig. 5.5, when two visual presentations are interchangeably good or ambiguous for the same idea or concept, when first encountering these icons, how do end users make a decision on their meanings if they do not have access to their text definitions?

Often adding an additional graphic element to an icon will change its taxonomy (Wang et al. 2007) and meaning in design (Setlur et al. 2005) at the same time. Unfortunately, there is never a direct quantitative measure of an icon's meaningfulness other than tools of evaluating its visual complexity (cf. Forsythe 2003; Byrne 1993), detectability, and interpretability (cf. Webb et al. 1989; Barr et al. 2003) in comparisons against other icons in similar designs. The answer is never absolute and objective, but comparative or subjective. This representational issue indicates concerns of icon independence in conveying a stable content of a GUI because an image can signify many meanings (cf. Haramundanis 1996; Pedell 1996) and it is important that an information system designer remains aware of this issue.

Designers will always face the problem of putting propositional meanings into icons (cf. Abdullah and Hübner 2006; Barr et al. 2003; Ferreira et al. 2005; Ferreira et al. 2006; Mitsock 1994; Payne and Starren 2006). Even though system designers have addressed the representational issue by achieving the optimal presentation of visual elements of an icon, they still need to deal with the issue of how end users will use and interpret it.

When an icon is created, the designer will assign one official label that defines its functional or operational meaning. Having access to an icon's text definition will at least minimize the possibility of a user's unexpected interpretations of linguistic and non-linguistic expressions of an image that leads to incorrect interactions with the system. Therefore, when the user is using an icon, the user is building the lexical access of a certain icon to a certain signified text that is a noun, a verb or a short phrase

Fig. 5.5 Changes in representations and meanings of icons

that is suggested by the label, in the internal lexicon. Although this designer-perspective presumption does not yield the possibility that an icon can still be interpreted differently by the user (indeed, it can help only speakers of the language the label is written in), we inevitably need to assume that through learning and retention activities, users can establish efficient connections between icons and their designed meanings (Wiedenbeck 1999).

Despite the fact that users can learn to use certain icons and be familiar with their contextual meanings through times of exposure, neither does this fact ultimately solve the user diversity issue suggested by the semiotic model of HCI, nor should the user diversity issue be taken lightly in the case of icon design. In fact, creating an icon that, without explanation, communicates a concept across culture is very difficult. Studies of Walton et al. (2002), Kim and Lee (2005), and Wang (2007) showed that factors of visual literacy, culture differences and language efficiency of end users all contributed to challenges and obstacles in the internationalization of interfaces and universal icon recognition.

Many cultural symbols are well perceived because of many years of reinforcement so that people who are familiar with them can immediately recognize them without accompanying text or other explanation (Watzman and Re 2008). For example, the skull symbol on a bottle is well perceived as poisonous or deadly substance in many cultures because the symbol is often associated with death. Another instance is that the Nazi symbol and the Swastika symbol are the same, but they represent different meanings and provoke different emotions for different groups of people in different places and periods of time. The possibility of different interpretations of the same symbol raises the concern that every representation does not necessarily have a consistent and transcending meaning. The answer to such a question relies on addressing *the user diversity issue* and the relation to *the representational issue*, with a focus on by what design criteria that people will perceive and use icons more effectively and efficiently in a system (Hemenway 1982).

To complete a semiotic analysis of icon design and to know how or how well end users respond to visual representations and understand the content, observations and evaluations must be done to address *the usability feedback issue*. As Barr et al. (2003) indicated, although there are many design guidelines for visual representations, a formal analysis of the concept of what icons do and are to users is rare, and semiotics can provide principles in icon evaluation and improve usability of icons. Studies have shown that applying semiotic principles and analyses in design and evaluation of icons helps by (1) providing postulate design guidelines for information visualization, (2) reinforcing usability principles to know the user better, (3) improving communication power that will require less redesign and prototyping, and (4) obtaining better understanding of users' potential responses and interpretations of unknown icons and graphics (cf. Barr et al. 2003; Ferreira et al. 2005, 2006; Payne and Starren 2006).

When system designers are designing an information system that facilitates the dynamics of interactions between end users and interfaces, as previously discussed in the semiotic model of HCI, they must address *the representational issue, the user diversity issue,* and *the usability feedback issue.* Traditionally, these issues were often tackled or investigated independently in HCI studies, which Carroll (2003) indicated as a magnificent challenge for an individual professional to attain such a breadth of working knowledge in information science, computing, cognitive/social psychology, and anthropology. Nevertheless, the strength of HCI studies also lies on its multidisciplinarity of the huge intellectual scope in both theoretical concepts and empirical approaches. We believe that the semiotic analysis of dimensions of HCI can help providing a more holistic view without deliberately insulate ourselves from some portion of the field's activity and knowledge. In fact, in the next session, we would like to extend the discussion of *the usability feedback issue* in the semiotic model of HCI and introduce the neuroergonomic approach (cf. Parasuraman 2003) that is currently thriving in HCI and ISD communities.

5.4   Current Status: Toward a Neuroergonomic Approach of Usability in HCI

With the growing number of users who wish to take advantage of the rapid growth of availability in computing and as CMC affects many aspects of people's lives, the need for more usable and intuitive systems becomes even more important today. Given the explosion of computing, and the concomitant variety of interfaces (e.g., drive-up kiosks, smart phones, GPS devices, and so many more), we are novices, and novices anew, in more and more systems.

The design of effective HCI is essential. An ineffective human-computer interface will hinder users from greater productivity, increase frustration, and increase overhead costs such as user training (Bias and Mayhew 2005). It is important that an effective HCI offers a computing environment that is maximally efficient to use, easy to learn, and satisfying to use by paying attention to its usability. However, making a complex information system appear simple and sensible to users is in fact a very difficult task for the developer (Butler and Jacob 1997).

Although most human-machine interactions are situated actions that are carefully designed by calculated plans of user flow, crossing the human-artifact boundary (represented by the dotted lines illustrated in Fig. 5.2) and allowing users to achieve their goals without resistance is never easy. Often the experience of the user is not predetermined but neither is it random, and it requires constant reconfiguration of interactions between the user and the computing environment within the constraint of the interface (Suchman 2007).

During the early years, users often needed elaborate training and experience in order to operate the machine interface proficiently. Since the 1940s, when equipment complexity began to exceed the limits of human ability for safe operation, the principles of applying human factors to machine interface became critical in order to reduce fatal human errors (Vicente 2004). Designs that take such factors in ergonomics into account not only reduce the chances of fatal human errors in demanding working environments but also improve the effectiveness and efficiency of user performance across all manner of systems. Similarly, the complexity of computing environments poses additional needs when physical panels are partially or utterly replaced by today's GUIs. Increased attention to usability in computing and software development has also become an engineering paradigm that can be generalized to a technical approach with the purpose of "making sure that something works well: that a person of average (or even below average) ability and experience can use the thing … for its intended purpose without getting hopelessly frustrated (Krug 2000)." With the march of technology, it is certain that the computing environment will become more complex than ever, and a well-designed and humane interface will spell success or failure more clearly than any other feature because it determines how effective the HCI will be and how usable the system will be.

Usability of HCI in the process of ISD has to do with people. Unlike functional requirements that are directly associated with a system's functions such as its inputs, system behaviors, and outputs, usability represents an example of non-functional requirements that embodies the qualities of a system that are determined by operations and experiences of the user (Wiegers 2003). Evaluations of system usability cannot be done directly on the system, and the measures must be collected from users of the system. Usability evaluation evolves based on understanding of the psychology of HCI where information about human performance gets involved in the design of user interfaces. It is part of the design philosophy of user-center design (UCD) (cf. Vredenburg et al. 2002) where the insight of an end user's needs and limitations take shape in an iterative design process by studying empirical data about human performance, theories of performance, and methods of observing and analyzing HCI (Abras et al. 2004). Approaches such as GOMS and the human information processor model (or model human processor, MHP) are examples of modeling human abilities and cognitive processes in HCI, which allow for different aspects of an interface and user responses to be studied and accurately predicted (Card et al. 1983). These techniques cannot be done without keeping the focus on understanding how a human responds to different stimuli provided by the interface in various computing environments.

Beyond behavioral modeling, HCI researchers have been adapting new methodology to study how people respond to different stimuli provided by the interface in various computing environments. For instance, studies applying analyses of event-related potentials (ERPs) in HCI have shown benefits of using neuroimaging methods to understand human factors such as fatigue and depletion and attention of cognitive resources during HCI tasks (e.g., Trimmel and Huber 1998). These findings have demonstrated great potential for using neuroimaging methods to evaluate aspects of HCI that conventional behavioral testing tools cannot probe into. Application of cognitive neuroscience in HCI has been advocated under the heading of neuro-ergonomics. According to Parasuraman (2003), "Neuro-ergonomics focuses on investigations of the neural bases of mental functions and physical performance in relation to technology, work, leisure, transportation, health care and other settings in the real world (p. 5)." The goal of neuroergonomics is to use the knowledge of brain functions that relates to certain behavioral responses to design interfaces and systems that are sensitive to the end user's neurophysiologic signals with the intent of increasing the efficiency and safety of human-machine systems (Proctor and Vu

2008, p. 47). By this neuro-ergonomic approach, a better understanding of how humans establish the connections between representations of the information system and their contextual meanings seems more promising than before.

As Ferreira et al. (2005) suggested, "The user interface can be seen as a complex sign made up of many smaller signs (buttons, scroll bars, images, etc.) all contributing to the process of communication, with each of the smaller signs having their own triadic relation (p. 48)." Expanded from Fig. 5.2, Fig. 5.6 further illustrates a theoretical framework of HCI research and design. Figure 5.6 stresses the importance of usability engineering as an equivalent and vital part of the development lifecycle in the design of a dynamic system (cf. Bias and Mayhew 2005; Mayhew 1999). The design of information representation is addressed by the syntactic approach by seeking the optimal solution of system design. The pragmatic approach identifies the potential variables of end-users' characteristics and individual differences through a thorough investigation of user experiences regarding the system. Finally, usability or neuroergonomic feedback can further refine and control the quality of system outcomes.

The semiotic approach of HCI demonstrates that, unless the user's perceptions of contextual meanings of the system are identified, the one-way communication between the user and system-mediated representations will lead to insufficient results. This neuroergonomic framework also indicates that designing HCI according to end-users' perceptions of system contents and subsequently incorporating usability feedback in the design process can considerably reduce the end user's uncertainty of interpreting system-mediated representations and therefore increase the probability of design success.

The distinctive difference between human intelligence and machine calculation is that human brains have the unique capability of creating contextual meanings

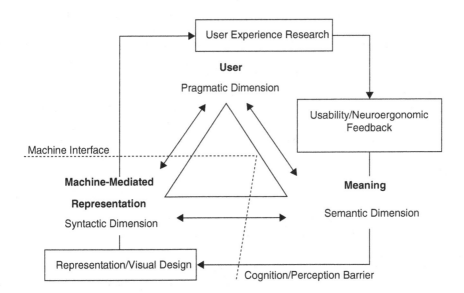

Fig. 5.6 A semiotic framework of HCI research

during interactions with information perceived in a given environment. Even with all of our advances in technology, this special ability is still exclusive to humans and cannot be duplicated by artificial devices (Freeman 2000, 2002). The question of why and how humans create meanings remains mostly unexplored territory. Moreover, an accurate measure of meanings is shown to be an improbable application of mathematic precision; it is seemingly impossible to explain the origin of intellectual execution except via probing into the neural mechanisms of the brain.

The diversity of human factors is also a difficult element to manage within systematic controls. Because of the complexity of unpredictable humanistic implications, reducing the uncertainty of obtained meanings of system-mediated information relies on direct consultation with the end users and on their unreliable introspective ability to gain insight into their own thought processes (Freeman 2002). Consequently, from a practical viewpoint, the neuroergonomic approach affords considerable integration in linking the user-defined meanings to the representational patterns and promises to provide valuable usability feedback to calibrate system performance.

The design of the interface plays a critical role that determines whether the machines can be used efficiently and intuitively. Systems will be easier to learn if designers can apply knowledge of neural basis of human cognitive processing and principles of semiotic signs in designing the system's symbolic contents. This new insight of converging brain activities and physical behaviors in interface design also opens up new directions to develop HCI that are beyond the current GUI paradigm (cf. Baldwin 2003; Kortum 2008).

Sarter and Sarter (2003) discussed the opportunities and challenges of merging neuroscience with ergonomics in hope of developing neuroadaptive interfaces that will achieve human-automation cooperation. For example, people can use their neurophysiologic signals to control the system and the system will automatically adjust its settings according to different users in real time. Such neuroadaptive interfaces, according to Hettinger et al.'s (2003) definition, are human-machine systems that can dynamically adapt different users' variations in perceptive and cognitive states according to corresponding neural sources of information from the user.

As related neuroergonomic studies have been carried out to investigate the human brain that controls physical work activities in computing (Karwowski et al. 2003), the future of this neuro-ergonomic approach "has the potential to improve not only the performance of human-machine systems, but also to improve the quality of life while enhancing our understanding of brain function" (Hancock and Szalma 2003, p. 247).

5.5 Conclusion

Computers are no longer simple, stand-alone, interactive tools and artifacts. As they have the ability to host communications and such complex interactions as computer-supported cooperative work (CSCW), they have become an important medium and feature of daily life, work, and education. This paper endeavored to illustrate a theoretical framework of HCI research and design based on semiotic principles of human information processing (Fig. 5.6). This framework emphasizes the importance of system optimization, user experience research, and usability engineering, with the addition of the neuroergonomic approach. These entities are equivalent and vital parts of the development lifecycle in the process of designing an information system. The semiotic model of HCI suggests three key dimensions (the end user, the representation, and the content) of the information system to be analyzed. This paper also indicates that the understanding of relations among these dimensions will also help ISD attain a more holistic scope and working knowledge of HCI. The semiotic framework of HCI demonstrated here serves to encourage more researchers and practitioners to focus on usability engineering, end-user studies, and human factors in system design in order to promote better ISD in the future.

References

Abdullah, R. and Hübner, R. (2006). *Pictograms, Icons & Signs: A Guide to Information Graphics.* London: Thames & Hudson.

Abras, C., Maloney-Krichmar, D., Preece, J. (2004). User-Centered Design. In Bainbridge, W. *Encyclopedia of Human–Computer Interaction.* Thousand Oaks, CA: Sage.

Andersen, P. B. (1991). A semiotic approach to construction and assessment of computer system. In H. E. Nissen, H. K. Klein & R. Hirschheim (Eds.), *Information System Research: Contemporary Approaches and Emergent Traditions.* North-Holland: Elsevier Science.

Andersen, P. B. (1997). *A Theory of Computer Semiotics: Semiotic Approaches to Construction and Assessment of Computer Systems.* (2nd ed.). Cambridge: Cambridge University Press.

Baldwin, C. L. (2003). Neuroergonomics of mental workload: New insights from the convergence of brain and behavior in ergonomics research. *Theoretical Issues in Ergonomics Science, 4,* 132–141.

Barr, P., Noble, J. and Biddle, R. (2003). Icons r icons. *Proceedings of the AUIC'03 Conference, Adelaide, Australia, 18,* 25–32.

Bias, R. G. and Mayhew, D. J. (Eds.). (2005). *Cost-justifying Usability.* (2nd ed.) Boston, MA: Academic Press.

Butler, K. A. and Jacob, R. J. K. (1997). Human-computer interaction: Introduction and overview. *CHI 97,* 22–27.

Byne, M. D. (1993). Using icon to find documents: Simplicity is critical. *Proceedings of the InterCHI'93 Conference,* Amsterdam, pp 446–453.

Calway, B. A. (1995). Semiotic approach for object abstraction. In E. D. Falkenberg, W. Hesse, and A. Olive. (Eds.). *Information Systems Concepts: Towards a Consolidation of Views. Proceedings of the IFIP International Working Conferences on Information Systems Concepts.* London: Chapman & Hall.

Caplin, S. (2001). *Icon Design: Graphic Icons in Computer Interface Design.* New York: Watson-Guptill.

Card, S. K., Moran, T. P., and Newell, A. (1983). *The Psychology of Human-Computer Interaction.* Erlbaum: Hillsdale.

Carroll, J. M. (1997). Human-computer interaction: Psychology as a science of design. *Annual Review of Psychology, 48,* 61–83.

Carroll, J. M., Ed. (2003). *HCI Models, Theories, and Frameworks: Toward a Multidisciplinary Science.* San Francisco, CA: Morgan Kaufmann.

Chandler, D. (2001). *Semiotics: The Basics.* New York: Routledge.

Chen, P. (1976). The entity-relationship model: Toward a unified view of data. *ACM Transactions on Database Systems 1* (1): 9–36.

Chu, J., Goldstein, M. and Anneroth, M. (1999). Icon size as a function of display screen. *Proceedings of the CHI'99 Conference*, Pittsburgh, Pennsylvania, USA. May 15–20, 1999 pp 314–315.

de Souza, C. S. (1993). The semiotic engineering of user interface languages. *International Journal of Man-Machine Studies, 39*, 753–773.

de Souza, C. S. (2005). *The Semiotic Engineering of Human-Computer Interaction.* Cambridge: The MIT Press.

Everett, S. P. and Byrne, M. D. (2004). Unintended effects: Varying icon spacing changes users' visual search strategy. *Proceedings of the CHI'04 Conference, Vienna, Austria, 6(1)*, 695–702.

Fairthorne, R. A. (1954). The theory of communication. *Asilb Proceeding 6*, 255–267. Reprinted in Fairthorne, R.A. (1961) *Towards Information Retrieval.* Butterworth: London. pp 64–79.

Ferreira, J., Barr, P. and Noble, J. (2005). The semiotics of user interface redesign. *Proceedings of the AUIC'05 Conference, Newcastle, Australia, 40*, 47–53.

Ferreira, J., Noble, J. and Biddle, R. (2006). A case for iconic icons. *Proceedings of the AUIC'05 Conference, Hobart, Australia, 50*, 97–100.

Forsythe, A., Sheehy, N. and Sawey, M. (2003). Measuring icon complexity: An automated analysis. *Behavior Research Method, Instruments, & Computers, 35(2)*, 334–342.

Freeman, W. J. (2000). A neurobiological interpretation of semiotics: Meaning, representation, and information. *Information Science, 124*, 93–102.

Freeman, W. J. (2002). How and why brains create meaning from sensory information. *International Journal of Bifurcation and Chaos, 14(2)*, 515–530.

Gonzales, R. (1997). Hypermedia data modeling, coding and semiotics. *Proceedings of the IEEE 85*, 1111–1140.

Gorn, S. (1983). Informatics (computer and information science): Its ideology, methodology, and sociology. In F. Machlup & U. Mansfield. (Eds.). *The Study of Information: Interdisciplinary of Messages.* New York: Wiley.

Hancock, P. A. and Szalma, J. L. (2003). The future of neuroergonomics. *Theoretical Issues in Ergonomics Science, 4*, 238–249.

Hansen, W. J. (1971). User engineering principles for interactive system. *Proceeding to Fall Joint Computer Conference, 39*, 523–532.

Haramundanis, K. (1996). Why icons cannot stand alone. *Asterisk Journal of Computer Documentation, 20(2)*, 1–8.

Hemenway, K. (1982). Psychological issues in the use of icons in command menus. *Proceedings of the 1982 Conference on Human Factors in Computing Systems*, Gaithersburg, MD, pp 20–23.

Hettinger, L. J., Branco, P. Encarnacao, L. M. and Bonato, P. (2003). Neuroadaptive technologies: Applying neuroergonomics to the design of advanced interfaces. *Theoretical Issues in Ergonomics Science, 4*, 220–237.

Hodge, R. & Kress, G. (1988). *Social Semiotics.* Cornell University Press, Ithaca, NY.

Horton, W. (1994). *The Icon Book: Visual Symbols for Computing Systems and Documentation.* New York: Wiley.

Jagacinski, R. J. & Flach, J. M. (2003). *Control Theory for Humans: Quantitative Approaches to Modeling Performance.* Mahwah, NJ: L. Erlbaum Associates.

Johansen, J. D. (1993). *Dialogic Semiotics: An Essay on Signs and Meaning.* Bloomington, IN: Indiana University Press.

Kamba, T., Elson, S. A., Harpold, T., Stamper, T. and Sukaviriya, P. (1996). Using small screen space more efficiently. *Proceedings of the CHI'96 Conference, Vancouver, Canada*, pp 383–390.

Karwowski, W., Siemionow, W. and Gielo-Perczak, K. (2003). Physical neuroergonomics: The human brain in control of physical work activities. *Theoretical Issues in Ergonomics Science, 4*, 175–199.

Kim, J-H. and Lee, K-P. (2005). Cultural difference and mobile phone interface design: Icon recognition according to level of abstraction. *Proceedings of the MobileHCI'05 Conference, Salzburg, Austria*, pp 307–310.

Kortum, P., Ed. (2008). HCI beyond the GUI: Design for Haptic, Speech, Olfactory, and Other Nontraditional Interfaces. Burlington, VT: Morgan Kaufmann.

Koskinen, I., Battarbee, K., Mattelmaki, T. Eds., (2003). Empathic Design: User Experience in Product Design. ITPress, Helsinki, Finland.

Krug, S. (2000). *Don't Make Me Think! A Common Sense Approach to Web Usability.* Indianapolis, IN: Macmillan.

Kurniawan, S. H. (2000). A rule of thumb of icons' visual distinctiveness. *Proceedings of the CUU'00 Conference, Arlington, VA,* pp 159–160.

Liu, K. (2000a). *Semiotics in Information Systems Development.* Cambridge: Cambridge University Press.

Liu, K. (2000b). *Semiotics in Information Systems Engineering.* Cambridge: Cambridge University Press.

Liu, K., Crum, G. & Dines, K. (1998). Design issues in a semiotic description of user responses to three interfaces. *Behaviour & Information Technology, 17,* 175–184.

Liu, K., Alderson, A., Shah, H., Sharp, B. & Dix, A. (1999). Applying semiotic methods to requirements recovery. In N. Jayaratna. (Ed.). *Methodologies for Developing and Managing Emerging Technology-based Information Systems.* Springer, London.

Mai, J. (2001). Semiotics and indexing: An analysis of the subject indexing process. *Journal of Documentation, 57*(5), 591–622.

Markman, A. B., & Gentner, D. (2001). Thinking. *Annual Review of Psychology, 52,* 223–247.

Mayhew, D. J. (1999). *The Usability Engineering Lifecycle: A Practitioner's Handbook for User Interface Design.* San Diego, CA: Academic Press.

Mitsock, M. (1994). What icons communicate. *Asterisk Journal of Computer Documentation, 18(2),* 21–24.

Morris, W. C. (1938). *Foundations of the Theory of Signs.* Chicago, IL: Univ. Chicago Press.

Moyes, J. (1994). When users do and don't rely on icon shape. *Proceedings of the CHI'94 Conference, Boston, MA,* pp 283–284.

Nielsen, J. (1994). *Usability Engineering.* San Francisco, CA: Morgan Kaufmann.

Norman, D. A. (1983). Design principles for human-computer interaction. *Proceedings of CHI'83,* Boston, Massachusetts, United States December 12–15, 1983 pp 1–10.

Norman, D. A. (1986). Cognitive engineering. In D. A. Norman & S. W. Draper (Eds.). *User Centered System Design: New Perspectives on Human–Computer Interaction* (pp 31–61). Hillsdale, N.J.: Lawrence Erlbaum Associates.

Noyes, J. & Baber, C. (1999). *User-Centered Design of Systems.* London: New York.

Ogden, C. K. & Richards, I. A. (1923). *The Meaning of Meaning.* London: Kegan Paul.

Parasuraman, R. (2003). Neuroergonomics: Research and practice. *Theoretical Issues in Ergonomics Science, 4,* 5–20.

Payne, P. R. O. and Starren, J. (2006). Presentation discovery: Building a better icon. *Proceedings of the CHI'06 Conference, Montreal, Canada,* pp 1223–1228.

Pearson, C. & Slamecka, V. (1983). Perspectives on informatics as a semiotic discipline. In F. Machlup & U. Mansfield, (Eds.). *The study of information: Interdisciplinary of messages.* New York: Wiley.

Pedell, B. (1996). Toward a declaration of icon independence. *Asterisk Journal of Computer Documentation, 20(2),* 18–21.

Proctor, R. W. and Vu, K-P. L. (2008). Human information processing: An overview for human-computer interaction. In Sears, A. and Jacko, J. A., Ed. (2008). *The Human-Computer Interaction Handbook: Fundamentals, Evolving Technologies and Emerging Applications, 2nd Edition.* pp 43–62. New York: Lawrence Erlbaum Associates.

Resnik, P. (1999). Semantic similarity in a taxonomy: An information-based measure and its application to problems of ambiguity in natural language. *Journal of Artificial Intelligence Research, 11,* 95–130.

Sarter, N. and Sarter, M. (2003). Neurergonomics: opportunities and challenges of merging cognitive neuroscience with cognitive ergonomics. *Theoretical Issues in Ergonomics Science, 4,* 142–150.

Setlur, V., Albrecht-Buehler, C., Gooch, A. A., Rossoff, S. and Gooch, B. (2005). Semanticons: Visual metaphors as file icons. *Eurographics, 24(3)*, 647–656.

Shneiderman, B. (1998). *Designing the user interface: Strategies for effective human-computer interaction.* Reading, MA: Addison-Wesley.

Stamper, R., Liu, K., Hafkamp, M. & Ades, Y. (2000). Understanding the roles of signs and norms in organizations – a semiotic approach to information systems design. *Behaviour & Information Technology, 19(1)*, 15–27.

Suchman, L. A. (2007). *Human-Machine Reconfigurations: Plans and Situated Actions, 2nd ed.,* Cambridge: Cambridge University Press.

Trimmel, M. and Huber, R. (1998). After-effects of human-computer interaction indicated by P300 of the event-related brain potential. *Ergonomics, 41*, 649–655.

Vicente, K. (2004). *The Human Factor: Revolutionizing the Way People Live with Technology.* New York: Routledge.

Vredenburg, K., Isensee, S., and Righi, C. (Eds.). (2002). *User-centered design: An integrated approach.* Englewood Cliffs, NJ: Prentice-Hall.

Walton, M., Vukovic', V. and Marsden, G. (2002). 'Visual literacy' as challenge to the internationalization of interfaces: A study of South Africa student web users. *Proceedings of the CHI'02 Conference, Minneapolis, MN,* pp 530–531.

Wang, H. (2007). Are icons used in existing computer interfaces obstacles to Taiwanese computer users? *Proceedings of the ECCE'07 Conference, London, UK,* pp 199–202.

Wang, Q-Y., Hsieh, T., Morris, M. R. and Paepcks, A. (2006). Visual information piles for small screen devices. *Proceedings of the CHI'06 Conference, Montreal, Canada,* pp 345–350.

Wang, H-F., Hung, S-H. and Liao, C-C. (2007). A survey of icon taxonomy used in the interface design. *Proceedings of the ECCE'07 Conference, London, UK,* pp 203–206.

Watzman, S. and Re, M. (2008). Visual design principles for usable interfaces: Everything is designed: Why we should think before doing. In Sears, A. and Jacko, J. A., Ed. (2008). *The Human-Computer Interaction Handbook: Fundamentals, Evolving Technologies and Emerging Applications, 2nd Edition,* pp 329–353. New York: Lawrence Erlbaum Associates.

Webb, J. M., Sorenson, P. F. and Lyons, N. P. (1989). An empirical approach to the evaluation of icons. *SIGCHI Bulletin, 21(1)*, 87–90.

Wiedenbeck, S. (1999). The use of icons and labels in an end user application program: an empirical study of learning and retention. *Behaviour & Information Technology, 18(2)*, 68–82.

Wiegers, K. E. (2003). *Software Requirements 2: Practical techniques for gathering and managing requirements throughout the product development cycle,* 2nd Edition. Redmond, WA: Microsoft Press.

Chapter 6
Information Systems Development as an Intellectual Process: Designers' Perceptions of Users

Hannakaisa Isomäki

6.1 Introduction

The modern society is transformed by digital convergence towards a future where technologies embed themselves and disappear into the fabric of everyday life. This ongoing merging of social and technological infrastructures provides and necessitates new possibilities to renovate past notions, models and methods of information systems development (ISD) that accommodates humans as actors within the infrastructure.

The idea in human-centred ISD is to take into account the qualities of human users' being and preferences regarding the new system being built by information systems (IS) designers as a tool for the users. According to Iivari et al. (2004), the most essential issues regarding users in ISD are the mutual alignment of IS and the organizational and social context in which the artifact is to be used, identifying and specifying the needs of people who are assumed to use the system, organizational implementation of the new systems, and the evaluation of these artifacts and related changes due to the new IS. Thus, the need for a variety of means for taking humans into account in ISD is evident.

However, the inclusion of users in ISD appears as one of the most challenging issues in the field of IS. Despite a long lasting research interest in user participation (Iivari et al. 2010), there is no simple solution for the humanisation of IS, and in the practice of systems development the users' view is often overlooked (e.g. Bygstad et al. 2008). As mentioned in the Introduction of this book, the perspectives of human-centred ISD are traditionally discussed from different viewpoints of ISD methodology. Yet these formalised guidelines reflect only the espoused theories in the field of ISD (cf. Argyris and Schön 1978) or canonical practices in contemporary ICT companies (Brown and Duguid 1991). Although systems development is a complex process which needs to be supported with different tools, the dominant way of considering the goals of ISD through conceptual structures in formal documents,

H. Isomäki (✉)
Department of Mathematical Information Technology, University of Jyväskylä, Finland
e-mail: hannakaisa.isomaki@jyu.fi

H. Isomäki and S. Pekkola (eds.), *Reframing Humans in Information Systems Development*, Computer Supported Cooperative Work 201, DOI 10.1007/978-1-84996-347-3_6, © Springer-Verlag London Limited 2011

such as the ISD methodologies, ignores IS designers as active, creative and thinking creatures whose vision and subsequent actions actually make up IS applications. This way these traditional viewpoints on the process of ISD do not reflect the actual way that IS are developed in the practice of ISD.

In this study the issue of human-centred ISD is approached by investigating the IS designers' perceptions of human users during ISD. This way ISD is understood as knowledge work: IS design flows from designers' understandings (Introna and Whitley 1997), thus, it is an intellectual and personal process which takes its form and consequences according to the conceptions of the performers of the process (e.g. Heiskanen and Newman 1997; Mathiassen 1998). This way IS may exhibit emergent features as an outcome of socially constructed actions during ISD, in particular designers' interpretations, but these features cannot be derived or forecasted from any a priori design (Sein et al. 2007). Therefore, the designers' views of users are important regarding the goals of human-centred design. The specific research question of this study is what are IS designers' conceptions of the human being as a user of computerized IS? There are two particular standpoints underpinning the question. First, the user is seen as a human being. This means that users are understood in terms of the physical, cognitive, emotional, social and cultural constituents of people instead of the traditional task- or role-related view (Cotterman and Kumar 1989; Grudin 2005). Second, IS designers conceptions of the user are seen as primary tools for human-centred ISD. Thus, these perceptions are considered as intellectual capital that can be put to use to create new innovative IS products (cf. Quinn 1992). In the following sections the method, results and discussion of this study are illustrated.

6.2   Method

This study merges with the principles of a qualitatively oriented method of empirical research with particular focus on investigating human thought in a certain context: phenomenography (Marton 1981; Booth 1992; Uljens 1993; Francis 1993; Bowden 1994; Marton and Booth 1997; Järvinen 1999; Wright et al. 2007). Phenomenography is about individual meaning construction, which results in a conception. Thus, a conception refers to conceiving and understanding something. People form their conceptions while experiencing the world, however, people are not constructing the world nor is the world being imposed upon them. Rather, humans and the world are merged with each other by the act of an experience. Experiencing refers to a recurrent mental act, and therefore, a conception is also regarded, on the one hand, as forming the foundation for the human construction of meanings, and on the other hand, as acting as mediator between an individual and the surrounding world (Uljens 1992). This way people's conceptions reveal what they have been conceiving while acting in a certain context. Moreover, conceptions act as interpretative schemes because they contribute to the individual construction of meanings concerning the surrounding world. In other words, conceptions are regarded as acting as ground for action (Säljö 1994). In this study, a conception is also referred to as a perception, a view, and a conceptualization.

6.2.1   Data Collection

Data was collected with a thematic qualitative interview procedure, which was planned in conformity with the principles of phenomenography: the procedure included both conceptual and contextual questions that were presented in a form that was assumed to promote the respondents' reflection and thought. In addition, projective questioning was included in order to minimize interviewer bias. The interview procedure was revised in accordance with a pilot study especially with respect to the phases and practice of ISD: the questions aiming at clarifying the designers' views of humans as users of IS were placed in the phases of ISD process: planning, design and implementation. In addition, some general questions were asked. During interviews authentic and mutual understanding was sought (Klein and Myers 1999).

6.2.2   Selection of Respondents

The process of selecting respondents can be described using Patton's (1990, 169) definition of purposeful sampling, together with what is known as theoretical sampling (Glaser and Strauss 1967, 45–49). The technique of snowball sampling was also used (Arber 1993). In addition, the selection strategy followed the idea of 'the common person' (Plummer 1995). In accordance with these principles, a group of 23 IS designers was selected as potential respondents in terms of accessibility (voluntary participation), commonness (work experience as IS designers in firms), and presumed information intensiveness (experience in working with users). None of the respondents had specialised education in human-centred ISD or human-computer interaction. In brief, the respondents meet with common characteristics of an IS professional but are also unique persons with a life history of their own. They are also involved with actual ISD practices, and thus their views indicate the theory-in-use of current IS work within different business domains. This way the possibility of gaining multiple interpretations within a group of designers was pursued (Klein and Myers 1999).

6.2.3   Data Analysis

The transcripted interviews were analysed with respect to those utterances by which the designers describe their perceptions, experiences and concepts, and which result from a process by which an individual gives meaning to certain phenomenon. These meanings are created with the aid of the two aspects of phenomenography: the referential and structural aspects, which express the intentionality of human thought. The data was first analysed with respect to the referential aspect, i.e., what is the focus of thought in the designers' perceptions of human users of IS.

Second, the data was analysed in regard to the structural aspect, i.e., how the referential aspects were seen. During the analyses an intellectual coding paradigm was used to facilitate both to maintain the context-dependent view of ISD and the content of the phenomenon under study in terms of physical, cognitive, emotional, social and cultural human qualities. The coding paradigm acted also as an aid in bracketing away any researcher-originating preconceived ideas of what the IS designers' views might be like (Francis 1993). Data analysis was accomplished by iterating first between the meaning of single statements, their surrounding statements and the data as a whole, and second, iterating between the interdependencies of these meanings (Klein and Myers 1999). The analysis was settled after employing ATLAS. ti –software (Muhr 1995).

6.3 Results

The comprehensive analysis resulted in altogether three forms of thought, namely separatist, functional and holistic (Isomäki 2007). In this paper the holistic form of thought is reported in more detail: it is the way of thinking that discloses IS designers' perceptions of authentic human characteristics. In the following three viewpoints humans are seen in the light of deliberate and emergent anthropomorphism, knowledge sharing and organisational learning as well as balancing emotions.

6.3.1 Deliberate and Emergent Anthropomorphism

One thread of the IS designers' views is that they reveal technology centred anthropomorphist conceptualisations while discussing about humans. Thus these views also disclose a tendency to adhere to technology while acknowledging human characteristics. IS are then considered to embody human features such as intelligence, human-like figures or avatars, communication, and precision. An essential distinction in these descriptions is the explicitness with which these human qualities are seen to be materialised in IS. On the one hand, the IS designers describe human characteristics as being deliberately embedded into the form and functions of IS. These conceptualisations reveal deliberate anthropomorphist predispositions. On the other hand, the designers refer to IS as conveying human qualities rather than explicitly including them. These descriptions signify understandings according to which human interpretation of the form and function of IS plays a central role. These latter views reveal emergent anthropomorphist orientations.

Anthropomorphism or metaphorical personification refers to the ascription of human-like attributes and characteristics to an otherwise non-human object (Stebbins 1993). The designers reveal such conceptualisations when understanding intelligence and reasoning as properties of technology:

R: What, to your mind, is the factor in them [IS] that users prefer?

D2: It's that you don't have to do everything by yourself but the system could be like an artificial intelligence, kind of, so it could realize in some way what you're thinking.

These comprehensions mirror views common in the field of Artificial Intelligence (AI), which traditionally has aimed to incorporate human cognitive capabilities, such as problem solving, reasoning and learning, into computers (e.g., van Someren and Reimann 1995). Traditional AI researchers focus on developing systems, such as reasoning programs and rule-based expert systems, which imitate cognitive human qualities in their functions (Lewin 2001). Then human characteristics are deliberately built in as embodied parts of IS. In other words, human-like cognitive features are coded into the software and cached into the computer's memory structure.

Another stance within AI emphasizes the inclusion of human emotions into IS. Picard (1997), for instance, stresses that emotions are essential to people's intelligent day-to-day functioning, and thus, computers need to be able to recognise and respond to humans' affective signals in a real-time way in order to function with intelligence and sensitivity toward humans. This aspiration necessitates the inclusion of emotion into computers or robots in a concrete form, such as software architecture for recognition and synthesis of affective patterns as well as for expressing affect according to those patterns (Picard 1997; Michaud et al. 2001). Furthermore, the IS designers describe human-like figures or avatars in user interfaces in an anthropomorphist manner that renders technology as having emotional features, as bringing a human sense to technology. Often this is the particular goal for constructing computer interfaces with human-like features: the interaction between people and computers is then seen to be enriched with dialogues that convey both the rational and emotional meaning of the information in question (e.g. Nakazawa et al. 2001):

R: What kind of user interface do you think that people would want to use?

D4: I strongly believe that 3D interfaces are coming. They could offer kind of human-like facial gestures as agents, which would bring a human sense to the systems. The third dimension could also be utilised so that interfaces become tangible and accessible.

These views suggest that human features which are deliberately constructed into computers render the interaction between users and IS as resembling the interplay with the cognitive, emotional, and social features of the interaction that occurs between humans. However, recent research has produced inconsistent results as to whether people perceive the anthropomorphic features of systems, such as gaze, gestures and vocal inflection of the virtual agents, as providing human-computer interaction with human characteristics in a similar manner that is expected in human-human interaction. For example, Fogg and Nass (1997) found that flattery generated by a computer can produce the same general effects in people as flattery experienced within communication between humans. That is to say, the participants in their experiment perceived emotionally shaded information emanating from a computer in a similar manner to that emanating from humans. However, opposite findings are provided, for instance, by Bonito et al. (1999), who questioned the results of prior research suggesting that on average humans are more likely to be influenced by computer agents than by human partners. In their experiments they found that in a decision-making task interaction with humans was more expected and valued than interaction with computers including human-like qualities. Even the addition of anthropomorphist features to interfaces did not increase positive evaluations of computer interaction (Bonito et al. 1999). In other words, people did not find anthropomorphic features of computers similar enough to the aspects that were experienced when interacting with humans. This gives some reason to assume that users do not always perceive human features that are deliberately incorporated in software in a human-like sense similar to that which was intended by the designers of those systems.

Another case of deliberate anthropomorphism within the designers' conceptions is suggested by the fact that 1S are understood to convey different ways of communicating. Then the human need for communication is seen as various document templates, keyboards and other such technical devices:

R: Could you define further what you mean by users' needs?

D7: At present we are replacing and adapting a version of Microsoft Office and in this project making an easy system from the end-users point of view is quite easy to accomplish. There are prepared document templates for different use situations, so one does not have to create them separately. So, for example, if one wants to make a memo, there is a document template already available.

Yates and Orlikowski (1992) combine human communicative action with technology with the concept of genre. They define a genre in the context of organisational communication as a typified communicative action invoked in response to a recurrent situation. The recurrent situation is seen as a socially defined need that includes the history and nature of established practices, social relations, and communication media within organisations. Similar substance and form typify a genre, which results as a response to the socially defined need. Substance refers to the social motives, themes, and topics being expressed in the communication whereas form denotes the observable physical and linguistic features of the communication. Form is seen as structural features of a genre, such as lists and fields for delineating text, as communication medium, e.g., face to face, and as language or a system of symbols, which would include linguistic features, such as formality and the specialised vocabulary of technical jargon. Yates and Orlikowski (1992, 302) illustrate the above definition by describing the meeting genre. The substance of such a genre consists of the participants' joint execution of assigned tasks and responsibilities. The form includes the prearrangement of time and place, the face-to-face medium, and an agenda as well as the chairperson's role as structuring devices. In other words, the genre of organisational communication incorporates the human need for communication in social activity, which is mediated through particular media. The role of technology is then solely as a supporting media, and the social communication is the actual substance.

Further, Yates and Orlikowski (1992) stress the social nature of genres by positing that genres are enacted through social rules, which associate appropriate elements of substance and form with particular recurrent situations. These genre rules may operate tacitly, through socialised or habitual use of communicative form and substance, or they may be codified into specific standards. In particular, genre rules may be standardised and embedded in a medium, such as electronic document templates with particular structural features, by making the tacit genres explicit, i.e., hardening the genres (e.g., Karjalainen and Salminen 2000). In this sense genres elucidate a case of deliberate anthropomorphism: rules of human communicative action are explicitly and deliberately embedded in technology. In the above anthropomorphism appears in a concrete form: technology, such as software agents and electronic documents, is deliberately and explicitly built to embody human-like features and action. Yet features of emergent anthropomorphism are also revealed in the IS designers' conceptions.

> R: Do you see that kind of progress [installation of package systems] going on?

> D14: Yes, it's due to the fact that at least the bigger firms are acting multinationally and have several offices around. Then a package method is the key to common systems. This means that systems are not tailored as multilingual and multicultural. Instead, German precision, like SAP/3R, is embedded everywhere.

Here the designers associate human-like attributes such as culture with technology which, however, may not be constructed on purpose to include those qualities. Instead, the designers' experience of human characteristics in technology emerges from their interpretations concerning the features of that technology. Referring to such interactions between humans and IS, Lyytinen and Ngwenyama (1992) define an interpretive mode of use, which implies that the semantics of data are not fixed beforehand and coded in the system's formal structure but that the meaning of data originates from users' interpretations of those systems. In the same vein, Sein et al. (2007)) argue that IS may exhibit emergent features as an outcome of socially constructed actions during ISD, in particular designers' interpretations, but these features cannot be anticipated from any a priori design. This is evident in a statement according to which a design methodology, SAP/R3, is seen to convey different culturally rooted types of action.

In particular, the designer criticises the methodology for forcing all the designers in a multinationally operating firm to design systems in a way that is typified as German precision. Because SAP/R3 is intended particularly for process optimisation and aimed at global markets, and is not equipped with deliberately incorporated cultural features (Information Technology Toolbox, Inc. 2001), this conceptualisation may be considered as an explication of information technology's capacity to inform its users of the nature of those activities, events and objects that they encounter when using that particular technology (cf. Zuboff 1988). In nature, then, this conceptualisation resembles emergent rather than deliberate anthropomorphism. Here the designer's experience of the cultural characteristics that are conveyed by a certain technology emerge from his interpretation concerning the use of that technology. That is to say, human qualities are not seen to be deliberately actualized in technology but they get a new form within the human-technology interaction which is shaped according to the dynamic affordances on the one hand offered by the human cultural quality, and on the other hand, supported or neglected by the features of a technology (cf. Cook and Brown 1999). Obviously, the designer had been engaged in an activity which was informed or 'disciplined' by knowledge, i.e., the use of theories, rules of thumb, and concepts concerning the purpose of building IS with the help of SAP/R3. In addition to possessing and using this knowledge, the designer clearly had been simultaneously engaged in an activity of knowing, which makes use of tacit knowledge as a tool for action (Cook and Brown 1999). In this case the design activity appeared as a process within which the conscious goal of that activity was less tacitly intertwined with the cultural human quality because the designer, as an outcome of the design activity, had created a conception concerning the cultural features of the technology in question. Thus, the activity of using SAP/R3 dynamically afforded the non-German IS designer the opportunity to acquire the conscious idea of German precision incorporated in that technology.

In a similar vein, but with respect to the social human quality, Orlikowski (2000), with reference to Giddens (1984), asserts that while technology can be seen to embody certain symbol and material properties, it does not embody social structures because these are only instantiated in human activity inherent in particular social practices. Rather, social structures that emerge within humans' use of technology are constituted as people regularly interact with particular properties of technology. The resulting recurrent social practice then produces and reproduces certain social structures within the use of that particular technology. In other words, human activity is seen to be shaped within human-technology interaction in terms of the acts of use based on humans' interpretations of the features of that technology, which may then be understood as having social features. It is worth noticing, however, that while Orlikowski (2000) assumes the use of technology as happening recurrently, as a fluently ongoing process, the designer criticises the cultural features implied in SAP/R3 in a way that suggests dissatisfied or even terminated use of that technology.

6.3.2 Humans as Organisational Learners and Knowledge Sharers

Another thread that is woven into the IS designers' conceptualisations of humans is in regard to knowledge sharing and organizational learning. The user is then understood in accordance with the cognitive, emotional, social human qualities. In particular, the behavioural affordances revealed within these conceptualisations refer to different features considered inherent in the activity of learning. Moreover, the designers express two different perspectives on the level at which learning are seen to happen: organisational and interpersonal. The designers depict changes in organisational work processes which are due to the learning that occurs during ISD: the examination of work processes teaches the involved organisation about its own activity and, thus, a new insight into the processes of work is created:

> D8: [Users] needs are prone to change rapidly, especially after the implementation of the system, because they teach an organization a lot about itself, and an organisation's self-knowledge

increases and usually needs change in a more clever direction. Then there very quickly happens a sort of 'learning leap', which is often experienced as if the system is not valid at all although it is a question of the organisation's increased knowledge of its own activity.

Here human behaviour is described by referring to organisational work-related learning, in which the organisational process of work is the source, learner and outcome of learning. In other words, learning is seen to occur beyond the individuals who make up the organisational process of work. Rather, it is considered that the learner is to be the organisation. This conception is in conformity with the perspective adopted by Robey et al. (2000), who define learning as an organisational process, and regard an organisation's own experiences as providing a base of knowledge for guiding the deployment of IS effectively. Then the examination of an organisation's own processes is seen to provide appropriate knowledge for developing IS and their use in the organisation, as suggested by the IS designers. However, as underlined by Fiol and Lyles (1985), considering organisations as learners suggests that organisations are cognitive entities, capable of observing their own actions, and modifying their actions according to their observations (Robey et al. 2000). This notion raises a question: are organisations human entities in their own right? Particularly, are organisations capable of learning independently of individuals and their learning, and thus, possessing a cognition of their own? Jones (1995) does not accept that organisations are disembodied cognitions and identifies three possible types of such organisational learning that can be differentiated from individual learning. The first of these highlights organisations as the site of learning, which denotes organisations as the environment for learning, rather than as the learner itself. The second type signifies organisational learning as a metaphor, which is derived from theories of individual learning in order to provide a reflection ground for developing the notion of organisational learning (Kim 1993). The third type regards all learning as social, being shaped by an individual's social context. Lave and Wenger (1991), for example, regard learning as equal to changes in the ways that an individual participates in social practices. They assume that learning is more effective when an individual's participation in a community of practice is emphasised. In addition, organisations are not seen to possess cognitions of their own but information and knowledge may be stored and accessed in a number of repositories, both human and artefact (Walsh and Ungson 1991). Consequently, organisations and their learning are not seen as independent of individuals but as a combination of individual, group and organisational learning. For instance, the notion of distributed cognition highlights a process in which cognitive resources are socially shared – in face-to-face situations or virtually – in order to extend individual cognitive resources or to accomplish something more than what individuals could achieve alone (Cobb and Bowers 1999). Crossan et al. (1999) stress that organisational learning occurs within four processes, intuiting, interpreting, integrating, and institutionalising, which link together the three levels of individual, group and organisational learning. These processes aim to make tacit knowledge explicit, which is the main idea of organisational knowledge creation defined by Nonaka and Takeuchi (1995), who emphasise that an organisation creates new knowledge through converting tacit knowledge into explicit knowledge in shared collaborative situations.

A particular human feature that is often overlooked in the theories of organizational learning is, nevertheless, recognised by the IS designers, namely, power relations inherent in organisational activity influence learning during ISD:

> D14: The most central issue in the planning phase is that the real needs of the real users are being worked on. I believe that an experienced IS designer can make the system according to the real needs when they are known. Often there are sort of two issues jumbled together and this is because – like in my last work assignment – the real users are not involved with the planning but there is traditionally some departmental or divisional superior involved with the work. Often this person acts as a bully to the real users although s/he is not the real expert concerning the work. This is, to my mind, often a central issue: that which is supposed to be needed has been designed but not the things that are actually needed.

The designers depicted situations in which the actual issues for IS development expressed by the users are often displaced with other interests by the users' superior. Similarly, Huysman (2000) argues that, contrary what is often assumed within studies of organisational learning, people in organisations are not always free to choose what to learn. The dominant coalitions within organisations have a stake in deciding what knowledge will be considered as an appropriate target for organisational learning.

Furthermore, the IS designers' perceptions open up views of learning by specifying interaction between users and designers as essential. In particular, the capabilities of communicating understandably and taking another's perspectives into account form the core of this conception, which highlights knowledge sharing as a particularly important instance within the processes of organisational learning:

> R: Are you interested in users' problems after implementation?

> D8: ...To my knowledge no systems have been completed by the implementation phase. Rather, the glitches aren't ironed out until just after implementation. I think that implementation is an inherent stage in the process of systems development. If it is done by different people than the actual developers, a lot is wasted.

> R: What is being wasted?

> D8: Firstly, the personal relationship between users and designers is wasted. Well, not everybody considers this as a bad thing. But, anyway, then all the discussions during development are wasted, especially all the information that has not been written in the minutes is lost.

The above extract shows well how designers value mutual information sharing during ISD. Given the change process view of ISD (e.g. Hirschheim et al. 1995) knowledge sharing between users and designers is an essential ground for successful systems development. Interpersonal learning has also been found essential by Bødker and Grønbæk (1996) who emphasise the significance of cooperative activities in the development of IS. Knowledge sharing is important also in that it is the link between individual and group learning, and signifies the expansion of individuals' cognitive maps into shared understandings (Crossan et al. 1999). The ability to take the perspective of others into account is an indispensable prerequisite for knowledge sharing (Boland and Tenkasi 1995). Buber (1993) ascertains that in order to be able to fully take into account others' perspectives, i.e., to share authentic information with other persons, one has to treat others as equal human beings and respect the current circumstances of others. The equal relationship between humans is then actualised as an I-You relationship, which refers to authentic mutual understanding within an interaction in which humans face each other with respect to the entire human being. In these kinds of relationships emotional features, such as care, trust, and security, need to be acknowledged and combined with cognitive and social abilities (Nonaka et al. 2000; von Krogh et al. 2000). Similarly, Häkkinen et al. (2000) state that mutual respect and the experience of equality are essential in authentic relationships, which build up the processes of collaborative learning. In this way empathy is an important feature of knowledge sharing. Also, it seems that the designers embracing this conception have overcome adherence to superfluous self-interest which is, according to Constant et al. (1994), a common factor that reduces willingness for knowledge sharing.

6.3.3   Balancing Emotions

A final thread within the IS designers human-centred views is that they conceptualise humans with respect to emotional characteristics. This is evident in that the continuity of customer relationship is regarded as relying on the client's satisfaction or contentment, and that skilful users are seen to behave in a peaceful, balanced way. Also, the aspiration of a designer regarding user interfaces reveals a need for a feeling of mastery gained through an interface. These perceptions disclose understandings of the human being as an emotionally diverse phenomenon with respect to IS and their development. In particular, humans are seen to cope with varying feelings, and these emotional experiences, in turn, seem to have the potential for facilitating the task people face in constructing a positive image of themselves within technological environments. Within these views emotions have a balancing role within human activity related to ISD.

The IS designers emphasise the significance of customer satisfaction in regard to the continuity of the customer relationship. They adduce a human characteristic, satisfaction, which is regarded as important to the client-deliverer relationship:

R: Are you interested in users' problems concerning use after implementation?

D10: Yes they do interest me. On the one hand, it is a crummy feeling if you've made a system for them and then it does not work. On the other hand, we cannot act if we don't do after-care. It could be that we want to sell something else to them, too.

A similar notion has been presented by Koivumäki (2001), who found that customer satisfaction predicts customer retention and the amount of purchases in an on-line environment. Aside from strengthening customership within electronic commerce, the feeling of satisfaction or contentment has significance in regard to the interaction between humans and their life situations – including ISD. As Fredrickson and Branigan (2001) point out, the positive emotion referred to as contentment is of special importance because it prompts individuals to savour their current life circumstances and recent successes, and helps people to integrate recent events as well as achievements into their overall conception of themselves. Thus, the feeling of contentment may appear as a balancing factor also between humans, their increasingly technological life circumstances and their self-perceptions.

Another conception which emphasises the adapting role of people's emotions in the interaction between the technical environment in which an individual operates, his or her perceptions, and behaviour, is referring to a feeling of mastery:

> D11: Well, it should make my life easier so that I don't have to recall any of those things that I have put in it to circulate. There should be this idea – particularly if we think about the whole organisation's action: if we have the information existing somewhere so we don't have to put the same information in from many places – that I could have a feeling that I'm in control of my work with just that tool [interface].

The designer mentions that the interface should help her in remembering things, both in regard to her own information needs and with respect to the other workers in the organisation, i.e., interpersonal information needs. She sums up the properties of the interface by referring to a feeling of being in control of her work with the system. That is to say, the properties of the system, in particular the user interface, should contribute to a feeling of mastery, which is due to individuals' perception of the successful accomplishment of particular tasks within a certain technological environment. In this way the designer is aspiring for a positive sentiment of computer self-efficacy.

Computer self-efficacy (CSE) refers to a continuous triadic interaction between the technical environment in which an individual operates, her cognitive-emotional perceptions, and behaviour (Compeau and Higgins 1995; Compeau et al. 1999). CSE derives its roots from the concept of self-efficacy, which originates from Bandura's (1986) social cognitive theory. Self-efficacy (SE) is a generative capability in which cognitive, social, emotional and behavioural subskills must be organised and effectively orchestrated to facilitate the various actions of individuals. Individual self-efficacy beliefs operate as a key factor in the generative system of human competence. Thus, skills can be easily overruled by self-doubts to the extent that even highly talented people rnake poor use of their capabilities within circumstances that impair their beliefs in themselves (Bandura 1997).

CSE as a self-perception about one's efficacy is based on four principal sources of information: enactive mastery, vicarious experiences, verbal persuasion, and physiological state (Bandura 1986, 399–401; Bandura 1997, 79–113; Marakas et al. 1998). These factors occur simultaneously and intertwine within a person's experience while using computers. The first factor, enactive mastery, refers to cognitive appraisal of enactive performance accomplishments. It seems to be an influential source of efficacy information because it is based on authentic mastery experiences, and is also aspired to by the designer. Yet information that is relevant for evaluating one's capabilities with respect to IS – whether conveyed enactively, vicariously, persuasively, or physiologically is not informative of its own accord; it becomes such only through humans' thought (Bandura 1997, 79). The felt CSE will depend on cognitive appraisal of a number of informative factors, which in this case are perceived through a user interface. The most commonly established are the difficulty of the task, the amount of effort expended, the number of situational supports and the rate and pattern of success. Successes raise efficacy appraisals and, respectively, failures lower them. Efficacy appraisals are partly influenced by vicarious experiences, which are mediated through modelled behaviour, i.e., people tend to model their behaviour according to others' successful performance (cf. Lee et al. 2006). This is the case particularly in situations where there are no absolute measures of adequate performance. Respectively, organisational support has been found to have a strong direct effect on CSE (Igbaria and Iivari 1995).

Often standard norms of how well representative groups perform certain activities are used to determine one's relative standing (Bandura 1997, 88–90). In this case the interface should convey this kind of informative traces to the user. For instance, social navigation techniques rely on guiding users by other people's actions and the traces they leave in the information space under navigation (Munro et al. 1999). Moreover, groupware applications and other software serving as organisational memories may include several social affordances for users, as well as act as a support for an individual's memory (cf. Walsh and Ungson 1991). However, vicarious experiences are often less influential than enactive experiences (e.g., Marakas et al. 1998). Verbal persuasion contributes to perceived self-efficacy in that people who are persuaded to believe that they have the capabilities to master given tasks are likely to mobilise greater sustained effort than if they have self-doubts (Bandura 1997, 101). However, the influence of social persuasion alone to create enduring increases in CSE is dependent on whether the heightened appraisal is within realistic bounds. Recent research shows that persuasion may also be included in software in various ways. This is because technologies may include several persuasive features or employ persuasive methods, designed either deliberately or unintentionally (Berdichevsky and Neunschwander 1999).

The emotional nature of CSE is evident in that people form their beliefs about CSE on the basis of their physiological state, which means that individuals interpret their capabilities according to their emotional arousal (Bandura 1997, 110–111). This arousal may be a concern of stress, fear reactions or anxiety in taxing situations. However, positive emotional arousal builds up a positive sentiment of CSE (Webster and Martocchio 1992). A special feature regarding CSE which the designer embraces but which is not usually included in the study of CSE is that usually CSE has been studied as individual reactions to computers in different environments while the role of technology's features has not been incorporated in the analyses (cf. Marakas et al.1998). However, as aspired to by the designer, CSE should be examined also with respect to the features of a user interface.

Further, a third notion which emphasises the balancing role of people's emotions in the interaction between their environments, their cognitive-emotional perceptions, and behaviour is revealed in regard to users' skills:

R: What is a skilful user like?

D8: …a skilful user always has such peace of mind and attitude. S/he kind of has a better tolerance for stress, and an ability to cope with contradictions in a better way than others.

> For some reason this kind of attitude leads to a particular resourcefulness and an ability to use the system in a more natural way...

Here the IS designer consider a skilful user as a human who is able to deal with contradictions, i.e., things that may cause conflicting feelings, and who appears as well as behaves (with IS) in a peaceful, balanced manner. In this way the designers see emotional coping in the light of positive outcomes (cf. Folkman and Moskowitz 2000). While ISD is often seen as a stressful process which requires an ability to endure changing emotional experiences, such as interest and frustration (Newman and Noble 1990) in recurrent situations of failure and subsequent success (Robey and Newman 1996), it is understandable that the designers regard as skilful people who are able to regulate their emotions successfully in particular in ISD situations. According to Pulkkinen (1994), emotion regulation refers especially to the internal cognitive-affective, but also external social and cultural, factors that redirect, control, and shape emotional arousal in such a way that an individual is able to act adaptively in emotionally activating situations. Within this interaction involving internal and external factors, the internal processes of emotion regulation consolidate and stabilise during human development as traits of personality (Pulkkinen 1996). However, despite its significance for human presence and behaviour, the often tacit ability of emotion regulation is not usually regarded as a skill because the concept of skill has no referent in describing the functions of emotion systems and stabilised patterns (Izard et al. 2000). In addition, conceptualisations that imply human emotional coping are also found in expressions in which designers highlight people's abilities to make long term commitments. Thus, the designers emphasise people's balanced cognitive emotional behaviour as essential in order to maintain long-term attachments to the process of ISD. In the same vein, Abrahamsson (2001) underlines that users' ability to sustain commitment is of utmost importance in order to endure the hardships of a process improvement effort.

6.4   Discussion

The IS designers' perceptions of users appear versatile and indicate also sensitivity towards humans as users of IS (cf. Friedman et al. 2007). First, they associate humanlike characteristics with technology. These conceptualisations appear as anthropomorphist in two different ways. Deliberate anthropomorphist perceptions denote a conscious and purposeful way of incorporating human features in technology, which may, however, be interpreted also in ways that were not anticipated by the designers of those technologies. Emergent anthropomorphist conceptualisations, in turn, signify that humans interpret human meanings conveyed by IS, which have been built without the intention to embody human features. This implies, as suggested by Zuboff (1988) and also Orlikowski (2000), that while an IS automates certain activities, it has the ability to translate the automated activities into a form that renders work processes, objects, events and behaviours so that they become visible, knowable and sharable for people. That is to say, within the interaction of humans and IS, people actively observe, interpret and share the information which is mediated to them by IS. Often this interpretation occurs in the context of task information and is influenced by various implications of the human characteristics.

Further, the designers conceptualise humans with respect to learning. On the one hand, they consider learning as an organisational process, which enables the improvement of organisational work processes. They also stressed the impact of learning during ISD – "a learning leap" as essential to the adequate design of the system being developed. On the other hand, they show sensitivity towards interpersonal learning and regard mutual understanding and empathy as important in human relationships that aim at knowledge sharing. However, these conceptions do not include features of individuals' cognitive learning processes. For example, how much knowledge or how well organised knowledge individuals seem to possess or acquire in ISD situations, or, how the information needed for knowledge construction is obtained (cf. Anderson 2000). This defect within the designers' thought is seen also in the current theories of organisational learning in that they do not clarify what kind of knowledge is being learned. Instead, these theories concentrate on the questions revealed by the analysis of Huysman (2000): who learns and how in organisational situations, as well as when and why learning occurs.

In summary, within the designers' perceptions the human being is seen in a multifaceted way. Cognitive features and rules of human communicative action are seen to be deliberately embedded as explicit features of technology. The interaction between humans and IS is seen in the light of emergent human characteristics, the conceptualisation of which flows from users' interpretations of the form and functions of IS. Within such interactions, IS are also seen to have the potential of facilitating people's task of constructing a positive belief of their capabilities with computerised tasks. In this way the designers reveal understandings which imply that IS are positioned more as human-like actors than as merely machines or 'neutral' tools. Further, the designers consider learning as an organisational process which enables the improvement of organisational work processes. They also regard mutual understanding and empathy as important in human relationships that aim at knowledge sharing. Moreover, human emotion is understood as a diverse phenomenon with respect to IS and their development. People's emotional experiences are seen to result in positive sentiments such as contentment and commitment in regard to ISD. In addition, humans are regarded as skilful in coping with varying feelings, which is appreciated in order to endure the hardships of ISD.

The results imply also challenges for ISD practice and education. First, the designers' views can be seen as intellectual capital regarding user knowledge that could be put into ISD practice in order to design systems that take into account users' qualities and preferences. However, do the ISD methods or other work conditions allow for the inclusion of IS designers' views into the design process? Second, the education of IS professionals does not necessarily facilitate in taking into use designers' own knowledge of users. For example, the ACM and IEEE curriculum 2008 does not encourage educational institutions to train IS professionals with abilities to incorporate knowledge of human users to ISD. Yet it seems that IS professionals would need further knowledge especially of individual, organizational and interpersonal learning, group dynamics, social interactions, power relations and emotional coping such as CSE. This task should not be left as happening randomly in the working life but should be accomplished during IS professionals' education. Third, noteworthy is that the designers clearly are able to obtain both explicit and tacit knowledge of users and their interactions with IS in various contexts of use during the ISD process. Do they need new means and methods to put their knowledge into actual designs?

References

Abrahamsson, P. 2001. Rethinking the concept of commitment in software process improvement. *Scandinavian journal of Information Systems* 13, 69–98.

Anderson, J.R. 2000. Cognitive psychology and its implications. New York: Worth & Freeman.

Arber, S. 1993. Designing samples. In Gilbert, N. (Ed.) *Researching social life*. London: Sage, 68–93.

Argyris, C. & Schön, D. 1978. *Organizational Learning*. Englewood Cliffs, N.J.:Prentice-Hall.

Bandura, A. 1986. *Social foundations of thought and action: A social cognitive theory*. Englewood Cliffs, N.J.: Prentice-Hall.

Bandura, A. 1997. *Self-efficacy: The exercise of control*. New York: W.H.Freeman & Co.

Berdichevsky, D. & Neunschwander, E. 1999. Towards an ethics of persuasive technology. *Communications of the ACM* 42(5), 51–58.

Bødker, S. & Gronbæk, K. 1996. Users and designers in mutual activity: An analysis of cooperative activities in systems design. In Y. Engeström & D. Middleton (Eds.) *Cognition and communication at work*. Cambridge: Cambridge University Press.

Boland, R.J. & Tenkasi, R.V. 1995. Perspective making and perspective taking in communities of knowing. *Organization Science* 6(4), 350–372.

Bonito, J.A., Burgoon, J.K., Bengtsson, B. 1999. The role of expectations in human-computer interaction. *Proceedings of the international ACM SIGGROUP conference on supporting group work*. New York: ACM Press, pp 229–238.

Booth, S.A. 1992. *Learning to program: a phenomenographical perspective*. Acta Universitatis Gothoburgensis. Göteborg studies in educational sciences.

Bowden, J.A. 1994. Experience of phenomenographic research: A personal account. In Bowden, J.A. & E. Walsh (Eds.) Phenomenographic research: Variations in Method. The Warburton Symposium. *The Royal Melbourne Institute of Technology*: Melbourne, 44–55.

Brown; J.S. & Duguid, P. 1991. Organizational learning and communities-of-practice: Toward a unified view of working, learning and innovation. *Organizational Science* 2(1), 45–57.

Buber, M. 1993. *Sinä ja minä* [I and Thou]. Juva: WSOY.

Bygstad, B., Ghinea, G. & Brevik, E. 2008. Software development methods and usability: perspectives from a survey in the software industry in Norway. *Interacting with Computers* 20, 375–385.

Cobb, P. & Bowers, J. 1999. Cognitive and situated learning perspectives in theory and practice. *Educational Researcher* 18(2), 4–15.

Compeau, D.R. & Higgins, C.A. 1995. Computer self-efficacy: Development of a measure and initial test. *MIS Quarterly* 19(2), 189–211.

Compeau, D.R., Higgins, C.A. & Huff, S. 1999. Social cognitive theory and individual reactions to computing technology: A longitudinal study. *MIS Quarterly* 23(2), 145–158.

Constant, D., Kiesler, S. & Sproull, L. 1994. What's mine is ours, or is it? A study of attitudes about information sharing. *Information Systems Research* 5(4), 400–421.

Cook, S.D.N. & Brown, J.S. 1999. Bridging epistemologies: The generative dance between organizational knowledge and organizational knowing. *Organization Science* 10(4), 381–400.

Cotterman, W. & Kumar, K. 1989. User cube: A taxonomy of end-users in management of computing. *Communications of the ACM* 32(11), 1313–1320.

Crossan M.M., Lane, H.W. & White, R.E. 1999. An organizational learning framework: From intuition to institution. *Academy of Management Review* 24(3), 522–537.

Fiol, C.M. & Lyles, M.A. 1985. Organizational learning. *Academy of Management Review* 10(4), 803–813.

Fogg, B.J. & Nass, C. 1997. Silicon sycophants: the effects of computers that flatter. *International Journal of Human-Computer Studies* 46, 551–561.

Folkman, S. & Moskowitz, J.T. 2000. Positive affect and the other side of coping. *American Psychologist* 55(6), 647–654.

Francis, H. 1993. *Advancing phenomenography: Questions of method.* Nordisk Pedagogik 13, 68–75.

Fredrickson, B.L. & Branigan, C. 2001. Positive emotions. In Mayne, T. and G. Bonanno (Eds.) *Emotions: Current issues and future directions.* New York: Guilford Press, pp 123–151.

Friedman, B., Kahn, P. & Borning, A. 2007. Value sensitive design and information systems. In P. Zhang & D. Galletta (Eds.) *Human-computer interaction in Management Information Systems: Foundations.* New York: M.E. Sharpe.

Giddens, A. 1984. *The Constitution of Society: Outline of the theory of structure.* Berkeley, CA: University of California Press.

Glaser, B.G. & Strauss, A.L. 1967. *The discovery of grounded theory. Strategies for qualitative research.* London: Weidenfeld and Nicolson.

Grudin, J. 2005. Three faces of human-computer interaction. *IEEE Annals of the history of computing*, Oct–Dec, 2–18.

Häkkinen, P., Linnakylä, P. & Lensu. A. 2000. Kollaboraatio teknologian tukemissa oppimisympäristöissä [collaboration in technology supported learning environments]. In Panzar, E. (Ed.) *Informaatio, tieto ja yhteiskunta. Raportti Tiedon tutkimusohjelman II tutkijaseminaarista 8.-9.2000.* Suomen Akatemian Tiedon tutkimusohjelman raportteja 4, pp 87–98.

Heiskanen, A. & Newman, M. 1997. Bridging the gap between information systems research and practice: the reflective practitioner as a researcher. In Kumar, K.& J.J. DeGross (Eds.) *Proceedings of the 18th International Conference on Information Systems*, December 15–17, Atlanta, Georgia, pp 121–131.

Hirschheim, R., Klein, H.K. & Lyytinen, K. 1995. *Information systems development and data modeling. Conceptual and philosophical foundations.* Cambridge: Cambridge University Press.

Huysman, M. 2000. Rethinking organizational learning: Analyzing learning processes of information system designers. *Accounting, Management & Information Technology* 10(1), 81–99.

Igbaria, M. & Iivari, J. 1995. The effects of self-efficacy on computer usage. *Omega* 23(6), 587–605.

Iivari, J., Hirschheim, R., & Klein, H.K. 2004. Towards a distinct body of knowledge for information systems experts: coding ISD processes knowledge in two IS journals. *Information Systems Journal* 14, 313–342.

Iivari, J., Isomäki, H. & Pekkola. S. 2010. The user – the great unknown of systems development: reasons, forms, challenges, experiences and intellectual contributions of user involvement. Editorial. *Information Systems Journal* 20, 109–117.

Information Technology Toolbox, Inc. 2001. *SAP/R3.* <URL: hup://sap.ittodbox.com>.

Introna, L. & Whitley, E. 1997. Against method-ism. Exploring the limits of method. *Information Technology & People* 10(1), 31–42.

Isomäki, H. 2007. Different levels of information systems designers' forms of thought and potential for human-centred design. *International Journal of Technology Human Interaction* 3, 30–48.

Izard, C.E., Ackerman, B.P., Schoff, K.M. & Fine, S.E. 2000. Self-organization of discrete emotions, emotion patterns, and emotion-cognition relations. In Lewis, M.D. & I. Granic (Eds.) *Emotion, development, and self-organization: Dynamic systems approaches to emotional development.* New York: Cambridge University Press, pp 15–36.

Järvinen, P. 1999. *On research methods.* Tampere: Opinpaja Oy.

Jones, M. 1995. Organisational learning: Collective mind or cognitive metaphor. *Accounting, Management & Information Technology* 5(1), 61–77.

Karjalainen, A. & Salminen, A. 2000. Bridging the gap between hard and soft information genres. In Khosrowpour, M. (Ed.) *Challenges of information technology management in the 21st century. Proceedings of the information resource management association (IRMA) conference.* Hershey, USA: IdeaGroup Publishing, pp 92–95.

Kim, D.H. 1993. The link between individual and organizational learning. *Sloan Management Review* 35(1), 37–50.

Klein, H.K. & Myers, M. 1999. A set of principles for conducting and evaluating interpretive field studies in information systems. *MIS Quarterly* 23(1), 67–94.

Koivumäki, T. 2001. Flow experience: Consumer behaviour in an online environment. *Presentation in the 11th Jyväskylä Summer School,* July 30th–August 17th, 2001. University of Jyväskylä. Department of Computer Science and Information Systems.

Lave, J. & Wenger, E. 1991. *Situated learning: Legitimate peripheral participation.* Cambridge: Cambridge University Press.

Lee, Y., Lee, J. & Zoonky, L. 2006. Social influence on technology acceptance behaviour: self-identity theory perspective. *ACM SIGMIS Database* 37(2–3).

Lewin, D.I. 2001. Why is that computer laughing? *IEEE Intelligent Systems,* December–October 2001, 79–81.

Lyytinen, K. & Ngwenyama, O.K. 1992. What does computer support for cooperative work mean? A structurational analysis of computer supported cooperative work. *Accounting, Management & Information Technology* 2(1), 19–37.

Marakas, G.M., Yi, M.Y. & Johnson, RD. 1998. The multilevel and multifaceted character of computer self-efficacy: Toward a clarification of the construct and an integrative framework for research. *Information Systems Research* 9(2), 126–163.

Marton, F. 1981. Phenomenography – describing conceptions of the world around us. Instructional Science 10, 177–200.

Marton, F. & Booth, S. 1997. *Learning and awareness.* Mahwah, N.J.: Lawrence Erlbaum.

Mathiassen, L. 1998. Reflective systems development. *Scandinavian Journal of Information Systems* 10(1 & 2), 67–118.

Michaud, F., Audet, J., Létourneau, D., Lussier, L., Théberge-Turmel, C. & Caron, S. 2001. Experiences with an autonomous robot attending AAAI. *IEEE Intelligent Systems,* December–October 2001, 23–29.

Muhr, T. 1995. ATLAS.ti, release 1.1E. In Weitzman, EA. & M.B.Miles (Eds.) *Computer programs for qualitative data analysis. A software sourcebook.* Thousand Oaks, CA: Sage, pp 217–229.

Munro, A.J., Höök, K. & Benyon, D. (Eds.) 1999. *Social navigation of information space.* London: Springer-Verlag.

Nakazawa, M., Mukai, T, Watanuki, K. & Miyoshi, H. 2001. Anthropomorphic agent and multimodal interface for nonverbal communication. In Avouris, N. & N. Fakotakis (Eds.) *Advances in human-computer interaction I. Proceedings of the PC HCI 2001,* Athens, Greece, pp 360–365.

Newman, M. & Noble, F.1990. User involvement as an interaction process: A case study. *Information Systems Research* 1(1), 89–110.

Nonaka, I. & Takeuchi, H. 1995. *The knowledge-creating company – how Japanese companies create the dynamics of innovation.* Oxford: Oxford University Press.

Nonaka, I., Toyama, R. & Konno, N. 2000. SECI, Ba and leadership: A unified model of dynamic knowledge creation. *Long Range Planning* 33, 5–34.

Orlikowski, W.J. 2000. Using technology and constituting structures: A practice lens for studying technology in organizations. *Organization Science* 11(4), 404–428.

Patton, M.Q. 1990. *Qualitative evaluation and research methods.* Newbury Park, CA: Sage.

Picard, R. 1997. *Affective computing.* Cambridge: The MIT Press.

Plummer, K. 1995. Life story research. In Smith, J.A., Harré, R.& L. Van Langenhove (Eds.) *Rethinking methods in psychology.* London: Sage, pp 50–63.

Pulkkinen, L. 1994. Emootion säätely kehityksessä [Emotion regulation during human development]. *Psykologia* 29, 404–418.

Pulkkinen, L. 1996. Female and male personality styles: A typological and developmental analysis. *Journal of Personality and Social Psychology* 70(6), 1288–1306.

Quinn, J.B. 1992. The intelligent enterprise: A new paradigm. *Academy of Management Executive* 6(4), 48–63.

Robey, D. & Newman, M. 1996. Sequential patterns in information systems development: An application of a social process model. *ACM Transactions of information systems* 14(1), 30–63.

Robey, D., Boudreau, M.-C. & Rose, G.M. 2000. Information technology and organizational learning: a review and assessment of research. *Accounting, Management & Information Technology* 10(1), 125–155.

Säljö, R. 1994. *Minding action. Conceiving the world versus participating in cultural practices.* Nordisk Pedagogik 14, 71–80.

Sein, M.K., Rossi, M. & Purao, S. 2007. Exploring the limits of the possible. *Scandinavian Journal of Information Systems* 19(2), 105–110.

Stebbins, S. 1993. Anthropomorphism. *Philosophical studies* 69(2–3), 113–122.

Uljens, M. 1992. *Phenomenological features of phenomenography.* University of Göteborg. Reports from the department of education 3. Göteborg.

Uljens, M. 1993. The essence and existence of phenomenography. *Nordisk Pedagogik* 13, 134–147.

van Someren, M. Reimann, P. 1995. Multi-objective learning with multiple representations. In Reimann, P. & H. Spada (Eds.) *Learning in humans and machines. Towards an interdisciplinary learning science.* Oxford: Elsevier, pp 130–153.

von Krogh, G., Ichijo, K. & Nonaka, I. 2000. *Enabling knowledge creation. How to unlock the mystery of tacit knowledge and release the power of innovation.* New York: Oxford University Press.

Walsh, J.P. & Ungson, G.R. 1991. Organizational memory. *Academy of Management Review* 16(1), 57–91.

Webster, J. & Martocchio, J. 1992. Microcomputer playfulness: Development of a measure with workplace implications. *MIS Quarterly* 16(2), 201–226.

Wright, A., Murray, J.P. & Geale, P. 2007. A phenomenographic study of what it means to supervise doctoral students. *Academy of Management Learning & Education* 6(4), 458–474.

Yates, J. & Orlikowski, W.J. 1992. Genres of organizational communication. A structurational approach to studying communication and media. *Academy of Management Review* 17(2), 299–326.

Zuboff, S. 1988. *In the age of the smart machine: The future of work and power.* New York: Basic Books.

Part II
Methodology

Chapter 7
Participatory Design in Information Systems Development

Keld Bødker, Finn Kensing, and Jesper Simonsen

7.1 Introduction

This chapter deals with IT design in an organizational setting – be it a medium sized service company, a large industrial company, a small entrepreneurial knowledge company, or a public company or institution. In such work settings we often find a complex organizational structure, including several management levels, diverse professional groups, workplace cultures, and established working relations where new IT projects challenge the established ways-of-working. This is also the domain of 'classic' information systems development (ISD) approaches. This chapter presents the principles, key ideas, and experiences from using the participatory design method known as the 'MUST method'[1], developed by the authors (Bødker et al. 2004).

Iivari et al. (2009) identify three fields where system development has been the topic of research: Software Engineering (SE), Information Systems (IS), and Human Computer Interaction (HCI). User involvement has not been the topic of research in SE, but the topic is well researched in IS and HCI. However, Iivari et al. (2009) note as an important aspect that the literature is not clear on *how* user involvement should be integrated with current approaches to system development: While agile methods include ways of incorporating customer requirements, Ballejos and Montagna (2008) demonstrate that they fail to support stakeholder identification; DeMichelis et al. (1998) show limitations towards the design and management of organizational change; and Coughlan and Macredie (2002) illustrate insufficiencies in negotiations of requirements between different stakeholder and user groups.

---

[1] MUST is a Danish acronym for initial participatory design activities.

K. Bødker (✉) and J. Simonsen
Roskilde University, Denmark
e-mail: keldb@ruc.dk; simonsen@ruc.dk

F. Kensing
University of Copenhagen, Denmark
e-mail: kensing@citi.ku.dk

H. Isomäki and S. Pekkola (eds.), *Reframing Humans in Information Systems Development*, Computer Supported Cooperative Work 201, DOI 10.1007/978-1-84996-347-3_7, © Springer-Verlag London Limited 2011

In this chapter, we describe the participatory design approach, presented by Bødker et al. 2004, illustrating *how* to engage *which* users in *what* type of design activities.

The MUST method is a 'meta-method' providing resources that has to be applied specifically to a situated IT design project. The method provides four types of resources: *Concepts* for the designer to understand and frame the situation, *principles* forming the backbone of the method, suggestions for how to *organize* the design project, and finally, a *toolbox* of techniques and presentation tools to support the various activities, see Fig. 7.1.

In the remaining part of the introductory section our interpretation of the concept of *design* is discussed. Section 7.2 discusses the most central concept – the user. *Who* is the user, and how can we identify and include them in design activities? Section 7.3 describes the four *principles* that form the backbone of the MUST method – illustrated by small vignettes from industrial projects. We use the vignettes to illustrate condensed experience describing typical situations or challenges faced in specific situations. Each vignette is identified by a number. Space does not allow for a thorough description of how to organize the design project according to clearly identified decision points, let alone the techniques and tools. For further details please see (Bødker et al. 2004). Section 7.4 compares the MUST method to other methods and approaches. Section 7.5 concludes the chapter by discussing implications for industry, education, and research.

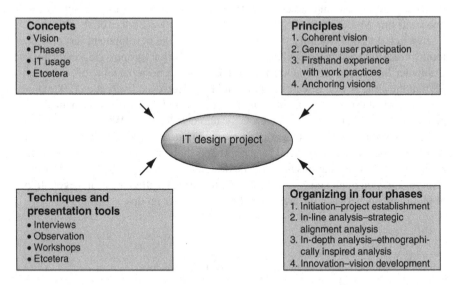

Fig. 7.1 Four types of resources for IT design using the MUST method[2]

---

[2] Bødker, Keld, Finn Kensing, and Jesper Simonsen, Participatory IT Design: Designing for Business and Workplace Realities, Figure 1.3 © 2004 Massachusetts Institute of Technology, by permission of The MIT Press.

7.2   What Is IT Design?

Our understanding of IT design and design activities in relation to an overall IT project is inspired by better established design traditions, such as architecture. In architecture architects analyze clients' wishes and needs, designing a building's form and function over several iterations taking an appreciation of the context into account. At first they design at a general and conceptual level, then in greater detail – in order to develop design ideas and prepare the construction process.

In the construction industry, traditions and experience have developed over centuries, stipulating how the construction process is conducted and how architects cooperate with the client and the many trade groups that, at one time or another, are drawn into a construction project. Over many years, a wealth of experiences has been gained and overall standards have been established in many areas of the construction process for example regarding division of work, as well as in terms of the content and detail of various specifications developed in the process. Traditions are less developed in the IT world. A marked difference is the construction industry's established interfaces between phases, enabling calls for tenders to be issued at several different points and with varying scope. For example, many large projects start by pre-qualifying a small number of architects who then for a small budget is asked to develop their design for an architectural competition. The winner is then awarded the project, and more detailed design is carried out. At a later stage another call for tenders is opened based on a detailed design for the construction, and the winner is awarded the contract for the construction of the building.

We understand IT design as similar to the activities of architects in the construction industry: Initial activities of analysis and design that outline visions for future IT usage and support decisions about which visions best meet business goals and user needs for IT support in their work. An IT design project thus constitutes an important element in an organizational clarification process leading to visions for one or more sustainable uses of IT. An explicit upfront design component of an IT project is important. This can be realized in many ways. In most projects, it is necessary to divide an IT project into a design project and an implementation project, separated by a call for tenders, see Fig. 7.2. In fact, this is the case with all large public IT projects in Europe according to the European Union rules for invitations to tender and award contracts. This model is used as a reference for identifying the IT design project throughout this chapter. The MUST method, including its techniques and presentation tools, may be used in other contexts as well. For example, product development companies may use the method when they prepare proposals for implementation of their generic IT products for potential customers.

The IT designer is defined as the professional actor responsible for the IT design project, underscoring the importance of the element of design in such projects and, in turn, the analogy to the function of the architect in construction. The MUST method

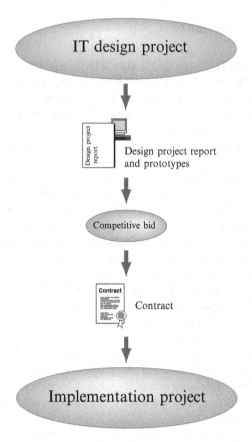

Fig. 7.2 Model of an IT project[3]

provides a perspective on IT design that takes a broad view of IT usage. This involves situating IT systems within the work organization context of which they will be part, and considering also what new qualifications will be required for users to contribute to desired changes. An important characteristic is the extensive participation of humans – that is, the management and the future users of new IT systems, along with any internal IT designers who will be participating in the implementation.

An IT design project, or design project for short, will produce a foundation for deciding how to undertake implementation projects. An IT design project is defined as a *project identifying problems, clarifying goals, and outlining solutions.* This involves:

– Analyzing the company's business and IT strategies, as well as its present goals, needs, and potentials as seen by the management and the future users of new IT systems.

---
[3] Bodker, Keld, Finn Kensing, and Jesper Simonsen, Participatory IT Design: Designing for Business and Workplace Realities, Figure 1.1 © 2004 Massachusetts Institute of Technology, by permission of The MIT Press.

- Designing one or more visions for overall change.
- Aligning the design visions in relation to the company's business and IT strategies.
- Setting down a strategy and plan for technical and organizational implementation, including cost estimates.
- Guaranteeing continued feedback from all relevant stakeholders.

The result of an IT design project is a report outlining one or more coherent visions for change in terms of technology, work organization, and required employee qualifications. The report may be supplemented by prototypes or (foam) mock-ups of any digital gadgets (Halse 2008). Moreover, the report includes an evaluation of the effects of implementing the visions, a cost estimate, along with a strategy and plan for implementing the visions. The report is the basis for a decision about implementation projects. This decision is typically followed by a call for tender and contract negotiations with the chosen supplier(s) that will be implementing the changes, including the IT systems.

One or several implementation projects can then be conducted in cooperation with the chosen supplier. The goal of the implementation projects is to perform the technical and organizational implementation of the chosen visions based on the design project. This will typically be done in a series of iterations, see Fig. 7.3. A vision outlines guidelines for the implementation through the documentation of goals, needs and potentials as well as through the proposed solutions. After an implementation project, or at other points in time, it is possible to evaluate achieved results in relation to the listed visions. Due to for example new solutions or problems emerging in the implementation project, parts of a

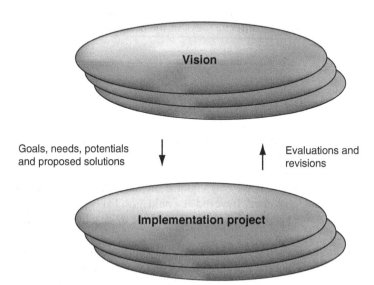

Fig. 7.3 The role of visions in a company's IT projects

vision may be revised as the result of an evaluation leading to a new foundation for succeeding implementation projects. Or an evaluation may result in a decision that a goal that was not met in the first implementation project is reformulated and set up for the next implementation project.

7.3 The Concept of 'User' in Participatory Design

A central contribution from the Scandinavian approaches to Participatory Design and Information System Development is the elaborate understanding of the user. Contrary to well known approaches like for example Contextual Design (Beyer and Holtzblatt 1998) that only talks about the 'customer', it is relevant to make several distinctions focusing not only on the relation between humans and the technology, but also to differentiate between:

– The *user*, who applies the technology for certain purposes versus the *customer* who orders and pays for it. In projects for very small companies they may be the same, but typically they are not – having sometimes very different sets of needs and goals for IT support for their work.
– *Employees* and *management*. IT design is also a political process involving conflicts and dilemmas. The resources offered by a method in terms of general principles, tools, and techniques, etc. need to reflect this.
– People having *first-, second- and third-hand knowledge* of use-processes. This entails consequences for the tools and techniques that are helpful and relevant to apply in bringing that knowledge to bear.

The premise of our participatory design method is that all types of users of a new system must be involved in different ways in the design of the relevant parts of a system.

7.3.1 User Versus Customer

Beyer and Holtzblatt (1998) present Contextual Design in which the 'customer' is defined as "anyone who uses or depends on a system." Customer is considered more inclusive than user, "which we'll use only for those who interact with the system directly" (ibid, p. 2). We may endorse the latter definition of users, while we do not talk about 'customer'. If we did, it would most likely refer to management, as customers in Beyer and Holtzblatt's vocabulary are those who pay for the system to be delivered.

When designing for workplace settings, users should explicitly be distinguished from the customer. They have different roles and competencies in organizational life in general and more specifically in IT design projects. Blurring such a distinction makes it harder for the IT designers to figure out who should be involved in which activities, how, and for what purpose (Kensing et al. 1998b, p. 175; Bødker et al. 2004, pp. 75–79). In many projects in larger companies, users from different organizational units, or from different professional groups, will also have diverging sets of needs and requirements for IT support. In such circumstances the designer needs to be able to identify the different groups and their needs, and further to see that conflicts are dealt with and negotiated in a professional and transparent manner. Further, in larger companies it is often useful to consider also the needs of the company's external suppliers and customers, who may or may not "interact with the system directly". If they do, we would treat them as user groups. If they do not, we would treat them as important stakeholders, which again leads to other considerations about who should be involved in which activities, and for what purposes.

7.3.2 Employees Versus Management

With the distinction between employees and management the MUST method stresses the differences in terms of power and other resources available to the two groups respectively. Participatory Design (PD) have argued for user participation and suggested concrete techniques for this, as discussed by Kensing and Blomberg (1998), while IS researchers and IS methodologies traditionally have been more concerned with finding ways for IT specialists to produce basis for decisions relevant for managers.

Clement and Van den Besselaar (1993), in a review of ten PD projects, reiterate three basic requirements for participation outlined by Kensing (1983): (1) access to relevant information, (2) the possibility for taking an independent position on the problems, and (3) participation in decision making, adding two additional requirements, (4) the availability of appropriate participatory development methods and (5) room for alternative technical and/or organizational arrangements. The participation of the intended users in IT design is seen as one of the preconditions for good design. Making room for the skills, experiences, and interests of employees in system design is thought to increase the likelihood that the systems will be useful and well integrated into the work practices of the organization. Of central importance is the development of meaningful and productive relations between those charged with technology design and those who, as users, must live with its consequences. PD researchers hold that design professionals need knowledge of the actual use context, and the employees need knowledge of possible technological options. The epistemological stand of PD is that these types of knowledge are developed most effectively through active cooperation between the different user groups and designers within specific design projects.

The appraisal of which organizational members should be involved in IT design and implementation has changed over time. In the early days of PD, the central concern was to increase the participation of workers and their unions or those with little say over technological and organizational design issues affecting the workplace.

Managers rarely participated in these projects. Even today the role of management in PD projects is sometimes intentionally restricted. Some have worried that management's participation would silence the voices of employees and undermine the goal of their influence in working conditions. Bødker (1996) reports that while managers participated in some seminars and meetings during the course of an IT project, they were asked not to take part in a future workshop because their presence would make employees reluctant to express their views honestly.

Increasingly, however, people positioned throughout the organizational hierarchy (including management) and with various relations to the IT design effort are included in PD projects. Kensing et al. (1998a) report on a project in which the participation of managers, internal design professionals, and users was considered a core condition for the success of the project. Korpela et al. (1998) argue for the need to involve community members who will be served by the system under development and not solely end users. In a discussion of PD in consulting, Gärtner (1998) reports: "Customers [those funding the project] will support and pay [for the project] only if they consider risks involved to be acceptable with respect to expected outcome." In this case the involvement of the funding managers was required to secure the resources needed for the project to move forward.

7.3.3   First Versus Second and Third Hand Knowledge

First hand knowledge of a given work practice is obtained by actually performing or experiencing it. Second hand knowledge is the result of being informed of the work practice for example by interviewing the employee performing the work. Third hand knowledge is the result of for example interviewing the manager of a work group, who knows about the work from interactions with his employees. The point with this distinction is that all too often the designers, who are concerned with "getting the requirements right" or "developing a proper understanding of users' needs and concerns", rely primarily on second or third hand knowledge of the work context and daily practices that an IT system is designed to support, reorganize, substitute, or create. The reason is that it is often considered too costly or too cumbersome to become involved with the employees who actually perform the job. They may have different or even conflicting needs or interests. This is exactly why it is important to get to know what these are and why. Because needs and interests do not disappear – people will relate to new IT systems based on such needs and interests.

"Not getting the requirements right" is among the primary reasons for unsuccessful IT projects (Schmidt et al. 2001). Our position is that it is – in this light – *less* costly and cumbersome to have IT designers experience users' work practices first hand when dealt with by proper tools and techniques, and with an open attitude towards how to deal with conflicts. As described below, the principle of first hand experiences with work practices prescribe observations of users in as genuine situations as possible. This should be viewed not in contrast to, but rather as supplement to the conventional data gathering approach.

7.4   Four General Principles for Human Participation in IT Design

This section outlines four general principles for human participation in IT design that are indispensable for all participatory approaches. The principles express an overall perspective built into the MUST method and into the participatory design projects where the method is used. Applying the four principles implies a reframing of humans as compared to contemporary ISD approaches. The principles concern (1) the development of a coherent vision; (2) ensuring genuine user participation; (3) experiencing work practices first-hand; and (4) anchoring the visions with different users and stakeholders. The principles, and how they have been implemented in real-life projects, are illustrated by giving small vignettes from a number of practical cases and experiences from industry. For each principle we state the basic critical factors for achieving the principle based upon our experience.

7.4.1   The Principle of Coherent Vision for Change

A design project is carried out in a company with the aim of designing sustainable IT usage that accommodates the company's current goals and needs, enabling growth without jeopardizing its future development potential. Accordingly, IT usage should contribute to a balance of a company's resources – staff members, with their qualifications and experiences, its financial foundation and technology (including IT). For instance, the information systems should enable staff members to utilize and continue to develop their qualifications when handling their tasks. The design project should thus strive for sustainable visions, in the sense that the applications should contribute to obtaining a balance between the development, utilization, and protection of the resources of the organization.

The result of any design project is one or more coherent visions for change in the company in question and in relation to its environment. The proposed change should meet the company's revealed goals, needs, and opportunities within its business and IT strategy – which may itself need revisions as part of the project. With *coherent* we mean that the following three elements of an IT application are designed so that they each and in combination support the vision: (1) IT systems, (2) work organization, and (3) the qualifications users need to perform their job with the help of the proposed IT systems in the proposed work organization, see Fig. 7.4.

A basic, but critical, factor for this is that the customer, i.e. the person(s) commissioning the design project, accepts that these issues are dealt with in the project

Vignettte 1

A large-scale design project was conducted in order to change the production technology at a national radio station from analogue to digital technologies (Kensing et al. 1998a). Three activities had a particularly relevance to the principle of coherent vision of change: Visiting other radio stations, developing scenarios and developing and testing prototypes.

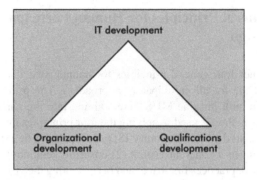

Fig. 7.4 Three elements of a coherent vision[4]

Early in the project two radio stations in Europe were visited where they used state-of-the-art digital technologies for radio production. The project group observed the radio production throughout one day and made video recordings. The video recordings documented the organization of work using the digital technologies. For example the traditional division of work between journalists and technicians was changed; journalists' selection of music was automated by using selection-programs, and parts of the program to be broadcasted during the night was prerecorded during daytime. The design visions were presented with prototypes and scenarios. The scenarios were written by the journalists who participated in the design project. In these scenarios they emphasized how management might use the new technologies to direct requests for coverage of specific events directly to the journalists and subsequently monitor the production right up to broadcasting – by having access to the material during the entire production process. Prototypes were developed with "make public" buttons illustrating how the journalists could allow management access to the material. Prototypes were distributed to all 140 employees and management at the radio station where they could interact with the proposed user interface for the envisioned systems. This way journalists and other groups could envision and to some degree experience the technology and how it might be used.

7.4.2 The Principle of Genuine User Participation

In many IT projects, the aim and focus of user participation are unclear. As a result, participation may be handled in ways that do not afford users opportunities to develop and express their needs, ideas, and visions for IT usage. If users' participation is limited to serving as informants, for instance in interviews about their work and IT needs, or to taking part in systems testing, or if participation is limited to middle

---

[4]Bodker, Keld, Finn Kensing, and Jesper Simonsen, Participatory IT Design: Designing for Business and Workplace Realities, Figure 2.1 © 2004 Massachusetts Institute of Technology, by permission of The MIT Press.

managers or executives, who may excel at representing the company's overarching goals for the project there is little chance that the resulting systems cover the users' actual needs. Such projects lacks the insight into day-to-day routines, including what factors may be complicating the work or what useful alternatives could be.

The principle of genuine user participation calls for the active participation of user representatives influencing the process of design as well as the visions it results in. There are two rationales for this, a pragmatic and a political. The pragmatic arguments rest on the need for mutual learning between users and IT designers: IT designers need knowledge about the work environment that is the domain of the design project, and users need knowledge about technological options. That end is most effectively attained by organizing activities that enable the two groups to learn from each other. Users can contribute innovative and constructive suggestions for change when they have the right conditions for doing so. The political arguments revolve around the users' right to influence their own working conditions, which are often significantly affected by IT projects. Modern companies rely on professionals, i.e. highly skilled, autonomous, and knowledgeable employees. Consequently, it is a core HR strategy to ensure staff members' influence on their own working conditions and working environment in order to keep (and attract) competent and ambitious staff members.

One should also note that in most real-life projects the user community is so large and diverse that the IT designer must rely on *representatives* of users to be involved in a design project. Thus, the selection of representatives becomes a crucial element in the design project, where compromises have to be made. Often there is a wish to include experienced persons capable of thinking out-of-the-box who are also well respected by their colleagues. However, in the daily business these people are busy and in short demand.

Genuine user participation increases the potential of visions produced by a design project to reflect the users' true situation and needs. And it further increases the potentials of the systems to be used according to their intentions. A basic critical factor is that sufficient time and resources are set aside for this (Clements and Van den Besselaar 1993).

Vignette 2

A design project was conducted by a large IT vendor to improve clinicians' overview of patients at intensive care units. A series of workshops were conducted where nurses and physicians from three intensive care units participated in designing the system. During these workshops, the physicians repeatedly stressed the importance of having graphical representations of results from the ongoing samples and measurements (blood pressure, oxygen levels, temperature, pulse rate, etc.). Much effort was directed to the design of different types of graphs, their colors, forms, configurability, etc. These representations constituted a major resource of developing the system. When the system was implemented and evaluated it was observed that the graphical representations were almost never used. It turned out, that the practical measurements and on-going monitoring of the patients' vital parameters was conducted by the nurses – and they did not use or appreciate graphical representations. Instead they measured and recorded the actual measurements and used the actual figures on the forms and charts to maintain the status of their overview of the patients. The physicians' statements represented second-hand knowledge of the work processes conducted by nurses. Due to their different ranks in the hierarchy, the nurses did not object to the design requirements voiced by the physicians. From this project the vendor learned that they had to claim an influence on who the customer put at the disposal for the design workshops and to insist on having users with first-hand knowledge of the work processes in question present – without they are compromised by second-hand or third-hand users with higher rank or management-like status.

7.4.3   The Principle of First Hand Experience with Work Practices

There are three different ways, basically, of obtaining new insight into subject matters relevant to a design project. You can read up on the subject, you can ask knowledgeable people to tell you about it and, finally, you can put yourself in a situation where you experience the subject first hand. The first two ways are most commonly used in ISD methods in general, and they reflect second-hand or third-hand knowledge. This implies descriptions of work in terms of processes and procedures reflecting an ideal work flow. This is different from how the work is actually carried out as pointed out by Suchman: Users act in a situation and do not follow plans and procedures in any narrow sense (Suchman 1983, 1987). Thus, there is a need to also include first hand experiences. A major tenet of this principle is that work is a socially organized activity where the actual behavior differs from how it is described, prescribed, or envisioned.

Ethnographically inspired observations are the primary means to realize the principle. In a design context the aim of ethnography is to develop a thorough understanding of work practices as a basis for the design of IT systems (Simonsen and Kensing 1997, 1998; Simonsen 2009). Using ethnography in design has been acknowledged especially within the fields of Participatory Design, e.g. (Greenbaum and Kyng 1991; Schuler and Namioka 1993; Bødker et al. 2004) and Computer Supported Cooperative Work (CSCW), e.g. (Sommerville et al. 1992; Hughes et al. 1993; Luff et al. 2000).

The principle of first hand experience implies that studies of work practices must include observations, possibly supported by video analyses. The work practices include existing work practices (users performing their regular business prior to system implementation) or new envisioned work practices (users trying out proto-types in situations as realistic as possible, or visits to other companies where similar technologies are in use). An obvious critical factor for this principle is to get access to the relevant work practices. Often this includes negotiations with management and/or the work groups to establish the conditions. In some design projects however, there is no current work practice, i.e. in projects dealing with radical new products or in new domains. In such projects we may have to "create the work practice" by simulating work and IT tools by prototyping and enacting scenarios.

Vignette 3

A design project included the design of IT support for the production manager and for the editors from the Danish Film Institute (Simonsen and Kensing 1997). From the beginning, it was voiced that "everybody should be able to see all information in the system." After we had observed the editors for some time, they became confidential with us and suddenly – at a follow up interview – one of them entrusted in us that there was a (legitimate but manifest) conflict between the production manager and the editors who all had a budget for their area: complete openness of all information in the system would favor the production manager and weaken the editor's influence in the organization. For example, financial support of productions considered by the editors should be strictly confidential. None of the editors' personal calculations (about which productions they were considering to fund and with how much) should be public unless made so by the editor managing the production. If this part of the system was open to all, the editors simply would not use it for this complex task. We had to carefully contemplate how to bring up this issue without taking part in the conflict. We decided to present two alternative design proposals: One implicitly in favor of the production manager and one explicitly supporting the editors, who had confided in us. At a steering committee meeting the proposal supporting the editors was chosen – though not without controversies.

7.4.4 The Principle of Anchoring Visions

The anchoring principle means ensuring that stakeholders understand and support the design project's goals, visions, and plans. Involving and informing relevant stakeholders is a key issue in ISD, especially with regard to top management and the staff of involved sections. Top management involvement and the development of strong relationships with top management continue to be reported as the uttermost important challenge within IS, see for example (Xia and Lee 2004) and (Schmidt et al. 2001).

In a design project, the project group develops various representations of the existing situation and visions of desired changes. Such representations are perceived and interpreted individually and differently by the people to whom they are presented. An important means of anchoring is to communicate representations that provide the most coherent image, as interpreted by the project group, to other relevant stakeholders that are not directly involved in the project. The principle of anchoring visions focuses on three stakeholder groups: (1) (top) management, who has the power to decide whether or not the proposed visions will be implemented, (2) employees and other interested parties, who will either use the IT systems in question or be effected by them, and (3) internal and external groups that at a later stage become involved in the technical and organizational implementation of the proposed visions.

Anchoring visions encompasses informing about and promoting understanding and backing for the relevance of the design project and its goals and visions. This includes inviting stakeholders to discuss, review, challenge, and reformulate the project groups' arguments for how a specific IT-based proposal solves an experienced problem or supports an important business need. The principle prescribes that stakeholders must be informed and involved in various ways to be able to evaluate the consequences of the proposed changes, as seen from each of their perspectives. This needs to occur in time for the project group to incorporate their reactions into the final design proposals.

To achieve the envisioned changes, continuity is a critical factor. This is why it is important to anchor the visions with the staff of involved departments and sections as well as with (top-) management. This is also why it is important to have central actors from the design project take part in the implementation and/or have central persons from the implementation team involved in the anchoring activities of the design project.

Vignette 4

A large international vendor of an enterprise system conducted a design project with a potential customer in order to clarify if the customer was in a situation where he could benefit from implementing (major parts of) the system (Simonsen 2007). Thirteen selected employees representing different areas of the customer's organization and business processes were interviewed. The vendor's IT designers were very experienced within the business domain of the customer. Based on the interviews they were able to develop a convincing generalization of the situation, which identified and characterized relevant problem domains. Their image of the situation was tied together by a string of assumptions and hypotheses generalizing the information gathered from the interviews. The IT designers presented the results of their interviews at a full day workshop for the customer's top-management including the CEO, CFO, and CIO. They systematically went through each argument chain relating identified problems or needs with proposed IT solutions specifying each problem or need, identifying its causes, the (undesirable) consequences it led to, and the ideas for its solution. The workshop acquainted the management group with the IT designer's analysis and diagnosis of the current state of affairs and involved them in a structured discussion of each line of argument related to an identified problem or need, and invited them to challenge central suppositions, assumptions, and hypotheses related to the causal relation between problems and solutions. The workshop disclosed the IT designer's experience and knowledge within the business domain as well as the customer's specific context and situation. In this way, it provided the customer management confidence in the vendor's competence and in the relevance of the proposed IT solutions, and hereby it anchored the visions.

7.5   Comparison with Other Methods

The issues and concerns dealt with by the MUST method are also addressed by other contemporary ISD approaches. This section outlines significant similarities and differences with regard to agile methods, RUP, Contextual Design, BPR, and Lean.

Contemporary approaches have abandoned the classic waterfall model with predefined phases. Rapid Application Development, or "agile" methods like Extreme Programming, focuses on fast deliveries of potentially operative systems and incremental development, relying on project models with strong iterative elements controlled along the time dimension by time boxes. These approaches differ in various ways, but they share a strong focus on programming and implementation aspects. A basic assumption for a project following these approaches is that a decision to build a system of a particular kind has already been made. In contrast to this, we specifically propose an upfront design project to establish the foundation for such a decision. Also, these methods are not intended for larger projects involving multiple systems, some of which are customized systems integrated within an existing system portfolio. Methods like modern object-oriented software engineering methods such as Rational Unified Process (RUP), focus on building systems from scratch. RUP, in turn, does incorporate early design activities – in the inception and elaboration phases. These activities are integrated into a software engineering method with a strong focus on modeling, specifications, and implementation, striving for the classic virtues of robustness and maintainability.

Contextual Design (CD), as formulated by Beyer and Holtzblatt (1998) and Holtzblatt et al. (2004), has a scope similar to MUST referred to as front-end design, requirement engineering, or systems analysis. However, CD does not distinguish between the users – those that will interact directly with the systems – and the customers – those that order and pay. In addition, the method does not suggest ways of handling potential conflicting interests. An IT design project may involve politics and we must be explicit about the different roles and competencies in organizational life in general and in IT design projects in particular. While a CD process aims at specifications meant for developers or coders, including detailed object oriented models of the system functionality and structure, the MUST method involves a separate design project where such specifications are deferred until a decision has been made on what to build or buy. In this way, MUST is inscribed in an overall project model where it is assumed that not all IT systems are built from scratch and where the implementation of customized systems will most likely be outsourced. The rationale of CD seems to be that the same group of people proceeds all the way to implementation, in which case this type of detailed description is valuable. But detailed technical descriptions are superfluous for those systems that the company in question decides to buy as standard systems, those that are outsourced for a vendor to deliver, and those that are decided not to be pursued any further.

Business Process Reengineering (BPR), in its original form as proposed by Hammer and Champy (1993), has the same scope as the MUST method. Both address the early analysis and design activities in an IT design project as well as project management. Both aim at formulating one or more visions for the future use of IT, while the technical and organizational implementation is considered outside the scope of these methods. BPR and MUST consider the relations between a design project and an organization's business and IT strategies, which are either neglected or considered outside the scope of many current methods – with potentially damaging results. While radical change, including downsizing, is a major part of the rationale of BPR, it does not deal with ethical or practical issues in relation to users. MUST states explicitly that if management aims at job cuts or other drastic changes, this should be announced up front. If users know and accept these objectives, we still recommend a participatory approach. Instead BPR suggests an expert strategy, neglecting the knowledge, experience, and interests of users, thereby risking that the visions developed do not meet real needs. BPR orients its deliverables primarily toward management, offering no help in understanding, developing, or presenting relations between IT and users' work practices. The content and the form of the reports and prototypes resulting from a MUST process are meant for management to prioritize further directions for the subsequent implementation activities. They also allow users to understand the consequences – as to their work practices – of the proposed coherent visions for change.

Lean represents an approach partly associated with BRP. Lean is a management philosophy originally developed at the Toyota Corporation and Lean is sometimes referred to as the "Toyota Way". The method's application area is thus by origin manufacture, but according to Womack and Jones (1996) the method is generally applicable to organizational innovation and change processes. As the name implies, the idea is to make processes 'lean' by removing or reducing all activities that are not producing value for the customer. Even though the objective of design is to create something new, MUST incorporates 'lean-thinking' by establishing the objective of the design project in relation to the context of the company as well as other ongoing projects early in the project. MUST does not stipulate how and where to lean the processes; instead the aim of the general principles for example on how to involve the human actors, the methodological guidelines and the techniques and tools is to create sustainable solutions.

7.6 Implications

This concluding section discusses implications and potential further directions when participatory design is taken out of the "research lab" and is applied in real life settings. First some of the lessons learned from assisting IT practitioners integrating PD into their work practice, and from teaching PD to students, are reflected upon. Then we conclude by briefly outlining some directions from our current research related to the MUST method, where it is applied in new contexts.

The MUST method, of which the four general principles and some of its main ideas have been described in this chapter, has been developed as part of a research program organized around 14 projects in Denmark and the US. Over more than 10 years we have cooperated with private and public organizations in the development of the method. Further, as the method was developed in an explorative and incremental way, our undergraduate and graduate students tried out various elements of the method in their course work and master thesis projects – some of which were also carried out in cooperation with external partners. Thus, dissemination activities were conducted hand in hand with the explorative and incremental development of the method.

7.6.1 Bringing PD to IT Practitioners

Integrating new methods in established work practices is difficult and therefore the introduction of new methods often fails (Bansler and Bødker 1993). However, it is indeed possible for IT practitioners to change their work practice and start using the MUST method (Kensing 1999, 2003), (Bødker et al. 2002, 2004). A short introduction (1 or 2 days) may work as a kick-off workshop for starting using the method – but this has to be supplemented. An approach to method dissemination must be based on two basic premises:

1. Introduction of a new method should be coupled with a joint appreciation of actual challenges in real design projects.
2. Traditional teaching cannot stand alone in method dissemination.

These premises have emerged from numerous projects in collaboration with IT practitioners. A successful dissemination process should comprise a combination of lectures, reflections on current and emerging practices, apprenticeship relations, and supervision of technical skills as well as personal competences. The central point is to get beyond a mode of detached reflection in the interaction between the IT practitioners and the person responsible for the dissemination endeavor (in our case, us as researchers).

Practitioners who are simply given a general presentation of a new technique are left on their own when trying to integrate the technique into their work practices. And a disseminator who is simply told about events and changes in a recent project is left with the question about what really happened.

So, to get beyond this problem (of second- and third-hand knowledge), the disseminator must get involved in the work of the IT practitioners through observations or ultimately through working together on a project. This makes it possible for the disseminator to relate to problems in the practitioners' current practices when presenting a new technique or proposing changes in their design practice.

7.6.2 Bringing PD to Students

The Danish version (Bødker et al. 2000, 2008) and English version (Bødker et al. 2004) of the MUST book has been used as the primary textbook in introductory design courses for graduate students in IS. The general format of these courses is designed based on the premise that students need to practice and develop these skills in order to learn to master the elements of participatory design. Half of the course is traditional lectures by the professor, whereas the other half is devoted to a project assignment. Here students work in groups of two to four persons on a project where they have to solve a real world IT design task. The students are asked to engage with a small company, a public institution, a non-profit organization, or a department or section within a larger corporation. Below, two lessons are presented: the first related to the structure of the course, the second related to what is learned by the project work.

Students enter the course with prerequisites in programming and requirements modeling from SE courses. In an introductory course, students need some kind of 'structure' to guide their learning process from reading about the method to start practicing a situation-specific combination of the resources provided, as depicted in Fig. 7.1. The guiding structure that has proven most efficient is the organization of a design project into separate activities.

The first part of the lectures is organized as a step by step walkthrough of a design project. The lectures highlight which techniques were chosen in order to follow each of the four principles and to help meet the requirements set for the results of each of the phases. This structure is also recommended to guide the students' first PD-project. However, when supervising subsequent PD-projects, students should be advised to also include their appreciation of the design situation at hand to inform the ways in which they combine the resources provided by the method. Even though the method includes guidelines for how and when for example to reduce a phase into an activity in the preceding phase, it takes more experience to master these types of decisions.

7.6.3 Ongoing Research

Research in relation to PD and the MUST method is still ongoing. These years we investigate, elaborate, and expand our approach within two directions: (1) How to manage participatory approaches applied throughout the design and organizational implementation of especially large-scale systems, referred to as a 'sustained' participatory design (Simonsen and Hertzum 2008, 2011), and (2) supporting communication and collaboration across organizational boundaries and between organizational members and individuals (patients), (www.cith.dk). We conduct experiments in an explorative and experimental way working with (close to) real life projects, and we expect this to lead to modifications and clarifications of various elements of the method and an evaluation of how it fares in the new contexts.

References

Ballejos, L. C. & Montagna, J.M. (2008) Method for stakeholder identification in interorganisational environments. *Requirements engineering* 13, 281–297.

Bansler, J and Bødker, K. (1993) A Reappraisal of Structured Analysis: Design in an Organizational Context. *ACM Transactions on Information Systems,* 11(2), 165–193.

Beyer, H. & Holtzblatt, K. (1998) *Contextual Design. Defining Customer-Centered Systems.* Morgan Kaufmann Publishers, Inc, San Francisco, CA.

Bødker, S. (1996) Creating Conditions for Participation: Conflicts and Resources in in Systems Development. *Human-Coomputer Interaction,* 11(3), 215–236.

Bødker, K., Kensing, F. & Simonsen, J. (2000) *Professionel IT-forundersøgelse – grundlaget for bæredygtige IT-anvendelser.* Samfundslitteratur

Bødker, K., Kensing, F. & Simonsen, J. (2002) Changing Work Practices in Design. In *Social Thinking – Software Practice* (Eds, Dittrich, Y., Floyd, C. & Klischewski, R.) MIT Press, Cambridge, MA, pp 267–285.

Bødker, K., Kensing, F. & Simonsen, J. (2004) *Participatory IT Design. Designing for Business and Workplace Realities.* MIT press, Cambridge, MA.

Bødker, K., Kensing, F. & Simonsen, J. (2008) *Professionel IT-forundersøgelse – grundlag for brugerdrevet innovation (2 udg.).* Samfundslitteratur

Clement, A. & Besselaar, P.V.d. (1993) A Retrospective Look at PD Projects. *Communications of the ACM,* 36, 29–37.

Coughlan, J. & Macredie, R.D. (2002) Effective Communication in Requirements Elicitation: A Comparison of Methodologies. *Requirements Engineering* 7, 47–60.

DeMichelis, G., Dubois, E., Jarke, M., Matthes, F., Mylopoulos, J., Schmidt, J. W., Woo, C. & Yu, E. (1998) A three-faceted view of information systems, *Communications of the ACM,* 41(12), 64–70.

Gärtner, J. (1998) Participatory Design in Consulting. *Computer Supported Cooperative Work – A Journal of Collaborative Computing*, 7(3–4), 273–289. Kluwer Academic Publishers, Dordrecht, The Netherlands.

Greenbaum, J. & Kyng, M. (Eds.) (1991) *Design at Work: Cooperative Design of Computer Systems* Lawrence Erlbaum Associates, Chichester, UK.

Halse, J. (2008) *Design Anthropology: Borderland Experiments with Participation, Performance and Situated Intervention.* Ph.d. dissertation. IT University of Copenhagen, Copenhagen, 2008.

Hammer, M. & Champy, J. (1993) *Reengineering the Corporation. A Manifesto for Business Revolution.* HaperBusiness/HaperCollins, New York.

Holtzblatt, K., BurnsWendell, J. & Wood, S. (2004) *Rapid Contextual Design: A How-to Guide to Key Techniques for User-Centered Design.* Morgan Kaufmann Publishers Inc, San Francisco, CA.

Hughes, J.A., Randall, D. & Shapiro, D. (1993) From Ethnographic Record to System Design: Some Experiences From the Field. *Computer Supported Cooperative Work (CSCW): An International Journal*, 1, 123–141.

Iivari, J., Isomäki, H., and Pekkola, S., (2009). The User – the Great Unknown of Systems Development: reasons, forms, challenges and intellectual contributions of user involvement, *ISJ special issue introduction*, to be published.

Kensing, F. (1983). The Trade Unions Influence on Technological Change. In *Systems Design For, With and By the Users.* U. Briefs et al. (eds.), North Holland Publishing Company, New York.

Kensing, F. and J. Blomberg (1998) PD meets CSCW – Issues and Concerns. *Computer Supported Cooperative Work*, 7, 167–185.

Kensing, F. (1999). Method Design and Dissemination. In J. Pries-Heje et al. (eds.): Proceedings of The Seventh European Conference on Information Systems, Copenhagen, Denmark.

Kensing, F., Simonsen, J. & Bødker, K. (1998a) Participatory Design at a Radio Station. *Computer Supported Cooperative Work*, 7, 243–271.

Kensing, F., Simonsen, J. & Bødker, K. (1998b) MUST – a Method for Participatory Design. *Human-Computer Interaction*, 13(2), 167–198.

Kensing, F. (2003). Methods and Practices in Participatory Design. ITU Press.

Korpela, M., H.A. Soriyan, K.C. Olufokunbi, A.A. Onayade, A. Davies-Adetugbo & D. Adesanmi (1998): Community Participation in Health Informatics in Africa: An Experiment in Tripartite Partnership in Ile-Ife, Nigeria. *Computer Supported Cooperative Work – A Journal of Collaborative Computing*, 7(3–4), 339–358. Kluwer, Norwell, MA.

Luff, P., Hindmarsh, J. & Heath, C.C. (2000) *Workplace studies: recovering work practice and informing system design.* Cambridge University Press, Cambridge.

Schmidt, R., Lyytinen, K., Keil, M. & Cule, P. (2001) Identifying software project risks: An international Delphi study. *Journal of Management Information Systems*, 17, 5–36.

Schuler, D. & Namioka, A. (Eds.) (1993) *Participatory Design: Principles and Practices* Lawrence Erlbaum Associates, London, UK.

Simonsen, J. (2007) Involving Top Management in IT Projects: Aligning Business Needs and IT Solutions with the Problem Mapping Technique. *Communications of the ACM*, 50, 53–58.

Simonsen, J. (2009) The Role of Ethnography in the Design and Implementation of IT Systems. *Design Principles and Practices, an International Journal*, 3(3), 251–264.

Simonsen, J. & Hertzum, M. (2008) Participatory Design and the Challenges of Large-Scale Systems: Extending the Iterative PD Approach. *Proceedings of the 10th anniversary conference on Participatory Design: Experiences and Challenges, September 30–October 4, 2008, Bloomington, IN, USA*, pp 1–10.

Simonsen, J. and M. Hertzum (2011): "Iterative Particpatory Design", in Simonsen, J., J.O Bærenholdt, M. Büscher, and J.D. Scheuer (Eds.) *Design Research: Synergies from Interdisciplinary Perspectives,* Routledge, London.

Simonsen, J. & Kensing, F. (1997) Using Ethnography in Contextual Design. *Communications of the ACM*, 40, 82–88.

Simonsen, J. & Kensing, F. (1998) Make Room for Ethnography in Design! *The Journal of Computer Documentation*, 22, 20–30.

Sommerville, I., Rodden, T., Bentley, R. & Sawyer, P. (1992) Sociologists can be surprisingly useful in interactive systems design. *Proceedings of HCI'92, York University, September 1992, People and Computers*, VII, 341–353.

Suchman, L.A. (1983) Office Procedure as Practical Action: Models of Work and System Design. *ACM Transactions on Office Information Systems*, 1, 320–328.

Suchman, L.A. (1987) *Plans and Situated Actions: The Problem of Human-Machine Communication*. Cambridge University Press, Cambridge, NY.

Womack, J.P. & Jones, D.T. (1996) *Lean Thinking: Banish Waste and Create Wealth in Your Corporation*. Simon and Schuster, London.

Xia, W. & Lee, G. (2004) Grasping the Complexity of IS Development Projects. *Communication of the ACM*, 47, 69–74.

Chapter 8
Reflecting, Tinkering, and Tailoring: Implications for Theories of Information System Design

Dirk S. Hovorka and Matt Germonprez

8.1 Introduction

The design and embedding of technical artifacts in complex task, social, and organizational environments is fundamental to IS. Yet in Design Science Research (DSR) and in the information system development process, the role of the humans who will use the system has been marginalized to that of a source in a require-ments elicitation process, a subject in participatory design, or worse, a "user" of the designed technological artifact (Bannon 1991). While recent research (Kensing et al. 1998; Kensing and Blomberg 1998; Grudin and Pruitt 2002) has positioned end-users as participants involved in the design process, this work has largely focused on the primary design phase of technology artifacts. We have not seen a conscious, research driven approach which posits people as free, intelligent, and intentional designers in the ongoing recreation of information systems through a process of secondary design in the context of use. The hegemony of artifact design is so strong that workers' deviation from prescribed uses of infor-mation systems and the creation of workarounds is frequently viewed as resistance (Ferneley and Sobreperez 2006) rather than as a secondary design process to tailor a system to fit the user's situated tasks, metaphors, and use patterns. Although a number of recent special journal issues have addressed Design Science Research, few researchers focus attention on the activities of the humans using the systems. Nowhere is the human actor considered a designer in her own right. Yet an increasing number of technologies are intended to be tailored for the creation of information environments, where actors in the information process reflect on the context, tasks, and technologies to tinker with the system and tailor it to suit their own metaphors and use patterns (Germonprez et al. 2007). Although

D. Hovorka (✉)
Bond University, QLD, Australia
e-mail: dhovorka@bond.edu.au

M. Germonprez
University of Wisconsin-Eau Claire, WI, USA
e-mail: germonr@uwec.edu

H. Isomäki and S. Pekkola (eds.), *Reframing Humans in Information Systems Development*, Computer Supported Cooperative Work 201, DOI 10.1007/978-1-84996-347-3_8, © Springer-Verlag London Limited 2011

researchers have recognized that technology and behavior are in fact inseparable in an information systems (Hevner et al. 2004), the focus in literature on the structure of design theory and what guidelines must be followed has obscured and undervalued an important phenomenon in design theory: human activity. DSR is becoming dominated by a functionalist perspective (Butler and Murphy 2007) which privileges method and structural form over understanding and support for the behaviours of the actors who will use the artifacts. Despite multiple paradigms for design theory (Hirschheim and Klein 1989) the functionalist problem-solving approach is widely used and contributes to an "appliance mentality" (Lee 2001) of design which does not account for the tailoring of the system to make it useable (Bannon 1991; Germonprez et al. 2007).

The emphasis on guidelines and anatomical structure tends to provide a false sense of *good theory* based on fulfilling a checklist rather than a design theory's ability to account for the phenomenon it is applied to investigate. A case in point comes from Hevner et al. (2004), whose definition of artifact design states the following: "we do not include people or elements of organizations in our definition nor do we explicitly include the process by which such artifacts evolve" (p 82). Researchers operating under these guidelines are likely to privilege the technical artifact over processes of secondary design in their theorizing. But it is impossible for a primary design effort to completely specify all possible system uses *ex ante*.

Current structural specifications and guidelines for design theory fall short of creating theories that account for the end-users' reflections, tinkering, and subsequent tailoring of information systems in a process of secondary design. It has long been recognized that the model of the task domain held by users is often not shared by the designers (Dourish 2001) and that information systems are frequently used in unanticipated ways for unforeseen tasks (Winograd and Flores 1986). The emergence of unanticipated and even previously unknown uses of information systems is a result of multiple forces. Users may tailor information systems in the context of use to fit changing tasks and contexts, to accommodate greater competence and learned use patterns, or to fit the user's metaphors or functional needs. This is due, in part, because systems are not designed to adapt to dynamic reassessment of situations, to accommodate altered plans, or to mediate non-typical, independent, or cooperative work (Ferneley and Sobreperez 2006). Research on resistance suggests that creation of adaptable, reconfigurable or accommodating systems requires that designers, developers, and managers reframe their views of workarounds as resistance, and critically analyze their systems' designs (Ferneley and Sobreperez 2006). Design can over-determine the coupling of a system to the situated world because designers do not understand that many aspects of the work itself are underdetermined until apprehended *in situ* (Robinson 1993). By necessity, end-users modify the actual information processes to complete their realized, contextual work.

In this chapter we argue that when using an information system, it is not the participants' goal to *use information technology*. Instead, the goal is to produce, collect, analyse, retrieve, store, or communicate *information* in an interactive and frequently ideographic process involving the actor, the technology, and other people. As a result, we contend that design theories must account for the processes by which the system actors interact with technology to produce and consume information. Early work on information system tailoring (Henderson and Kyng 1991) focused on the alteration of the artifact by the user. We extend and build on this basic idea to expand the conception of design research itself to include the entire constellation of associations that combine to create situated information processes, not just a single, stable artifact. The object of design becomes the information process and the actor's reflection and action as mediated by the technology. This requires reframing human actors in the design process as *users-as-designers* (Germonprez et al. 2007; Henderson and Kyng 1991) in a process of secondary design. Therefore the creation of the technological artifact is only one-half of the design process. The other and perhaps more important half, is understanding and designing for the cognitive, subjective, and embodied interactions (Butler and Murphy 2007) of reflection, tinkering, and tailoring which actors engage in during information technology use.

This suggests an interactionist perspective on IS design which draws upon Dourish (2001), Winograd and Flores (1986), and Bannon and Bødker (1991), and interpretive design epistemologies from Introna and Whittaker (2002), McKay and Marshall (2005, 2007) and Niehaves (2007). To move from an artifact to a contextually oriented, unique, and innovative set of processes in the production of new information systems requires an expanded view of human action in design theory. We examine the implications for design theory as we shift from theorizing about an artifact to theorizing about design of holistic information processes. We argue that design theory itself must account for and support the activities of the human actor, which creates an evolutionary trajectory for the information process. We propose the addition of environments which organize kernel theories, providing insight regarding interaction and influence in different use contexts. In addition, reflection along the lines suggested by Introna and Whittaker (2002) has long been an issue surrounding systems that engage and encourage the user to look, touch, and work with parts in the creation of a larger whole. Many researchers have considered the reflective component critical if we are to interact with and ultimately innovate on component parts.

8.2 Theory in Design Science Research: Status Quo

Many researchers ascribe the origins of the current conceptualization of DSR to Herb Simon's *Sciences of the Artificial* (1969). There has been a strong effort to establish DSR as a legitimate scientific approach to knowledge creation within IS. Current research has resulted in guidelines for the procedural steps required to qualify as DSR (Hevner et al. 2004), the identification of structural elements of design theory (Gregor and Jones 2007; March and Smith 1995), and discussions of the role and necessity of theory in design science (Venable 2006). Throughout all of this published work, there is an underlying rationale that privileges the artifact and relies on a designer-centric approach.

As a consequence, there is a schism between DSR, which "has to do with the systematic creation of knowledge about, and with design" (Baskerville 2008, p 441) and the practice of information system development (ISD) which emphasizes functional artifacts. Traditional systems analysis and design methods are often supplemented with participatory design, user-centered design, or activity-based design. Yet even in ISD, personas (Pruitt and Grudin 2003), activity-based design (Andersen 2006), and human-centered design emphasize the importance of the end-user for the primary design process, and they all firmly position the user as external to the instantiation of the final information process or the actual work for which the system is used. The information system is something designed for them to use. There continues to exist a "software culture based on the notion of trying to achieve perfect software, which of course is an in-your-face manifestation of designer-centered design" (Koopman and Hoffman 2003, p 74).

Our current conceptualization of *design theory* is modeled after the natural sciences in which there are highly predictable and regular phenomena. DSR has been constituted in a number of ways, but generally incorporates some version of 'problem identification-build-evaluate-theorize' (Winter 2008). Each of these steps is performed *by the designer*. One implication of this model is the belief that "people will encounter technology as something that is encountered just as it was designed, to be appropriated or incorporated into practice" (Dourish 2006, p 6). There are certainly classes of information systems for which this may be largely true. Corporate ERP systems, enterprise accounting software, and medical reporting systems may provide examples where inflexible IS may be desired, so that information system use and outputs are standardized, and users will all have similar experiences with the system. But at the other end of the spectrum are an increasing number of information systems and services which are intended to be tailored in the context of their use (Germonprez et al. 2007). These systems provide information environments where actors in the information process reflect on the context, tasks, and technologies, and tinker with system to eventually tailor it to suit their own metaphors and use patterns. Human actors who tailor information processes are acting as secondary designers in the ongoing creation and recreation of information environments. This is fundamental human activity currently not recognized in most design theorizing.

The everyday engagement in an information process "shows unexpected consequences: events, behaviors, and features of systems and the people who use them fall outside the scope of the original specifications" (Ciborra 2002, p 44). It also tells us that system use patterns are irregular, often contradictory, untidy, and subject to approximation. Current design science theory separates the design of the artifact from the teleological goal of the artifact (i.e. its use in ongoing but changing information processes) while at the same time declaring that these two aspects are inseparable. It is impossible for a primary design effort to completely specify an information process *ex ante*.

This seemingly obvious omission from design science theory begs for resolution. To begin, we assume that the purpose of information systems is to enable human participants to accomplish goals related to information or decision making, and are not ends in and of themselves. The information manipulated by an actor engaged with an information system is intended to be consumed by human actors in some fashion, rather than to satisfy the whims of a technology or an *a priori* design.

This places technology firmly in the role of mediation, which enables and constrains human activity, and expands the system design boundary beyond the technological artifact. Technology provides and imposes structure, context, and negotiation between participants and a system. The emphasis shifts from objective artifacts to the co-constitutive nature of information systems composed of technologies, participants, and contexts (Huizing 2007). We also adopt Bannon's (1991) vision that humans are active and intentional actors, and not merely collections of cognitive processes and characteristics. Thus we extend the stream of research which views people as intelligent actors, into the domain of secondary design of information systems in use. In the remainder of this chapter we use the term *actor* so that emphasis is placed on the person as an "autonomous agent that has the capacity to regulate and coordinate his or her behaviour, rather than being a passive element in a human-machine system" (Bannon 1991, p 29).

8.3 Expanding Design Theory: Reflection, Action, Technology

Ciborra (2002) argues that the everyday informal modes of teleological use involve tinkering, hacking, and serendipitous outcomes from information systems. This informal tinkering, rather than a formal top-down design process, has led to numerous instances of strategically advantageous information systems, with the most noteworthy example being the Internet itself. Recent research has begun to address this phenomenon, including a theoretical approach to the design of tailorable technologies (Germonprez et al. 2007) which identified a dual-phase design process. Additionally, Gregor and Jones (2007) note the system characteristic of mutability, which describes the ways in which artifacts emerge, evolve and develop interdependencies with socio-economic contexts as a key unresolved issue for design.

The secondary design activities enacted by human actors are a crucial element in the way information systems are encountered in practice. To encompass these phenomena, design research and design theory must extend their boundaries to include the reframing of human users as intentional actors in the design process, outside formal procedural design roles. Behavioural science can inform such expanded design theory by identifying behavioural theories which account for common patterns of reflection, information sharing, creation, and attachment of meaning to situated objects, secondary design, and which sensitise researchers to ideographic or revolutionary designs. To assume a more defining role in the new class of information systems, our focus needs to shift from the management of outcomes measures through rigid coupling of systems to performance measures and towards identification of use patterns and motivations for system tailoring. In considering the role of design theory, researchers are tending to be accountable only for the characteristics of the technology, not for the design of the teleological goals of the technology. We start by framing the initial design activities of these interactionist cognitive-technical systems in different rhetorical terms, and construct theories which account for actors' interactions in a life world created with these emerging technologies. Thus we eliminate the dichotomy between 'designing the artifact' and 'using the artifact' and focus instead on designing information processes.

We identify three major characteristics essential to design theorizing about secondary design: the technological environment, the reflective environment, and the active environment in which actors undertake intentional actions (Germonprez et al. 2007). Although each of these characteristics has been examined separately, and some research has sought to integrate two components, our conceptualization of design theory must expand to incorporate and understand the interactions of each of the environments (Fig. 8.1).

We view reflection, action, and technology as distinct aspects of the phenomenon, in the sense that we can design from a technology perspective (i.e. software engineering), or take a more reflection-based approach. Where we begin in the framework is not important. The combination of these three environments reciprocally shape and constrain the manner in which users-as-designers can innovate with tailorable systems. The relationships in Fig. 8.1 indicate bi-directional processes, not cause-effect directionality, as actors engage with different information environments, different material aspects of the technology, and reflect on different subjective meanings and experiences. We now look at each one of the environments and consider them as part of the larger framework.

Human interactions with technology may be initiated through either action or reflection so Fig. 8.1 does not specify a sequence or order for interactions. Reflection about the technology environment may lead to tailoring, which then leads to additional reflection on the newly configured technology. Or tinkering without a specific goal in mind may lead to a desirable design state which then engenders further reflection. The actor may first encounter a primary design from a rational development process, or she may first encounter a secondary design

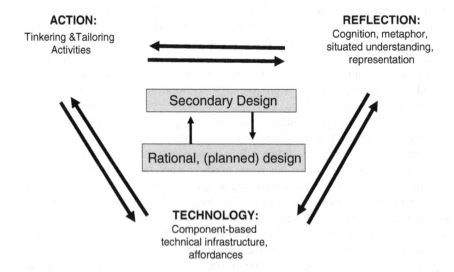

Fig. 8.1 Framework for extending design theory through secondary design

which was tailored by another actor. In either case, the three environments exist and support secondary design. These interactions have no specific end as actors tailor and distribute innovations that others may further modify, or developers may subject to a more formal design process.

The critical issue to consider when working with each of the environments is that they shape not only the primary design of a tailorable technology (Germonprez et al. 2007), but they also shape the ability of an actor to engage in secondary design. In providing a tractable framework, we are attending directly to what we have argued as a deficiency in design science research: human activity.

8.3.1 Reflection

The theory of tailorable technology design (Germonprez et al. 2007) posits two distinct environments embedded in the technology that each of the primary and secondary designers access: reflective and active environments. The reflective environment exposes design principles with which the actor can engage and begin a conversation which "includes the essential elements of situated directedness and ongoing dialectical movement (to and fro) as an exemplar of cognition and action" (Introna and Whittaker 2002, p 166). This aptly supports the activity of tinkering as the actor is simultaneously *acting upon* and *acting with* technical system components, engaging, distancing, and reengaging, and communicating with components and other actors.

The reflective environment provides the cognitive lenses we use to make sense of situations, and emphasizes the structural coupling of the system with the world and the creation of meaning for the activity, system use, and information. This meaning is frequently shared with other participants, or may serve to construct their own personal future realities (Ramiller 2007). Thus reflection changes our rhetoric from *design* to *disseminate*. In their actions as secondary designers, human actors are not describing to others a formal design activity. Rather, they are engaged in identification of goals and actions, and the dissemination of the resultant activities through the action of creation. This changes the design metaphor from instrumental design of a product or appliance, to communicative actions and creation.

The reflective environment is rooted in the fact that human action is not determined by a set of rules, nor is it based on unchangeable edicts. Winograd and Flores (1986) emphasize that over-determination of the designed structural coupling of system rules with the real world restricts actors' ability to meaningfully reflect on the horizon of possibilities presented by the system. From the perspective of phenomenology, thoughts are not independent events prior and separate from action (Introna and Whittaker 2002). Reflection is something which occurs continuously, and is shaped by the situated environment and context. The information technology artifact is not something 'out there' as it is used. Rather it is part of the actors' sense of *being in the world* (Heidegger 1962) and provides perceived possibilities for action which inform the actor's intentions. In the same way an actor does not have to explicitly consider the pencil in order to write, the possibilities for action understood from the information system emerge as relevant as part of reflective awareness of the situated environment containing the user's goals and the technological artifact. Ongoing use, such as navigating the internet, sending email, or writing a manuscript, are embodied cognitive actions that occur against the backdrop of constant reflection on what was just done, and what the actor intends to do. But occasionally all users will encounter breakdowns when the technology does not fit within expectations or use patterns. The sudden awareness of the existence of the system as separate from the activity shifts what Heidegger (1962) referred to as the *ready-at-hand* experience to a *present-at-hand* experience. When designing mediating information technologies for human action, designers must resist the temptation to determine rules which limit user goals and possible action. Greater plasticity of information systems may be desirable in some domains and can be achieved by enabling reflection and the capacity for secondary design so that people can create new structural couplings to overcome breakdowns in the context of use. We must recognize human action as originating a reflective process, whether mediated by technology or not, and pursue design that does not overly constrain users' reflections by enforcing over determined procedures. Computer mediated interaction should not provide a new domain where rules become a constraint for how action is determined (Craib 1992). Rather, our design theories become more comprehensive when they are explicit about the degrees of freedom of that human action and reflection embedded in the technology.

Human activity typically follows patterns in order to achieve outcomes (Wittington 1992). People apply patterns in the completion of outcomes *but* these patterns should not be constrained by a predetermined set of rules in the form of determined technology. These two seemingly incompatible issues of *no rules* and *needed patterns* are, in fact, quite complementary. Considered in order, people use patterns to produce outcomes. There is a pattern to completing this paper, there is a pattern to teaching a class, and there is a pattern to shopping for bread. Variability exists in these patterns to the extent that each person applies their own, similar yet distinct, pattern (Boland et al. 2007). The application of an individual pattern itself is variable. One day an individual may apply one pattern to achieve an outcome while the next day applying a different pattern to achieve of the same outcome. The individual variability results from changing contexts, new information, or experience. Considered and mindful interaction with technology suggests that people must reflect on their surroundings each and every time they apply a pattern in the production of an outcome. If information systems are designed to simply apply rules to control the patterns that people apply in the production of outcomes, we undermine human action as a reflective process. Technology must maintain a reflective environment, so that human action is supported in the accomplishment of desired and variable outcomes. All this must be done without over-specifying the individual actions associated with the production of outcomes.

8.3.2 Action

From a design perspective, action must be considered as divisible into three separate aspects. First, there is the *situated being-in-the-worldness* (Heidegger 1962) in which ongoing, embodied and situated cognition is action, and action is cognition (Introna and Whittaker 2002). From this perspective, an actor already knows what to do with a system within a context, without having to think of it as an external object to be confronted and manipulated. Her experience, skills, and use patterns make the technological environment ready-at-hand for actions without extended moment-by-moment decisions. The second aspect of action occurs when an actor engages the horizon of possibilities of the technological environment in a non-random set of actions that have no specified outcome. This tinkering (Ciborra 2002) or fiddling (Introna and Whittaker 2002) with system components and functions, without having a specific task in mind, creates possibilities of meaningful use that may result in subsequent intentional actions as new configurations emerge and are recognized. Prior experience with systems in the world, and the affordances and perceived affordances (Gibson 1977; Greeno 1994; Norman 1999) of the system themselves present transcendental possibilities in which the reflective user may create new uses or applications through actions. Thirdly, action may take the form of what is thought of as cognition or imagination, as an actor envisions new configurations based upon knowledge and reflection of the *possibilities for* presented by the technological environment.

Tailoring and tinkering are activities which overcome cognitive and normative barriers, and allow human actors to see, appreciate and utilize all the potential applications already present (Ciborra 2002).Thus tinkering and tailoring are key actions resulting from reflection on the situated tasks and on the resources embedded in the technology, or mediated through the technology. Thus an actor may not see the technology as something to use as much as a necessary *mediation* to access information or to communicate/collaborate with other people. The affordances (real or perceived) provided by functional characteristics, components, and conventions enable the user-as-designer to tinker and reconfigure the system. This may be as simple as modifying the presentation of a desktop, or engaging pre-determined service sources, or more complex tailoring such as linking portlets, or linguistic tailoring where users define the content of a system. Furthermore, systems should be designed to provide multi-dimensional mechanisms such as peripheral awareness, implicit communication, and double-level language (Robinson 1993) that were not explicitly specified in the original design, but which emerge through action in the performance of work practices.

By adopting Latour's (1995) viewpoint that technologies are assemblages of people and things, we see that design and innovation are processes of modifying the chain of associations between constituent parts in the system. In doing, so we remove the subject-object dualism, and view technology as contextualized tools for signifying meaning, understanding, and representation (Huizing 2007). These modifications may tailor the functions, presentation, services, or language in the system. But the actor's actions also may change the associations among representations, meanings, contexts, and people. For example, use of a wiki will entail linguistic tailoring as participants negotiate shared representations of world objects through a technical system, in an ongoing dynamic recreation of representations through language use and the patterns of interaction mediated through technology. Language actions are supported and mediated by a technology which eventually represents the totality of the participant's actions. In the process of supporting language, the technology becomes a historical record of interaction (i.e. different forms of communicative action) Habermas (1981) as well as a manifestation of the object of discussion (representation).

As we consider action in relation to technology we must consider it as having a frame that contributes to the interaction with the participant in the form of what a human actor *has done* and *might do*. As the horizon of possibilities emerges, the participant must have clear signals from technology on how to realize the desired structural coupling of the system to their world. This can be done through referencing a set of design principles including existing tools, recognizable conventions and components, and established metaphors (Germonprez et al. 2007). By tailoring systems in accordance with their own actions, human actors maintain an engagement with the technology, other actors, and themselves.

8.3.3 Technology

Current design theories and rhetoric largely assume that the technical specifications of information systems are fixed and finished objects which can be optimized. The research goal is to design, model, service, and evaluate systems in relation to a set of preconceived goals and operators. In this way, we can manipulate the system so that we explain the greatest variance in a specific selection of performance measure. But, given that actors are going to tinker with systems, and tailor them where possible (including the development of workarounds which enable work in praxis), design theory needs to address the characteristics of the technology which either enable, or inhibit, secondary design (Germonprez et al. 2007). Principles found to be important in the primary design of tailorable systems (Germonprez et al. 2007) are presented in Table 8.1 as positioned in their respective active and reflective environments. These principles help define the conditions which enable an interaction between an actor, technology, and their environment. These affordances (Gaver 1991; Gibson 1977; Greeno 1994; Norman 1999) represent inherent possibilities for action. Reframing the human actor in design theory will aid research regarding the affordances these principles offer (whether or not they are perceived) and the manner in which they are perceived or sequenced by actors.

Affordances provide support for secondary design through a human actor manipulating attributes of the technological environment which were not originally intended to be combined. This action expands the horizon of possibilities where

Table 8.1 Principles in the primary design

Environment	Principle	The technology supports...
Reflective	Task setting	Variable tasks and problems
	Recognizable components	Components from existing technologies
	Recognizable conventions	Use patterns from existing technologies
	Outward representation	The context that it will likely be used in. This includes individual, group, and organizational
Active	Metaphor	Symbolic representation
	Tools	Existing design tools
	Methods	Existing design methods
	Functional characteristics	Functional requirements
	User representation	The representation of users

tailoring is likely to occur in new appearance, representation, or functionality deemed desirable to an actor.

However, consideration of physical affordances in design theory must not focus solely on the artifact. The components to be acted upon must be compatible with what the actor contributes to the interaction. Snow (1992) refers to this as *aptitude* and Greeno (1994) refers to it as *ability*. Here we again see the need for deeper understanding of the aptitude of actors in their different phases and contexts of use and provide appropriate technology in support. This must consider the dimension of competence as an actor progresses from learning, to interacting with the technology through to habitual interactions which do not require focused attention. Technology must also support actors' situated focus, which can vary depending on whether the task is goal driven work or casual interaction, while attending to other matters simultaneously. There is a growing need to better understand actor behaviours, intentions, and emergent actions for design theory to provide guidance for design of these types of technology.

8.4 Conclusions

In this chapter we present the argument that the use of information systems involves the human actor as an intentional agent in the secondary design of information processes mediated by technological artifacts. Therefore, our design theories must be extended beyond the narrow focus on the IT artifact to explain and predict the activities of human actors and the processes by which information processes and the mediating artifacts are tailored and evolve. We contend that to separate the design theory of the physical artifact from consideration of its instantiation, engagement, and use by actors in the world reduces the evaluation of design theory to trivial verifications. We suggest that design theory should improve knowledge of the technologically mediated human information process rather than merely determining that the technology performs better along some domain specific performance measure. In this view, human communication and information processes become the objects of design.

This is no trivial task, one that extends far beyond this paper. Additional methodologies are required to pursue this agenda. Phenomenological and ethnographic accounts are necessary to understand the actors' intentions and perspectives on their actions. As Galliers notes, "The many *problematiques* (defined here as a nexus of inter-related problems) facing individuals, organizations and society in the age of 'modernity' are such as to require 'requisite variety' in our approach to research, in the literature we cite in developing our arguments, and in the subject matter we choose to research" (2008, p 334). Design theories must be considered as composite theories composed of kernel theories (March and Smith 1995) or justificatory knowledge (Gregor and Jones 2007). Although positivist theories frequently inform design theory (Hevner et al. 2004; Kuechler and Vaishnavi 2008; Walls et al. 1992), qualitative and interpretive approaches can also be used effectively (Germonprez et al. 2007; Romme 2003; Winograd and Flores 1986). This pluralist approach opens the range of system evaluation and refinement to include perspectives such as Actor-network theory (Latour 1995), affordances (Gibson 1977), and the studies of situatedness (Ciborra 2006; Gasson 1999; Suchman et al. 1999).

Calls for design theories are dominated by the underlying assumption that theory is a set of procedural rules for how to build something, rather than a set of principles which enable designers to explain and support a desired phenomenon. This has frequently been interpreted as designing an artifact to solve a problem. This may be an appropriate approach for automated systems and repetitive work activities, but from a broader perspective, a system mediates the human activity and enables human actors to solve their own, contextualized problems. This changes the focus from how does the artifact solve the problem, to how does this artifact enable a human actor to reflect and act in a meaningful way. The focus becomes interactive use rather than mechanistic problem solving, and recognizes the innovative tinkering, tailoring, and reflection which users apply to work-arounds and unforeseen solutions to the *human's* problems.

Theorizing about design theory can also be extended to account for observed phenomena and attaining the ability to make novel predictions. If design theories only prescribe procedures building an artifact, these theories are subject to a continuous state of trivial verification, and are unable to predict novel observations, which have been either undreamt of, or possibly contradict previous research (Lakatos 1973). We argue that if design theories are not to degenerate to procedural, rather than theoretical knowledge, the design theories must expand to predict novel facts and observations (Hovorka and Germonprez 2009). This may be accomplished by reconsidering the role of the human actor as a critical part of the ongoing design, and by identifying and fostering use patterns; in essence reminding the human actor of prior patterns. As recognizable patterns become individually favorable, they may be shared and distributed to peers and colleagues. *Recognizable patterns* may also represent a secondary design manifestation of the primary design principles of *recognizable conventions* and *recognizable components* as presented by Germonprez et al. (2007).

For researchers to reclaim a more defining role in the new class of information systems, our focus needs to shift to the identification of use patterns and support for information processes, which the actors create through reflection, action, and tailoring of systems. Currently, most design theories account only for the characteristics of the technology, not for the design of the mediation of *human information processes* via technology. There is a constant morphing of new technologies, information, and communications processes often at the hands of the actors. Our design theory must account for these observations or lose credibility as theory.

This research provides the foundations for a significant set of issues to consider as design theory is extended to account for secondary design. We have argued and expressed our astonishment that the issue of secondary design has remained quiescent in spite of the emerging and active design science community. By synthesizing and articulating an argument drawn from extensive prior but fragmented literature, we hope to promote a reframing of the human actor as an active and reflective user-as-designer who has a necessary place in future design theory. By testing the accepted boundaries of design theory we engage in the scientific process of scrutinizing and expanding the foundations for good theory, which will be broad in scope and fruitful for future research and practice.

References

Andersen, P. (2006) Activity-based Design. *European Journal of Information Systems* 15(1) 9–25.

Bannon, L. (1991) From Human Factors to Human Actors: The Role of Psychology and Human-Computer Interaction Studies in System Design. in: *Design at Work: Cooperative Design of Computer Systems*, M. Kyng and J. Greenbaum. (ed.), Lawrence Erlbaum, Hillsdale, NJ.

Bannon, L., and Bødker, S.; (1991) Beyond the Interface: Encountering Artifacts in Use. In: *Designing Interaction: Psychology at the Human-computer interface*, J. Carroll (ed.), Cambridge University Press, New York.

Baskerville, R.; (2008) What Design Science is Not. *European Journal of Information Systems* 17(5) 441–443.

Boland, R.J., Lyytinen, K., and Yoo, Y.; (2007) Wakes of Innovation in Project Networks: The Case of Digital 3-D Representations in Architecture, Engineering, and Construction. *Organization Science*, 18(4) 631–647.

Butler, T., and Murphy, C.; (2007) Understanding the design of information technologies for knowledge management in organizations: a pragmatic perspective. *Information Systems Journal*, 17(2) 143–163.

Ciborra, C.; (2002) *The Labyrinths of Information*. Oxford University Press, Oxford.

Ciborra, C.; (2006) The mind or the heart? It depends on the (definition of) situation. *Journal of Information Technology*, 21(3) 129–139.

Craib, I.; (1992) Anthony Giddens. Routledge, New York.

Dourish, P.; (2001) *Where the Action Is: The Foundations of Embodied Interaction*. MIT Press, Cambridge, MA.

Dourish, P.; (2006) Implication for Design, *Proceedings ACM Conference on Human Factors in Computing Systems* CHI, Montreal, Canada.

Ferneley, E., and Sobreperez, P.; (2006) Resist, comply or workaround? An examination of different facets of user engagement with information systems. *European Journal of Information Systems*, 15(4) 345–356.

Galliers, R.; (2008) A Discipline for a Stage? A Shakespearean reflection on the Research plot and Performance of the Information Systems Field. *European Journal of Information Systems*, 17(4) 330–335.

Gasson, S.; (1999) A social action model of situated information systems design. *ACM SIGMIS Database*, 30(2) 82–97.

Gaver, W.; (1991), Technology affordances. *Proceedings of the SIGCHI conference on Human factors in computing systems: Reaching through technology*, Montréal, Québec, Canada, pp 79–84.

Germonprez, M., Hovorka, D., and Collopy, F.; (2007) A Theory Of Tailorable Technology Design. *Journal of the Association of Information Systems*, 8(6) 351–367.

Gibson, J.J.; (1977) *The Theory of Affordances.* Lawrence Erlbaum Associates, Hillsdale, NJ.

Greeno, J.G.; (1994) Gibson's Affordances. *Psychological Review*, 101(2) 336–342.

Gregor, S., and Jones, D.; (2007) The Anatomy of a Design Theory. *Journal of the Association of Information Systems*, 8(5) 312–335.

Grudin, J. & Pruitt, J.; (2002) Personas, participatory design, and product development: An infrastructure for engagement. *Proc. PDC* pp 144–161.

Habermas, J.; (1981) *The Theory of Communicative Action*, London: Beacon Press

Heidegger, M.; (1962) *Being and Time*. Basil Blackwell, Oxford.

Henderson, A., and Kyng, M.; (1991) There is No Place Like Home: Continuing Design in Use. In: *Design at Work: Cooperative Design of Computer Systems*, J. Greenbaum. and M. Kyng (eds.), Lawrence Erlbaum Associates, Hillsdale, NJ.

Hevner, A.R., Ram, S., March, S.T., and Park, J.; (2004) Design Science in IS Research. *MIS Quarterly*, 28(1) 75–106.

Hirschheim, R., and Klein, H.K.; (1989) Four Paradigms for Information Systems Development. *Communication of the Association for Information Systems*, 32(10) 1199–1216.

Hovorka, D., and Germonprez, M.: (2009) Tinkering, Tailoring, and Bricolage: Implications for Theories of Design, *15th Americas Conference on Information Systems*, San Francisco CA.

Huizing, A.; (2007) The Value of a Rose: Rising above objectivism and subjectivism. *Perspectives on Information Management – Information Management: Setting the Scene* A.a.E.J.d.V. Huizing, E.J (ed.), Elsevier, Amsterdam.

Introna, L.D., and Whittaker, L.; (2002) The Phenomenology of Information Systems Eval-uation: Overcoming the Subject Object Dualism. *Proceedings of IFIP WG 8.2*, Barcelona. pp 155–175.

Kensing, F. and Blomberg, J.; (1998) Participatory Design: Issues and Concerns, *Computer Supported Cooperative Work* 7(3–4), 167–185.

Kensing, F., Simonsen, J., and Bødker, K.; (1998) MUST – A Method for Participatory Design, *Human-Computer Interaction*, 13(2) 167–198.

Koopman, P., and Hoffman, R.; (2003) Work-arounds, Make-work, and Kludges. *IEEE Intelligent Systems*, 18(6) 70–75.

Kuechler, B., and Vaishnavi, V.; (2008) On Theory Development in Design Science Research: Anatomy of a Research Project. *European Journal of Information Systems*, 17(5), 489–504.

Lakatos, I.; (1973) Science and Pseudoscience. *Philosophy of Science: The Central Issues*, M. Curd and J.A. Cover (eds.), W.W. Norton, New York 20–26.

Latour, B.; (1995) A Door Must Be Either Open or Shut: A Little philosophy of Techniques. *Technology and The politics of Knowledge*, Feenberg, A and A. Hannay (ed.), Indiana University Press, Bloomington, IN, p 272.

Lee, A.; (2001) Challenges to Qualitative Researchers in Information Systems. *Qualitative Research in IS: Issues and Trends*, E. Trauth (ed.), IDEA Group, London, pp 240–270.

March, S.T., and Smith, G.S.; (1995) Design and Natural Science Research on Information Technology. *Decision Support Systems*, 15(4) 251–266.

McKay, J., and Marshall, P.; (2005) A Review of Design Science in Information Systems. *16th Australasian Conference on Information Systems*, Sydney, pp 1–11.

McKay, J., and Marshall, P.; (2007) Science, Design, and Design Science: Seeking Clarity to Move Design Science Forward in Information Systems. *18th Australasian Conference on Information Systems*, Sydney, pp 1–11.

Niehaves, B.; (2007) On Epistemological Diversity in Design Science – New Vistas for a Design-Oriented IS Research? *Twenty Eighth International Conference on Information Systems*, Montreal, CA.

Norman, D.; (1999) Affordance, conventions, and design. *Interactions*, 6(3) 38–43.

Pruitt, J., and Grudin, J.; (2003) Personas: practice and theory, *Proceedings of the 2003 conference on Designing for User Experiences* San Francisco, CA, pp 1–15.

Ramiller, N.C.; (2007) Virtualizing the Virtual. *Virtuality and Virtualization*, IFIP International Federation for Information Processing (Crowstow, K., Sieber, S. and Wynn, E. eds.), (236) Springer, Boston, MA, pp 353–366.

Robinson, M.; (1993) Design for unanticipated use. *Proceedings of the Third European Conference on Computer Supported Cooperative Work.* G.de Michelis, Simone, C. and Schmidt, K. (eds.), Kluwer, Milan, IT, pp 195–210.

Romme, A.G.L.; (2003) Making a Difference: Organization as Design. *Organization Science*, 14(5), September–October 558–573.

Simon, H.A.; (1969) *Sciences of the Artificial*. MIT Press, Cambridge, MA.

Snow, R.E.; (1992) Aptitude Theory: Yesterday, Today, and Tomorrow. *Educational Psychologist*, 27(1) 5–32.

Suchman, L., Blomberg, J., Orr, J., and Trigg, R.; (1999) Reconstructing Technologies as Social Practice. *American Behavioral Scientist*, 43(3) 392–408.

Venable, J.; (2006) The Role of Theorizing in Design Science Research. *DESRIST*, Claremont, CA.

Walls, J.G., Widmeyer, G.R., and El Saway, O.A.; (1992) Building an Information System Design Theory for Vigilant EIS. *Information Systems Research*, 3(1) 36–59.

Whittington, R.; (1992) Putting Giddens into Action: Social Systems and Managerial Agency, *Journal of Management Studies*, 29, 693–712.

Winograd, T., and Flores, F.; (1986) *Understanding Computers and Cognition: A New Foundation for Design*. Ablex Publishing Corporation., Norwood, NJ.

Winter, R.; (2008) Design Science Research in Europe. *European Journal of Information Systems*, 17(5) 470–475.

Chapter 9
Evolutionary Application Development: Tools to Make Tools and Boundary Crossing

Anders I. Mørch

9.1 Introduction

When I use the term end user, I mean people who use computer applications in their daily activities, without being interested in computers per se (Costabile et al. 2003). In the rest of this paper "user" will sometimes be used instead of "end user" whenever it is clear that the reference is to end users. End-User Development (EUD) is software development conducted by end users, which allows them at some point to create or modify a software artifact. This activity is different from professional software development on the one hand and user-generated content in new media on the other, though it can be explained as a combination of the two. EUD is the (further) development of tools (rather than content) and carried out by users (rather than software engineers and programmers), while Evolutionary Application Development (EAD) is the type of EUD profiled in this paper. At InterMedia, University of Oslo we have developed demonstration prototypes and a conceptual framework for EAD. Here, I present four "snapshots" in the development of the EAD framework, which includes system-building efforts and results from empirical studies. The following research themes are explored

1. Design for tailorability
2. Design with tailorability
3. Incentives for end-user participation
4. Integration of specific and general development

They have been put in chronological order since each theme addresses one or more shortcomings from the previous theme, and the research covers technical and organizational issues in EAD.

The paper starts with an overview of end-user development, which is organized into three perspectives: (1) human-computer interaction, (2) software engineering, and

A.I. Mørch (⊠)
InterMedia, University of Oslo, Norway
e-mail: anders.morch@intermedia.uio.no

H. Isomäki and S. Pekkola (eds.), *Reframing Humans in Information Systems Development*, Computer Supported Cooperative Work 201, DOI 10.1007/978-1-84996-347-3_9, © Springer-Verlag London Limited 2011

(3) information systems. I then present the development of EAD by proof-of-concept prototypes (end-user tailoring, application evolution) and findings from two empirical studies (super users, mutual development). The findings are summarized as a set of concepts (application unit, application evolution, application growth control, mutual development, predecessor artifact, resemblance relation, and super user), which form the components of the first version of a conceptual framework for EAD. Lastly, the concepts are compared with related concepts, which have inspired the current research (boundary crossing, emergence, meta-level interface, multi-level development, mutual learning, and stable intermediate form).

9.2 Overview of End-User Development

Researchers in end-user development were inspired by research that dealt with languages and tools to improve information technology such as scripting languages (Ousterhout 1998) and meta-level (modification) interfaces (Mehandjiev and Bottaci 1998). EUD gained broader visibility and became a research topic with its own agenda in the European EUD-Net project (2002–2003), which defines EUD as "a set of methods, activities, techniques, and tools that allow people who are non-professional software developers, at some point to create or modify a software artifact" (Lieberman et al. 2006). The different approaches to EUD vary with respect to how they emphasize methods, activities, techniques and tools, and whether they focus on the creation and/or modification of software artifacts. The software artifacts addressed in previous work include: applications, application development environments, design models, program code, software components and user interfaces. For example, end-user tailoring concerns methods, techniques and tools for the further development of software applications based on the direct activation of tailoring tools by end users (Mørch 1995; Wulf and Golombek 2001). Thus, EUD is both a multi-disciplinary topic and emerging field, which intersects human-computer interaction, software engineering and information systems.

From a human-computer interaction perspective, EUD is about leveraging the deployment of easy-to-use applications and turning them into easy-to-develop systems (Costabile et al. 2003; Lieberman et al. 2006; Mørch et al. 2004; Wulf et al. 2008). The goal has been to bridge the gap between the use and design of application systems, which has been addressed by the concept of "gentle slope." What is meant by this concept is that in order to modify an application through its user interface, end users should only have to increase their knowledge by an amount in proportion to the complexity of the modification (Fischer and Girgensohn 1990; MacLean et al. 1990), and simple modifications should not require programming, and more complex tailoring tasks should be possible with user-oriented programming languages and building blocks (Fischer and Girgensohn 1990; MacLean et al. 1990; Mørch et al. 2004). Two techniques we have experimented with are direct activation (Mørch 1995; Wulf and Golombek 2001) and different levels of tailoring (Mørch 1997). Direct activation means that tailoring functionality should be available at the location where the need for tailoring occurs, with different levels of tailoring available upon demand (see section on end-user tailoring of application units).

From a software engineering perspective, EUD supports the trend of constructing generic applications (multifunctional systems), applying software engineering techniques to correct end-user-developed programs (Burnett et al. 2004), and leveraging the potential of component-based software development (Mørch et al. 2004; Wulf et al. 2008). The term "generic" refers to functionality that can be configured to different user needs such as application generators or domain-independent tools like groupware and generic drawing programs or methods and tools that support users in creating new applications (Fischer and Scharff 2000; Fischer et al. 1992). In addition, even though many users are willing to write programs to create new applications or to modify existing ones, their lack of experience in programming will cause their programs to contain more errors than professionally developed programs. Techniques for identifying and repairing these errors become important, and research in this area is collectively known as end-user software engineering (Burnett et al. 2004). Component-based systems have been proposed as a framework to support EUD (Wulf et al. 2008), e.g. JavaBeans components can be integrated and edited by direct manipulation techniques in visual builders and embedded in Integrated Development Environments (IDEs) (Mørch et al. 2004).

From an information systems perspective, the rationale for EUD is associated with organizing end-user development activities (Andersen and Mørch 2009; Mehandjiev et al. 2006), with user diversity found in organizations employing advanced ICT (Costabile et al. 2003; Åsand and Mørch 2006) and the means for formalizing user participation in development activities (Pekkola et al. 2006). Users have various cultural, educational, training and employment backgrounds, including novices and experienced computer users (e.g. super user), range from the young to the mature who have many different abilities and disabilities.

Some organizations within Scandinavia use the term "super user" in conjunction with the role required of end-user user developers, and train super users to address the information overload problem associated with the introduction of advanced information systems and new practices such as end-user tailoring. Supers users are selected to take part in this activity based on their skill in using the new system, their knowledge of the application domain, and their ability to teach other employees to use the system effectively (Kaasbøll and Øgrim 1994). In light of this, end-user development can be defined in terms of the multiple roles that exist in the continuum from regular use to professional development (Fig. 9.1):

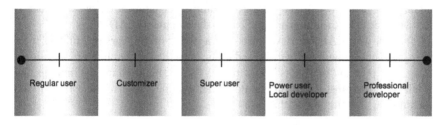

Fig. 9.1 The multiple roles in end-user development span regular use to professional development

- *Regular user*: workers who are not interested in tailoring a system, but who want to use the system's various productivity and computational tools to accomplish their required tasks.
- *Customizer*: a person who does more than merely use a system, i.e. making persistent changes without any programming. It could be to download pictures to change a desktop background, modify default appearance in applications, and set parameters to configure a computer.
- *Super user*: domain-trained workers who are also skilled with computers, interested in exploring tools for tailoring if there is time allocated for this and who like to teach other users how to use the system. Super users are boundary spanners and translators between regular users and developers.
- *Power users, local developer*: domain-trained workers who have more computer skills than super users. They know how to program using high-level (scripting) languages (e.g. JavaScript, PHP, Tcl), have more responsibility than super users, and will often be asked to coordinate the organization's EUD activities. They communicate directly with professional developers in regard to development tasks that cannot be accomplished locally.
- *Professional developer*: IT workers who develop a new software application or a new version of an existing application. These developers work in software houses or consultancy companies, and are trained as software engineers and/or programmers who write programs in general-purpose programming languages such as C, C++ and Java. Professional developers can be grouped into specialized roles as well, and some of them overlap those presented here. For example, customizing is also an activity in software engineering (Dittrich et al. 2009).

9.3   Evolutionary Application Development

From our point of view, EUD is not a stand-alone activity, but instead is part of a larger process of building software applications. In order to position EUD within this process, we distinguish between general and specific development, which is represented by the activities of amateur (end-user) and professional (paid) developers, respectively. When they interact constructively, opportunities for cross-fertilization and innovation emerge as a result of the overlap of multiple perspectives that extend the boundaries of either activity on its own. The conceptual framework for understanding this constructive interaction of multi-level application development is what we refer to as evolutionary application development (EAD).

Our work with EAD has developed over a period of 10 years by building tools and experimenting with techniques, and doing empirical research in organizational settings. We present "snapshots" of the process below, highlighting the findings that we felt were the most interesting and/or generating new research questions to aid in setting the direction for further work:

- End-user tailoring of application units (Mørch 1995, 1997, 1998)
- Application evolution (Mørch 1996, 2003; Mørk 2004)
- Super users to organize EUD activity (Mørch et al. 2004; Åsand and Mørch 2006)
- Mutual development (Andersen and Mørch 2009; Mørch et al. 2009; Nygård and Mørch 2007)

This line of development starts with concrete examples (prototypes of tools), which are followed by empirical studies and a discussion of emerging concepts. The overall aim here is to explore multiple means for empowering end-user developers to contribute towards a more democratized software design process.

9.3.1 End-User Tailoring of Application Units

The interface of a computer application is composed of user interface objects. The actual mechanism that will transform user input (keyboard press, mouse action) into system functionality is the *event handler* that we have also defined for signaling tailoring events at various levels of abstraction. Based on this, we have suggested a user interface that combines hierarchical and non-hierarchical objects: a hierarchy extended with user-oriented views. The resulting UI objects are referred to as *application units* (Mørch 1995). Three application unit aspects can be independently selected and modified of each UI object: user interface, rationale, and program code. One proof-of-concept of such an application is BasicDraw (Fig. 9.2), a tailor-enabled drawing program that allows a user to create basic shapes (lines, rectangles, ovals and polygons) and to manipulate them by the use of basic operations (copy, move, rotate and scale).

Figure 9.2 shows a screen dump of BasicDraw with two aspects (rationale and program code) of the "Rotate Rectangle" application unit exposed. To access these aspects, a user holds down a modifier key (alt, shift or ctrl) while performing the normal interaction gestures on the UI object. The two arrows labeled shiftMouseUp and ctrlMouseUp are two events generated by modifier keys that open the Rationale viewer and Implementation viewer, respectively.

The end-user tailoring of application units (Mørch 1997) is accomplished on three levels associated with the three aspects described above and are referred to as

- Customization
- Integration
- Extension

Customization is the modification of attribute values of user-interface objects. By opening a presentation editor, the "look and feel" of user interface objects can be changed (Fig. 9.3).

Integration is the modification of rationale by comments, diagrams and pictures in the Rationale viewer (see Fig. 9.2) to document the rationale for the application

User interface

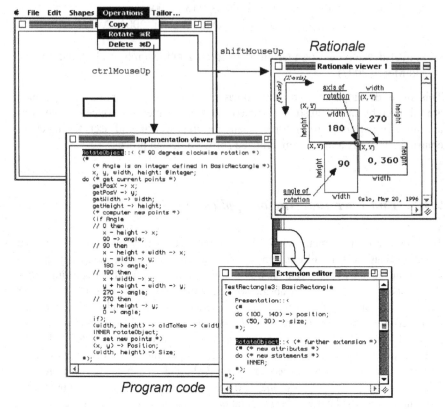

Fig. 9.2 BasicDraw is a tailor-enabled application; each application unit can be "opened" and modified at three different levels of abstraction: user interface, rationale, and program code

unit's program code, although the application cannot interpret its rationale. The main function of the rationale is to provide answers to user-oriented questions about the program code behind the application units.

Extension means to modify the program code underneath application units, which is accomplished in an extension editor (see Fig. 9.2). The new code does not replace, but rather builds on (i.e. extends) the old code. As a result, none of the old codes in BasicDraw can be discarded. This prevents users from accidentally destroying program code that already works (Mørch 1998). It is a feature of the underlying programming language that methods (and not only classes) can be inherited and extended (Kristensen et al. 1987).

Customizing the user interface requires end-user developers to use skills that are different from those required when extending the program code. In order to write programs, end-user developers need to be power users or local developers (see Fig. 9.1). To tailor the user interface, the tailor needs to be concerned about how to best support user tasks, which can vary from user to user, as well as be

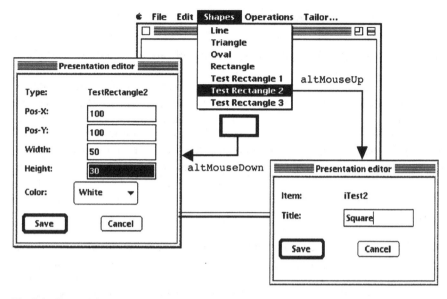

Fig. 9.3 Customizing application units. The presentation editor is opened by holding down the alt key while performing the normal interaction gesture on any user interface object

Table 9.1 Techniques for accessing, viewing, and modifying application units

Aspect	Access	Viewer	Modification
User interface	Alt-key	Presentation editor	Customization
Rationale	Shift-key	Rationale viewer	Integration
Program code	Ctrl-key	Implementation viewer	Extension

open-ended and informal compared to programming. Therefore, customizers and supers users can accomplish this. Some super users will also be able to integrate new application units with an existing application and capture the rationale for an application unit's functionality (Mørch 1996; Mørch et al. 2004). Table 9.1 summarizes the tailorability support (tools and techniques) in BasicDraw.

In sum, the strengths and limitations of end-user tailoring of application units to support end-users development are as follows:

- *Strength* for developers: A demonstration of design for tailorability by integrating tailoring tools with an ordinary application
- *Strength* for users: Direct access to tailoring tools from an application's user interface (tools bundled within application units)
- *Limitation* for developers: Extra work to create APIs, domain-specific languages and IDEs to be integrated with an application; increased memory consumption
- *Limitation* for users: Tailoring is often perceived as a one-time activity, often after installment of a new application to tweak, adjust or improve certain features, but with little impact outside the application and its instantiation context

9.3.2 Application Evolution

In the work following the experiments with BasicDraw, we addressed one of the limitations of end-user tailoring, namely to demonstrate that tailoring can go beyond a one-time local adaptation. This is illustrated by three system-building efforts, one of a commercial nature, and two developed as a proof-of-concept.

An early example of visual application development with user-oriented software components is HyperCard (Fig. 9.4). HyperCard is not in use today, but was a success soon after it was launched with Mac OS in 1987, and other platforms have subsequently adopted some of its innovative features for application development, including PowerBuilder, which is a popular tool for creating database applications in finance and business domains.

HyperCard supported "cloning" when invoked by the Command-D operation with a mouse click on a UI object. The example in Fig. 9.4 shows how to create an input field by cloning an existing field. This circumvents the conventional approach to application development, which is to select a tool from a palette/menu and apply it to objects inside a work area. New application units are created with cloning based on the resemblance and modification of existing application units (Mørch 2003; Mørk 2004). When invoking a cloning operation on an object (referred to as source), a copy of the selected application unit is instantiated in the user interface (referred to as a clone), and performs the same function, without replacing the source. This allows experimentation on the clone without side effects, and modifications to it can be performed until a satisfactory new behavior has been achieved. In a second stage, the end-user developer can choose to replace the source with the clone to avoid redundancy.

Two examples of how to accomplish this are shown below: SimpleBuilder and KitchenDesign.

SimpleBuilder. Taking UI property sheets and the HyperCard cloning operation as inspiration and using JavaBeans and Sun Bean Builder IDE as platforms, we

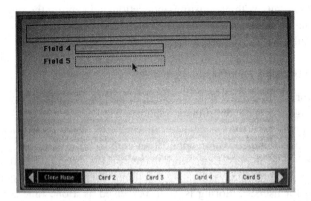

Fig. 9.4 HyperCard application development using "cloning:" A new UI object (Field 5) is created from another one (Field 4) by a single command within the context of a running application

developed the SimpleBuilder design environment for cloning and customizing JavaBeans components (Mørk 2004). In order to clone a component, it first needs to be selected, which can be done directly from the runtime environment or from a catalog of examples in a JAR format. The clone just created is then placed into a design environment (top-right window in Fig. 9.5), where it can be modified by direct manipulation of its attributes by a JavaBeans property sheet (not shown). A modified component can again be saved as a JAR file, which is accomplished by writing its configuration to a disk using the LTP mechanisms of Java 1.4. The file name is automatically constructed from the class name and appended with the hash value. The component will be associated with an icon in a "Clones" tab in the user interface of the design environment, so that it can be reused in a new design session (bottom window in Fig. 9.5). The tab is stored as an XML file in a "clonedir" directory and restored the next time SimpleBuilder opens. All components stored as clones will be available for later projects; thus, cloning supports the evolution of the design environment with incrementally added functionality (Mørk 2004). SimpleBuilder is a crude prototype of this behavior.

KitchenDesign. Evolutionary application development with application units is illustrated by the transformation of BasicDraw into KitchenDesign (Mørch 1997). The two screenshots in Fig. 9.6 show both before and after stages of this process, which were accomplished with the tailoring tools integrated with BasicDraw (Mørch 1997; 1998). When using these tools, an end-user developer can modify the selected

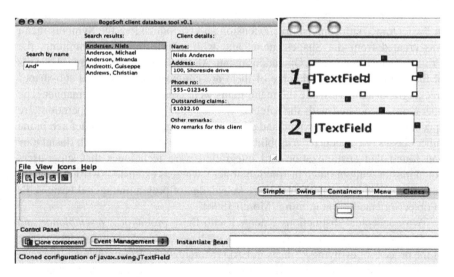

Fig. 9.5 Cloning a JavaBeans component using SimpleBuilder: *Top-left* window shows the application, the *bottom* window displays a set of available components, predefined (Simple, Swing, etc.) and Clones (one clone is displayed), and the *top-right* window shows the work area for cloning a text field component

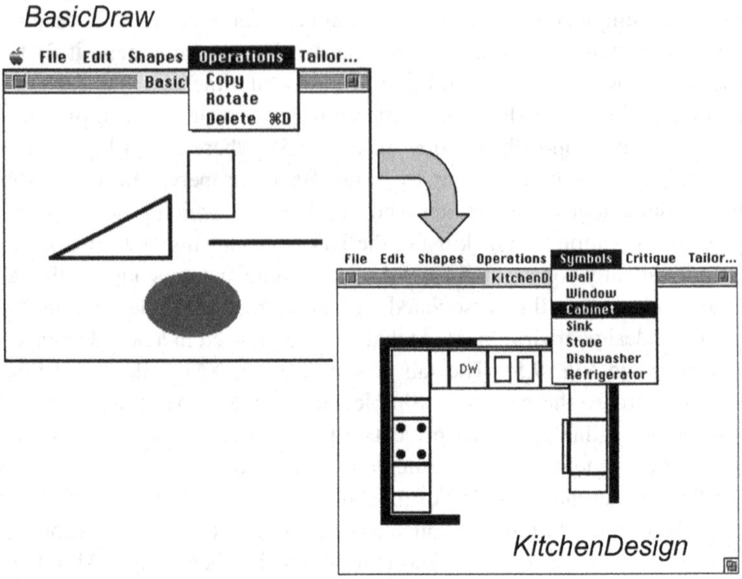

BasicDraw

KitchenDesign

Fig. 9.6 Evolving BasicDraw into KitchenDesign by tailoring individual components (application units). The basic shapes of BasicDraw are "predecessor artifacts" in the KitchenDesign symbols

application units at different levels of abstraction (user interface, design rationale and program code) by the use of the techniques shown in Figs. 9.2 and 9.3.

The menus and shapes in KitchenDesign are subclasses of the menus and shapes in BasicDraw. With some simple extension and customization, the Symbols menu was created from the Shapes menu, and with a little more programming, the Critique menu extended the Operations menu. All the kitchen symbols are subclasses of the rectangle shape, and some of them are composed of additional sub-shapes (rectangle, oval, text), while the menu items were created in a similar manner. The operations associated with the kitchen symbols, such as the scale operation, are specialized methods that extend and constrain the original operations defined in the super-classes. We conducted a usability test of end-user development with BasicDraw and found that customization and integration were techniques that super-users could master without much instruction or help, whereas extension (writing program code in method bodies) required more knowledge of programming and basic skills in object-oriented programming (Mørch 1996).

Two conceptual distinctions emerged with these prototypes: *resemblance* and *predecessor artifact*. Using these concepts, we have achieved a better understanding of the process of evolving artifacts in EAD (Mørch 2003). Resemblance is the relation between the two components of source and clone (e.g. new text field created by cloning another; rectangle shape implicit in a kitchen symbol). The resemblance-relation is a user-oriented relation between two visual components, and is modeled after the inheritance relation between class and subclass in object-oriented programming

(Kristensen et al. 1987). Resemblance allows users (not only developers) to perceive and create new behavior by reusing existing behavior.

Predecessor artifacts are "disabled" application units, e.g. the source of a clone once the clone has replaced the source as the executable object. One example of this is the clone of an input field that has been modified by customization in order to improve the functionality of the source (Figs. 9.4 and 9.5), while another is the rectangle shape contained within the kitchen cabinet symbol (Fig. 9.6).

In some situations, it will be advantageous to remove the source of a clone because the clone makes the source redundant, which can help to reduce complexity and free memory space. For instance, the rectangular shape of a kitchen design unit is not an active object in BasicDraw, but instead a kind of abstract object (i.e. object without any event handler). In other cases, predecessor artifacts should remain available since the source retains old but working functionality and can serve as a backup. For example, when new functionality is not working, a re-enabled predecessor artifact can resume old functionality until a problem has been repaired.

The two prototypes implement resemblance in different ways. In KitchenDesign, it is the *inheritance* relation between two object classes that defines the relation, whereas in SimpleBuilder, it is the *versioning* relation between two component instances, which are represented by their component files. Further work should be undertaken in order to investigate ways of improving the second approach and make versioning into a user-oriented class-subclass relation between visual software components since sub-classing and method modification are both demanding and error-prone for end-user developers (i.e. requires programming expertise).

In sum, the strengths and limitations of application evolution to support end-user developers are as follows:

- *Strength*: A demonstration of design with tailorability
- *Limitation*: Programming is more difficult than customization and integration, and most end-users are not willing to put the time and effort into tailoring their applications (it diverges from the required work) unless it yields favorable benefits or improved personal development
- *Limitation*: The clone of a component in SimpleBuilder is generated from its class, but successive cloning will repeatedly call the same class, supplemented each time by accumulated data from an initialization file. Alternatively, successive cloning could be generated from "accumulating subclasses." In biological terms, this corresponds to the distinction between "Darwinian" and "Lamarckian" evolution, although the latter seems a better model for evolving artifacts (i.e. acquired properties are inherited from parent to offspring)

9.3.3 Super Users to Organize EUD Activity

We conducted a case study to follow the activities of super users and local developers during the adoption of a new business application by an accounting firm in Scandinavia

(Åsand and Mørch 2006). The firm (hereafter known as the Company) launched a program to train super users to help with this process because of the complexity of the new system: a generic, multi-purpose application system replacing several older, non-integrated systems. The new system, Visma Business (VB), is a comprehensive financial and accounting application delivered as a set of components that need to be configured for domain-specific tasks, depending on which clients the accountants will interact with. We documented their activities both empirically and analytically, using interviews to obtain data and drawing on aspects of Activity Theory (Engeström 2004; Kaptelinin and Nardi 2006) for the conceptual framework for analysis.

The super users we studied took on a contract-based role assigned to them by the company they worked for, which was in contrast to the previous research reported in the literature. The EUD actors emerged (selected or volunteered) from a group of regular users as those who demonstrated proficiency in using a system and who showed an interest in helping other users learn to use it efficiently as well. In a study reported in the literature (Volkoff et al. 2002), boundary spanners ended up taking on two roles even though there were few rewards for the extra role. The authors suggested the need for "system sponsors" to provide special incentives for boundary spanners in order to help them maintain credibility in both communities, but in the companies reported on (Volkoff et al. 2002), this was not achieved. Taking on a contract-based role assigned to them by the company is a form of formalizing user participation in information systems development activities (Pekkola et al. 2006), which is quite common in the Nordic countries.

The Company decided to have one super user for every ten employees who were chosen from among the ordinary employees (regular users) in the local offices. The corporate management formalized the criteria for being a super user in the form of a contract, which both the local office manager and each super user had to sign. The contract lays out the duties and expectations of the super user role as follows:

- The super user must be both professionally and technically competent, with an emphasis on mastery of the profession-oriented accounting language.
- The super user must set aside time for training and for sharing knowledge, e.g., conducting workshops for their office colleagues.
- The super user must provide all employees in their local office with the necessary training to use the new VB application for their specific accounting needs and to manage a specific schedule for such training. The latter requirement was of great importance and was made explicit in the contract since without scheduled presentations, the training may not be as effective.

By use of this contract, the Company formalized the super user role, which conferred legitimacy and visibility on the time and effort invested by the super users. After they signed the contract, the super users received training in VB, which focused on the more technical aspects of the application, particularly the EUD features.

The business solutions created by VB are meant to be tailored to the clients the offices do business with. The changes are made locally to each installation of the VB application, but those found to have company-wide applicability could also be enabled "globally" by a local developer in the company. Possible changes include choosing which functions to make available and creating, or modifying menus and fields (Åsand and Mørch 2006).

Our main findings from the analysis are two organizing principles for EUD (Åsand and Mørch 2006):

- *Institutionalization of the role of super user*: EUD became institutionalized in the Company as a result of the strategic decision to involve super users in the implementation process in a more formalized way in response to a complex and multi-purpose system (VB). The role of super users was established through a contract, which guaranteed that the super users had time to perform the end-user tailoring activities the role required.
- *Double grounding*: The Company chose to have a distributed network of super users located at all of its offices (one super user for every ten accountants). Thus, the grounding for sustaining the super user initiative was accomplished in two ways: (1) the geographical distribution of super users and (2) the utilization of super users with a background in the same profession as that of the regular users.

In sum, the strengths and limitations of having super users in a contractual agreement to support the EUD work in a company-wide adoption of a complex business application are:

- *Strength*: A demonstration of incentives for end user participation.
- *Strength*: Most end users are not willing to do EUD on top of ordinary work unless specific incentives exist, including a work description for a super user role and time assigned to do the work.
- *Limitation*: There is a versioning incompatibility latent in EAD because a locally adapted version of a system may be incompatible with a future release, unless measures are taken to ensure local extensions are version compatible to future releases.

9.3.4 Mutual Development

Versioning incompatibility is a thorny issue for EAD and can arguably be best resolved if end-user developers are able to discuss EUD problems and solution strategies directly with developers. We designed a case study to investigate this issue, which we formulated as an integration of specific and general software development.

We contacted a company that is known for their customer initiated product development approach, i.e. close interaction with customers to develop tailor made software products (Andersen and Mørch 2009; Nygård and Mørch 2007) (take out, redundant clause) in the area of project planning and management, and provides consultancy services in using its products. At present, the company employs 25–30 people, yet despite its small size, is recognized as a major player in the business of project planning tools, and its primary customers are in oil and gas and construction in the Nordic countries. They have several hundred customers, and have long-term commitments with many of them, e.g., one of their recent products is an add-in for the Microsoft Project application.

The company's customers are encouraged to report problems, share information about innovative use, and assist in local development to the company's developers. The developers have provided communication and information sharing tools for customer interaction, which has been stimulated through long-term relationships (maintenance contracts) and user forums. The main meeting ground is an annual showcase in which customers are invited to communicate with the company's employees. As researchers, we were invited to interview employees and customers in order to collect data, and in return, we gave advice on how to improve knowledge management practices. Our main research question was formulated around how customers and professional developers engage in mutual development mediated by shared software tools (products and support systems).

We used a qualitative approach as part of a case study and open-ended interviews recorded by video and/or audio, while following a grounded theory and open coding approach to categorize data, iterating between data and preliminary categories in multiple rounds. We ended up with the following five categories (sub-processes) of customer-initiated product development (listed here alphabetically) (Andersen and Mørch 2009):

- *Adaptation*: This is when a customer requests an improvement to an existing product and the company chooses to fulfill that request which becomes an adaptation just for this customer. Sometimes, the customer has to pay for this, sometimes not.
- *Generalization*: This occurs when a new version of an existing product is released and is available to more than just one customer.
- *Improvement Request*: This is when customers make a request from the company for extra functionality, to report bugs and usability problems, which are viewed from the customers' perspectives.
- *Specialization*: This is when the professional developers at the company create in-house builds. This could potentially result in new features, but most often it entails removing bugs, reorganizing program modules, and perfecting the product when time allows.
- *Tailoring*: This is about active end-users (customizers, super users, local developers) who make adaptations on their own.

We justified these various stages using data extracts and analysis (Andersen and Mørch 2009; Mørch et al. 2009). Our findings are summarized as a model of mutual development, which is shown in Fig. 9.7 and is our first attempt to construct a model that integrates professional development and end-user development.

The overall (integrated) systems development process goes through an elaborate process of specialization (refinement), adaptation (domain orientation) and

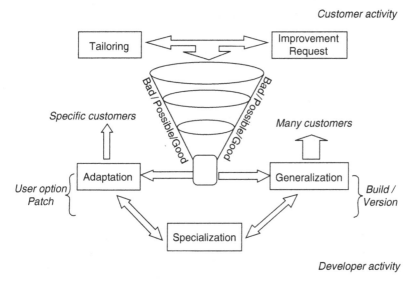

Fig. 9.7 Mutual development is when developer activity and customer activity co-evolve. The arrows indicate dependencies. Specialization is not addressed because it does not interrelate directly with end-user activities. The software engineering aspects of Adaptation and Generalization are outside the scope of the work presented here

generalization (one too many instances), starting with a stable (non-optimal) version that is gradually improved by uptakes of locally developed extensions, user options and patches. These are initiated and/or informed by customers through improvement requests and end-user tailoring, and are categorized as either good, bad or possible. Those that are good or possible (i.e. paid for) will be part of the new builds. When multiple builds become unwieldy (i.e. too many different sites to coordinate), the system is rebuilt in-house. The new system may be introduced as a new version if it will benefit the company and not jeopardize existing customer contracts. The interaction between the stages is bidirectional since new versions may lead to new local development and improvement requests, which repeat the process.

In sum, the strengths and limitations of mutual development are as follows:

- *Strength*: A demonstration of integrating specific and general development
- *Strength*: Open (funnel shaped) channels of communication, information sharing, coordination, collaborative design, company open forum, and shared tools between developers and end users for joint benefit
- *Limitation*: Crossing over into a domain in which one is no longer an expert can create situations that lead to misunderstandings and information overload since the user becomes a learner in the new domain
- *Limitation*: We cannot rule out that there may be sub-processes that have not been identified in the mutual development model, some that may have to be modified, and yet others that need to be elaborated, based on more research

9.4 Towards a Conceptual Framework

The approach to evolutionary application development (EAD) profiled in this chapter reveals tools, user roles, processes, techniques and work activities that can be named and analyzed. They have been summarized here for comparison with related work, as these concepts form the cornerstone of a conceptual framework for EAD and serve as the result of the work presented here. The basic concepts have emerged out of system-building efforts and empirical research, but were also inspired by the work of others and are as follows:

- *Application unit*: This is the basic building block of EAD-enabled applications, and combines interaction and functionality as multiple views of the same visual software component. In the same way as a UI object on the screen can be selected to perform a well-defined function (interaction), the same object can be selected for modification of functionality. The tools for tailoring an application unit are invoked by holding down one or more modifier keys while interacting with the application unit.
- *Application evolution*: Applications may require modification at multiple levels of abstraction and granularity in successive stages, with effects that range from surface adjustment to transformation of a tool to perform a new task. Each application unit may be modified in several rounds in a cumulative manner, resembling how evolution is understood in other domains when aided by human intervention.
- *Application growth control*: Application evolution may lead to increased complexity as a result of a cumulative build-up of features for all types of tasks, but users' cognitive processing capabilities for interacting with the applications do not keep pace. To better cope with this discrepancy, measures must be taken to reduce feature complexity in the technology; otherwise, users may abandon a given system and seek out alternative means to accomplish their tasks. Growth control refers to techniques to adjust a system's image (an application's perceived complexity) so as to align it with the ceiling of users' information processing capabilities.
- *Predecessor artifact*: A programmer's technique for controlling complexity is to "hide" functionality, which can be realized in user interface of applications by grayed out menus. With cloning as a technique used to generate functionality, the source of a clone is a candidate for hiding. Related to this is user deactivation, which means to give end-user developers' access rights to hide unused functionality from the user interface. Predecessor artifacts are "permanently" hidden application units, while professional developers should have the access right to re-activate them.
- *Resemblance relation*: When an end-user developer creates an application unit by copying and/or extending an existing one, the relationship between the two is referred to as resemblance, and is a resemblance based on perception and behavior in use.
- *Super user*: A domain-trained worker who is also skilled with computers, interested in exploring tools for tailoring if time allows, and who likes to teach other

users how to use the system. Super users are boundary spanners and translators between regular users and more advanced users and developers.

– *Mutual development*: There is a range of end-user development activities (from use to design) taking place in the interaction between end-user developers and professional developers. We proposed a model for this interaction, which has five components: adaptation, generalization, improvement requests, specialization and tailoring.

9.4.1 Comparison to Related Work

The set of concepts, ideas and techniques from related work, which have inspired this work, including the conceptual framework, are

– *Boundary crossing*: Experts operate in and move between multiple activity systems (Engeström 2004), e.g. during collaborative design activities. One example of this could be a situation in which a software house wants to increase sales, so to accomplish this it may seek out new markets to reach out with a new product or to adapt an existing product. When customers (domain expert users) participate by raising issues or proposing improvement requests, boundary crossing is needed in order for communication to succeed and mutual understanding to result, i.e. to take the perspective of the other side when reconciling differences and to move proposals forward (Ludvigsen et al. 2003; Nygård and Mørch 2007).

– *Emergence*: According to George Herbert Mead, it is "the presence of things in two or more different systems in such a fashion that its presence in a later system changes its character in the earlier system or systems to which it belongs" (Mead and Murphy 1932, p. 62). Furthermore "Emergence involves a reorganization, but the reorganization brings in something that was not there before." (Mead and Morris 1934, p. 198) In plain language this means the total is more than the sum of parts. Emergence can help us to better understand how predecessor artifacts are more than "parts," and can be identified in application units and linked by the resemblance relation.

– *Meta-level interface*: Software design researchers have pointed out that for tools to be truly modifiable they need to provide interfaces at a level of abstraction which is different than the regular (user) interface. Notions such as meta-level protocol (Kiczales 1991), meta-design (Fischer and Scharff 2000), languages of design (Ehn 1990) and tailoring interfaces (Wulf et al. 2008) have been proposed. They share the same goal of modifying a tool by use of another tool (i.e. tools to make tools), although they approach it differently, including new programming techniques (Kiczales 1991; Lindeberg et al. 2002), methods for re-design (Fisher and Scharff 2000), grounding design in everyday activity (Ehn 1990), and multiple user interfaces and access rights (Wulf et al. 2008).

- *Multi-level development*: Development occurs on multiple levels of abstraction. In biological systems, two basic levels of development are phylogeny (species evolution) and ontogeny (individual development), which have inspired our distinction of general (product, software house, formal) development and specific (end-user, organizational, informal) development.
- *Mutual learning*: A technique for participatory design (PD) that is commonly acknowledged as a prerequisite for collaboration across professional boundaries, and is most often associated with users learning about software design from professional developers, as well as developers learning the professional language of domain-expert users (Bratteteig 1997). The goal here is to support collaboration between developers and users.
- *Stable intermediate form*: This is a term coined by Herbert Simon (1996) to describe the basic building block (part) of hierarchic systems and an intermediate stage in evolutionary development. Simon said that complex systems will evolve from simple systems much more rapidly if there are stable intermediate forms than if there are not (Simon 1996). Stable intermediate forms are subassemblies (parts) that both contain and hide smaller units, thereby allowing analysis and design to proceed by a combination of focus shifts (choosing the level of abstraction) and composition (detailing a subassembly). Predecessor artifacts are a type of stable intermediate form in evolutionary application development.

9.5   Summary and Conclusions

The French philosopher Henri Bergson wrote a famous book entitled *"Creative Evolution"* in which he used the phrase "tools to make tools," to characterize the development of the human intellect. He opposed Darwin's theory of evolution from a perspective on creative evolution, because of its dependency on randomness in the two interacting systems (individual organism, environment). Instead of adapting an organism by random mutation to an environment that also changes randomly, Bergson believed that humans co-evolve with their environment in a more constructive manner and can impact evolution by intervention and acts of creative life.

In the field of software engineering, tools to make tools has been taken to mean the tools software developers use when they build or improve upon systems, though the phrase can also mean tools for collective activity generation to stimulate and leverage everyday creativity by multiple stakeholders. The meaning of the phrase used in this chapter is a combination of the two, and is the creative activity at a collective level of using software tools to adapt and evolve existing tools that need to be easily available and simple to use in order for end-user developers to make constructive use of them.

This chapter has presented successive stages in the development of the first version of a conceptual framework for evolutionary application development (EAD), which emerged in response to building prototype tools, proposing techniques for EAD, and studying end-user development activities in organizations. The main contribution of this work to research is to provide concrete examples of EUD that reveal strengths and weaknesses in terms of technological and Organizational issues, which I have addressed by drawing on and contributing to research in HCI, SE & IS. When it comes to practice, the work presented here suggests that user-driven innovation of professionally developed software is an area that will benefit EUD support, and is an area in which one can expect more activity in the near future.

The end result of this work is a preliminary set of concepts (application unit, application evolution, application growth control, mutual development, predecessor artifact, resemblance relation and super user) that will hopefully enhance the reader's understanding of how software applications can evolve by active user involvement, tools for tailoring, and interaction across organizational borders in addition to what challenges remain to make this a reality outside the prototyping lab and case studies presented here. Limitations and open issues for further work include

- If a local adaptation of an application in a user organization is not accepted for incorporation in the next release of a common system, it may lead to several layers of ad hoc solutions to this version, thus causing an unstable system, or an adaptation without much impact.
- The complexity of application evolution and EAD may render them unfit for EUD. For example, a tailorable commercial software product that is complex to EUD-enable, or requires major effort to adapt is not likely to succeed.
- Many tailoring tasks are not simple to accomplish in current EUD environments and require end-user developers to join forces with other users and developers and/or learning to program and use developer environments (IDEs). Further studies should identify the various options that managers can choose from to make decisions in this regard so as to better stimulate collaboration both locally and trans-organizational, educate end-user developer, switch from a difficult to use system to a simpler system, etc.
- The current version of the EAD framework is in its infancy and is likely to be improved in the future, based on new system building efforts and empirical work. Consequently, some of the concepts may have to be modified or withdrawn and new ones added.

Acknowledgements Many students and colleagues have contributed to the work presented here. In particular Balder Mørk who programmed SimpleBuilder, Hege-Rene Hansen Åsand who studied super users, Renate Andersen and Kathrine Nygård who studied super users in commercial software development. The work received financial support from Research Council of Norway (LAP project) and European Commission's IST program in FP6 (KP-Lab project).

References

Andersen, R., Mørch, A. I.: Mutual Development: A Case Study in Customer-Initiated Software Product Development. Pipek, V., Rosson, M.B., de Ruyter, B., Wulf, V. (eds.) *Proceedings 2nd Int'l Symposium on End User Development (IS-EUD 2009)*. LNCS 5435, pp. 31–49. Springer, Berlin (2009)

Bratteteig T.: Mutual Learning: Enabling Cooperation in Systems Design. *Proceedings 20th Information Systems Research Seminar in Scandinavia (IRIS 20)*, pp. 1–20. Dept. of Informatics, University of Oslo (1997)

Burnett, M., Cook, C., Rothermel, G.: End-User Software Engineering. *Comm ACM* 47(9), 53–58 (2004)

Costabile, M., Foglia, D., Fresta, G., Mussio, P., Piccinno, A.: Building Environments for End-User Development and Tailoring. *Proceedings IEEE Symposium on Human Centric Computing Languages and Environments*, (pp. 31–38). IEEE Computer Society, Auckland, NZ (2003)

Dittrich, S. Vaucouleur, S. Giff, S.: ERP Customization as Software Engineering: Knowledge Sharing and Cooperation. *IEEE Softw* 26(6), 41–47 (2009)

Ehn, P.: Work-Oriented Design of Computer Artifacts. Laurence Erlbaum, Hillsdale, NJ (1990)

Engeström, Y.: New forms of learning in co-configuration work. *J Workplace Learn* 16, 11–21 (2004)

Fischer, G., Scharff, E.: Meta-design: Design for Designers. *Proceedings 3rd International Conference on Designing Interactive Systems (DIS'00)*, pp. 396–405. ACM Press, New York (2000)

Fischer, G., Girgensohn, A.: End-User Modifiability in Design Environments. *Proceedings Conference on Human Factors in Computing Systems (CHI'90)*, pp. 183–192. ACM Press, New York (1990)

Fischer, G., Girgensohn, A., Nakakoji, K., Redmiles, D.: Supporting Software Designers with Integrated Domain-Oriented Design Environments. *IEEE Trans Softw Eng* 18(6), 511–522 (1992)

Kaptelinin, V., Nardi, B. A.: *Acting with Technology: Activity Theory and Interaction Design.* MIT Press, Cambridge, MA (2006)

Kiczales, G.: Towards a New Model of Abstraction in Software Engineering. *Proceedings International Workshop on Object Orientation in Operating Systems*, IEEE Press, pp. 127–128. (1991)

Kristensen, B.B., Madsen, O.L., Møller-Pedersen, B., Nygaard, K.: Classification of Actions, or Inheritance also for Methods. *Proceedings of First European Conference on Object-Oriented Programming (ECOOP'87)*. LNCS, vol. 276, pp. 98–107. Springer, Berlin (1987)

Kaasbøll, J., Øgrim, L.: Super-Users: Hackers, Management Hostages or Working Class Heroes: A Study of User Influence on Redesign in Distributed Organizations. *Proceedings of the 17th Information Systems Research Seminar in Scandinavia (IRIS-17)*, pp. 784–798. Dept. of Information Processing Science, University of Oulu, Finland (1994)

Lieberman, H., Paterno, F., Wulf, V. (eds.) *End-User Development: Empowering People to Flexibly Employ Advanced Information and Communication Technology.* Springer, Springer, Dordrecht, NL (2006)

Lindeberg, O., Eriksson, J., Dittrich, Y.: Using Metaobject Protocol to Implement Tailoring: Possibilities and Problems. *Proceedings of the 6th World Conference on Integrated Design and Process Technology (IDPT-2002)*, pp. 1–8. Society for Design and Process Science, Pasadena, CA (2002)

Ludvigsen, S.R., Havnes, A., Lahn, L.C.: Workplace Learning Across Activity Systems: A Case Study of Sales Engineers. Tuomi-Gröhn, T., Engeström, Y. (eds.) *Between School and Work: New Perspectives on Transfer and Boundary-Crossing*, pp. 292–310. Elsevier Science, Amsterdam (2003)

MacLean, A., Carter, K., Lovstrand, L., Moran, T.: User-Tailorable Systems: Pressing the Issues with Buttons. *Proceedings of Human Factors in Computing Systems* (CHI'90), pp. 175–182. ACM Press, New York (1990)

Mead, G.H., Murphy, A.E. (ed.) *The Philosophy of the Present.* Open Court, Chicago (1932)

Mead, G.H., Morris, C.W. (ed.) *Mind, Self, and Society.* University of Chicago Press, Chicago (1934)

Mehandjiev, N., Bottaci, L. (eds.) End-User Development: Special Issue of the *J End User Comput* 10 (2) (1998)

Mehandjiev, N., Sutcliffe, A. G., Lee, D.: Organizational Views of End-User Development. Lieberman, H., Paterno, F., Wulf, V. (eds.) *End User Development: Empowering People to*

Flexibly Employ Advanced Information and Communication Technology, pp. 371–399. Springer, Dordrecht, NL (2006)

Mørch, A.I.: Application Units: Basic Building Blocks of Tailorable Applications. *Proceedings 5th Int'l East-West Conf. Human-Computer Interaction*, LNCS, vol. 1015, pp. 45–62. Springer, London (1995)

Mørch, A.: Evolving a Generic Application into a Domain-Oriented Design Environment. *Scand J Inform Syst* 8 (2), 63–90 (1996)

Mørch, A.: Three Levels of End-User Tailoring: Customization, Integration, and Extension. Kyng, M., Mathiassen, L. (eds.) *Computers and Design in Context*, pp. 51–76. MIT Press, Cambridge, MA (1997)

Mørch, A.I.: Tailoring Tools for System Development. *J End User Comput* 10(2), 22–30 (1998)

Mørch, A. I.: Evolutionary Growth and Control in User Tailorable Systems. In: Patel, N.V. (ed.) *Adaptive Evolutionary Information Systems*, pp. 30–58. IGI Publishing, Hershey, PA (2003)

Mørch, A.I., Nygård, K.A., Ludvigsen, S.R.: Adaptation and Generalisation in Software Product Development. In: Daniels, H. et al. (eds.) *Activity Theory in Practice: Promoting Learning Across Boundaries*, pp. 184–205. Routledge, London (2009)

Mørch, A.I., Stevens, G., Won, M., Klann, M., Dittrich, Y., Wulf, V.: Component-Based Technologies for End-User Development. *Comm ACM* 47(9), 59–62 (2004)

Mørk, B.: *Evolution by Resemblance in Component-Based Visual Application Development.* Master's thesis, Dept. of Informatics, University of Oslo, Norway (2004)

Nygård, K.A., Mørch, A.I.: The Role of Boundary Crossing for Knowledge Advancement in Product Development. *Proceedings Int'l Conf. Computers in Education (ICCE 2007)*, pp. 183–186. IOS Press, Amsterdam (2007)

Ousterhout, J.K.: Scripting: Higher-Level Programming for the 21st Century. *IEEE Comput* 31(39), 23–30 (1998)

Pekkola, S., Kaarilahti, N., Pohjola, P.: Towards Formalized End-User Participation in Information Systems Development Process: Bridging the Gap Between Participatory Design and ISD Methodologies. *Proceedings of the Ninth Conference on Participatory Design (PDC'06)*, pp. 21–30. ACM Press, New York (2006)

Simon, H.A.: *The Sciences of the Artificial: Third Edition.* MIT Press, Cambridge, MA (1996)

Volkoff, O., Strong, D. M., Elmes, M.B.: Between a Rock and a Hard Place: Boundary Spanners in an ERP Implementation. *Proceedings of the 8th Americas Conference on Information Systems*, pp. 958–962 (2002)

Wulf, V., Golombek, B.: Direct Activation: A Concept to Encourage Tailoring Activities. *Behav Inform Tech* 20(4), 249–263 (2001)

Wulf, V., Pipek, V., Won, M.: Component-Based Tailorability: Enabling Highly Flexible Software Applications. *Int J Hum-Comput Stud* 66(1), 1–22 (2008)

Åsand, H.-R., Mørch, A.I.: Super Users and Local Developers: The Organization of End-User Development in an Accounting Company. *J Organ End User Comput* 18(4), 1–21 (2006)

Chapter 10
Design Science Research for User-Centeredness

Juhani Iivari and Netta Iivari

10.1 Introduction

We would like to discuss three interesting contributions to the present book: Bødker et al. (2010), Hovorka and Germonprez (2010) and Mørch (2010). All the articles fit nicely into the theme of this book within the role of (end-) users in information systems development.

The article of Bødker et al. (2010) is refreshing during these times when much of the focus lies in agile systems development methods that tend to omit the upfront design of the system. The MUST method is placed in increasingly common situations where the system is likely to be implemented using an application package or the implementation will be outsourced. In this respect the MUST method addresses a significant problem. We also have the impression that many organizations tend to take this upfront design lightly and are therefore ill equipped to proceed to the acquisition of an application package or the contract negotiation with potential vendors. To our knowledge there are not many widely known systems development methods that are specifically targeted to this niche of IS development. Perhaps the authors could have emphasized this more in the title of their article.

Hovorka and Germonprez (2010) is a rich philosophical treatise of tinkering and tailoring of information systems and IT artifacts. Mørch (2010) also addresses tailorability under the umbrella of "evolutionary application development", but at a much more concrete level, introducing some highlights of his research program that has continued for more than 10 years.

Hovorka and Germonprez (2010) frame their article in Design Science Research (DSR) terms, making a number of critical comments on the current understanding of DSR. The DSR perspective is very appropriate in this context, since all three articles, and especially those of Bødker et al. (2010) and Mørch (2010), are essentially summaries of DSR contributions. On this understanding, it is interesting to consider to what extent they confirm the criticism of Hovorka and Germonprez.

J. Iivari (✉) and N. Iivari
Department of Information Processing Sciences, University of Oulu, Finland
e-mail: juhani.iivari@oulu.fi; netta.iivari@oulu.fi

H. Isomäki and S. Pekkola (eds.), *Reframing Humans in Information*
Systems Development, Computer Supported Cooperative Work 201,
DOI 10.1007/978-1-84996-347-3_10, © Springer-Verlag London Limited 2011

However, before this we will attempt to make sense of the three articles from the viewpoint of user-centered design.

10.2   User-Centeredness

Based on an extensive literature analysis of "user-centered design" Iivari and Iivari (in press) identify four dimensions of user centeredness with a number of questions and positions related to the dimensions. Table 10.1 uses this framework to make sense of the focus of the three articles.

In the case of user focus, we interpret that all the articles focus mainly on real users. However, Mørch (2010) introduces a detailed classification of actors on a continuum from regular use to professional development (regular user – customizer – super user – power user – professional developer). This can be interpreted as a typification of users. Although he may not have a priori targeted his "tools to make tools" to specific user categories, at least in hindsight he evaluates them in terms of these user categories. An interesting finding of Mørch (2010) is that most users are not willing to do end-user development (including tailoring) on top of ordinary work unless specific incentives exist. The question is not only about skills, but also about division of labor. Therefore, we wonder if research into end-user development is to some extent based on "fictive users" – users who exist but perhaps not in such large numbers as may be assumed.

Among the three articles only Bødker et al. (2010) pays special focus to the work of prospective users. The MUST method seems to be an attempt to reconcile holistic work process modeling ($\approx$ business process reengineering) and local work practices (ethnographically inspired observations of existing work practices). This is a challenging ambition not only because of the scope (organization wide business processes and related local work practices), but also because of the orientation (possible radical reengineering versus respect for the existing practices), objectives and consequences of change (streamlined processes, intensified work, job cuts, new skill requirements versus preserving jobs and skills, quality of working life) and politics (management pushing the change versus workers responsible for the existing work practices). Although this article does not describe in detail how to reconcile the two, it is an admirable ambition.

Despite the fact that Hovorka and Germonprez (2010) refer to negotiation of shared representations while tailoring, they do not specifically view tinkering and tailoring in the wider context of organizational work, to what extent it – to be efficient, effective, adaptive and innovative – may require tailoring, and to what extent it may constrain the freedom and possibilities of tailoring. One gets the impression that they assume that individual users make tinkering and tailoring independently of each other in their local work contexts. Mørch (2010) is still less explicit about the wider work context, but we interpret that this focus in the local work context is also implicit in his work.

Table 10.1 The focus of the three articles and user-centeredness

Dimension	Different views	Bødker et al.	Hovorka and Germonprez	Mørch
User focus	How can one identify and represent users? • Real user – human factor – average or typical user – fictive user	Real users	Real users	Real users Typical users (user categories)
Work-centeredness	How can one conceptualize and represent work? • Local work practices – holistic work models	Local work practices and holistic work processes	Tinkering primarily as a part of local work practices	Tinkering primarily as a part of local work practices
	What are the drivers of change in the work domain? • Technology driven – interactive – work process driven – emergent	All	Especially emergence emphasized	
User involvement	Why should users be involved? • Democratic – functional em-powerment of users	Democratic and functional	Democratic and functional	Democratic and functional
	How should users be involved? • Direct – representative – surrogate • Informative – consultative – participative	Direct or representative Participative	Direct and participative (users as secondary designers)	Direct, representative and surrogate Participative (users as secondary designers)
	Who has the power to decide about changes? • Users – developers – managers – intermediaries	Managers	Users in the case of tailoring	Users in the case of tailoring
System personalization	Adaptive – adaptable		Adaptable	Adaptable

Admitting that Bødker et al. (2010) are not very explicit, we interpret that they consider technology, work processes and their interaction as possible drivers of change, also recognizing that the process is emergent. In the case of Hovorka and Germonprez (2010), and Mørch (2010), we deduce that the idea of tailoring is largely based on the idea of emergent changes. Hovorka and Germonprez (2010), for example, point out that 'everyday engagement in an information process' may result in unexpected consequences and that 'system use patterns' are irregular, contradictory and untidy. They also reconceptualize designing information systems as 'designing information processes', seen as an emergent process carried out by intentional, intelligent user-designers who try to make the system fit their specific contexts, tasks and use patterns.

We interpret that all three articles justify user participation as a democratic right and as functional empowerment, noting that Hovorka and Germonprez (2010) is not explicit in this regard. They also assume direct and participative user involvement, Bødker et al. (2010) also referring to representative participation. Quite interestingly, Mørch (2010) offers some insights into the issue of representative (or even surrogate) user involvement while discussing contracted 'super users' as boundary spanners and translators between 'regular users' and 'developers'. In the case study presented in their article the super users were domain experts chosen from among the employees to train the other employees and to take part in the tailoring activities, the situation thus resembling representative user involvement. However, it might be that in certain cases, especially during the longer time span, this kind of 'super users' get very distanced from the actual work practices and settings, and instead get immersed in the world of technical development. As a result, it may not be appropriate to regard them as user representatives anymore (cf. Hedberg 1975), but rather as 'surrogates' of 'regular users', delivering domain knowledge to the tailoring activities as well as translating the technical solutions in an understandable manner to the 'regular users'. This brings us to the research topic of mediation between design and use – carried out by different kinds of intermediaries in varied kinds of IS settings – which offers highly interesting avenues for future research, including studies on user involvement in contemporary IS contexts (see Iivari et al. 2009).

Neither Hovorka and Germonprez (2010), nor Mørch (2010) refer to personalization. Yet, we surmise that tailoring is mainly done because of personalization reasons, although Hovorka and Germonprez (2010) especially, recognize that tailoring can also be a more social and collective phenomenon, implying that the way of tailoring may be negotiated and information about individually tailored versions may be distributed to peers.

Table 10.1 summarizes our interpretations of three articles from the viewpoint of user-centeredness. We are pleased to observe that together the three articles form a quite rich illustration of user centeredness as postulated by Iivari and Iivari (in press), whilst at the same time pointing out clear differences between the articles. We hope that Table 10.1 clarifies some of their assumptions, focuses and biases. Bødker et al. (2010), for example, has a strong work orientation, acknowledging both local work practices and holistic work models, and both understanding current and designing future work practices. In addition, user involvement is positioned as an integral element in the MUST method discussed in the article. However, the focus on users (as human beings) seems to be less strong (just as in Contextual Design). The primary interest of Hovorka and Germonprez (2010), and Mørch (2010), is more narrowly in personalization, but they also make their own assumptions.

10.3   Design Science Research

Hovorka and Germonprez (2010) start their article with a strong critical ethos towards the current understanding of Design Science Research (DSR), at the same time illustrating the confusion that characterizes much of the discussion of DSR. They speak about Design Science Research and Design Research without making it clear if they are synonyms or not (although they likely consider them to be synonyms). The latter could also be interpreted in the sense of Cross (2007). Although Cross does not elaborate his "Design Research", based on his other writings we would guess that it would cover his "Scientific Design", "Design Science" and "Science of Design" (Cross 2001). "Science of Design" would broaden "Design Research" to cover phenomena that do not imply building any innovative artifacts at all, but would include purely descriptive-explanatory studies of the design activity (see Iivari 2010 for a mapping between DSR and Cross 2001). In the following, we will refer by DSR to the research orientation outlined by Walls et al. (1992) and Hevner et al. (2004), for example.

A second source of confusion in Hovorka and Germonprez (2010) is the loose use of the concept of "design theory". It is not very clear whether they use it in the sense of Gregor's (2006) "theory for design and action", since they expect that design theories should "predict novel facts and observations". How does this notion of "design theory" differ from "theories for predicting" and "theories for explaining and predicting" in Gregor (2006)? Yet, the concept of "design theory" is pivotal to their argumentation, since normally "design theories" refer to the central outcomes of DSR. The core of "design theory" is the innovative artifact (Walls et al. 1992; Gregor and Jones 2007), although they can be associated with various supplementary components. Therefore it is usually clearer to write about the nature of the core IT artifact of "design theory" (e.g. a systems development methods) than about design theories in general.

Our question is whether there is anything in the current understanding of "design theory" in the sense of Gregor and Jones (2007), for example, that in some way excludes "secondary design"? Walls et al. (1992) and also Hevner et al. (2004) are very explicit that the artifacts (design theories) produced by DSR are not concrete IT applications, but rather meta-artifacts that help develop the concrete IT applications (Iivari 2003). Walls et al. speak about meta-requirements and meta-design to make the point and Hevner et al. (2004) remark that "artifacts constructed in design science research are rarely full-grown information systems used in practice" (p. 83).

This insight leads us to extend the two-level model of design in Hovorka and Germonprez (2010) to include an additional level:

- Level 0: Design of IT meta-artifacts in DSR.
- Level 1: Design of an IT artifact adapted to the specific organization or problem ("primary design" in Hovorka and Germonprez 2010), possibly applying meta-artifacts of Level 0.
- Level 2: Tailoring the Level 1 system by a user to fit his/her work and preferences ("secondary design" in Hovorka and Germonprez 2010).

One should note the view of DSR advocated by Hevner et al. (2004), for example, does not represent any design at Level 0, but introduces a research framework for DSR. Therefore it is understandable that it does not address specific design problems of information systems at Level 1 (e.g. its tailoring or tailorability).

The remaining two articles (Bødker et al. 2010 and Mørch 2010), on the contrary, introduce results of notable DSR efforts. We are not aware if the authors in question have explicitly framed their earlier articles using the existing DSR frameworks, but we do not see any fundamental difficulty in doing so. In our view the artifacts introduced in the two articles (the MUST method and the tools for tailoring) are artifacts produced by DSR in any case. Mørch (2010) explicitly addresses secondary design proposing tools to support it. Bødker et al. (2010) introduces the MUST method as a "meta-method" (corresponding to Level 0 above) that provides resources to be applied to a situated design project corresponding to Level 1 above.

In conclusion, based on the above argumentation and the two counterexamples, we are not confident that there is anything in the current understanding of DSR that would be incompatible with the idea of secondary design in the sense of Hovorka and Germonprez (2010). In fact, we do not find their quote from Hevner et al. convincing – "we do not include people or elements of organizations in our definition nor do we explicitly include the process by which such artifacts evolve" (Hevner et al. 2004 p. 82) – since it concerns their interpretation of artifacts as outcomes of DSR research (i.e. constructs, models, methods and instantiations), not the design process at Levels 1 and 2.

10.4   Conclusion

The three articles provide examples of DSR for user-centeredness. We would encourage the authors to continue and possibly strengthen their DSR orientation. In our view, the existing DSR frameworks might be very useful in guiding future research efforts in the area and in structuring their research outcomes. Before closing, let us make a few additional remarks.

Contrary to Bødker et al. (2010), we do not see the MUST method as different from the Contextual Design method as they do. Particularly related to the discussion on users and customers, the Contextual Design method seems to differentiate them in a way similar to the MUST method. However, an obvious feature of the Contextual Design method is its management orientation; the method has been criticized as a 'realization of Scandinavians worst fears' (Spinuzzi 2002). The MUST method could contribute to this aspect. The current article, however, does not specify in detail how the method deals with the 'IT design as a political process involving conflicts and dilemmas' (Bødker et al. 2010). Actually, the method seems to be positioned to serve two masters: the top managers AND the employees. This may be realistic in practice, but presupposes a harmony view of organizations.

Mørch (2010) introduces a detailed classification of actors on a continuum from regular use to professional development – regular user – customizer – super user – power user. This seems a practically useful framework. Yet, his empirical case of super users in the EUD activity leads us to wonder to what extent the classification is dynamic so that a user can migrate from one class to another. In addition to an upward movement (e.g. from a super user to a power user), can one also conceive of downward migration because of changes in the work environment and rapid technological change, for example. What are the implications of these migrations from the viewpoint of representing the user, personal image of a user, etc.? These are interesting issues to be investigated in the social milieu of the user community. In addition, the descriptions on tinkering and tailoring by Mørch (2010), and Hovorka and Germonprez (2010), both imply that from the viewpoint of user-centeredness there are interesting avenues for future work targeting the field of EUD, taking into account its collective, emergent and bidirectional qualities (see also Iivari et al. 2009).

References

Bødker, K., Kensing, F. and Simonsen, J., Participatory design in information systems development, 2010 (*in this book*)

Cross, N., Designerly ways of knowing: Design principle versus design science, *Design Issues*, 17(3), 2001, 49–55

Cross, N., Forty years of design research, *Design Studies*, 28(1), 2007, 1–4

Gregor, S., The nature of theory in information systems, *MIS Quarterly*, 30(3), 2006, 611–642

Gregor, S. and Jones, D., The anatomy of a design theory, *Journal of the AIS*, 8(5), 2007, 312–335

Hedberg, B., Computer systems to support industrial democracy, in Mumford, E. and Sackman, H. (eds.), *Human Choice and Computers*, North-Holland Publishing Company, Amsterdam. 1975, pp. 211–230

Hevner, A.R., March, S.T., Park, J. and Ram, S., 2004, Design science in information systems research, *MIS Quarterly* 28(1), 75–105

Hovorka, D. and Germonprez, M. (2010) Reflecting, tinkering, and tailoring: Implications for theories of information system design, 2010 (*in this book*)

Iivari, J., The IS core – VII: Towards information systems as a science of meta-artifacts, *Communications of the Association for Information Systems*, 12, 2003, 568–581

Iivari, J., Twelve theses on design science research in Information Systems. In Hevner A. and Chatterjee, A. (eds), *Design Research Information Systems*, Springer, Heidelberg/Berlin, 2010, pp. 43–62

Iivari, N., Karasti, H., Molin-Juustila, T., Salmela, S., Syrjänen, A.-L. & Halkola, E., Mediation between design and use – revisiting five empirical studies, *Human IT – Journal for Information Technology Studies as a Human Science* 10(2), 2009, 81–126

Iivari, J. and Iivari, N., Varieties of user-centeredness: Analysis of four systems development methods, *Information Systems Journal* http://onlinelibrary.wiley.com/doi/10.1111/j.1365-2575.2010.00351.x/full

Mørch, A.I., Evolutionary application development: Tools to make tools and boundary crossing, 2010 (*in this book*)

Spinuzzi, C., A Scandinavian Challenge, a US Response: Methodological Assumptions in Scandinavian and US Prototyping Approaches, *Proceedings of SIGDOC*, 2002, pp. 208–215

Walls, J., Widmeyer, G.R. and El Sawy, O.A., 1992, Building an information system design theory for vigilant EIS. *Information Systems Research* 3(1), 36–59

Chapter 11
"20 Years a-Growing"[1]: Revisiting *From Human Factors to Human Actors*

Liam J. Bannon

> ...the study of information systems in their social and organizational context remains at the heart of the discipline of informatics.
>
> Kristen Nygaard[2]

11.1 Introduction

Almost two decades ago, I published an article entitled "From Human Factors to Human Actors" (Bannon, 1991) in the book "Design at Work: Cooperative Design of Computer Systems" (Greenbaum and Kyng 1991). This short polemical essay on the need to re-formulate our goals in the fields of information systems design and human-computer interaction to take account of people's general motivation and abilities, as well as their work setting, seemed to strike a chord. The article was anthologized in the popular HCI collection "Readings in Human–Computer Interaction" (Baecker et al. 1995) and is still, somewhat to my surprise, cited today. (witness the reference in the Chapter by Hovorka and Germonprez, this Section).

The reason for re-visiting the theme of this 20 year-old article again is because I believe that, with recent developments in both computing hardware and software, we are at a unique moment in the history of computing where, finally, this human-centred perspective on information technology can become a more mainstream perspective within the information systems (IS) and related fields. So, precisely for this reason, I very much welcome the appearance of this edited collection of papers concerning the re-framing of the "human factor" in the field of IS.

---

[1] The phrase "Twenty years a-Growing (Fiche blíain ag Fás)" is the title of a well-known Irish memoir by Maurice O'Sullivan from Great Blasket Island, first published in Irish and English in 1933. It is also the first line of a well-known Irish proverb about the stages of life.

[2] In his Foreword to the book, *The Labyrinths of Information* (Ciborra 2002).

L.J. Bannon (✉)
Department of Computer Science and Information Systems, University of Limerick,
Limerick, Ireland
e-mail: liam.bannon@ul.ie

H. Isomäki and S. Pekkola (eds.), *Reframing Humans in Information Systems Development*, Computer Supported Cooperative Work 201, DOI 10.1007/978-1-84996-347-3_11, © Springer-Verlag London Limited 2011

In the early days of computing, the goal of the computing field was to answer the question "What can be Automated?" Indeed a large review of the Computer Science (CS) field some years ago was explicitly titled thus – the COSERS report (Arden 1980). As a result, the human and social side of computing has usually been seen as, at best, a sideshow, a minor aspect to be treated in several disparate, peripheral, areas – such as "user requirements" or user need surveys, interface design issues, or more general professional topics, e.g. ethics, organizational issues in implementation of information systems. There have been attempts over the years by a small band of academics, consultants, and researchers, from a variety of perspectives, to change this techno-centric paradigm towards a more human-centred one – e.g. Gerald Weinberg's early work on developing software teams (Weinberg 1971), Rob Kling's work on Social Informatics (Kling 2003), Kristen Nygaard's work on systems development with unions (c.f. Bjerknes et al. 1987), Peter Naur's work on human aspects of programming (Naur 1992) and Enid Mumford's socio-technical systems approach (Mumford 1983). However, despite such a sampling of illustrious names, it would be safe to say that until quite recently the standard view of computer science and information systems did not place much emphasis on human, social, organizational, political or cultural factors as co-constitutive of the very field of CS and IS. This view is slowly changing as a result of both internal and external pressures. From within, voices such as Denning (1992), Winograd (1997), Wegner (1997), as well as other names listed above have argued for a more comprehensive approach that puts the human aspects of the design and use of technology as an integral part of the conceptual and empirical foundations of the CS and IS disciplines.

This alternative view of computing has lead to the slow emergence of what is beginning to be termed, in some quarters, "human-centred" computing or human-centred design. The label may appear somewhat meaningless, as who would subscribe to an alternative "system-centred" computing label? But, just as the label "user-centered design" in the field of human–computer interaction hit a chord in the 1980's, it may be the case that the "human-centred computing" label will have a similar re-orienting effect on the field of computing in the early decades of the 2000s. Concerns expressed in such emerging areas as the "new informatics", and "interaction design" are, in my opinion, examples of shifts in perspective, in the information systems and human–computer interaction communities respectively, towards a more wholistic view of human-systems interaction that begins to privilege the human, social and cultural aspects of computing. Note that these are not simply surface changes, nor should they be viewed simply as ancillary issues in relation to the dominant computational approach, but rather they raise foundational issues for the field of computing per se. The very field of computing is being transformed as a result of hardware and software innovations. The remarkable rise in the development of ubiquitous technologies has lead to a re-thinking of the role of computer technology in our lives. No longer is the focus on educating people to be "computer-literate", rather the emphasis is how do we think about computationally-enhancing artefacts, environments and services for human use. The open software movement has provided a powerful paradigm for opening up access to proprietary software systems and applications, thus allowing people to add, mix, edit and adapt code for all kinds of purposes not intended by the original developers. The advent of Web 2.0 technologies and services allows for the emergence of new forms of social media that encourage these forms of what has been termed "open innovation".

11.2   A Human Activity-Centred View of Computing[3]

My personal view of computing is one that views the technology from a tool, and also a medium, perspective. This approach focuses on understanding human activity, in all its guises, in order to provide useful and pertinent observations on human action in the world. What is shared in this approach is a highlighting of the user perspective, examining how people accomplish their goals – with and through other people, and at times, other media. While technology may play an important role in these human activities, often the use of the technology is as an intrinsic mediating influence, rather than being the goal of the activity. The relevance of this approach to technology development is that it provides a distinct perspective that encompasses many of the key issues being faced by computing technology developers today – issues such as *awareness, context, interaction, engagement, emotion.* All of these aspects concern the activities of human actors in a (variety of) setting(s). I have been involved, over the years, in attempting to extend the design boundaries of HCI (Bannon 1985), grappling with issues of context and with alternative frames for theorizing about human–computer interaction (Bannon and Bødker 1991; Bannon and Kaptelinin 2000), developing our understanding of cooperative work in CSCW (Bannon and Schmidt 1991), understanding the role of work practices in organizational learning and memory (Bannon and Kuutti 2002), and more recently, in working on a framework to understand the field of interaction design, dealing with issues of meaning, engagement and emotion (Aboulafia and Bannon 2004). What might appear to be somewhat unrelated topics, taken from one perspective, can be seen to be integrated from another.

   This perspective is one that takes the term "human-centred" to mean more than simply "considering the user" in technology development, but rather places our understanding of people and their practices to the forefront in the design of new technology. The issue here is not simply one of values, although explication of the underlying values inherent in technological designs is certainly important, but requires us to understand human activity in the world. This perspective is inspired by a number of theoretical perspectives, including phenomenology. Applying phenomenological methodology (and hermeneutics) to design was suggested by Winograd

---

[3] This section outlines a formulation first expressed in Bannon (2005).

and Flores (1986), whose work has had a significant influence on the development of recent "human-centred" approaches to computing. Moran and Anderson (1990) have proposed as a specific paradigm for design, the Workaday World, which 'puts the technology in proper perspective', the perspective of the lifeworld (lebenswelt) of people working. This paradigm, also motivated by phenomenology, draws on the works of such figures as Husserl, Habermas, Heidegger, Schutz and Luckmann. The notion of 'lifeworld' is defined as the sphere of practical activity and common-sense reasoning (derived from Husserl). It is a description, from the view of a particular 'actor', which captures the experience of that actor, involving three aspects: technology, social relationship, and work practice. Ehn's notion of 'work-oriented design' (Ehn, 1988) within the participative design tradition also draws on this phenomenological account. Ehn argues that a Heideggerian approach to design creates a new understanding of the process of designing computer artefacts, that 'help focus on the importance of everydayness of use as fundamental to design'.

The Scandinavian work on participatory design in systems development – from the late 1970s onwards- has had a significant influence in "opening up" the computing and more general information systems fields to aspects of human activities relating to the design and use of technology. Another of the major conceptual frameworks that we have found helpful in developing our understanding of certain computer-related issues, specifically in human–computer interaction, is what is commonly termed (cultural-historical) activity theory. This framework shifts attention away from the interface per se and focuses on computer-mediated activity. We believe that this shift in focus is extremely important if we are to develop truly useful and usable systems that support people in their everyday activities. The framework emphasizes the concept of mediation in all human activities, and its strongly his-torical approach provides us with a powerful tool for viewing the computer system as yet another, albeit much more powerful and flexible, mediational device that is used by people to accomplish certain goals. While the conceptual framework can be at times obscure, it provides a useful conceptual tool for understanding such issues as user goals, mediational means, work context or environment, and collec-tive human activities. What is of interest in this approach is a more theoretical framing of certain issues which are difficult to conceptualize within, for example, traditional information-processing accounts of human behaviour. For example, the problem of context, which has become more and more recognized as a crucial issue for useful theory and empirical work, is built into the very basis of the theory, in terms of activities. "An activity system comprises the individual practitioner, the colleagues and co-workers of the workplace community, the conceptual and practical tools, and the shared objects as a unified dynamic whole" (Engeström 1991).

11.3   Further Perspectives

The three chapters in this section provide a number of distinct vantage points from which to understand how we might move towards the goal of developing more human-centred information systems. The Chapter by Bødker, Kensing and Simonsen provides an account of their participatory design framework – labelled the MUST method, which they note is a really a "meta-method" that provides resources (concepts, principles, project organization, and a toolbox of techniques) for handling any specific IT design project. Here the focus is on how to go about introducing technical change into organizations, where one must deal with complex socio-political issues, and different professional groups with different ways-of-working. The paper discusses some of the issues around the concept of design in the context of developing IT systems, and explores our understanding of the term "user", emphasizing the importance of ensuring genuine user participation, and the involvement of real users – those people who have first-hand experiences of the work practices that are being changed or augmented. The authors also discuss how their approach differs from other extant approaches such as RUP, Contextual Design and Lean and BPR approaches. Again, the work is ongoing, both with practitioners in the field and with student projects, so the corpus of knowledge and experience with the method is always expanding. It also draws on the insights and pioneering work of many systems development groups engaged in participatory design projects in Scandinavia over a period of years.

Next, the Chapter by Hovorka and Germonprez critically examines a topic that has generated considerable interest within the information systems community in recent years, namely Design Science Research (Hevner et al. 2004). They note how this approach surprisingly omits reference to the human actors involved in actually making design work. Drawing on a tradition that extends back to my own paper mentioned at the start of this article on human actors, and on the extensive writings of the late Ciborra (2002), they show how crucial is the role of the human actor in making systems fit into practice, as design is intimately tied up with an ongoing practice. They make a plea for the central role that human agency should play within any information systems tradition that claims to study how systems are taken into practice through forms of appropriation and adaptation. Ciborra, deeply rooted in the work of Heidegger, has provided a rich tapestry of concepts and ways of thinking about various aspects of information systems design and use that eschew more formal models and methods that are the mainstream of the IS tradition. Rather he points us to the phenomenological philosophical tradition, and shows how such concepts as hospitality, *bricolage*, *Gestell*, drift, improvisation, feelings and moods can provide a new vocabulary and way of looking at human action in the world, and help provide insight into how systems become part of our practice. Ciborra celebrates the role of active users as *bricoleurs*, taking, shaping, and adapting what is *at-hand* (Heidegger) to fit our purpose.

Finally, the Chapter by Mørch provides a comprehensive overview of an area that has been around for some time, namely End User Development (EUD), where users modify and adapt existing systems to their own practice. Mørch positions this field between professional software development on the one hand, and the burgeoning area of user-generated content production for new media on the other. His focus is on tool development, not content, here. Mørch provides a detailed account of the evolution of the field, from human–computer interaction (HCI), software-engineering, and information systems perspectives. As well as exploring the "tailoring" work of various kinds of users and super-users, he examines the ways in which these roles can be used in organizations to enhance the tailoring activities of the whole user community, before moving on to outline a comprehensive conceptual framework for understanding the field of evolutionary application development (EAD), involving such terms as boundary crossing, stable intermediate forms, emergence, and mutual learning (between developers and users) as discussed in participative design approaches mentioned earlier.

11.4 Conclusions

Returning for a moment to the Chapter by Hovorka and Germonprez, the renewed interest in understanding the art of the *bricoleur* seems most *apropos* at this moment in time, where information systems are moving from monolithic closed bespoke systems towards more open, flexible, extendible library and application packages that can be re-assembled and adapted by a variety of people - from hackers to application developers to more traditional "end–users", in innumerable ways. Open source software packages provide a plethora of opportunities for people to take, re-make, shape and tailor software, and increasingly even hardware, to fit their particular purposes. In so doing, they are also contributing to the growth of the open source movement, and adding to the community know-how and expertise embedded within the corpus of open software libraries and packages available to all. What we are seeing is a fundamental shift away from proprietary systems towards a more open, flexible, collaborative infrastructure and application environment where individuals, groups and communities as active agents can appropriate and shape information tools and media to fit their needs. The development of 3D prototyping machines and low-cost fabrication labs (e.g. Gershenfeld 2005), the explosion of open platforms such as Arduino, etc. has provided a plethora of possibilities for people to develop innovative applications and services at low cost. Within such an active, open community space, the need for us to develop more innovative concepts and methods to understand and support these practices is clear. There is a renewed interest in understanding bottom-up innovative practices in general, where people are taking a closer look at such vernacular expressions of "making-do" with resources at hand in areas with resource scarcity, such as *Jugaad* in India and *Riquimbili/Rikimbili* in Cuba (Jana 2009; Ortosa 2009). These kinds of tinkerings and tailorings with mechanical technology show the power of the old adage: "necessity is the mother of invention". They also point out the ingenuity and capability that can be found amongst people of all walks of life, and not only well-educated software professionals! The emerging paradigm of creative collaboration and innovation that we see in, for example, Web 2.0 and social media, requires us to re-think our conceptual frameworks concerning IT design, development and use. Foremost in this re-framing must be the (re-)emergence of human and social actors. The articles in this book are a modest beginning towards this re-conceptualization and it is time for the broader information systems community to engage with these exciting developments.

References

Aboulafia, A., & Bannon, L. (2004). Understanding Affect in Design: An Outline Conceptual Framework. *Theoretical Issues in Ergonomics Science.* Taylor & Francis, Volume 5, Number 1/January–February 2004, pp. 4–15.

Arden, B.W. (Ed.) (1980). What Can Be Automated? The Computer Science & Engineering Research Study (COSERS). *MIT Press series in Computer Science*: 3, Cambridge, MA: MIT Press.

Baecker, R., Grudin, J., Buxton, W., & Greenberg, S. (Eds.). (1995). *Readings in Human-Computer Interaction: Towards the year 2000*, 2nd edn. San Francisco: Morgan Kaufmann.

Bannon, L. (1985). *Extending the Design Boundaries of Human–Computer Interaction.* San Diego: Institute for Cognitive Science, University of California, ICS Technical Report 8505. (Extracts from this report appear as 3 Chapters. In D.A. Norman & S.W. Draper (Eds.) (1986) *User Centered System Design: New Perspectives on Human-Computer Interaction.* Hillsdale, NJ: Lawrence Erlbaum Associates.

Bannon, L. (1991). From Human Factors to Human Actors: The Role of Psychology and Human–Computer Interaction Studies in Systems Design. In J. Greenbaum & M. Kyng (Eds.) *Design at Work: Cooperative Design of Computer Systems.* Hillsdale: Lawrence Erlbaum Associates, pp. 25–44.

Bannon, L. (2005). A human-centred perspective on interaction design. In A. Pirhonen, H. Isomäki, C. Roast & P. Saariluoma (Eds.) *Future Interaction Design.* London: Springer, pp. 31–51.

Bannon, L., & Bødker, S. (1991). Beyond the Interface: Encountering Artifacts in Use. In J. Carroll (Ed.) *Designing Interaction: Psychology at the human-computer interface.* Cambridge: Cambridge University Press, pp. 227–253.

Bannon, L., & Kaptelinin, V. (2000). From Human-Computer Interaction to Computer-Mediated Activity. In C. Stephanidis (Ed.) *User Interfaces for All: Concepts, Methods, and Tools.* Mahwah, NJ: Lawrence Erlbaum, pp. 183–202.

Bannon, L., & Kuutti, K. (2002). Shifting Perspectives on Organizational Memory: From Storage to Active Remembering. In: S. Little, P. Quintas & T. Ray (Eds.) *Managing Knowledge: An Essential Reader.* London: Open University/Sage Publications, pp. 190–210.

Bannon, L., & Schmidt, K. (1991). CSCW: Four Characters in Search of a Context. In J. Bowers & S. Benford (Eds.) *Studies in Computer Supported Cooperative Work: Theory, Practice and Design.* Amsterdam: North-Holland, pp. 3–16.

Bjerknes, G., Ehn, P., & Kyng, M. (1987). *Computers and Democracy – A Scandinavian Challenge.* Aldershot, UK: Gower.

Ciborra, C. (2002). *The Labyrinths of Information: Challenging the Wisdom of Systems.* Oxford: Oxford University Press.

Denning, P. (1992). Educating a new engineer. *Communications of the ACM*, 35(12), 83–97.

Ehn, P. (1988). *Work-Oriented Design of Computer Artifacts.* Hillsdale: Lawrence Erlbaum.

Engeström, Y. (1991). Developmental Work Research: Reconstructing Expertise through Expansive Learning. In M. Nurminen and G. Weir (eds.) *Human Jobs and Computer Interfaces.* Amsterdam, North-Holland.

Gershenfeld, N.A. (2005). *Fab: The Coming Revolution on Your Desktop – from Personal Computers to Personal Fabrication.* New York: Basic Books.

Greenbaum, J., & Kyng, M. (Eds.). (1991). *Design at Work: Cooperative Design of Computer Systems.* Hillsdale, NJ: Lawrence Erlbaum Associates.

Hevner, A.R., March, S.T., Park, J., & Ram, S. (2004). Design science in information systems research. *MIS Quarterly* 28(1), 75–105

Jana, R. (2009). India's next global export: Innovation. *Business Week*, December 2, 2009.

Kling, R. (2003). Social Informatics. In A. Kent, H. Lancour, W. Z. Nasri & J. E. Daily (Eds.) *Encyclopedia of Library and Information Science.* New York: Marcel Dekker, Inc.

Moran, T., & Anderson, R. (1990). The Workaday World as a Paradigm for CSCW Design. *Proceedings, ACM Conference on CSCW.* Los Angeles, CA, pp. 381–393.

Mumford, E. (1983). *Designing Human Systems – the ETHICS Method.* Manchester, UK: Manchester Business School.

Naur, P. (1992). *Computing: A Human Activity.* NewYork: ACM Press/Addison-Wesley.

Oroza, E. (2009). *Rikimbili: Une etude sure la désobéissance technologique et quelques formes de reinvention.* Cité du Design: Publications de l'Université de Staint-Étienne.

Wegner, P. (1997). Why interaction is more powerful than algorithms. *Communications of the ACM*, 40(5), 80–91.

Weinberg, G. (1971). *The Psychology of Computer Programming.* New York: Van Nostrand Reinhold.

Winograd, T., & Flores, F. (1986). *Understanding Computers and Cognition. A New Foundation for Design.* Norwood: Ablex.

Winograd, T. (1997). The Design of Interaction. In P. Denning & R. Metcalfe (Eds.) *Beyond Calculation: The Next Fifty Years of Computing.* New York: Copernicus/Springer, pp. 149–161.

Part III
Practice

Chapter 12
Three Levels of Failure: Analysing a Workflow Management System

Tom Gross and Samuli Pekkola

12.1 Introduction

In this paper we report on a case study of the introduction of a workflow management for travel management in a higher education organisation. We aim at addressing two central questions. Firstly, why did a workflow management system (WfMS), which was initially anticipated and welcomed, create complaints that go far beyond the well-known resistance towards the introduction of new systems? And secondly, why did the users regard this workflow management system and its introduction as a failure? The answers that we found to these two central questions are valuable lesson learned for the designers of user-friendly workflow management systems. And, they also have implications to the general organisational resistance discussion, where for instance Piderit (2000) asked for more individually oriented approaches to gain more understanding about cognitive ambivalences of individuals and their adaptation to new systems. Although we do not study cognitive processes, the study provides a basis to understand individual users and their roles and expectations in the organisational context.

In particular, we reflect on issues concerning the changes of processes induced by the system, concerning the functionality of the specific system used, and concerning the usability of the system used. This study provides insight from real-life introduction and use of a WfMS. These insights demonstrate that – although the technical systems design was basically properly developed – the neglect of organisational and user-centric issues inflicted the whole system to fail on three levels: process,

T. Gross (✉)
Faculty of Media, Bauhaus-University Weimar, Germany
e-mail: tom.gross@medien.uni-weimar.de

S. Pekkola
Department of Business Information Management and Logistics, Tampere University
of Technology, Finland
e-mail: samuli.pekkola@tut.fi

H. Isomäki and S. Pekkola (eds.), *Reframing Humans in Information
Systems Development*, Computer Supported Cooperative Work 201,
DOI 10.1007/978-1-84996-347-3_12, © Springer-Verlag London Limited 2011

functionalities and usability. Taking them in the socio-technical (Sarker and Lee 2002) context provides a simple three-tier checklist for systems designers.

At the same time, such an analysis shows the complexity of developing user-friendly systems. Focusing primarily on user interface related issues, and overlooking other issues such as organisational or functional issues, can lead to a system that is unusable in its context of use. Or, if moving to organisational level, user interface is underrated. Therefore, the case also emphasises the need for an integrated approach in human-computer interaction in general, following the early definitions of computer-supported cooperative work (CSCW) discipline and how the relationship between organisations and systems was seen. For instance, Grudin (1994, p. 19) writes: "*building technology was not enough. ... practitioners need to learn more about how people work in groups and organisations and how technology affects them*". Schmidt and Bannon (1992, p. 11) write along the same lines: "*CSCW should be conceived of as an endeavour to understand the nature and requirements of cooperative work with the objective of designing computer-based technologies for cooperative work arrangements.*" This dispersion has also been discussed in the context of HCI discipline (Grudin 2006) and of information systems (IS) discipline (Iivari and Iivari forthcoming; Iivari et al. 2010; Isomäki and Pekkola 2005). Grudin (2006) identified the existence of three different communities within the subject. Each of these communities has their own theoretical basis, questions of interest, and publication outlets, and little interactions between communities. Similarly Iivari and Iivari (forthcoming) analysed the varieties of human centeredness in IS literature. They identified four distinct dimensions (user-centeredness, work-centeredness, user involvement and participation, and systems personalization) that appear in varying extensions in different IS development methods. This, again, resembles the dispersion between the communities aiming at developing user-friendly systems.

WfMS and their usage have been discussed particularly in CSCW forum. Often those studies focus either on design or technical issues (such as access control or coordination mechanisms (Agostini and de Michelis 2000; Divitini and Simone 2000; Dourish et al. 1996; Kreifelts et al. 1993; Simone et al. 1995), WfMS's relationship to organisational processes (Abbott and Sarin 1994; Dourish 2001). Studies, where WfMS are analyzed in the light of their use in organisational settings, are few (ex. Bowers et al. 1995). However, such studies would offer new understanding about the challenges and practice of developing, using and introducing WfMS in organisations.

In the remainder of the paper we will provide the background of the study with relation to workflow management, organisational issues as well as related studies. We will then characterise the setting of the study and present some findings. We will discuss the lessons learned and draw conclusions.

12.2   Theoretical Background

In this section we briefly discuss WfMS and different perspectives that have been taken in their analysis and research, and frame the subsequent case study by briefly introducing organisational issues and requirements related to them.

12.2.1   Workflow Management Systems

Workflow management systems (WfMS) are software systems that support the management of processes in organisations, particularly business processes (Conery et al. 2005; van der Aalst and van Hee 2001). They have been discussed since industrialisation, particularly with the goal of increasing efficiency of routine work activities (Mentzas and Halaris 1999).

The international Workflow Management Coalition (WfMC) developed a reference model for WfMS in order to provide an interface and foster exchange among systems. The WfMC defines a workflow as *"the computerised facilitation of automation of a business process, in whole or part"* and a WfMS as *"a system that completely defines, manages, and executes workflows through the execution of software whose order of execution is driven by a computer representation of the workflow logic"* (WfMC 1995). In general, WfMS support users performing their tasks: they schedule resources and provide the information required in each step (Mangan and Sadig 2002). Furthermore, the WfMC specifies that a WfMS should provide support for three types of functions: for the definition and modelling of workflow processes; for the management of the workflows at runtime; and for the interaction of users with the respective applications at runtime (WfMC 1995).

WfMS typically support various types of workflows (Mentzas and Halaris 1999). Workflows can be distinguished according to the nature of the processes involved. Administrative workflows are characterised by their permanent structure and the strict rules they follow. Ad-hoc workflows do not follow rules – either because they deal with exceptions, or because they are unique and different from preceding processes. Collaborative workflows involve several users for the same process, which can lead to multistep procedures and iterations. Finally, production workflows are those processes that are mission-critical and central to the respective organisation.

According to Mangan and Sadig (2002) flexible WfMS should support adequate combinations of sequences (activities following after the preceding activity is completed), splits (two or more activities are executed simultaneously), joins (two or more split activities are re-joined in a coordinated way with transition control), exclusive or splits (a specific activity out of several thread is selected and executed), and exclusive or joins (two or more split activities are re-joined without coordination). Also, flexible WfMS should not only support administrative rule-based processes, but also ad-hoc processes and exceptions. The notion of expected exceptions is thus brought up (Casati et al. 1999; Saastamoinen 1995, 2005). With them the designer knows in advance that some processes will need human intervention. For instance, in a car rental company cars will mostly be returned without damage. Yet, accidents can and do occur. Or, in a global company up to 40% of incoming invoices are treated as exceptions (Saastamoinen 1995, 2005). So, the systems should provide an exception handler that allows the employees of the car rental company to react to this unlikely event (e.g., by giving assistance to the renter, organizing the repair of the car, cancelling and rearranging future rentals of the damaged car) or that allows non-standard invoices to be treated in an efficient way, as close to standard invoices as possible.

Sarker and Lee (2002) identified three different perspectives on WfMS and the redesign of business processes. They argued that these perspectives are used as theory of action or theory-in-use guiding the everyday work in the world of practice. The techno-centric perspective is rooted in technological determinism and departs from the idea that it is primarily the quality of the technology that causes a success or failure. Consequently the assumptions are that success can only happen if the approach is IT-driven, and that good design of technology guarantees success. The socio-centric perspective in contrast sees human motives and human action as the driving force and sees social processes (e.g., leadership, communication) as sources of success. Therefore, the assumptions are that success can only happen if the approach is driven by a good leadership and its vision, and that a balanced team does the redesign. The socio-technical perspective partly combines the other two perspectives and attributes success to a good interplay of actors, technology, and context. The assumptions are that technology and processes need to be understood per se as well as in their social context, and that processes need to be coupled based on technology and social enablers.

12.2.2   Organisational Studies

The organisational studies relevant for this paper range from the analysis of organisational settings before the introduction of a system, to the conception and implementation of a system, to the introduction of the system, to the process and study of actual use, as well as to the eventual adaptation of the system according to the finding in the study. Many studies on organisational issues related to WfMS can be found in the literature (cf. e.g., Abbott and Sarin 1994; Conery et al. 2005; Mangan and Sadig 2002; Mentzas and Halaris 1999; Orlikowski and Gash 1994; van der Aalst and van Hee 2001). We subsequently primarily want to give a broad overview of the theories that are applied in these studies and to provide some information concerning the models these studies produced.

For studying organisational issues surrounding WfMS several theories have been developed. They can roughly be divided into variance theories that are based on studies of independent and dependent variables, and into process theories that are based on the analysis of preceding circumstances and occurrences in order to explain the actual outcome (Kim and Pan 2006).

The variance theories often identify several loci where technology has an impact on (Prescott and Conger 1995). For instance, the information systems unit locus of impact (as the potential that information technology has on changes in the information systems department), intra-organisational locus of impact (as the potential of information technology for cross-departmental change; such as when introducing document imaging systems), and inter-organisational locus of impact (as the potential of information technology for cross-organisational change; such as when introducing inter-organisational workshop management systems) were identified.

The process theories have produced a considerable number of process models; they can be clustered into three groups (Kim and Pan 2006). Sequences of events identify and analyze processes on the basis of social actions in a row. For instance, Abbott (1990) as well as Robey and Newman (1996) analyzed sequences. These models provide means for a precise analysis of single-threaded and linear sequences, but have shortcomings with relation to the complexities that can occur in real-world situations. Structuration theoretical analyses study the relation and interaction between institutions and their properties on one side and members of the institutions and users on the other side. For instance, Orlikowski (1992a; 1994) studied institutions, key groups, and technology as central factors influencing the structuration during the conceptualisation and implementation of the system. Here simultaneous activities – that is, splits and joins of activities – are possible. Finally, the cognitive mapping approaches identify and analyze the structure and relation of factors by looking at influential processes among them. For instance, Abdel-Hamid and Madnick (1989) did a study on the management of software development projects and developed their own study paradigm. Overall, since many factors and processes can be relevant for describing the situation, cognitive maps can become quite complex.

Besides these general observations concerning the theories applied in the studies and the resulting process models we do not want to go into more details of individual studies, as there are problems there as we will show later. However, we want to bring up a concept of technological frames that are interpretations of technology by key groups in the respective organisation (Orlikowski and Gash 1994). The interpretations summarise the perception of the nature, value, and use of the system. Assuming that the interpretations strongly influence the behaviour towards and use of the system, knowledge about the interpretations can then provide early insight to the future acceptance of the system. The key groups are typically managers, users, and technologists. Whereas previous literature has emphasised the individual interpretations and the differences among them, more recent publications point out that "*shared cognitive structures*" (Orlikowski and Gash 1994, p. 176) can emerge. So, the group of technologists could have a shared interpretation about the nature of the technology, about the use of the current technology, and about a strategy on how technology can and should be used. Likewise, the group of users and the group of managers can also have shared interpretations about these issues. As a matter of fact, the shared interpretations of the specific groups can and in reality often will be different. For instance, while the functionality and use of a system might be very clear to the technologists, it can be less clear to the actual users. And, managers might be sceptical about the use of a system (e.g., Orlikowski and Gash 1994 report that managers were sometimes sceptical about sharing information via Lotus Notes). Also, the fact that often employees in organisations have to use a technology that management has chosen for them can lead to difficulties (Gallivan 2001).

12.2.3   Criteria for Organisations, Key Groups and Workflow Systems

Several criteria for organisations and key groups that are necessary as a prerequisite for the successful introduction of any type of cooperative information technology and WfMS in particular can be identified. Most of them have been formulate in a quite general manner (Karsten 1999; Orlikowski 1992b):

- The members of the organisation should cooperate
- The users should understand the value of the technology for the cooperative endeavour
- The organisation should allow for appropriate adoption of the system
- The organisational culture should facilitate cooperation

Furthermore, the following requirements for systems can be listed (Lin and Cornford 2000):

- The system should solve (some of) the existing problems and provide a fit to the existing infrastructure
- The system should be user-friendly and easy to learn for the users
- The system should be cost effective and enhance the state of the art for the management group

12.3   Case and Research Settings

This study is based on our observations from a WfMS supporting travel management in a higher education organisation. The system primarily supports repetitive administrative workflows, and is based on a Web-centric approach. As basic constructs for workflows, it supports sequences.

The study is based on our observations on the introduction and use of the system in an organisation over a time period of 1 year. The subjects of the study were employees working in this higher education organisation, using this system in their daily work; they (or researchers) were thus not paid for the study. Relevant processes are travelling, creating, accepting, and passing documents. We collected data from system logs and captured experiences, complaints, praises through numerous informal interviews and coffee-table discussions. In addition, six formal theme interviews to get "hard-data" and confirm our log and informal findings were conducted. We believe that the fact that one of the authors has also worked in this organisation leads to even deeper insights (Crabtree et al. 2000).

Subsequently we will briefly introduce the system and describe the workflow as it was before the introduction of the system and as it emerged through the use of the system.

12.3.1   The Workflow Management System

The workflow management system is a commercial Web-based system to support the management of travel claims in all levels of an organisation. At the time of purchase, it was tailored to fit into the organisation and its processes, and some processes were tailored respectively. This means that the consultants from the supplier-side made field studies in the target organisation and tailored the system accordingly. At the end, the system met the needs of the organisation and was appropriate for its employees – in an optimal case.

12.3.2   The Workflow Before the Introduction of the System

For years, travel plans (i.e., requests for permission to travel) and travel claims for refunding (i.e., demands for the payment of personal costs) were managed with a paper form (cf. Fig. 12.1). The form and several attachments were circulated in the following steps:

1. A person intending to travel – the traveller – fills in a travel plan form stating the reason and duration of the trip, estimated costs, and a project account where the costs are to be covered. Finally she signs the form.
2. The traveller's project manager evaluates the necessity of the trip and its budget demands, and advocates the trip by a signature.
3. The traveller's secretary checks the correctness of a project account and daily allowance, the acceptability of other costs, and places the initials.
4. The traveller's head of department evaluates the necessity of the trip and its budget demands again, and approves the plan by a signature. The original is delivered to the secretary, and copies to the central administration for advance payments, and back to the traveller.
5. After the trip, the traveller fills in another form, a travel claim, where she states all the costs and attaches appropriate receipts. The form is signed.
6. The traveller's secretary checks the project account, daily allowance, and correctness of all costs and potential currency conversions, and calculates the VAT. Finally she signs the form and attaches the original travel plan.
7. The traveller's head of department checks that all the costs are appropriate, and approves the claim by a signature.
8. The traveller's secretary makes a photocopy of all papers to departmental achieves and sends the plan, the claim and attachments to the central administration.
9. Another secretary in the central administration checks the costs and their appropriateness, and makes entries to the bookkeeping and accounts payable systems. She also signed the form before filing it.
10. The traveller receives the costs she has claimed to her bank account. A secretary at the department checks the ledger.

As can be seen, this process includes several overlapping tasks and complicated processes thus requiring a considerable amount of unnecessary work. It happened, for instance, that a person waited for his travel claim to be approved and paid for

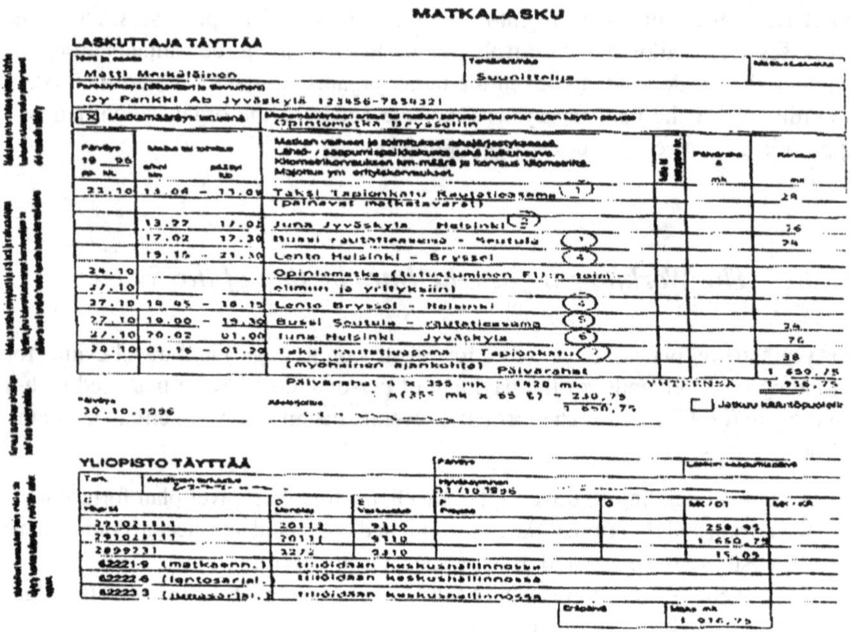

Fig. 12.1 Travel plan on paper

more than 2 months (phases 6–9). It was evident that a WfMS to manage and speed-up the process would be of great help.

12.3.3 The Workflow in the System

A commercial WfMS for managing travel plans and travel claims in higher education organisations was chosen. The consultants from a supplier studied the organisation and tailored a version for a trial use in two different departments and in the central administration. They gathered feedback and adjusted the system. After 6 months, the system was introduced into the whole organisation. Central administration informed the employees that no travel plans or travel claim would be dealt with on paper after a certain day.

The introduction of the new system changed the aforementioned processes as intended. Yet, it was impossible to get rid of paper forms. Legislation required that a person, who checks and approves plans and claims, could be juristically identified. Electronic signatures were not regarded to as juristically approvable. This resulted that all the forms were created by entering information into the WfMS and then printing out a copy for signing it. Handling the plans and claims as administrative activities, both versions, the paper and the one in the system, were treated simultaneously (we will come back to this later).

The WfMS forced the organisation to adapt processes and the following steps:

1. The traveller fills in a travel plan form in the system stating the reason and duration of the trip, estimated costs, and a project account where the costs are to be covered. Finally, she prints a paper copy and signs it.
2. The traveller's secretary checks the correctness of a project account and the acceptability of other costs and approves the copies ("a click" in the system, signature on a paper).
3. The traveller's head of department evaluates the necessity of the trip and its budget demands, and approves the plan in the system and by a signature on paper. The paper copy is then delivered to the secretary.
4. After the trip, the traveller converts the plan to a travel claim in the system, and changes the estimations to real costs. She then prints out a paper copy, signs it and attaches appropriate receipts.
5. The traveller's secretary checks the project account and correctness of all costs in the system. And, she signs the paper copy (reprints it if needed) and attaches the original paper-based version of a travel plan.
6. The traveller's head of department checks that all the costs are appropriate, and approves the claim in the system and by a signature.
7. The traveller's secretary sends the paper copies of the plan, the claim and the attachments to the central administration.
8. Another secretary in the central administration checks the costs and their appropriateness in the system, and signs the paper copy before filing it.
9. The traveller receives the costs she has claimed to her bank account. A secretary at the department checks the ledger.

As it can be seen, the process and the steps are slightly simpler regardless of the two versions of plans and claims that are handled hand-in-hand. However, from the users' perspective, the workload is (partially) heavier:

– Traveller: instead of filling in paper forms, the traveller uses the WfMS. This allows (re-) editing, etc. of travel plan and its automatic conversion to a travel claim thus reducing the amount of writing and typing. Also, as the process is speeded up, reimburse is quicker.
– Project manager: the project manager loses control of travel plans, as the plans are not circulated to him.
– Departmental secretary: The secretary's workload is reduced as VAT calculations and other parts requiring manual work are automated. The only major task left is to check the acceptability of the costs and the correctness of the project account.
– Head of department: The head of department has to make sure that both the paper version and the electronic version are identical and the costs there are acceptable and within budget. Partly the secretary already ensures this, but in practice those versions have to be approved at the same time. This, evidently, forces the head to do more work than before.
– Secretary in the central administration: As the costs are already checked several times, and most importantly manual calculations and entries to bookkeeping system are automated, the work of central administration secretaries has almost diminished.

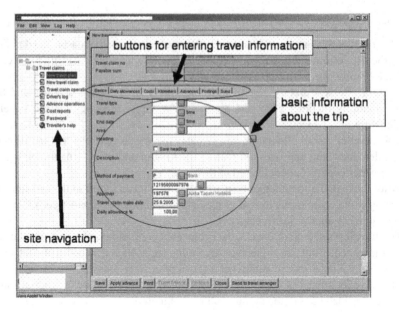

Fig. 12.2 User interface for a new travel plan

The user interface for creating new travel plans is illustrated in Fig. 12.2. The traveller enters information about the trip, its duration and description, and fills in appropriate types of costs (daily allowance, general costs (hotels, taxis, plane tickets, etc.) kilometre allowance), advance payments, and project accounts page by page. Entering data largely resembles former paper form. For travel claims, the user interface is the same with pre-entered information from the travel plan.

Similarly, the users who perform administrative activities on travel plans and claims – that is, the secretaries and the heads of department – use the Web-based system. Its user interface is illustrated in Fig. 12.3. There the person chooses the type of the status of the plan or the claim and makes appropriate activities (checking or correcting information, approving plans or claims). In other words, some of the former activities are automated and transferred to a Web-based system. Hence, the situation basically improves.

12.4 Findings

Although the introduction of a Web-based system aimed to improve the travel-claim management operations, there were several issues that the users did not confront. Partly this resistance can be explained with usual organisational resistance towards new systems (c.f. Orlikowski 1992b), partly because of improper system and its unsuccessful design and introduction. Next, these issues are dealt in details.

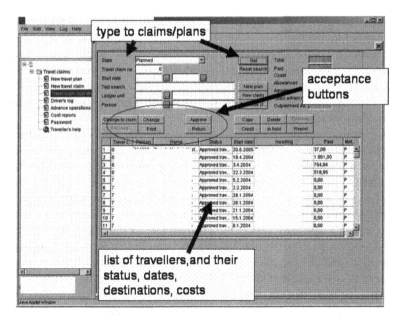

Fig. 12.3 User interface for managing travel claims and plans

12.4.1   Organisation Issues

The WfMS changed the work processes. However, although the changes reduced the work of secretaries and project managers, it also decreased the project managers' ability to keep an eye on their project budget. Thus some project managers developed their own sub-processes to preserve control. They insisted on signing the paper versions of the travel plans before passing them to the secretaries. The control was enabled by the essential use of both paper and electronic versions of the travel claim, as an electronic version did not support such a mechanism. However, the use of two versions is an interim solution before accepting only electronic signatures. Thus this solution is going to disappear.

The use of two different forms increased the work at the departmental level to some extent. Even though some activities were automated, the secretaries still had to make photocopies of the papers. And, even more encumbering, they had to check, at least briefly, both the paper and the electronic version of plans/claims to ensure their congruence. For the same reasons, the heads of departments became bound to their desks since otherwise it became impossible to keep track on approved/declined plans and claims.

Also the rights management created some confusion. The activity is centralised to central administration. Every now and then, when new employees are hired or there have been some changes with the administrative personnel (secretaries, head of departments), each department requests appropriate changes to the use rights of the WfMS. However, it may happen that a new employee has no rights to create a travel plan before the trip thus violating the travel regulations. Or, in case of plan/claim approvals, a person approving/handling them has no rights to do actions upon that plan/claim. Infrequent visitors and consultants, whose travel costs are to be paid by the organisation, are regarded similarly as regular employees. This obviously creates additional work when creating one-time-only users, increasing the number of users of the system rapidly.

Managing exceptional situations causes changes in the process. For instance, the travel plans/claims of a person working in a department but getting costs covered from two or more projects that have different remits, triggers departmental secretary to circulate the paper copy of the plan/claim to two different approvers. The WfMS does not support such trips or activities. Travellers working in multiple projects in multiple departments, have two (or more) system accounts. In a case of a combined business trip (one meeting for one project and another for the other), the WfMS does not allow the costs to be shared. Instead, the traveller is expected to make two separate plans and claims, and split the cost among the departments (e.g., ask one department to cover accommodation and the other to cover the flight tickets). Then both plans/claims are dealt as usual. The problem is that individual travellers necessarily have no idea about the budgets in different departments, nor secretaries have idea about the other plan/claim, nor heads of departments about the state of acceptance of the other plan. Coordinating the approval process of two plans/claims is an enormous extra work. Unfortunately these situations are not uncommon.

12.4.2   System Functionalities

The users log into the WfMS by using their employee number, which they use nowhere else. And, for multiple accounts, each account has unique id. For frequent users this creates no problems as it is just one more password (and user id) to remember, while infrequent travellers, or travellers with multiple accounts, face problems of forgetting and mixing up ids and passwords. The WfMS does not have a reminder feature, or automated method to receive the ids or passwords by email, but the super-user in the central administration need to be consulted.

The WfMS is designed for travellers and secretaries in the central administration. For them, all the necessary features (excluding keyboard shortcuts) are implemented, and, after a learning period (and learning the ambiguities), they are usable. Departmental secretaries and the heads of department need to use the system in an inefficient way. For example, there is no sorting feature implemented. Instead, the travellers are sorted alphabetically, thus, for instance when approving the plans, the secretaries and the head of department have to scroll back and forth the list of plans. All of them, no matter whether they are pending, approved, accepted, or waiting for activities, are listed there.

Another improperly implemented feature (from the departmental secretaries' point of view) is the calculation of the VAT. Although its calculation is automated, in certain cases an incorrect account-type, that cannot be changed, is used. Thus separate memos to correct the accounts, typically less than 1€, are circulated. An easy way round this would be to allow departmental secretaries to choose an appropriate account-type.

When a plan or claim is created or corrected, it is printed out for a signature. The print-feature utilises the built-in mechanisms of a Web-browser, and opens the form in a new browser window. For the users not using other Web-based applications this is obviously no problem, but for the others using (e.g., a Web-based email application or document management application) the print screen of a travel plan/claim appears on the same screen as the other application, replacing its former content. This forces them to log into the other system again after the printing.

12.4.3   User Interface

As said above, the WfMS does not support keyboard shortcuts. In other words, users have to use both the mouse and the keyboard to move between different fields and enter data. This is neither ergonomic nor efficient particularly for users accustomed with shortcuts.

The placement and naming of different input/output fields is not intuitive either. For the departmental secretaries and the heads of department, the mostly used buttons are grouped in the middle of the screen (see Fig. 12.3). This placement, with the choice of colourless buttons, makes it difficult to perform the activities smoothly. Similarly, the travellers have to move between upper menu bar, the input fields, and save/print-buttons at the lower menu bar. For instance, once a traveller has entered the daily allowance to an appropriate screen, she has to use mouse to save the screen (in the lower menu bar), switch the screen to general costs (upper menu bar), and select the line (in a new screen) where to enter the information (in the middle). All these movements are essential to ensure the information to be saved.

Default-values in the check boxes, drop-down menus and navigation bars provide values that are expected by the secretaries but are incorrect for other users. Even more irritating for the travellers is, in the words of a traveller, "the un-intuitiveness of the user interface". For example, to see a line for one cost (e.g., a hotel bill), one has to scroll it horizontally – the screen is too narrow – or to enter an explanation for a cost (e.g., sharing a hotel room with someone), one has to count the characters manually as the number of accepted characters in a line is limited to 40, the rest are just ignored, and in the case of longer explanations, to use mouse to add new lines as "enter"-button in the keyboard does not work.

This also points the difficulty to get a comprehensive view of the trip. A secretary, also travelling occasionally, had to use paper versions to get a complete picture of others trips: what costs are applied, whether there are any requests for advance payments etc. The multitude of windows, menus, and fields make it very difficult to understand what is actually happening. She said: "this is old-fashion. It resembles some applications from the 1980s with many windows that are created for fun."

12.5   Lessons Learned

The lessons learned can be classified into three categories: technological frames that can be identified and should be dealt with, techno-centric, socio-centric, and socio-technical requirements that should be met and balanced, and specific points with relating to the development and technology use.

From *technological frames* (Orlikowski and Gash 1994) perspective, the WfMS was created for secretaries in the central administration. The WfMS reflected the secretaries' interpretations of the perception of the nature, value, and use of the system. The system did not produce "*shared cognitive structures*" (Orlikowski and Gash 1994, p. 176) but remained as a perception of an individual user group. This resulted that the functionality and use of a system was clear to the technologists and secretaries, but less clear to other users. The WfMS automated secretaries work, but caused more or less extra work in different levels of the organisation.

From the Sarker and Lee's (2002) perspectives on WfMS and the redesign of business processes, the WfMS was techno-centric, emphasising the developers' idealism of technological determinism and separating "social"-component from "technical" as in socio-technical perspective. In this sense the case study presented the socio-technical perspective, missing its integrative approach. Socio-centric perspective was completely missing.

Two remaining issues concerning the role of the software developers and concerning the technology use can be identified.

The *role of software designers and developers* for WfMS is distinct from those developing other types of systems (Gallivan 2001). Whereas, traditionally they have been responsible for specifying, programming, and maintaining the systems (and not responsible for helping with problems related to software, hardware, and networks), the new role of designers and developers of software makes them responsible for solving business challenges, developing adequate concepts and systems, and maintaining systems as well as keeping business processes running. In our case the people selecting and adapting the system clearly did not have this latter broad perspective.

A final issue relates to the ongoing adaptation of the *technology* throughout its *use* (Bansler and Havn 2003). Since in most organisations the context of application of the WfMS is continually changing and since generally exceptions should be expected (cf. above), so-called technology-use mediation should in an ongoing process check if technology is still adequate and eventually adjust it. Unfortunately, this technology-use mediation was not done in the case reported.

12.6   Discussion

As the case demonstrates, the adaptation and introduction of a WfMS may result a failure in three interrelated levels: organisational issues, system functionalities and user interface. Improper consideration of the technological frames and the systems adaptation, different perspectives of WfMS and the roles of developers resulted that the system did not fully meet the needs and requirements of an organisation and its employees.

For example, the project managers' adaptation of the paper form signatures as an essential mechanism to maintain control will disappear when the electronic signatures are accepted. Yet, although the system already supports these checks, the users are not allowed to use them in the organisation. So, although technology provides new means for workflow management, the inflexibility of the organisational practices prevents its full exploitation. On the other hand, flexible and varying travel situation are supported in the organisational processes, but not considered when designing the WfMS. Most of these organisational and technical inflexibilities are due to an improper integration of socio-technical perspective in the system implementation causing the system fail at an organisational level.

Similarly, the choice of technological frames creates a failure on a system functional level. No one in the design team, apparently, has thought that other users apart from the secretaries may forget their passwords thus automated "if you forgot your password, email it"-feature is not implemented. Also, the miscalculations of VAT are not fixed. Users have complained about these issues at the departmental level, but as these issues are not problems for central administration, no progress has been taken. The parties just have different perspectives and conventions to the same issue (c.f. Mark 2002). This system functional level-failure is consequently also caused by a lack of representative user participation in the systems design stage.

The failure on a user interface level is due to biased technological perspective, where the technological advancement has been a dominant view. Simple, and often discussed issues in human-computer interaction literature (Dix et al. 2003; Nielsen 1994; Preece et al. 2002) are not considered in the WfMS design. For example, unnecessary mouse movements, illogical naming and placement of buttons, and overall un-intuitiveness could have been solved by traditional user interface design.

Mapping these failures to earlier listed criteria for organisations (Karsten 1999) and systems (Lin and Cornford 2000) provides another viewpoint. First, in the organisation-category the users' cooperation and understanding, and organisation's ability to adopt the system were improperly considered. Second, in the system-category requirements were incomplete on user-friendliness and cost effectiveness. In particular, in our case the use of two versions of the plans/claims, turned out to be cost-in-efficient. Everyone else's workload in the process was reduced, or it remained approximately the same, while the heads of departments have to do the evaluations of the necessity of the trip, and so forth, twice (on paper and on electronic version). Putting this addition of workload into the paycheck provides quite fascinating results: the heads are handling exactly the same number of plans/claims as are the secretaries, whose task was made easier by the introduction of a new system (see also Rogers 1996). So, despite the organisational culture facilitating the cooperation and the system to solve an existing problem, we argue the WfMS, as a whole, failed.

Fixing these sources of failures is not easy in every respect. The user interface level-failures are the easiest to fix, as they require "only" a user interface designer's and consultant's work. System functionality-level failures are slightly more difficult, as they require changes in the technological frames of several people and their influence on systems designers and developers. Organisational level issues are the most difficult since to repair them an organisation-wide business-process re-engineering is required. Socio-technical design needs to be done correctly.

Some issues of our lessons learned can be found in literature – still, we would like to point out that our case is important and relevant, as it clearly shows that in current projects several lessons from old cases have not been taken up. For a new system, one should not focus only on evident design issues such as user interface, basic functionalities, and organisational implementation and adaptation, but the system as a whole, meaning also its socio-technical component. Further layering of socio-technical, horizontal division (of organisation-category and systems-category) into vertical three-tier framework (user interface, functionalities, and organisational levels) gives an easily usable checklist. We argue that if one of these dimensions is missing, the system would ultimately fail.

Using the checklist is not only a responsibility of user interface designers. Instead, people working in any positions in the development process should cooperate to minimise resistances both on organisational level and individual level. However, to do that, a shift in designers' minds has to be made. Yet this is nowadays not common as illustrated by our case and the study by Hansen et al. (2008). So, systems developers, designers, consultants, HCI researchers and every other participant involved in the systems development and introduction should bridge the borders between their own reference discipline and other disciplines, no matter whether their backgrounds are on computer science, organisation studies, information systems, or UI design, or other. Developing good, usable systems that fulfil the needs of users and of their organizational departments, and the organizations at large necessitates efficient cooperation between different communities.

This requirement for cooperation is not a new. However, it is again evident that it does not happen in practice. It is thus feasible to ask why learning does not take place even though the issue has been known for years. We have no answers, just speculation: education is siloed to traditional disciplines and there is no proer; old dogs do not learn "new" tricks; there is a lack of resources; development is e.g. schedule driven (not in this case); etc. This urges for more studies.

12.7   Summary and Conclusions

In this paper we have presented a case of a WfMS supporting travel management in a higher education organisation: we described the system, the workflows before the introduction of the system, and the workflow when using the system. We have also provided some background with respect to workflows and WfMS and with respect to related organisational studies. Finally, we have identified some major lessons that can be learned from combining the findings of the study with previous experience from literature.

The paper answers two key questions: why a WfMS, that was anticipated and welcomed, created more complaints towards a new system than expected; and why it turned out to be regarded to as a failure in its users' eyes. As the case illustrates, there were failures on several levels.

- The user interface had its problems.
- Functionalities were poorly implemented.
- Organisational issues were largely ignored.

Some of these issues are easy to fix, while others require more work. Now, retrospectively speaking, requirements specification for the system should have been done better. There should have been people involved in the design process that understand the whole context and concept, not just a part of it. Thus, for research communities aiming at developing user-friendly systems, there are several issues to consider as directions for future research and practice:

- Addressing user interface issues and good design with respect to effectiveness, efficiency, and satisfaction – as in their widest possible interpretation.
- Going beyond the user interface (e.g. expanding the scope of the field) by also addressing organisational change and resistance, and what are the implications to, and caused by, the user interface.
- Introducing or changing WfMS typically entails changes for a multitude of actors, and thus requires their involvement from the very beginning of the requirements gathering through to the design and implementation of the system up to the introduction and adaptation of the system in the real setting.
- Neither variance theories nor process theories provide explanations for the phenomenon here. Variance theories approach WfMS by identifying different loci where technologies have an impact on. These loci are individual points, which, according to our case are intertwined and even integrated. Thus variance theories provide only a partial view. Similarly process theories face challenges with complex socio-technical environment (c.f. Kaplan and Seebeck 2001) for instance in terms of exceptions and exceptional usage situations. There is thus a need for integrative theories.
- To our surprise, we could not find a publication discussing the impact of a user interface to organisational resistance, or vice-verse, the impact of organisational issues to the user interface design. In this perspective, both HCI and IS disciplines are still limiting its view to user interface and psychological issues related to it – as pointed out by Grudin (2006) and Iivari and Iivari (forthcoming).

References

Abbott, A. A Primer on Sequence Methods. *Organisation Science* 1, 4 (1990). pp. 375–392.
Abbott, K.R. and Sarin, S.K. Experiences with Workflow Management: Issues for the Next Generation. *Proceedings of the Conference on Computer-Supported Cooperative Work – CSCW'94* (Oct. 22–26, Chapel Hill, NC). ACM, N.Y. (1994). pp. 113–120.

Abdel-Hamid, T.K. and Madnick, S.E. Lessons Learned from Modelling the Dynamics of Software Development. *Communications of the ACM* 32, 12 (Dec. 1989). pp. 1426–1455.

Agostini, A. and de Michelis, G. A Light Workflow Management System Using Simple Process Models. *Computer Supported Cooperative Work: The Journal of Collaborative Computing.* 9(3–4) (2000). pp. 335–363.

Bansler, J.P. and Havn, E. Technology-Use Mediation: Making Sense of Electronic Communication in an Organisational Context. *Proceedings of the International ACM SIGGROUP Conference on Supporting Group Work – Group 2003* (Nov. 9–12, Sanibel Island, FL). ACM, N.Y. (2003). pp. 135–143.

Bowers, J., Button, G. and Sharrock, W. Workflow from Within and Without: Technology and Cooperative Work on the Print Industry Shopfloor. *Proceedings of the European Conference on Computer-Supported Cooperative Work.* Kluwer, Stockholm, Sweden (1995).

Casati, F., Ceri, S., Paraboschi, S. and Pozzi, G. Specification and Implementation of Exceptions in Workflow Management Systems. *ACM Transactions on Database Systems* 24, 3 (Sept. 1999). pp. 405–451.

Conery, J.C., Catchen, J.M. and Lynch, M. Rule-Based Workflow Management for Bioinformatics. *International Journal on Very Large Data Bases* 14, 3 (Sept. 2005). pp. 318–329.

Crabtree, A., Nicols, D.M., O'Brien, J., Rouncefield, M. and Twidale, M.B. Ethnomethologically Informed Ethnography and Information System Design. *Journal of the American Society for Information Science* 51, 7 (May 2000). pp. 666–682.

Divitini, M. and Simone, C. Supporting Different Dimensions of Adaptability in Workflow Modeling, *Computer Supported Cooperative Work: The Journal of Collaborative Computing* 9(3–4) (2000). pp. 365–397.

Dix, A., Finlay, J., Abowd, G.D. and Beale, R. *Human-Computer Interaction.* Prentice-Hall, Englewood Cliffs, NJ (2003).

Dourish, P., Holmes, J., MacLean, A., Marqvardsen, P. and Zbyslaw, A. Freeflow: Mediating Between Representation and Action in Workflow Systems. *Proceedings of the 1996 ACM conference on Computer supported cooperative work.* Boston, Mass (1996). pp. 190–198.

Dourish, P. Process Descriptions as Organisational Accounting Devices: the Dual Use of Workflow Technologies, *Proceedings of the 2001 International ACM SIGGROUP Conference on Supporting Group Work,* Sept. 30–Oct. 3 (2001), Boulder, CO, pp. 52–60.

Gallivan, M.J. Organisational Adoption and Assimilation of Complex Technological Innovations: Development and Application of a New Framework. *ACM SIGMIS Database* 32, 3 (Summer 2001). pp. 51–85.

Grudin, J. Is HCI Homeless? In Search of Inter-Disciplinary Status. *ACM Interactions* 13, 1 (Jan./Feb. 2006). pp. 54–59.

Grudin, J. Computer-Supported Cooperative Work: History and Focus. *IEEE Computer* 27, 5 (May 1994). pp. 19–26.

Hansen, S., Berente, N. and Lyytinen, K. Emerging Principles for Requirements Processes in Organizational Contexts. *Networking and Information Systems* 13 (2008). pp. 9–35.

Iivari, J., Isomäki, H., and Pekkola, S. The User – The Great Unknown of Systems Development: Reasons, Forms, Challenges, Experiences and Intellectual Contributions of User Involvement. *Information Systems Journal* 20(2) (2010). pp. 109–117.

Iivari, J. and Iivari, N. Varieties of User-Centeredness: An Analysis of Four Systems Development Methods. *Information Systems Journal* forthcoming.

Isomäki, H. and Pekkola, S. Nuances of Human-Centredness in Information Systems Development. *Proceedings of 38th Hawaii International Conference of System Sciences (HICSS38)* Jan. 3–6, (2005) Big Island, HI.

Kaplan, S. and Seebeck, L. Harnessing Complexity in CSCW. *Proceedings of the 7th European Conference on Computer Supported Cooperative Work.* Bonn, Germany (2001). pp. 359–378.

Karsten, H. Collaboration and Collaborative Information Technologies: A Review of the Evidence. *ACM SIGMIS Database* 30, 2 (Spring 1999). pp. 44–65.

Kim, H.-W. and Pan, S.L. Towards a Process of Information Systems Implementation: The Case of Customer Relationship Management (CRM). *ACM SIGMIS Database* 37, 1 (Winter 2006). pp. 59–76.

Kreifelts, T., Hinrichs, E. and Woetzel, G. Sharing To-Do Lists with a Distributed Task Manager. In Proc. *Third European Conference on Computer-Supported Cooperative Work - ECSCW'93* (Sept. 13–17, Milan, Italy). Kluwer. pp. 31–46.

Lin, A. and Cornford, T. Framing Implementation Management. *Proceedings of the Twentyfirst International Conference on Information Systems – ICIS 2000* (Dec. 10–13, Brisbane, Australia) (2000). pp. 197–205.

Mangan, P. and Sadig, S. On Building Workflow Models for Flexible Processes. *Proceedings of the Thirteenth Australasian Database Conference – ADC 2002* (Jan. 28-Feb. 1, Melbourne, Australia). ACM, N.Y. (2002). pp. 103–109.

Mark, G. Conventions and Commitments in Distributed CSCW Groups. *Computer Supported Cooperative Work: The Journal of Collaborative Computing* 11(3–4) (2002). pp. 349–387.

Mentzas, G. and Halaris, C. Workflow on the Web: Integrating E-Commerce and Business Process Management. *International Journal of E-Business Strategy Management* 1, 2 (Nov./Dec. 1999). pp. 147–157.

Nielsen, J. *Usability Engineering*. Academic Press, London, UK (1994).

Orlikowski, W.J. The Duality of Technology: Rethinking the Concept of Technology in Organisations. *Organisation Science* 3, 3 (1992a). pp. 398–427.

Orlikowski, W.J. Learning from Notes: Organisational Issues in Groupware Implementation. *Proceedings of the Conference on Computer-Supported Cooperative Work – CSCW'92* (Oct. 31–Nov. 4, Toronto, Canada). ACM, N.Y. (1992b). pp. 362–369.

Orlikowski, W.J. and Gash, D.C. Technological Frames: Making Sense of Information Technology in Organisations. *ACM Transactions on Office Information Systems* 12, 2 (Apr. 1994). pp. 174–207.

Piderit, S.K. Rethinking Resistance and Recognising Ambivallcence: A Multidimensional View of Attitudes Towards an Oranisational Change. *Academy of Management Review* 25, 4 (Oct. 2000). pp. 783–794.

Preece, J., Rogers, Y. and Sharp, H. *Interaction Design: Beyond Human-Computer Interaction.* Wiley, NY (2002).

Prescott, M.B. and Conger, S.A. Information Technology Innovations: A Classification by IT Locus of Impact and Research Approach. *ACM SIGMIS Database* 26, 2–3 (May/Aug. 1995). pp. 20–41.

Robey, D. and Newman, M. Sequential Patterns in Information Systems Development: An Application of a Social Process Model. *ACM Transactions on Office Information Systems* 14, 1 (Jan. 1996). pp. 30–63.

Rogers, Y. Exploring Obstacles: Integrating CSCW in Evolving Organizations. T.W. Malone (ed.): *Proceedings of the Conference on Computer Supported Cooperative Work*, Chapel Hill, USA, October 22–26 (1996). pp. 67–77.

Saastamoinen, H.T. Exception-Based Approach for Information Systems Evaluation: The Method and its Benefits to Information Systems Management. *Electronic Journal of Information Systems Evaluation* 8 (1) (2005). pp. 51–60.

Saastamoinen, H.T. *Exception Handling in Information Systems*, Ph.D. Thesis, University of Jyväskylä Press (1995).

Sarker, S. and Lee, A.S. Using a Positivist Case Research Methodology to Test Three Competing Theories-in-Use of Business Process Redesign. *Journal of the Association for Information Systems* 2, 7 (Jan. 2002).

Schmidt, K. and Bannon, L. Taking CSCW Seriously: Supporting Articulation Work. *Computer Supported Cooperative Work: The Journal of Collaborative Computing* 1, 1 (June 1992). pp. 7–40.

Simone, C., Divitini, M. and Schmidt, K. A Notation for Malleable and Interoperable Coordination Mechanisms for CSCW Systems. *Proceedings of Conference on Organisatinoal Computing Systems – COOCS'95* (Aug. 13–16, Milpitas, CA). ACM (1995). pp. 44–54.

van der Aalst, W. and van Hee, K. *Workflow Management: Models, Methods, and Systems*. MIT Press, Cambridge, MA (2001).

WfMC. *The Workflow Management Coalition – The Workflow Reference Model. Workflow Management Coalition Specification*. Brussels, Belgium (1995). http://www.wfmc.org/standards/docs/tc003v11.pdf

Chapter 13
When and How Do We Become a "User"?

Katarina Lindblad-Gidlund

13.1 Introduction

This chapter will begin with a critical examination of the thought of participation and representation in relation to the user concept in information systems design (ISD) theory and practice. The argument being put forward is that the thought of a participating representative user is problematic from several points of view. Firstly, the idea of a 'user' automatically holds a power dimension since the users are identified by someone in the design process i.e. the user is not an active subject in the selection process. They are being categorized and defined by someone and consequently run the risk of becoming passive in the construction. Secondly, the user concept is closely coupled with a specific information technology development context. As such, certain interests are enclosed and others are left behind. In addition, the process of enclosure is largely in the hands of someone other than the user himself/herself. Finally, this implies that the power relation between the user and the someone referred to above, is not equally distributed; there exists different positions in relation to design processes that hold explanatory value to some of the complications we are facing in ISD practice.

The objective of this chapter is to examine closely the above by using Feenberg's (1999) dominant and subordinate subject positions. The suggestion is that our understanding of power relations in ISD will benefit from the usage of the concept 'dominant and subordinate actors' and the actors' respective awareness of embedded meanings in technology, and as such it will be a contribution both theoretically and practically to the ISD field. Moreover, since applying a power analysis into ISD often entails static and unconstructive conclusions, the framework of primary and secondary instrumentalization (Feenberg 1999) is introduced in order to address change and alternative futures in design processes.

Before delving into the concepts by Feenberg a short section on the notion of a participating user in the design of information systems will be presented. Followed

K. Lindblad-Gidlund (✉)
CITIZYS Research Group, Midsweden University, Sweden
e-mail: katarina.lindblad-gidlund@miun.se

H. Isomäki and S. Pekkola (eds.), *Reframing Humans in Information*
Systems Development, Computer Supported Cooperative Work 201,
DOI 10.1007/978-1-84996-347-3_13, © Springer-Verlag London Limited 2011

by two sections (Sections 13.4 and 13.5) where the main critique in relation to the user concept i.e. the complex process of identification, the contextual enclosure and the relation between positions, will be related to earlier research. Thereafter, in Section 13.5, the dominant and subordinate positions, diverse awareness of the meanings embedded in technology, and the framework of primary and secondary instrumentalization by Feenberg will be presented and related to the critique points. Finally, the chapter ends with a short summary and conclusion.

13.2   The Notion of a Participating User

A participating user has reached an almost indisputable position in the design of information systems, and it is often claimed that the involvement of appropriate and representative users is critical to the success of a system. (Already in Ives and Olson (1984) made a literature review touching upon user involvement and indicators of system success, and since then many others have followed; Kappelman and McLean 1991; Hartwick and Barki 1994; Iivari and Igbaria 1997, among others.) The quest of finding "the right user" to participate is built upon the anticipation that users will be able to provide insights about requirements that need to be addressed, which in turn will guarantee that the technology is suitable and becomes frequently used (Mackay et al. 2000). With the concept "the right user" Mackay touches upon an interesting distinction related to user participation; are everybody's insights equally welcome or are there preconceived ideas about what kind of user should be given opportunity to formulate requirements, and who decides who should be listened to?

First, numerous research efforts focus on identifying user characteristics (see for example Cotterman and Kumar 1989; Schneiderman 1998; Noyes and Baber 1999; Redish and Wixon 2003). These characteristics draw upon studies from different disciplines such as psychology, human-computer interaction and marketing and the result is often a plentiful list of variables such as age, gender, education, cultural or ethnic background, training, motivation, goals and physical abilities (Schneiderman 1998). There is also a plethora of typologies and categorizations referring to the 'user', for example Friedman's six-category typology of patrons, clients, design inter-actors, end-users, maintenance inter-actors, and secondary users that covers the traditional information systems development cycle (Friedman 1989). Connected to these typologies are assumptions about who the user is and how he or she will behave. The aim of producing these variables is to identify efficient categorizations in order to choose appropriate representatives to participate (or by other methods extract needs and expectations), which in turn is anticipated to bring a deeper understanding of the needs of the whole user group. Such a standpoint is, however, selective in nature and rests upon an understanding that it is necessary to choose between 'all users' to get a manageable (and representative) group of users that could participate in the development process.[1]

---

[1]There is however a discussion among feminist researchers from an ontological perspective whether it is possible at all to represent something/someone and in Science and Technology Studies (STS) regarding the possibility to represent a category (or even create a category) (see e.g. Barad 2003; van der Tuin 2008).

Second, several methods and methodologies are based on the notion of a participating user; user participation (Mumford 1983), prototyping (Floyd 1984), participatory design (PD) (Greenbaum and Kyng 1991 among others), computer supported cooperative work (CSCW) (Schmidt and Bannon 1992), usability engineering (Nielsen 1993), and user-centered design (Gulliksen et al. 2003). These are all different ways of involving the user in some way, and to some extent. Taken together they all share the assumption that it is crucial that the voices of the users-to-be are present in the design process. The reasons behind this might vary from democratic reasons, such as work place democracy or counteracting discrimination, to purely economic reasons (i.e. it is necessary to be able to develop a product that will meet a market), and it is notable that there are several differences between them concerning how this should be done and why.

In addition, most user-focused studies (see e.g. Bødker et al. 1988) concentrate on the organizational individual since from the beginning the research was aimed at designing technology for workplaces (see e.g. Iversen et al. 2004). Work practices and professional use was a natural focal point due to the fact that the computer had not yet reached the private sphere to the extent it has today (see e.g. Beck 2002). Some of the difficulties the notion of a participating user creates today, (as in relation to the design of public e-services for example), were not yet an issue and as such were not shown in the methods and methodologies (Beck 2002). Moreover, since many systems today are often developed for very large user populations, it is hard, not to say sometimes impossible, to involve all users or to find suitable user representatives, or even to create fictive users (Mackay et al. 2000; Rose and Blume 2003). To create a useful set of fictive users or a useful number of representative users, we will have to extract a very large number of heterogeneous characteristics from a very small number of generalized characteristics. Such an extraction, resting on what is considered as important characteristics in the specific situation, might run the risk of losing what really matters during the process because the information is mistakenly perceived as beyond the scope.

However, the notion of a participating user as such, is seldom questioned. One reason might be that by doing so you run the risk of being perceived as an old-fashioned elitist, claiming that the user knows too little about the technological potentials to know what he or she might actually need in the future. Another reason might be that balancing the designer and producer (and the responsibility following on these roles) with a representative and participative user, (and thus moving some of the responsibility to the users since they "have had their say") appears so useful in practice, that by problemizing it, a too difficult to handle complexity evolves. Several aspects come into play and we are still too short of answers.

13.3   The Creative Agency – Chosen by Someone

Leaving aside the reasons for not questioning the notion and focusing on a critical analysis however, will provide us with knowledge about complexities experienced in practice when trusting the notion too much. The belief that complications will be dealt with by involving users in the design process, is often met by harsh reality when users nevertheless both experience and complain about systems not meeting their needs and expectations when implemented. So, the question evolves, why is the idea of giving voice to users-to-be not enough, and are there hidden difficulties in the concept?

The concept of 'user" is by no means novel. In innovation and economic studies early understandings of users showed a strong agency coupled with the concept of user. Users were thought of as highly active in the innovation process (Von Hippel 1976; Lundvall 1985, 1988) and important actors in design choices. And it also appeared in consumerism analysis during the 1960s (Hudson 1990) through the necessity to show value for money in public expenditure (Thompson 1988). In sociology of technology Cowan (1987) presented the concept of 'consumption junction', focusing on "the place and the time at which the consumer makes choices between competing technologies" (Cowan 1987:263) which today might be related to a market logic resting on a relation between competition and best product for the consumer, but was initially developed as a social constructivist understanding. According to Cowan, the consumption junction is after all the interface where technological diffusion occurs (or not) and (referring to early network theory by Law and Callon) she wants to analyze the consumer in the centre of the network in which the consumer is embedded, and do the analyzes from the consumer's point of view. By examples such as the one about the cast iron stove, she wants to open up the 'black box' of diffusion (in doing so Cowan claims to take 'unintended consequence' into consideration). The ideas of Cowan are part of the so-called SCOT (social construction of technology) approach, focusing on technologies interpretative flexibility and the process of closure, giving the social actor dominance by the idea that users as a social group are central in the construction of a technology (Bijker et al. 1987; Bijker 1995).

Since then several different approaches have been associated with the concept of user in innovation and design processes, ranging from users as active agents to users as restricted by technological artifacts.

An example of the latter is Steve Woolgar's well-known chapter in A Sociology of monsters, Configuring the user (1991), where Woolgar highlights the relation between the design process and the idea of the user, by stating that in the process of designing, the designer(s) configure the user whilst trying to capture what should be designed. Throughout the process the designers (in a broad sense i.e. architects, hardware engineers, product engineers, project managers, salespersons, technical support, purchasing, finance and control, legal personnel etc.) are contributing to a definition of the user and at the same time those definitions become built into 'the designed'. It is a process of investigation and negotiation where these different participants construct the user, while making assumptions about the user i.e. they define, enable and constrain the user. And in turn define "the division of responsibility or agency between the user and the machine" (Van House 2005:67).

Madeleine Akrich (1992) introduced a related idea with the concept of 'inscribing' where innovators are thought to inscribe the vision or script (about the world and about the user) into the technical object. "In the development phase of a new technology, innovators define the preferences, motives, tastes, and competencies of potential users and inscribe these views into the technical design of the new product. The inscription of representations of users and use in artifacts results in technologies that contain a script: they attribute and delegate specific competencies, actions, and responsibilities to users and technological artifacts" (Akrich 1992:208). According to Akrich, representations of users become materialized into the design, but she also points at 'antiprogram' and 'subscriptions and de-inscriptions' that describe the reactions of human actors to what is prescribed and proscribed to them.

Both Woolgar and Akrich have since then been frequently referred to in studies following on the theme of restrictions constraining users in terms of configuring (Woolgar) or inscribing (Akrich) and a more nuanced view on the division between active agent and constrained user developed. An example of this is where Mackay et al. (2000) further elaborate Woolgar's notion of a configured user with four arguments that need to be dealt with in the quest of understanding development of technology: a symmetrical notion of decoding (by users) and encoding (by producers); that designers indeed configure users but designers are also configured by users and organization; that the boundary between user and designer as such is fluid; and finally, an extended actor-network approach to understand that what is designed is not designed in isolation but is constructed in or through broad networks. By and large, Mackay et al. certainly give a lot of credit to Woolgar's 'configuring of the user' but they claim to take the next step i.e. to turn the analytical efforts not only to the concept of user, but also to the designer and to the environment where the design process takes place.

By doing so Mackay et al. emphasize that "the power of the designer is far more circumscribed than suggested by Woolgar's work on 'configuration'..." (Mackay et al. 2000:741). Moreover, there are several studies analyzing the circumstances that encompass the relation between the designer and the user from several perspectives (see for example the Greenbaum and Kyng 1991 discussion about the fact that designers complain that they do not know what users want and users complain about systems not giving them what they want). By such an argumentation Mackay et al. also highlight the drawbacks of a too immature idea of user configuration (see also Lamb and Kling 2003; Millerand and Baker 2009); that runs the risk of defining the user as merely a passive recipient of technology. This has also been a core issue for feminist scholars such as Wajcman (2000, 2007) and Suchman (2002) (among others) pointing out that the line between representing and controlling users is thin and unclear. Suchman's critical analysis of the borders between the designer, the designed and the users in terms of "design from nowhere" (the idea of an objective, non-situated, master view) asks for a politics of professional design practice in terms of 'located accountabilities' (or in Haraway's terminology, situated knowledges, 1988) that will be returned to in the section of contextual enclosure. "It is precisely the fact that our vision of the world is a vision from somewhere – that is inextricably based in an embodied, and therefore partial, perspective – which makes us personally responsible for it." (Suchman 2002:96)

In 1999 the Society for Social Studies of Science (4S) Annual Meeting at San Diego arranged a session on co-constructing users and technologies where 17 different papers were presented that eventually became a collection of readings edited by Nelly Oudshoorn and Trevor Pinch (Oudshoorn and Pinch 2003). The field of interest in the collection is how users consume, modify, domesticate, design, reconfigure, and resist technologies and also how users are defined and by whom, and the aim is to present studies of co-construction of users and technologies that go beyond technological determinist views of technology and essentialist views of users' identities. The texts cover the SCOT approach (users as agents of technological change through technology's interpretative flexibility), feminist approaches (capturing the diversity of users and the power relations between users and other actors in technological development), semiotic approaches (about configurations and scripts, how representations of users become materialized into the design), and cultural and media studies (focusing on consumption and domestication).

Their firm intention is to make clear "how the co-construction of users and technologies may involve tensions, conflicts, and disparities in power and resources among the different actors involved" since they claim that "a neglect of differences among and between producers and users may result in a romantic voluntarism that celebrates the creative agency of users, leaving no room for any form of critical understanding of the social and cultural constraints on user-technology relations" (Oudshoorn and Pinch 2003:16).

To sum up, many of these interactions between social theory and design acknowledge the user as a "competent practitioner" (Greenbaum and Kyng 1991:15) but the image of a restrained user (configured, meeting inscriptions etc.) is also present. However, as Oudshoorn et al. concludes:

> ...we should be careful not to replace a technological determinist view by a romantic voluntarism which celebrates the agency of users (Oudshoorn et al. 2004:55).

In celebrating the agency of users and making them equivalent to designers, producers, hardware engineers, product engineers, project managers, salespersons, technical support, purchasing, finance and control, legal personnel (to use the list provided by Woolgar 1991) we run the risk of foreseeing what Woolgar and Akrich initiated and Oudshoorn and Pinch reopen. That is that the positions are not exclusively equal, there exist power relations and complexities in relation to the concept of a representative participating user that need to be addressed and analyzed in order to avoid the pitfall of 'romantic voluntarism' as Oudshoorn and Pinch put it.

So, to return to questioning the notion of a participating representative user; recognizing the tensions and the unequal power relations might hold explanatory value to the understanding of practical experiences of complicated design processes and systems not meeting needs and expectations. Acknowledging that the user (however active in the design process) is chosen by someone also directs attention to how these inequalities are distributed and formalized, which will be returned to in Section 13.5 with the help of Feenberg's dominant and subordinate positions.

13.4   Defining 'Good' Usage – A Contextual Enclosure

The second point of critique is the suppression of the boundaries given by the specific design situation. It is of course attractive to keep the image of a strong and creative user representative choosing from innumerable possible solutions and future scenarios. But, a critical analysis might provide answers to experiences gained in practice by both users and designers.

The contextual approach in information systems was first put forward by the 'socio-technical' researchers in the 1980s (Land and Hirschheim 1983), followed by elaborations on social aspects and consequences of information systems in organizations (Kling 1980; Lyytinen and Lehtinen 1984) and today studies on social effects of new technologies are widespread (Baskerville et al. 1994; Orlikowski et al. 1996). The duality of technology (Orlikowski 1992), social constructionism (Bijker and Law 1992) and actor network theory (Callon 1991; Latour 1991; Akrich 1992; Law and Callon 1992) have all contributed to the interactive perspective on technology and organization.

In the same way that the relation between designer and user today is often presented regarding agency, i.e. symmetrical (co-constructive), the relation between technology innovation and organizational change has come forward as mutually shaping each other (co-designed) (Orlikowski 1992; Walsham 1993). Several other studies have also acknowledged the fact that organizational change in its turn is surrounded by other layers of contextuality, drawing upon Pettigrew's contextualist analysis (Pettigrew 1986). By focusing on the "the event in its setting" the history of changes in an organization is seen as shaped by the organization's social, economic, and political context (see e.g. Avgerou 2001; Walsham 1993). ICT implementation is then analyzed as being shaped in interplay with social and cultural aspects of both the organizational and the broader national environment (Avgerou 2001).

According to Avgerou "innovation inside an organization is rarely a result of its 'free choice' and action: it is to a large extent determined by events, trends, pressures, opportunities, or restrictions in the international and national arena" (Avgerou 2001:10). Such an argumentation highlights the pressure imposed on the designer by the design context, which in turn, emphasizes that certain interests are looked after and others left behind (according to Avgerou also colored by a too technical and rationalistic approach).

A parallel discussion, using the notion of 'good or bad usage', is found in Rose and Blume regarding citizens, the state and technological use. Rose and Blume claim that resisting "the configuring, and disciplining, effects of this and other technologies may be to protest the social policies implicated by the technologies themselves" (Rose and Blume 2003:106). In this way "individuals not only become inappropriate users of technologies, they also fail in their civic responsibilities to use them, or to use them appropriately; that is they become "bad" citizens" if not using the by the state promoted technology (Rose and Blume 2003:109). Such an argumentation is easily transferred to other contexts and the analytical contribution is plentiful since it emphasizes the contextual constraints. Both the designer and the user are enclosed by contextual factors and as such become restricted actors and these restrictions are displayed in diverse ways.

Besides the above, the wider contextuality (from local to national and international), another set of constraints are also imposed on the "right" choice when searching participative users: the image of 'inside and outside' and exclusive knowledge held by the organization. In turn this affects the view on users and user participation since it is possible to claim that they (the users), are less knowledgeable and might not know what is best for them. Woolgar touches upon the issue in his study on usability trials: "...although it was important to have an idea of who 'the user' was and what they wanted in the machine, users' views should not be unproblematically adopted in design...the suggestion was that design should respond instead to ideas about 'where the market was going' or 'where things were going'...there was no point in asking users what they wanted because they themselves didn't know - since the company tends to have better access to the future than users, it is the company's view which defines users' future requirements" (Woolgar 1991:74–75). As mentioned briefly earlier, such an image is however problematic to pursue due to the connection with an elitist standpoint considering the user-designer relation. Even if problematic, it is however present in information systems projects in practice.

From another angle, Markussen (1994) problemizes statements about users as experts on their context of work and participatory designers as technical experts since such an image hides the fact that the designers preclude some solutions because they already have some other solutions in mind or because there are many (professional) interests involved that go beyond the specific work site. This implies, in the same way as Woolgar, that even though we might celebrate the notion of a participating user, other factors are involved.

The claim here is that information technology is not developed in a vacuum, it is always situated, and the context shapes and affects the boundaries around the design process, which in turn affects the notion of a representative and participating user. Social structures, culture, economy and institutional prerequisites, etc. impinge the design choices throughout the process. This gives several demarcations on what is perceived as essential. The user (and in turn the choice of representative users) is as such analyzed and taken into consideration in relation to these contextual factors, and participation and representation is related to the prerequisites. The goals of the specific design situation provide a major part of the topics that are perceived as necessary to be taken into consideration.

In a situation where an information system is developed to support efficiency regarding work processes in an organization, much sharpened, good usage is productive usage from somewhere i.e. the point of view of the specific organization. Non-productive usage is, on the other hand, bad usage, however creative and innovative it might be. Actions and usage not related to the goals of the work organization become less important and may even sometimes be considered as non-important when studies and evaluations are made about the productivity of the IS implementation. As such, 'good' or 'bad' usage is not self-evidently interpreted in the same way by the users, since the organizational goals and the users' motivational factors are not necessarily indistinguishable.

Returning to the earlier discussion of situated knowledge regarding design actions, highlighting the contextual factors helps avoid a negligence about the structures "above" (or inside) both the designer and the user. To imply symmetry between actors by excluding contextual constraints precludes analyses on power relations between individual positions, and power relations on a structural level between contexts (specific and abstract) (see e.g. Haraway 1988).

13.5   Who Makes Technology – The Definer and the Defined

As highlighted by Oudshoorn and Pinch, with "a romantic voluntarism celebrating the creative agency of users" (Oudshoorn and Pinch 2003:16) ISD theory and practice run the risk of disregarding the social and cultural constraints on design situations. Acknowledging the complexity of the notion of a participating user, the different attempts of identifying the 'user', and good or bad usage illuminates the contextual dependency. Not only between the 'user' and his or her definer but also between the designed (technical solution) and the overall objectives present in the specific design context. This gives that the relations between the defined and the definer surface. Who defines whom and what? And what are the consequences of different interpretations and definitions of the process of defining?

To begin with the user concept, Feenberg highlights that we, as actors in a design process, start out from different positions; dominant or subordinate (Feenberg 1999). By using "subject position" Feenberg argues for a terminology that points out the differences and injustices between our different relations towards, or with, technological development. Feenberg claims that we ascribe different meanings to technology according to our positions, subordinate or dominant. The producers (not only producers of technology but also producers of ideas about technological development), or technological masters, are the dominant actors both in the manner in which they view technology and how they act when encountering technology. According to Feenberg, their view of technology is based on a rational, instrumental and efficiency oriented system and, because of their professional competencies, they are able to form the technological spaces in this manner.

The subordinate actors, are at the opposite end of the spectrum to the dominant actors and they are also the ones who "encounter technology as a dimension of their life-world…and… merely carry out the plans of others or who inhabit technologically constructed spaces and environments. As subordinate actors, they strive to incorporate the technologies with which they are involved and adapt them to the meanings that illuminate their lives. Their relation to technology is thus far more complex than that of dominant actors." (Feenberg 1999: preface: x).

The separation between dominant and subordinate positions is highly rewarding for understanding our different relations with technology and the embedded meanings, even though Feenberg's coupling with different views of technology (instrumental/ incorporated, etc.) possibly should be regarded as stereotypical images and not exclusive ones. The main contribution is the understanding of our different possibilities of approaching technology, the level of detachment or not and the preferential right of interpretation depending on position.

In addition, the relation between dominant and subordinate positions and their awareness of the meanings embedded in technology is not one-dimensional, it also acts the other way around. Since subordinate actors have to adjust to and incorporate the technologies, they are also closer to the embedded meanings. They are the ones discovering them throughout the process of technology taking concrete form: "the manager may see the new machine as more efficient, but the worker condemned to using it notices that it also removes skills and initiative from the shop floor" as Feenberg puts it (Feenberg 1999:preface:xiii). As such, the meanings embedded in technology are more immediately available to subordinate than dominant actors.

To then separate between dominant and subordinate positions facilitates an analysis of who defines what and the different ways of defining (level of detachment and availability of embedded meanings). Dominant actors might hold the preferential right of interpretation but at the same time they lose contact with its concretization. Whereas, the subordinate actors have to adjust to what is given, whilst on the other hand, they are the ones giving it meaning in concrete situations. If dominant actors are the ones choosing the frames, subordinate actors are filling the frame with colors and shape. Therefore, the proposed passivity of 'the user defined by someone' is never absolute, even if he or she is identified by someone in a design process and so becomes a user in relation to the specific design situation. There exists an activity space inside the frames that acts back on the definer since the definer has a harder time reaching awareness of the meaning embedded in technology. The definer might produce the frames, but when it comes to how it is given meaning and actual usage, it is held in uncertainty.

The concept of 'dominant and subordinate positions' as such clarifies the process of identifying the user (when and how we become a user) without losing the power dimension or being too static. Change and alternative possibilities remain present even if acknowledging our different possibilities. It also gives attention to the unequal relation between the positions and provides possibilities to analyze.

In addition, Feenberg provides a second tool for understanding the relation between the designed (technical solution), the overall objectives present in the specific design context, and actual usage by introducing 'primary and secondary instrumentalization' (see Fig. 13.1). Primary instrumentalization involves four stages: decontextualization, reductionism, autonomization and positioning resting on a functional world relation. Secondary instrumentalization is about realization through the four stages: systematization, mediation, vocation and initiative.

Whereas primary instrumentalization provides a thin frame of basic technical relations, secondary instrumentalization is necessary for a technique to become integrated with the natural, technical, and social environments that support its functioning. "In this process, technical action turns back on itself and its actors as it is realized concretely" (Feenberg 1999:205). Through systematization, mediation, vocation and initiative secondary instrumentalization constitute a reflexive metatechnical practice, which treats functionality as "raw material for higher-level forms of technical action" (Feenberg 1999:206). As such, the technical always,

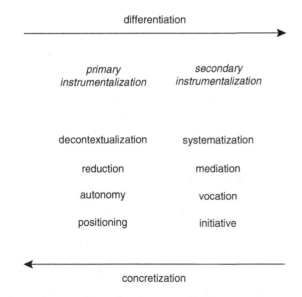

Fig. 13.1 Feenberg: primary and secondary instrumentalization

according to Feenberg, incorporates the social in its structure; "design internalizes social constraints, condensing technical and social relations" (Feenberg 1999:210). Moreover "secondary instrumentalizations, with sources in ideological visions, tradition, and democratic rationalization, continue to shape technical design" (Feenberg 1999:221). As such, technological future is by no means predetermined; there is a possibility of alternatives. As Feenberg puts it:

> A different type of social system that restored the role of secondary instrumentalizations would determine a different type of technical development in which these traditional technical values might be expressed in new ways (Feenberg 1999:223).

By secondary instrumentalization Feenberg recovers agency, without losing the power dimension. The social system is embedded in technology and as such reinforces and acts back on subordinate technological users, but at the same time it opens up alternative possibilities. As such, technology is constantly revised and advanced by incorporation of different values reflecting a broader range of interests.

By analytically distinguishing between different positions and meanings ascribed to technology, Feenberg provides a deeper understanding on both the power dimension and the contextual enclosure. Subject positions and meanings are related to both the configuring of the user and good and bad usage, and also offer a possibility to refine the analytical instruments. According to Feenberg there is "a single fundamental distinction among technical factors that enables us to link social to philosophical issues. This is the distinction between the dominant and the subordinate subject positions with respect to technological systems" (Feenberg 1999:x).

Resting on such an argumentation, what is attention grabbing is not the essence of technology but the meaning experienced by actors embodied in technological designs. "At any given stage in its development, a device will express a range of these meanings gathered not from 'technical rationality' but from past practices of its users" (Feenberg 1999:xii) (drawing upon Don Ihde's remark that "technology is only what it is in some use-context (Ihde 1990:128).

Moreover, the idea that awareness of the meanings embedded in technology is more directly available to subordinate than dominant actors is challenging. Subordinate actors are the ones trying to incorporate and adapt meaning of technology into their lifeworlds and as such they experience the meaning more explicitly. Technological masters, or dominant actors, are seldom faced with the same complexity, which also hinders them from getting closer to what is actually embedded. They definitely perform power by design actions but they might be less in contact with the intrinsic meanings inscribed in the design.

So, let us return to the two questions in the beginning of this section (i) who defines whom?, and (ii) who defines what? First, by using subject positions when analyzing a design situation we could better understand that the positions are not exclusively equal. Even if they are not fixed and static, there exists power imbalances in terms of positions and we need to acknowledge them in order to deal with them. These positions influence our relation with technology in certain ways and it is essential that we enhance our understanding of how. A subordinate actor is more inclined to be defined by a dominant actor since the dominant actor in different phases of the design process is the one with the position and objective to reduce and frame what should be accomplished or not. As such, the dominant actor defines both the overall goal of the design process and the users that should be a part of it. This means that the subordinate actors experience another relation with technology, being more inclined to search for how to appropriate it to the meanings that illuminate their lives (at work, at home or in public spaces, etc.). Accordingly, they experience the frames and what is defined (by someone i.e. the dominant actor) and become a 'user' in the process.

On the other hand, part of the defining also takes place when the subordinate actor adjusts to what is given, since the subordinate actor fills in the bits and pieces when trying to find the meaning embedded in the technological solutions. This is not primarily done by the dominant actor since the dominant position is 'above' and as such is more distant from the process of concretization. A certain amount of power is then lost for the dominant actor; how the design will be appropriated becomes partly out of reach. This part of the design process is when things happen that the dominant actor often experiences as inexplicable and unforeseen. What has been defined is adjusted by the ones chosen to participate, not primarily the definer.

13.6   Summary and Conclusions

Let us return to the initial argument about a power dimension in the construction of the user and a contextual enclosure of certain interests and not others. Feenberg's framework of 'dominant and subordinate subject positions' and 'primary and secondary instrumentalization' provides a possibility for deeper understanding about the logic behind technology design processes, without falling into one trap or the other (technological determinism or romantic voluntarism), but instead analyzing ISD processes through the distinction between the dominant and the subordinate subject positions. Such a distinction does not place subordinate actors without possibilities to intervene, but even so, dominant actors hold certain prerogatives that need to be acknowledged. They are the ones, using Akrich's terminology, who inscribe values and because of their professional competencies, are able to form the technological spaces in a, for them, suitable manner. And as such it is still significant to analyze what kind of values they convey.

Therefore, analyzing dominant actors in their context provides important insights. Analyzing their preconceived ideas about what they think they are supposed to design, and for whom, reveals important knowledge to understand what actually happens when the design will come into use. Dominant actors are "setting the scene"; they are the producers deciding on manuscript, scene, screenplay, actors etc. on different levels. As Oudshoorn et al. put it: "actors involved in the development of technologies need to articulate the subject identities of the future users. Users, in turn, need to articulate and perform identities that correspond with the identities anticipated by the innovators" (Oudshoorn et al. 2004:32). And, quoting Marc Berg: "why not embrace a substantive position, and, with that, embrace the newly found political actors for what they are" (Berg 1998: 480), but at the same time, not mislead oneself to believe that the analysis can stop there since the play is interpreted and translated and might take forms the producers never anticipated.

References

Akrich, M. (1992). The de-scription of technical objects. *Shaping Technology/Building Society*, ed. W. Bijker and J. Law. Cambridge, Massachusetts, MIT Press

Avgerou, C. (2001). The significance of context in information systems and organizational change. *Information Systems Journal*, Vol. 11, No. 1, pp. 43–63

Barad, K., (2003). Posthumanist performativity: toward an understanding of how matter comes to matter. *Signs: Journal of Women in Culture and Society*, Vol. 28, No. 3, pp. 801–831

Baskerville, R., Smithson, S., et al., Eds. (1994). *Transforming Organizations with Information Technology*. Amsterdam, North-Holland, Elsevier

Beck, E.E. (2002) P for political. *Scandinavian Journal of Information Systems*, Vol. 14, pp. 77–92

Berg, M. (1998). The Politics of Technology: On Bringing Social Theory into Technological Design. *Science, Technology, & Human Values*, Vol. 23, No. 4, Special Issue: Humans, Animals, and Machines (Autumn, 1998), pp. 456–490

Bijker, W.E., Hughes, T.P., & Pinch, T. (1987). *The Social Construction of Technological Systems*. Cambridge, Massachusets, MIT Press

Bijker, W.E., & Law, J., Eds. (1992). *Shaping Technology/Building Society*. Cambridge, Massachusetts, MIT Press

Bijker, W. E. (1995). *Of Bicycles, Bakelites and Bulbs: Toward a Theory of Sociotechnical Change*. Cambridge, Massachusetts, MIT Press

Bødker, S., Ehn, P., Knudsen, J., Kyng, M., & Madsen, K. (1988). Computer Support for Cooperative Design", *CSCW '88. Proceedings of the Conference on Computer-Supported Cooperative Work, September 26–28, 1988, Portland, Oregon*, ACM, New York, NY, 1988, pp. 377–394

Callon, M. (1991). Techno-economic Networks and Irreversibility. A Sociology of Monsters. *Essays on Power, Technology and Domination*, ed. J. Law. London, Routledge, pp. 132–161

Cotterman, W. W., & Kumar, K. (1989). User cube: a taxonomy of end users in management of computing. *Communications of the ACM*, Vol. 32, No. 11, pp. 1313–1320

Cowan, R. S., (1987). The Consumption Junction: A Proposal for Research Strategies in the Sociology of Technology. *The Social Construction of Technological Systems*, ed. W. Bijker et al. Cambridge, MA, MIT Press

Feenberg, A. (1999). *Questioning Technology*. London, Routledge

Floyd, C. (1984). A systematic look at prototyping. In: Budde, R., Kuhlenkamp, K., Matthiassen, L. and Züllighoven, L. (eds.) *Approaches to Prototyping: Proceedings of the Working Conference on Prototyping*. Berling, Springer-Verlag, pp. 1–18

Friedman, A. (1989). *Computer System Development: History, Organisation and Implementation*. Chichester, Hants, Wiley

Greenbaum, J., & Kyng, M. eds. (1991). *Design at Work. Cooperative Design of Computer Systems*. New Jersey, Lawrence Erlbaum Associates

Gulliksen, J., Göransson, B., Boivie, I., Blomkvist, S., Persson, J. and Cajander, Å. (2003). Key principles for user-centred system design. *Behaviour & Information Technology*, Vol. 22, No. 6, pp. 397–409

Haraway, D. (1988). Situated knowledges: the science question in feminism and the privilege of partial perspective. *Feminist Studies*, Vol. 14, No. 3, pp. 575–599

Hartwick, J., & Barki, H. (1994). Explaining the role of user participation in information system use. *Management Science*, Vol. 40, No. 4, pp. 440–465

Hudson, B. (1990). Free speech, not lip service. *Health Service Journal*, Vol. 21, pp. 918–919

Ihde, D. (1990). *Technology and the Lifeworld*. Bloomington and Indianapolis, Indiana University Press

Iivari, J., & Igbaria, M. (1997). Determinants of user participation: a Finnish survey. *Behaviour & Information Technology*, Vol. 16, No. 2, pp. 111–121

Iversen, O., Kanstrup, A., & Petersen, M. (2004). A visit to the 'new Utopia': revitalizing democracy, emancipation and quality in co-operative design". In: Proceedings of the Third Nordic Conference on Human-Computer interaction. NordiCHI '04, vol. 82. ACM Press, New York, NY, pp. 171–179

Ives, B., & Olson, M. H. (1984). User involvement and mis success: a review of research. *Management Science*, Vol. 30, No. 5, pp. 585–603

Kappelman, L. A., & McLean, E. R. (1991). The respective roles of user participation and user involvement in information system implementation success. *Proceedings, Twelfth International Conference on Information Systems*, New York, NY, pp. 339–349

Kling, R. (1980). Social analysis of computing: theoretical perspectives. *Recent Empirical Research in Computing Surveys*, Vol. 12, No. 1, pp. 61–110

Lamb, R., & Kling, R. (2003). Reconceptualizing users as social actors in information systems research. *MIS Quarterly*, Vol. 27, No. 2, pp. 197–235

Land, F., & Hirschheim, R. (1983). Participative systems design: rationale, tools, techniques, *Journal of Applied Systems Analysis*, 10, 91–107

Latour, B. (1991). Technology is society made durable. *A Sociology of Monsters. Essays on Power, Technology and Domination*, ed. J. Law. London. Routledge, pp. 132–161

Law, J. & Callon, M. (1992). The life and death of an aircraft: a network analysis of technical change. *Shaping Technology/Building Society*, eds. W. E. Bijer and J. Law. Cambridge, Massachusetts, MIT Press, pp. 21–52

Lundvall, B. (1985). *Product Innovation and User-Producer Interaction*. Aalborg University Press

Lundvall, B.-A°. (1988). Innovation as an interactive process: from user–producer interaction to the national system of innovation. In: Dosi, G. Freeman, C., Nelson, R., Silverberg, G., Soete, L. Ž. Eds., Technical Change and Economic Theory. Pinter, London, pp. 349–369

Lyytinen, K., & Lehtinen, E. (1984). On Information Modelling Through Illocutionary Logic. *Report of the Third Scandinavian Research Seminar on Information Modelling and Data Base Management*. H. Kangassalo. Tampere, University of Tampere, pp. 35–118

Mackay, H., Carne, C., Beynon-Davies, P., & Tudhope, D. (2000). Reconfiguring the user: using rapid application development. *Social Studies of Science*, Vol. 30, No. 5, pp. 737–757

Markussen, R. (1994). Dilemmas in cooperative design. *PDC'94: Proceedings of the Participatory Design Conference*, eds. R. Trigg, S. I. Anderson, and e. Dykstra-Erickson. Palo Alto, CA: Computer Professionals for Social Responsibility

Millerand, F., Baker, K. S. (2010). Who are the users? Who are the developers? Webs of users and developers in the development process of a technical standard. In Iivari, J., Isomäki, H., Pekkola, S., Eds., The user – the great unknown of systems development: reasons, forms, challenges, experiences and intellectual contributions of user involvement. Information Systems Journal. HYPERLINK "http://onlinelibrary.wiley.com/doi/10.1111/isj.2010.20.issue-2/issuetoc" Vol. 20, No. 2, pp. 137–161

Mumford, E. (1983). *Designing Human Systems for New Technology. The ETHICS Method*. Manchester Business School, Manchester

Nielsen, J. (1993). *Usability engineering*. Academic, Boston

Noyes, J., & Barber, C. (1999). *User-Centred Design of Systems*. London Springer

Orlikowski, W. (1992). The duality of technology: rethinking the concept of technology in organizations. *Organization Science*, Vol. 3, No. 3, pp. 398–427

Orlikowski, W., Walsham, G., et al. (eds.) (1996). Information Technology and Changes. *Organizational Work*. London, Chapman & Hall

Oudshoorn, N. & Pinch, T. (2003). *How Users Matter: The Co-construction of Users and Technology*, The MIT Press, Cambridge Massachusetts

Oudshoorn, N., Rommes, E., & Stienstra, M. (2004). Configuring the user as everybody: gender and design cultures. *Information and Communication Technologies in Science, Technology & Human Values*, Vol. 29, No. 1, pp. 30–63

Pettigrew, A., M. (1986) Contextualist research: a natural way to link theory and practice. *Research Methods in Information Systems*, ed. E. E. A. Mumford. Amsterdam, North-Holland

Redish, J., & Wixon, J. (2003). Task Analysis. *The Human-Computer Interaction Handbook: Fundamentals, Evolving Technologies, and Emerging Applications*, eds. J. A. Jacko and A. Sears. Mahwah, NJ, Lawrence Erbaum Associates, pp. 922–940

Rose, D. & Blume, S. (2003). Citizens as Users of Technology: An Exploratory Study of Vaccines and Vaccination. *How Users Matter, The co-construction of Users and Technology*, eds. N. Oudshoorn, & T. Pinch. New Baskerville, The MIT Press

Schneiderman, B. (1998). *Designing the User Interface Strategies for Effective Human-Computer Interaction*. Reading, MA, Addison-Wesley

Schmidt, K., & Bannon, L. (1992). Taking CSCW seriously: supporting articulation work. *Computer Supported Cooperative Work*, Vol 1, pp. 7–40

Suchman, L. (2002). Located accountabilities in technology production. *Scandinavian Journal of Information Systems*, Vol. 14, No. 2, pp. 91–105

Thompson, A. (1988). The practical implications of patient satisfaction research. *Health Services Management Research*, Vol. 1, pp. 112–119

van der Tuin, I. (2008). *Third Wave Materialism: New Feminist Epistemologies and the Generation of European Women's Studies*. Proefschrift Universiteit Utrecht

Van House, N., A. (2005). Science and technology studies and information studies. *Annual Review of Information Science & Technology*, Vol. 38, No. 1, pp. 1–86

Von Hippel, E. (1976). The dominant role of users in the scientific instrument innovation process. *Research Policy*, Vol. 5, pp. 212–239

Wajcman, J. (2000). Reflections on gender and technology studies: in what state is the art? *Social Studies of Science*, Vol. 30, No. 3, pp. 447–464

Wajcman, J. (2007). From women and technology to gendered technoscience. *Information, Communication & Society*, Vol. 10, pp. 287–298

Walsham, G. (1993). *Interpreting Information Systems in Organizations*. Chichester, Wiley

Woolgar, S. (1991). Configuring the user: the case of usability trials. *A Sociology of Monsters, Essays on power, technology and domination*. London and NY Routledge

Chapter 14
Use of Mobile IS: New Requirements for the IS Development Process

Bo Andersson and Stefan Henningsson

14.1 Introduction

A large corporate group in northern Europe within the heavy industry and haulage sector implemented a mobile service order system for their 280 service technicians in Sweden. Savings due to shorter lead-time from ordered service to sent invoice was one of the main reasons for developing and implementing the system. The desired benefits were achieved when the time from order to invoice was cut from 3 weeks to 3 days. The service technicians, however, deemed the system a failure owing to increased administration on their part from 20 to 90 min per day and lack of support for the service technician's vital information needs. Post-implementation evaluation showed that the production loss caused by the technicians spending more than an hour less per day actually performing service could have been avoided if the system had been adapted to how the technician performed service order administration in the field (Andersson 2008).

Similar stories in the business press and academic literature indicates that the example above is not an isolated anecdote but a typical example of how mobile information systems (IS) projects do not harness the potential due to failure in understanding the use situation (Allen and Wilson 2005; Blechar et al. 2005; Er and Kay 2005; Fussell and Benimoff 1995; Kay and Er 2005; Luff and Heath 1998; Marcus and Gasperini 2006; Norman and Allen 2005; Steinert and Teufel 2004, 2005). This is the motivation behind this chapter and its focal point in the concept of mobility and what characterizes mobile IS use from a developer's perspective. Much research has been done on mobile IS and mobility per se and some research issues have been raised (Dahlberg 2003; Jarvenpaa and Lang 2005; Kakihara and

B. Andersson (✉)
Department of Informatics, School of Economics and Management, Lund University, Sweden
e-mail: bo.andersson@ics.lu.se

S. Henningsson
Center for Applied ICT, Copenhagen Business School, Denmark
e-mail: sh.caict@cbs.dk

H. Isomäki and S. Pekkola (eds.), *Reframing Humans in Information Systems Development*, Computer Supported Cooperative Work 201, DOI 10.1007/978-1-84996-347-3_14, © Springer-Verlag London Limited 2011

Sørensen 2002; Kietzmann 2008; Kristoffersen and Ljungberg 1998; Lyytinen and Yoo 2002; Löfgren 2008; Perry et al. 2001; Weilenmann 2003), but the conceptualization of the term and what implication mobility has for the IS development process is still limited.

Different frameworks have been developed in order to describe or explain aspects of mobility and IS use in a mobile context. Zheng and Yuan's (2007) framework consisting of the entities *mobile workers, mobile context, mobile tasks* and *mobile technologies* describes differences between stationary and mobile context. Kakhira and Sörensen's (2002) discusses mobility and includes *temporal, spatial* and *contextual mobility* into mobility as a phenomena. Focusing on design Tarasewich (2003) suggests context to be divided into three categories: *activities, environment* and *participants*. These frameworks are important contributes to the field of mobile information systems, but the frameworks are not specifically developed and focused on the development of mobile applications.

The chapter is based on the proposition that mobile IS use has distinctive characteristics compared to traditional IS use. The more traditional mindset of desktop computing that can be considered as rampant in system development have limitations that can affect the development of information systems for the mobile user negatively (Fällman 2003). Our purpose is to develop a framework for capturing aspects of mobile IS use to be of importance during the analysis and design phases of mobile IS development. Consequently, pure technological aspects as platform proliferation, roaming, and handover are not dealt with. We are neither focusing differences in the IS content, i.e. potential distinction of what kind of IS applications are being used in traditional and mobile IS and by which purpose. We are interested in the use situation and its characteristics.

We ground our research on previous research on aspects on mobility and approaches to analyze mobile IS use in IS development. This is accounted for in the next. Based on the previous research we develop a tentative analytical framework for capturing the use aspects of mobile IS. We then test and validate the framework with a retrospective cases study of failed development of mobile IS to see if our suggested framework would had been able to capture the causes for failure. Finally, we draw conclusions on our research and discuss the generalisability of our findings.

14.2 Mobility and Mobile IS Use

Mobility and use of mobile computers or mobile devices are a large and versatile topic. What and whom are mobile? Mobility have a range of meanings, an application can be regarded as mobile in consideration that it is possible to move between different devices or platforms. Mobility can also be understood as "possible to carry" – meaning possible to run on mobile devices. Mobility can also be valid in respect of the user. The user is mobile and can use the same resource in different places at different nodes (Makimoto and Manners 1997; Weiser 1991). Another angle is the combination of a user and the device the user may use; i.e. a laptop at a desk being used for a task identical to the stationary metaphor. In this chapter mobile means that the user is mobile. He or she is outbound and works in different places using a handheld device to accomplish task due to information and data processing. We thus define mobility as a duality where both the user and the device are mobile.

14.2.1   Entities in Mobile IS Use

A considerable amount of work have been done on technological aspects of mobile IS; for example on processor capabilities (Clark 2002), migrating (Artsy et al. 1987; Artsy and Finkel 1989), battery capacity (Panigrahi et al. 2001), roaming (Minghui et al. 2004), positioning (Adusei et al. 2002) etc. Studies of technological limitations are relevant to mobile IS development since they define the boundary condition for mobile IS. In this chapter, however, the technological boundaries are regarded as somewhat fixed conditions that mobile IS development cannot alter but has to conform to. For mobile IS development such a feature as positioning is relevant if it exists and is accurate, how the positioning technically is managed is of minor concern.

Given the still formative vocabulary of mobile IS where most terms have different or ambiguous meanings any deeper discussion on the subject has to define what is meant by the key concepts addressed in the discussion. Our key concepts are the entities frequently employed in system development to depict the situation for which the system is developed for. Often used entities in system development is User, Application, Device (i.e. Platform), Operational System, Hardware and Connectivity (i.e. Network).

- The User can be a physical individual or another system. We regard only the physical individual as a user in this text.
- The Application is an application or a service, from our perspective there are no major difference between an application and a service. Regardless if it is a remote service that is called upon or a local application it is always some kind of software involved offering an interface to the user. The Application uses functions in the operational system to access hardware.
- The Device is dividable into the actual unit and the input and output devices. It can be a stationary computer, laptop or a handheld computer. The input devices can range from keyboard and pointers to microphones, touch screens, motion detectors etc. Due to the focus on handheld devices the limitations and features caused by the form factor is vital.
- The Operational System is the application platform performing request to and from application and hardware.
- Hardware is the built in electronic equipment in the computers.
- Within mobile computing the networking ability is of immense importance and as a consequence wireless connectivity an additional aspect that must be considered in greater extent than in wired computing.

Table 14.1 summarizes the entities and their importance within IS development.

Table 14.1 Entities of IS use

Entity	Description	Importance within IS development
User	A person using an application	Essential
Application (i.e. the software or service and its graphical interface)	The representation of the offered service or functionalities	Essential because the application in conjuncture with the Unit is the user experience of the mobile information system
Device (i.e. the physical interface)	The physical interface in form of keyboard, screen, touch screen and other I/O units	Essential, because it has features and constraints compared to a desktop environment
Operational system	The software that the application uses to access hardware	Are not of any concern in this text
Hardware	Components as processor, memory, battery etc.	Are conditions rather than aspects
Connectivity	Type of network technologies and properties	Essential

14.2.2 Additional Technologically Aspects of Mobile Computing

Apart from the general aspects that any kind of IS development has to consider, B'Far (2005) identifies seven additional aspect accentuated by mobility (Fig. 14.1). Active transactions identifies differences as in push and pull solutions where a system relies on actions from the user to initiate a process and is considered a passive system whereby a system that automatically starts a process is considered as an active system. Limited Device Capabilities concerns the restrictions caused by the small form factor of screen, keyboard etc. Wireless Connectivity regards unreliable networking conditions, when using a wired connection the quality of service are often known and high whereby in the case of wireless connectivity the quality of service is often not known and varying. Location awareness describes the mobile device possibility to know where it is at the present moment. Limited Power Supply concerns the reliance on battery to operate with demands on low power consumptions applications and strategies for applications to die gracefully when running out of power. Large Variety of platforms considers that there is not a homogenous platform environment; instead there exists an indefinite range of platforms and hardware combination affecting development of applications. Multimodal and Variant UIs describes the greater variety of input and output solutions compared to the desktop environment.

All dimensions in Fig. 14.1 are of interest to a developer, some of them are in fact restrictions and other are features of mobility and computerizing. In the following we elaborate the dimension that can be considered consist the features of mobile IS use: User, Application, Device or Connectivity.

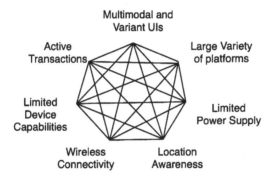

Fig. 14.1 B'Far (2005) identifies seven additional technological aspect accentuated by mobility

14.2.2.1   Conceptual Cleansing of Mobility

As said above, the label User in the continuance is a physical person with a role as a user of a computerized IS. Different user roles can be differentiated in the aspect of modalities. A person can be regarded as stationary when working at the desktop, but is still mobile in the sense of able to leave the desktop, travel and visit other sites. The point here is to what extent the user is mobile when using an IS. The ability of mobility ranges from non-mobile to completely mobile that is free of any physical limitations, such as buildings or geographical areas. In between there is a span different degrees of mobility.

To identify and categorize mobility is intricate if the context is not accounted for. A medical doctor (in a user role) may be stationary when using a desktop and mobile during ward round and using a PDA. If the doctor only can use the PDA on a specific ward or hospital she is not globally mobile, just locally mobile. The main argument is the typical use of IT within a certain role. We are not looking at persons but on roles. When writing of a person the role is the characteristic. The doctor in her office is one role and the doctor on round is another role. We argue that depending on type of role and its degree of mobility, different aspects have to be considered. Kristoffersen and Ljungberg (1998) coins the terms *travelling, visiting* and *wandering* in their reference model for mobile use of IT. Travelling is the transportation from place A to place B. It can range from car driving to airplane commuting. Visiting is spending time at a remote location for a period of time. It can be a visiting professor or a hired consultant working at another campus or at a costumer's office. Wandering is local mobility within a predefined area as a building. Exemplified with IT-support staff wandering around on a site helping users. From our perspective a key contribution by Kristoffersen and Ljungberg is that this is not different types of mobility, it is different modes that one and same user can appear in. But missing, or at least not obvious, in Kristoffersen's and Ljungberg's (1998) reference model is the *ranger* mode: a mode depicturing a user without any home base always on the move from place to place. An example is the field worker starting her work from home and visiting clients or sites to repair equipment. Therefore we replace

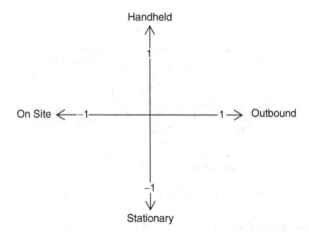

Fig. 14.2 Two dimensions of mobility: the users' mobility and the mobility of the device. 1,1 would depicture the "digital ranger" – an ever-outbound field worker using a handheld device meanwhile –1,–1 could depicture an office worker using a desktop computer. –1,1 could depicture support staff working in a specific building, i.e. wanderers. 1,–1 can depicture transport staff using vehicle mounted computers

the original model of Kristoffersen's and Ljungberg's (1998) with a model with two axels displaying the device ability to be mobile and the user's ability to be mobile in a certain use situation (Fig. 14.2).

Another known aspect of mobile IS use is *anywhere* and *anytime*. Anywhere describes the opportunity to access the IS from any place without restrictions to a certain location. Anytime describes the opportunity to access whenever the user needs a certain service or information. But this is not related to synchronous or asynchronous communication instead it is an aspect of omnipresence (B'Far 2005; El-Kiki and Lawrence 2008; Makimoto and Manners 1997; Perry et al. 2001).

14.2.2.2 Application

When accessing the IS the user's needs are of time-critical nature compared to stationary desktop computing. For example, a service technician's request for documentation on a certain machine just in time for the service. If the information is not accessible the service technician may be forced to wait until the information is available. This property is often labeled intermediacy or *immediacy* (B'far 2005; Frank 2006, Sacher and Loudon 2002). Considering the range of services available to the user the mobile IS is more often than the opposite the only IS available and as a consequence the user relies heavily on just that IS. File management, editing programs and other supplementing applications are seldom present in the same extent as in stationary computer use, making high *reliance on application* an important factor (B'far 2005). *Field use conditions* in form distortion as noise, different lightning conditions also come with mobile IS use because the variation of places is larger than compared to stationary desktop computing (B'far 2005; Lamming et al. 2000). Using different technologies the mobile device can calculate its position – it is context aware. The *context awareness* can be divided into region and place awareness (adapted from B'far 2005). The region concerns aspects as time zones, tax zones or legislations zones. Given a certain location some conditions are applicable. Place awareness describes the device ability to be aware of its actual position at a specific moment. The main difference between region and place is that region may be determined in advanced with some setting meanwhile place cannot be determined in advanced. But the application can easily store information of visited places and can communicate its position to other devices (B'far 2005; Froehlich et al. 2008; Marcus and Chen 2002). This will be categorised as *application/context*.

The technologically environment on an application for a handheld device is more varied compared to applications for stationary computers. Due to the vast range of operational system on handhelds and the vast range of hardware combinations, often labelled as *platform proliferation*. Different devices may interpret the same instructions in different ways making the development for cross platform applications cumbersome and error prone (B'far 2005). Even within the same manufacturer and product line differences may occur (Andersson and Hedman 2007). An application may be mobile in different dimensions. It can be used on mobile devices or that it can be moved along different devices. The user can access the functionality from different platforms and devices (Makimoto and Manners 1997). These aspects will be labelled *application/mobility*.

14.2.2.3   User

Another aspect of mobile IS use is *anywhere* and *anytime*. Anywhere describes the opportunity to access the IS without restrictions to a certain location. Anytime refers to access whenever the user needs a certain service or information. This is not related to synchronous or asynchronous communication instead it is an aspect of omnipresence (B'far 2005; El-Kiki and Lawrence 2008; Makimoto and Manners 1997; Perry et al. 2001; Zheng and Yuan 2007). The user may be in different *modes* of mobility; travelling, visiting, wandering or ranging (Kristoffersen and Ljungberg 1998; Marcus and Chen 2002). These aspects will be labelled *user/ mobility*.

When being mobile the user is often involved with other tasks than just using a computer. The mobile user can be considered as being *off-task* compared to a stationary user meaning that the main occupation is off the computer (B'far 2005; Frank 2006; Tarasewich et al. 2002; Zheng and Yuan 2007). And as the mobile user works in different places on the field the *lack of supporting technologies* such as photocopiers and faxes is a circumstance to consider (Perry et al. 2001). The user may also be *outbound* in the sense of a solitary mode with less opportunities to interact with colleagues (Orr 1996) These aspects will be labeled *user/context*.

14.2.2.4 Device

Device limitations as in limited processing capacity, limited memory capacity and limited power supply seems to be the most discussed topic within mobile computing and handheld devices. *Limited processing capacity* affects the calculating capacity making a calculating application slow or even impossible to run on a handheld device. The main reason is said to be the miniaturisation of the processor. Processes easily run on stationary computers are not certain to run smoothly on handheld devices forcing the developer to reduce the processor load. *Limited memory* capacity affects the possibilities to build applications requiring large amount of memory. Expansion memory may handle some storage problems but this type of memory is seldom suitable for running applications. *Limited power supply* is a crucial aspect though the intended use is without a wired power supply (B'far 2005).

The vast range of input and output variants or multimode compared to desktop or laptop affects how to build an application. At the desktop the keyboard, mouse and screen is used for interaction between the user and the application. The traditional mouse is often missing on mobile devices. Different models may have *different user interfaces* making the development more cumbersome compared to develop for one or fewer user interfaces. If existing, the keyboard is smaller and with few keys and the screen is considerably smaller due to the *small form factor* making input more cumbersome. The screen size restricts the amount of running applications, too many applications quickly clutters the screen making navigation cumbersome (B'far 2005; Böcker et al. 2006; Frank 2006; Holmquist 2007; Marcus and Chen 2002; Prammanee et al. 2006). These aspects will be labeled *device/attributes*.

As a consequence of the handhelds small form factor and intended use they are carried along in varying use situations. This making it *easy to loose* the device or that it becomes stolen. If critical information is reached trough the device or if the handheld device with its IS is vital this is a considerable security risk (Ravi et al. 2002). These aspects will be labeled *device/security*.

14.2.2.5 Connectivity

The quality of service regarding the wireless network is a crucial aspect of mobile computing. Type of connection (i.e. protocol), transmission rate and reliability is components of connectivity. A wired connection on a known location makes the quality of service stable. External aspects such as skip zones, solar flares, road tunnels, and large buildings make wireless connections *unpredictable and varying*. Wireless networks also rise concern of security in form of intrusion or distortion of information (Ravi et al. 2002). If the wireless network is preset it is easier to take security measures compared to the mobile users using different networks or providers making the transmission more vulnerable for *intrusion and distortion* (Ghosh and Swaminatha 2001; PTS 2006). These aspects will be categorised as *application/ connection*.

14.2.3   A Framework for Capturing Aspects of Mobile IS Use

Summoning the different aspects accentuated by mobility the AUCD-map is depictured in Fig. 14.3. AUDC stands for *Application, User, Device,* and *Connection.* This map may guide the developer in design considerations as what pattern or design proposal to elaborate further. We therefore suggest that it may be used as a framework for capturing aspects of mobile IS use to be used during the analysis and design phases of mobile IS development. All aspects are not likely to be mastered but the main point is to visualize the design space so the designer may do well argued design.

Some of the aspects in Fig. 14.3 are wicked or paradox problems (cf. Rittel and Webber 1973). When dealing with one aspect another aspect is negatively affected. For example, a strategy for dealing with unreliable connectivity is to develop on-deck applications. This strategy is restricted by the low processing capacity. Another dilemma due to the small form factor and its property to be carried along all the time is the increased risk of theft or accidental loss of the device if containing confidential information can be managed by setting password, encryption, automatically

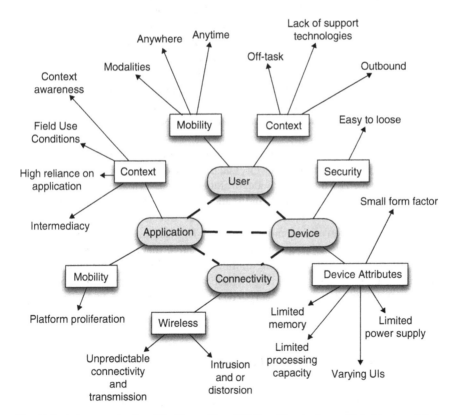

Fig. 14.3 A framework of mobile IS use. The AUDC entities depicture vital objects and their attributes that are accentuated compared to stationary computing

log-off procedures, but these strategies affect the off-task and intermediacy properties negatively. To use general strategies originating from desktop and wired computing is less successful. Another set of design principles is required.

14.3 Methodology

The research approach behind this chapter is mainly conceptual, integrating previous research into the AUDC framework. We then use a retrospective case study to
illustrate the usefulness of the framework.

14.3.1 Contribution and Research Approach

The theoretical contribution we want to make in this paper can be labeled as theory
for analyzing (Gregor 2006). Our outset, as described in the introduction, was to
develop a framework useful for identifying and describing aspects of mobile IS use.
The value of our contribution thus lay in that using it, important aspects currently
not considered in development of mobile IS can be identified. This is the overall
criteria for assessment of our contribution. Drawing on Gregor (2006), we conclude
that the usefulness of this type of theory may be refined to be evaluated by its completeness, distinctiveness, and simplicity. Completeness means that important categories
or elements should not be omitted from the classification system, that is, the framework should be able to capture all important resources. Distinctiveness means that
boundaries between categories and characteristics that define each category are
clear. The empirical phenomena encountered should be possible to categorize
according to these criteria without too much difficulty (Gregor 2006). Simplicity
refers to that which by making a model or framework too elaborated or comprehensive, it makes it hard to work with and in the end makes it useless for its purpose.

Our contribution in the form of a framework for aspects of mobile IS use clearly
has an implicit normative element. The distance from arguing that some aspects are
relevant in order to describe mobile IS use to arguing that these aspects should be
taken into account when developing mobile IS is not far. Our contribution is thus
implicitly leaning towards what Gregor (2006) refers to as theory for action, closely
related to the concept of design theory – design theory says "how to do something"
Gregor (2006).

14.3.2 Empirical Data Gathering

Developing theory for analyzing we are interested in whether our framework
enlightens aspects of mobile IS use that are currently not considered in the development process. Two approaches are possible in order to verify the degree to which

the framework meets this ambition. One way would be to study the development process and document all aspects considered during the process. A second, less resource demanding option was chosen. By investigating failed, or at least problematic, cases of mobile IS use we might investigate (a) if the aspects identified by our framework are taken care of, and (b) if doing so would have avoided to encountered problems. This way we will not be able tell whether or not the mobile IS under investigation would have function well using our framework but we will be able to tell whether or not our framework can help in avoiding some existing shortcomings. We thus use the retrospective case study approach to verify our framework.

The methods used to collect empirical data were a blend of several instruments, as suggested by Yin (2003) when carrying out case studies. Document studies, demonstrations of the system, system studies and interviews with users and back office staff was used to gather data. Over 250 pages of printed material in form of manuals, handbooks and teaching material available to the users were read and analyzed in order to establish a view of the structural features of the technology. Interviews were carried out with four users, one foreman (work dispatcher) and one clerk who handled the administration of service orders.

The data were analyzed by categorizing the information according to in which extent the different aspects in the AUDC framework. An elaborated description of the case is presented in Andersson (2008). The rich data collection enabled a retrospective application of our framework for mobile IS use.

14.3.3   The Object of Study

The case in this chapter is the order system presented in the introduction of the chapter. It is crucial that the company is kept anonymous in this study in accordance with the agreements made with the firm's executives.

The organization and system was chosen as an extreme case of mobile IS use. The users were a set of digital rangers, completely detached from their home base and always operating on the field. Another reason for selection was that the users' main occupation during work time was not to do administration or informational tasks; they were off task considering computer use.

The company is a Swedish subsidiary to a large conglomerate within the heavy industry and haulage sector. The company implemented a mobile service order system for the company's 280 service technicians (henceforth STs) in Sweden. Savings due to shorter lead-time from ordered service to sent invoice was one of the main reasons for developing and implementing the system. The desired benefits were achieved when the time from order to invoice was cut from 3 weeks to 3 days making the system a success from a managerial perspective. The STs, however, deemed the system a failure owing to increased administration on their part from 20 to 90 min per day and lack of support for the ST's vital information needs. An ST is the company's ambulatory repairmen who operate from the company's service trucks (each contains a small workshop and spare parts). Post-implementation

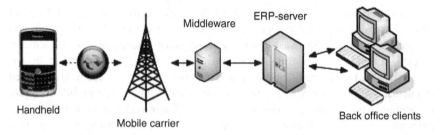

Fig. 14.4 IT architecture in the case

evaluation showed that the production loss caused by the technicians spending more than an hour less per day actually performing service could have been avoided if the system had been adapted to how the technician performed service order administration in the field.

The ordinary workflow for the ST is as follows; on a regular day, the ST leaves his (the ST is more often than not male) home, travels directly to the client's facility and starts working on the servicing of the client's machinery. After completing a day's work, the ST drives directly home. Ordering of spare parts is done by the IS and the postal service or a transportation firm delivers the spare parts. The ST most often operates by them self without any direct interaction with other STs or the dispatchers at the back office facility.

The mobile application used by the STs was built to run on the OS Windows Mobile 6 and deployed on a handheld devices designed for rough conditions. A touch sensitive screen with a stylus was used for input. The main functionality was to pick up service orders dispatched by customer service desk. The customer service desk personnel registered all orders in the company ERP system and a middleware developed by an IT-consultant company distributed the orders to the technicians using the built in Windows Sync function. To receive a service order the technician had to synchronize their handheld device with the ERP. The network used was the GSM-network offered by Vodafone. When a service order was finished the technician opened up the order and filled in time spent, mileage, spare parts, and other order details. The system also offered on-screen blue prints on machinery to help the technicians identify the correct spare part (Fig. 14.4).

14.4 Framework Application

We will validate the use of our framework by applying it on the above introduced case of mobile IS development. The presented case seems at a glance as a rather straightforward information-processing task. However, after the implementation the technicians suffered increased administration on their part from 20–90 min per day and lack of support for the service technician's vital information needs. How could the time spent on administration increase as much as it did? Several contributing reasons were identified. The use of Windows Sync caused major problem. Windows Sync apparently relies heavily on a stabile connection to function properly. The unpredictable transmission regarding connectivity was not considered appropriate. As a consequence the technicians were forced to keep double records, one on the handheld and one on paper. If or when the sync malfunctioned the customer service desks staff had to call the technician to correct the service order manually in the ERP. If the aspect of connectivity had been addressed most likely another synchronization technique had been chosen. For example state monitoring and a simple transaction engine had avoided these problems.

Complaints on tedious input was made and the reason was that the service technician often bought consumables in any nearby store, may it be electrical cable, oil, bulbs and other items not in the service truck spar part repository. These items was not on the spare part list in the applications database therefore a verbose round trip in the application was required consuming time and temper on the technicians behalf. The aspect of high reliance on application was not properly managed, an email function or an more flexible service order form had managed these problems by allowing other than registered spare parts to be included into the service order. The aspect of high reliance on application is further elaborated in Andersson and Carlsson (2009) where they depart from the AUDC framework and propose a design of flexible forms.

14.5   Framework Evaluation

As argued in the methodological section, the framework's raison d'être should be evaluated through the general criteria that identification of important aspects currently not considered in development of mobile IS should be possible. In more specific terms, evaluation should be effectuated along three lines of completeness, distinctiveness, and simplicity.

Completeness in this case would mean that no important aspects were missed by the classification categories in the framework. Regarding the case presented above, the problems discovered during the study were all covered by the framework and no immediate extension is required. However, as discussed in the methodological section it lays not within this study to verify that all problems could be solved by taking into account our identified aspects. We can say by applying the framework as above that some of the roots that later caused problems would have been identified by our framework.

Distinctiveness, referring to the ease with which elements (aspects) could be classified into the proposed categories, was not perceived by the authors as problematic. However, it should be noted that the authors are the formulators of the categories and have an extensive understanding of the theoretical concepts included. As discussed in the methodology section, IS developers are potential users of knowledge in the area of this study. But it is vital to recognise that IS developers would not be able to use the framework in its current shape as a set of design patterns. The categories would require elaborated explanation and suggestions how to solve restrictions. The main contribution is to expand the design space and introduce important aspects to the developers and be an analytical tool instead of a recipe on how to.

Finally, to maintain the simplicity of the framework, we choose to revolve the aspect round the four entities Application, User, Device, and Connection. In the application of the framework above naturally not all aspects are present. A single case study of this kind will not reveal if some categories do not exist in practice.

14.6 Conclusions and Lessons Learned

In this chapter we have introduced a framework for capturing aspects of mobile IS use to be of importance during the analysis and design phases of mobile IS development framework. Using the framework we identified and described which aspects of mobile IS use a failed development project had ignored. Considering these aspects during the analysis phase of the project would have made possible to avoid the encountered problems. It is outside the scope of this paper to verify if these were the only shortcomings of the investigated IS, or if taking these aspects into account the IS would still not be appropriately adjusted to the situation in which it is supposed to be used.

Evaluating the suggested framework along the lines of completeness, distinctiveness, and simplicity revealed that the framework needs to be further tested in different academic and business trials. Further validation is needed along all three lines. The natural extension of our research is through the principles of design science. Our framework consists an appropriate kernel theory to develop an analytical tool to be used in the analysis phase of mobile IS development. Reworking the framework to an actionable design theory would enable testing to reveal the framework's completeness. The rework process would require that information was given to practitioners on how to interpret the entities and associated aspects. The enabled real world testing should also reveal how the framework corresponds to the criteria of simplicity.

The most important lesson to learn from this paper is the acknowledgment that developing IS for mobile use will introduce an additional set of aspects that has to be considered during the design of the system. Following traditional development methods and practice based on experiences with traditional desktop computing will ignore these additional.

With this chapter we have provided a starting point for including the specific aspects of mobile IS use. Few doubts remains that as computer based IS no longer are limited to fixed, stationary settings they way IS are developed meets new challenges. These challenges are likely to be evolving as technology and application areas for IS evolves. It is therefore also likely that a framework such as the one suggested in this chapter never will assume a fixed and stable form that perfectly match the needs of the IS developers. The outset of capturing aspects of mobile IS use is the haunt for a moving target.

References

Adusei, I. K., Kyamakya, K. & Jobmann, K. (2002). Mobile positioning technologies in cellular networks: an evaluation of their performance metrics. *MILCOM 2002. Proceedings,* 2, 1239–1244.

Allen, D. & Wilson, T. D. (2005). Action, interaction and the role of ambiguity in the introduction of mobile information systems in a UK police force. *Mobile Information Systems-Bk,* 158, 15–36.

Andersson, B. (2008). About Appropriation of Mobile Applications – The Applicability of Structural Features and Spirit. *European Conference on Information Systems.* Galway.

Andersson, B. & Carlsson, S. A. (2009). Designing for Digital Nomads: Managing the High Reliance on Single Application. *Global Mobility Roundtable.* Cairo.

Andersson, B. & Hedman, J. (2007). Developing m-Services; lesson learned from a developers Perspective. *Communications of the Association for Information Systems,* 20.

Artsy, Y., Chang, H. Y. & Finkel, R. (1987). Interprocess Communication in Charlotte. *IEEE Software,* 4, 22–28.

Artsy, Y. & Finkel, R. (1989). Designing a Process Migration Facility - the Charlotte Experience. *Computer,* 22, 47–56.

B'far, R. (2005). *Mobile computing principles: designing and developing mobile applications with UML and XML,* New York, Cambridge University Press.

Blechar, J., Constantiou, I. & Damsgaard, J. (2005). The role of marketing in the adoption of new mobile services: Is it worth the investment? *ICMB 2005: International Conference on Mobile Business,* pp 370–376

Böcker, M., Von Niman, B. & Larsson, K. I. (2006). Increasing text-entry usability in mobile devices for languages used in Europe *Interactions,* 13, 30–35.

Clark, D. (2002). Mobile processors begin to grow up. *Computer,* 35, 22–25.

Dahlberg, P. (2003). Local mobility. Gothenburg studies in informatics Report, 27 Göteborg University. Sweden. Doctoral dissertation.

El-Kiki, T. & Lawrence, E. (2008). Mobile user needs: Efficient transactions. *Proceedings of the Fifth International Conference on Information Technology: New Generations,* 975–981.

Er, M. & Kay, R. (2005) Mobile technology adoption for mobile information systems: An activity theory perspective. *ICMB 2005: International Conference on Mobile Business,* pp 322–325.

Frank, B. (2006) Driving devices: lessons learned in the business of designing mobile UIs. *Interactions,* 13, 14–15.

Froehlich, P., Baillie, L. & Simon, R. (2008). Realizing the Vision of Mobile Spatial Interaction *Interactions,* 15.

Fussell, S. & Benimoff, N. (1995). Social and Cognitive processes in interpersonal communication: implications for advanced telecommunications technologies. *Human Factors,* 37, 228.

Fällman, D. (2003). In Romance with the Materials of Mobile Interaction : A Phenomenological Approach to the Design of Mobile Information Technology.

Ghosh, A. & Swaminatha, T. (2001). Software security and privacy risks in mobile e-commerce. *Association for Computing Machinery. Communications of the ACM,* 44, 51–57.

Gregor, S. (2006). The Nature of Theory in Information Systems. *Mis Quarterly,* 3, 611–642.

Holmquist, L.-E. (2007). Mobile 2.0. *Interactions,* 14, 46–46.

Jarvenpaa, S. & Lang, K. (2005). Managing the paradoxes of mobile technology. *Information Systems Management,* 22, 7–23.

Kakihara, M. & Sørensen, C. (2002). Mobility: An Extended Perspective. *35th Annual Hawaii International Conference on System Sciences (HICSS'02).*

Kay, R. & Er, M. (2005). Autopoiesis & mobile technology adoption: The case of wireless collaboration. *Mobile Information Systems-Bk,* 158, 303–310.

Kietzmann, J. (2008). Interactive innovation of technology for mobile work. *European Journal of Information Systems,* 17, 305–320.

Kristoffersen & Ljungberg (1998). Representing Modalities in Mobile Computing – A Model of IT use in Mobile Settings. *Proceedings of Interactive Applications of Mobile Computing.* Rostock.

Lamming, M., Eldridge, M., Flynn, M., Jones, C. & Pendlebury, D. (2000). Satchel: providing access to any document, any time, anywhere. *ACM Trans. Comput.-Hum. Interact.,* 7, 322–352.

Luff, P. & Heath, C. (1998). Mobility in collaboration. *Proceedings of the 1998 ACM conference on Computer supported cooperative work.* Seattle, Washington, DC, ACM.

Lyytinen, K. & Yoo, Y. (2002). Research commentary: The next wave of Nomadic computing. *Information Systems Research,* 13, 377–388.

Löfgren, A. (2008). *Making Mobile Meaning- expectations and experiences of mobile computing usefulness in construction site management practice.* KTH Industrial Engineering and Management.

Makimoto, T. & Manners, D. (1997). *Digital nomad,* Chichester, Wiley.

Marcus, A. & Chen, E. (2002). Designing the PDA of the future. *Interactions,* 9, 35–44.

Marcus, A. & Gasperini, J. (2006). Almost dead on arrival: a case study of non-user-centered design for a police emergency-response system. *Interactions,* 13, 12–18.

Minghui, S., Xuemin, S. & Mark, J. W. (2004). IEEE 802.11 roaming and authentication in wireless LAN/cellular mobile networks. *Wireless Communications, IEEE,* 11, 66–75.

Norman, A. & Allen, D. (2005). Deployment and use of mobile information systems. *Mobile Information Systems II,* 191, 63–78.

Orr, J. E. (1996). *Talking about machines : an ethnography of a modern job,* Ithaca, NY, ILR Press.

Panigrahi, T. D., Panigrahi, D., Chiasserini, C., Dey, S., Rao, R., Raghunathan, A. & Lahiri, K. (2001). Battery life estimation of mobile embedded systems. *VLSI Design, 2001. Fourteenth International Conference on,* pp 57–63.

Perry, M., O'hara, K., Sellen, A., Brown, B. & Harper, R. (2001). Dealing with mobility: understanding access anytime, anywhere. *ACM Trans. Comput.-Hum. Interact.,* 8, 323–347.

Prammanee, S., Moessner, K. and Tafazolli, R. (2006). Discovering modalities for adaptive multimodal interfaces. *Interactions,* 13, 66–70.

PTS (2006). Säkerhetshot mot mobiltelefoni – en lägesbedömning vintern 2005/2006. Post & Telestyrelsen.

Ravi, S., Raghunathan, A. & Potlapally, N. (2002) Securing wireless data: system architecture challenges. *Proceedings of the 15th international symposium on System Synthesis.* Kyoto, Japan, ACM.

Rittel, H. W. J. & Webber, M. M. (1973). Dilemmas in a General Theory of Planning. *Policy Sciences,* 4, 155–169.

Sacher, H. & Loudon, G. (2002). Uncovering the new wireless interaction paradigm. *Interactions,* 9, 17–23.

Steinert, M. & Teufel, S. (2004). European mobile data services 2003: Where are the promised innovations? *Innovations Through Information Technology, 1 and 2,* 152–155.

Steinert, M. & Teufel, S. (2005). The European mobile data service dilemma - An empirical analysis on the barriers of implementing mobile data services. *Mobile Information Systems II,* 191, 63–78.

Tarasewich, P. (2003). Designing Mobile Commerce Applications. Association for Computing Machinery. *Communications of the ACM,* 46, 57–60.

Tarasewich, P., Nickerson, R. C. and Warkentin, M. (2002). Issues in Mobile E-Commerce. *Communications of the Association for Information Systems,* 8.

Weilenmann, A. (2003). *Doing mobility,* Göteborg, Dept. of Informatics [Institutionen för informatik, Handelshögsk.] Victoria Institute.

Weiser, M. (1991). The Computer for the 21st-Century. *Scientific American,* 265, 94.

Yin, R. (2003). *Case Study Research,* Thousands Oaks, CA, Sage.

Zheng, W. and Yuan, Y. (2007). Identifying the differences between stationary office support and mobile work support: a conceptual framework. *International Journal of Mobile Communications,* 5, 107–123.

Chapter 15
Reframing Online Shopping Through Innovative and Organic User-Oriented Design

Anita Greenhill and Gordon Fletcher

15.1 Exploring Blogshops

The structure and form of the Web is defined by specific design elements; its protocols, the scope of acceptable file formats and the capability of clients. These elements are intentionally minimal constraints but nonetheless structure what can be achieved "through" the Web. With the increasingly standardised abilities of Web clients and wider application of accessible design principles increasingly emphasis shifts from the problem of creating and developing monolithic software systems towards concern for the integration and configuration of existing systems to meet specific social and cultural needs. The free availability of, for example, open source content management systems and blogging applications has increased the ability for individuals and closely geographically constrained highly specialised interest groups to more rapidly represent and express themselves through the Web. Importantly, the abilities provided by pre-built existing systems enables greater focus on reflecting and capturing the peculiar cultural sentiments of special interests.

This chapter explores innovative and organic user-oriented design found in the grass-roots ecosystem management (GREM) of Singaporean Blogshops. The intersection of Web2.0 integration tools and freely available open source systems coupled with self-motivated shopping practices introduces the capacity for direct conversation and immediate expression in social media that, in turn, produces unexpected forms of empowerment (Beer and Burrows 2007). The research presented here reveals how young Singaporean women are utilising blogging systems to fulfil their desires to possess identifiable "brand name" objects of fashion. Satisfying these desires requires exchange practices and communication that extend and increases their personal and financial capability to

A. Greenhill (✉)
Manchester Business School, University of Manchester, UK
e-mail: A.Greenhill@manchester.ac.uk

G. Fletcher
Salford Business School, University of Salford, UK
e-mail: G.Fletcher@salford.ac.uk

H. Isomäki and S. Pekkola (eds.), *Reframing Humans in Information Systems Development*, Computer Supported Cooperative Work 201,
DOI 10.1007/978-1-84996-347-3_15, © Springer-Verlag London Limited 2011

obtain goods. These practices are conducted in parallel with conventional commercial activities in the sense that these women maintain everyday desires for recognisable brand names and employ the rhetoric and imagery familiar to a commercially oriented style sentiment. However, the mechanism by which they seek to obtain these goods is undertaken outside what is seen as conventional shopping practice. The bottom-up motivations of Blogshops illustrates how user-oriented design does not necessitate originality and the personal desire to accumulate currently fashionable items mitigates towards reuse and repurposing of conventional mainstream imagery and rhetoric in conjunction with localised vocabulary and practices.

By utilising empirical data gathered from a selection of Blogshops we present contemporary examples of polymorphic and interactive design practices (Cooley 1987). Our research asks whether online design practices necessarily adopts a separation of designer and developer from use and users and whether online design practice is always, even necessarily, audience-focused. We argue that Blogshops consciously represent the interests of the individual Blogshop hosts designed by them on their terms and in a style that appeals primarily to them personally. This perspectives enables the hosts to be the designers for a primary audience of one; themselves. This observation is albeit unsurprising with the context of blog authorship but counter-intuitive to the commercial need for a buying audience. The Blogshops, however, remain relevant and even enticing for a secondary audience, of other teenage Singaporean girls, because of shared (micro) cultural understandings and worldviews. Blogshops cannot be seen as directly attentive to the requirements of a clearly articulated mass audience or alternatively 'simply' be seen as examples of unconsciously ironic anti-design (Whiteley 1993).

The research presented in this chapter problematises the classification of user in distinction from that of designer and the implication that these categories could be mutually exclusive or readily differentiated aspects of an individual experience, cultural experience or capacity. The term "bottom up" participation has previously been utilised primarily in relation to governance, democracy and community oriented organisational practices. Weber (2003) in referring to grassroots ecosystem management (GREM) states, "instead of a system premised on hierarchy and commands from above, GREM emphasizes non-hierarchical, place-based networks … expertise is substantially redefined to include local expertise and community-based folk knowledge. Canas (2009) reminds us that the human and the technology depend on each other and cannot be studied separately. He states that 'the term human–machine interaction refers to the design of the interface where a person and a machine interact during the execution of a task'" (2009, 55). Weber contends that designers work in either academic or industrial environments, where an academic's primary role is to explain interactive behaviour and industry-based designers are commissioned to design for a need-specific context by providing solutions, for example, to reduce costs or obtain benefits within short-term projects. The hosts as the designers of Blogshops are neither academics nor situated in a conventional industrial environment but instead exist between a range of roles and understanding as the creators of home-grown eCommerce ventures. The examples drawn from this study present everyday adaptation of Web technologies, where conventional ideas of human–computer design are reframed and reduced to a scale that benefits individual purposes and motivations.

Blogshops are an online shopping phenomenon that can currently be most clearly observed in Singapore. We have previously suggested that the Blogshop phenomenon emerged through the symbiotic relationship of technology adaptation and design with specific geographic conditions including public transport infrastructure (Greenhill and Fletcher 2009). The public visibility and clarity of Blogshop exchange events constitutes Singapore as an experimental viewport for understanding a partially Web-based practice in situ. Similar online shopping sites that deviate from conventional perspectives of eCommerce design and implementation can already be identified within activities based in the United Kingdom (UK) and United States (USA). However, Singaporean Blogshops, as the primary location of the most completely articulated concept expressed through well-established sites presenting the widest variety of goods, frames contemporary technology-mediated experiences within a specific and identifiable social and cultural group. Unlike many discussions concerning Web technologies and the general level of uncertainty surrounding the identity of its users (Beer 2008), Blogshops can be precisely identified within the domain of female teenagers (usually around the age of 16) who are 'middle class' college students living primarily in the outlying suburbs of Singapore. This group is thoroughly immersed within a particular technoscape (Crang et al. 2007) that incorporates daily engagement with innovative and organic design practices, social networking and eCommerce as well as the more mundane day-to-day practicalities of attending a college and constant exposure to a globalised mainstream fame-obsessed culture. The influences of this environment coalesce within the form of Blogshops. While a Blogshop ostensibly uses the blog to sell fashion objects for personal financial gain such a primarily economic observation obscures more subtle design and cultural issues. Blogshops adopt a unique iterative and polymorphic design sentiment by drawing upon a rich assemblage including Web and mobile technologies, innovative and creative design skills, easy access to major international export centres of consumable goods, access to 'middle class' levels of disposable income, Singaporean-specific cultural knowledge and an efficient urban public transport system. The combination of available open source technology with a desire to sell for specific personal and cultural motivations presents a critique of prescriptive design practices (He and King 2008) including, for example, received understanding of what is necessary to enable an eCommerce payment system or the stated requirement for Web sites to have mechanisms 'designed in' that cultivates a purchaser's trust (Jarvenpaa et al. 1998). By largely ignoring the presence of an external audience hosts overcome these apparently essential design concerns by effacing the distinction between the role of user from that of developer (Greenbaum and Kyng 1991).

15.2 Designing Blogshops

Blogshops are readily defined from a technology point-of-view as virtual shop fronts that utilise third party hosted blogging systems. But this neat statement belies the complexities of Blogshop practice. Blogshops use multiple blogs to construct different "departments" for separate classes of items as well as specific events including sales and sprees. A hallmark of the most established Blogshops are the number of individual blogs being maintained and are part of their evolving design from a conventionally purposed weblog. However, Blogshop departments are themselves critiques of conventional shopping and its rarely questioned classifications. For example babys-candy-new.blogspot.com offers departments such as 'pretty', 'instock' and 'itemssold'. Utilising multiple blogs for what is ostensibly a single purpose could be dismissed as naivety on the part of the hosts and the apparent naivety of the hosts is itself a hallmark of Blogshops. However, the subtlety and regularity of the multiple blog form, as well as other aspects of hosts' activities, reveals a collective deeper understanding of the workings of blogging systems and the application of effective methods for obtaining maximum personal benefit from their exploitation. As a single web page a single blog can only accommodate a single thread of discussion whereas the better established Blogshops are constantly engaged in multiple threads of different conversations with different 'types' of buyers. The simplicity of setting up a blog on the hosted systems generally preferred by the hosts makes creating additional blog pages easy and more importantly a hosted system also helps to manage the styles and themes that are applied across an entire Blogshop. Constructing a separate 'terms and conditions' blog is an example of how the hosts have independently developed an understanding of the need to reduce repetition and maintain consistency across many individual blog pages. By linking to a separate terms and conditions page their consolidated capture of experience and knowledge is fully applied to all transactions within the Blogshop rather than requiring duplication within each separate department. Thejewelhaus takes a slightly different approach by offering a single image that is hosted on photobucket.com to cover all of its terms and conditions (Fig. 15.1).

Blogshops often incorporate a 'wants list' of desired items as a side panel to their main blog or as a separate blog entirely. The items wanted are usually the most recent fashion items and hard to obtain or exclusive brand name lifestyle accessories but often more mundane needs are also listed such as 'a black bag'. Wants lists on Blogshops are not confined to those items wanted by the host herself and can extend to include sisters, friends and sometimes other buyers. As an example of a general 'want' on Wednesday, July 16, 2008,

Wants

URGENT!

Looking for Hei Tang Qun Xia Zhuan (Legend of Brown Sugar Chivalries) collectibles; OST, pictorial, the like. Below SGD 30, or swaps would be great!

Please email fahrenheitstuffs@hotmail.com if you have these items, thank you (: (from fahrenheitmerchandise.blogspot.com/2008/07/urgent-looking-for-dbsk-five-in-black. html).

The collective wants lists point to the (sometimes unintentional) cooperative nature of many Blogshops and the ways in which social networking activities are intertwined and complemented by the physical acquisition of desired items. Hosts and buyers are drawn together to exchange and buy goods outside mainstream circuit of Singaporean shopping but are simultaneously drawn into a broader set of practices

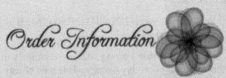

*To order an item, leave a comment with your email address or email me at thejewelhaus@gmail.com and state the item that you wish to purchase.
*Comments are screened to ensure the privacy of our customers.
* Once you receive a confirmation email, it is considered as ordering the item.
*If you change your mind after ordering an item, please notify me. Backing out at the last minute without notifying me would cause you to be listed on the Dead Buyers List.

* I do not do meetups so payment is made via ibanking and bank transfer
* For ATM fund transfer users, please provide a clear snapshot of your receipt.
* Payment is to be made within 48 hours after the confirmation of your order.
* If payment is not made by then, the order will be cancelled and the item will be put up for sale again.
* Strictly no refunds.

* Prices stated do not include postage fees.
* Normal postage costs S$0.50–S$1.00
* Registered postage costs S$2.50
* I will take no responsibility for the loss of any items.

Fig. 15.1 The terms and conditions of thejewelhaus.livejournal.com that is an image hosted on photobucket.com

that results in mutual trust through star buyers and sellers lists and mutual distrust by sharing 'dead' and 'MIA' buyers lists. All of these lists refer to the buyers and hosts by their online identity and presume that while the identity is assumed by the individuals themselves it will remain immutable across time, separate blogs and multiple transactions.

A further feature of many Blogshops is the use of handmade items including cards, jewellery and ceramics (for example jjsshoppe.blogspot.com) – with the occasional hint that the facilities of the hosts' college were involved – as well as more unusual items such as cakes (bubblegum-x.blogspot.com).

Dear Prince & Princess...

http://photos1.blogger.com/blogger2/3869/4312/1600/264a.0.jpg[264] Handmade "Purple Outer Space" Swarovski Earring

A brand new pair of Handmade Earring. All my earrings will be mailed and carefully packed in bubble bag to prevent any damage. This pair of earring is made with Authetic Swarovski Crystals 4mm (Violet Opal, Light Amethyst & Amethyst) and Cat's eye oval beads. Condition:Excellent.

P&H: FREE LOCAL NORMAL POSTAGE

Selling @ S$4 /- (Sold Out)

(from www.babygodz.blogspot.com accompanied by a photograph of the earrings on a wineglass).

Handmade items reflect the relationship that hosts have to mainstream economic practice. By applying their own labour to relatively low cost and readily obtained materials additional value can be realised and this can then be applied to buying higher value and more highly desired commercial brand name items. Many aspects of the most established Blogshops include references to one or more of the colleges or high schools in Singapore and indicate that hosts come from generally financially secure family backgrounds. Their activities reflect the frustration of most teenagers who do not have direct access to disposal cash but rather to the accoutrements of middle class backgrounds such as, for instance, a college with a pottery kiln as well as digital cameras and mobile phones. All of these features reinforce the additional networks that bind and shape the design sentiment adopted by Blogshop hosts and their imprecise roles that never constitutes them as designer but similarly they cannot simply be described as a 'user'.

We're the lady bosses LYDIA and VALERIE . We're going on 14 and we study at RIVER VALLEY HIGH SCHOOL . You can make enquires at the tagboard, mail us at

twocarrots-@hotmail.com, or sms or valerie [912510##] / call lydia [822284##]

For meetups already scheduled at the east side, contact valerie. West side, contact lydia. meetup available @

{foc}

(at our convenience)

mrt stations:

- woodlands
- yewtee
- choachukang
- boonlay to bugis
- habourfront

others:

- outside RVHS
- queensway shopping center

you can mail us to request for other locations :D we'll consider . we are nice people :D you might have to pay a small sum though.

Please do not be late, latecomers will be charged $1 for every 10minutes late.

Also, if you wish to change the meetup time or place please inform us at least 4hour earlier.

meetup twice, once for payment, once for collection.

if you only want to meetup once; want us to pay for you first, state in the order form. We'll consider, depending on whether we're rich or poor at that point in time ;D You'll probably have to pay a small sum – also depends on how rich we are then ;D (twocarrots.blogspot. com)

Each Blogshop is hosted by one or two female teenagers generally still at college. This affiliation with full-time education is repeatedly confirmed during exams periods while hosts take a break to undertake 'O' level or higher level examination preparation. For example, "We are also getting few instocks ;] Bag spree #2 is opened now, closing on 8 oct, sry, but tht is when my exam is over. getting more designs too =D" (www.reminisce-x3.blogspot.com). The connection of the hosts with individual education institutions also reveals that they have an immediate network of buyers – who in many cases are also hosts – which is supported by very close proximity and allows the school grounds to act as a trading floor. Posts in Blogshops refer to these practices in ways that assume relatively good levels of inside knowledge regarding the daily routine of the college as well as specific locations on campus. What is equally evident from the messages and information on each Blogshop is the relationship of this 'virtual' operation to one or more of the stations physically located on Singapore's Mass Rapid Transport (MRT) system and the integrated use of mobile phones to confirm arrangements and finalise sales and purchases. The use of the public transport network enables hosts (as a buyer) to reach buyers (as hosts) outside the closed circuit of her own college and interact with buyers and hosts associated with other colleges who may hold slight variations of fashion preferences and priorities. The procedures for obtaining items purchased from a host through the MRT network, the need to conform to her delivery arrangements and the conditions associated with pickups including payment penalties for a late appearance, and wasting a host's time, are very detailed and specific. The stringency and precision of the conditions, particularly on those that are longer established, reveal one of the ways in which Blogshop design has continuously evolved through personal and newly learned experiences and the means that the host employs to ensure that she will enjoy some form of benefit from any exchange – even if this is simply to minimise the time and hassle spent disposing of items she no longer wants and to which she has ascribed only minimal economic value. The changing personal circumstances of the hosts can invoke a change of terms and conditions. For example, one host only does exchanges in one MRT station during weekdays, which is close to her parent's home; however, on weekends her MRT station of choice changes to reflect the fact that she spends weekends with her grandmother in a different part of Singapore. Individual hosts have also developed the design of Blogshops from solely one of one to one exchange. The most common trajectory has been the development of a separate spree blog. The spree is a mechanism by which groups of buyers can introduce new and hence more highly desirable items into the relatively closed circuits of Blogshop exchange. By subscribing to a spree the buyer gives money to a host who then places an order with an offshore wholesaler and then once they are received redistributes the items to the subscribers. While the most obvious means for personally benefitting from this exchange is to place a mark-up on the amount each subscriber puts into the spree many organisers do not take a monetary profit but rather use the additional funds to buy items for themselves effectively gaining the highly desired items for little cost other than the time it takes to organise a group of friends, associates and trusted buyers.

Sprees are successful and popular with hosts and many Blogshops specialise in this form of exchange – with, again, specific and clear terms and conditions – as they have the benefit of utilising bulk meetups at MRT stations to distribute the goods and have already received an upfront payment from subscribers. But even this specialism can force a further iteration in design of the Blogshop as the host recognises the need, once again, to dispose of items as they become unfashionable.

The various pulls of different social and cultural networks both online and within the daily experiences of Singaporean high school life ensures that the aesthetic aspects of the Blogshops are not particularly distinctive, they retain the general look and feel of an 'amateurish' teenage blog – long pages bloated with images inappropriately over-sized for web-delivery. However, this approach is now employed by more mainstream and popular blogs where less consideration is given to load times and there is an increasingly active resistance to the multi-page advertising laden above-the-fold approach adopted by daily newspaper and print magazine Web sites (Nielsen, 1999). Many of the images for the Blogshops are taken from mobile phone cameras and are not resized, optimised or even re-orientated. Hosts regularly also make regular use of third-party free photo hosting sites such as photobucket.com to host their images. Blogshops are further complemented with tools such as cbox.ws, a chat and tagging service, as well as code from javascript.nu and dynamicdrive.com, which are both remotely hosted Javascript libraries. The Blogshop technically becomes a front end to a collection of tools, capabilities and systems that are brought into service by the host as required. As the sophistication and size of the Blogshop expands the need for third-party subsystems to control navigation and maintain consistent styles becomes increasingly necessary. Other elements are drawn upon to craft and provide the expected elements of all Blogshops including link lists, shout boxes as well as kitsch effects such as black snowflakes falling down the screen (taken from www.24fun.com). Longer established Blogshops tend to adopt cleaner design principles and more disciplined use of imagery as well as more diverse hosting of photographs.

A feature of Blogshops distinctive from more conventional blogs or eCommerce sites is the levels and forms of personal identity being revealed. Hosts include photos with obscured faces, utilising hands and legs as the platform to model available items (Riegelsberger et al. 2003; Fig. 15.2). In contrast, buyers will include 'snapshot' images of themselves and their friends at a range of identifiable locations including restaurants and daytrips. Buyers and hosts of newer Blogshops also offer commentary and observations about their daily lives. Hosts also make 'liberal' use of images taken from printed and online fashion catalogues and other Blogshops to complete their

Fig. 15.2 Kisses-shoes.blogspot.com adopts the advantage of introducing handmade items in the Blogshop exchange circuits and describes the host as "I dont make shoes for a living, i am a full time student, part time shoes Maker. =)" and reveals less reluctance to show her face than many hosts

design. The scanned and copied images are undoubtedly a 'budget' and home brew approach to showing their available items. These design elements mimic strategies employed by conventional eCommerce to facilitate trust by creating an association with the prestige and quality of the brands displayed, however, the choice of imagery reflect the personal preferences and currently owned items of a host rather than forming a design strategy. One of the few examples of hosts incorporated in full length unobscured photos was myrunway-boutique.blogspot.com where all three hosts include full length pictures and also reveal that they are students at the National University of Singapore making them among the oldest hosts that can be identified. This Blogshop includes (in May 2009) photographs of Lady Gaga with one of the hosts imitating the pose in a matching dress creating an association with popular media celebrity and the clothes available. The Blogshop also constructs an arbitrary classification scheme for a series of popular houndstooth dresses with the red version described as 'love', the black version as 'hate' and brown as 'apathy'. With the exception of the first term these are descriptions rarely used for selling fashion items. Within the mainstream fashion and fame conscious teenage culture that the majority of Shopblogs exist there is a clear temptation to 'be' or become a model. Association of individual desired fashion items with the commercial imagery being displayed encourages this ambition and further reinforces the desire to mimic. At least, in part, as a consequence of the desire to imitate and 'be' models many hosts include 'mirror photos' – photographs they have taken of themselves with the aid of a mirror. The results are variable but generally poor; "sorry it's unclear, my camera was dying" (clearplease.blogspot.com). The use of mirror photos by the hosts in

Singapore is itself an naive technological adoption and re-purposing of youth culture activities found elsewhere such as the US and UK where 'sexting' (Muscari 2009) is a more common use for mirror photos in which teenagers take sexually explicit photographs of themselves and text them to friends.

Singaporean Blogshops are hallmarked by their close relationship to the Singaporean Mass Rapid Transit (MRT) public transport system that covers the island and is the mechanism for many physical exchanges. Meeting up is a contentious activity for hosts with many expressing complete distrust for them or at least presenting such an onerous set of terms and conditions that would discourage all but the most enthusiastic buyer. Some conditions are relatively polite such as "No meetups/reservations as we're really busy these days" (community.livejournal.com/sgflea/34572582.html) or "NO meetups, unless there is really a need." (littlehappyshop.blogspot.com). Hosts' enthusiasm for spreeing is also partially explained by this distaste for individual meetups as the mass meetups conducted at the end of a spree enable many exchanges to happen at the same time in a context where the buyers (who have already paid) must meet the conditions of the host in order to receive their ordered items. None of the hosts acknowledge the risk to their personal safety in conducting an individual meetup with an unknown buyer and this reveals the tacit support provided by the broader networks complementing the social networks of Blogshops as well as the authoritarian form of Singaporean government that embeds greater provision for protection of personal security and policing presence. Where a host is prepared to meetup with buyers they are generally prepared to travel to only one to three MRT stations for the free delivery of items (FOC). Additional information offered on the blogs such as the high school they attend or the stations they will travel to for free changes on weekdays shows how closely the location of the 'free delivery' stations relate to hosts' own homes. A smaller number of hosts are prepared to travel further for free. However, this generosity should not be interpreted as client orientation or an attempt to gain competitive advantage over rival hosts but is more mundanely connected to the possession of a different travel pass and is consequently an insight into slightly different lifestyles of individual hosts. The MRT system also enables hosts to break away from the network of a single college or high school to take advantage of neighbouring networks of Blogshops to acquire rarer items not easily found within these closer networks. The rapid development of Blogshops across Singapore and with so many distinct exchange networks prohibits discovery of the original source although some Blogshops indicate that they originally had a connection with the National University of Singapore's (NUS) Students Business Clubs. And a recent posting on a discussion board about $SG 2,000 fines being applied to making trades over the MRT fare barrier bemoans, "And yet our govt encourage us to be entrepreneurs." (www.sgclub.com/singapore/pay_goods_over_136371_3.html) highlighting the important cultural influences being received from education and government by potential and current hosts to adopt a spirit of free entrepreneurship. The earliest Blogshop that can be definitely dated is daisyloves.livejournal.com – "Want to be like her?? Korean Big Piece Clip On" and on her Bio, "Hi! I am a heavy shopper who buys clothes on impulse. They are either all brand new or worn less than

2 times. My aim of opening this blogshop is to lessen my closet load as it is really too packed. No intentions of earning profits at all. So i am selling them at very cheap prices. U take a fancy in it, u buy it. :)" – from June 2005, however, the majority of Blogshops have starting dates from 2007 onwards. Blogshops at this point in their early development clearly identified a social need and desire rather than the discovery of an unrealised technological capability hidden embedded within blogging systems. The longer term advantage of using both livejournal and blogspot has been the longevity of the systems themselves, the level of support available and the active development that continues on the themes/skins available to novice users. Both systems are owned by large companies, in the case of the latter it is Google, and have been in continuous development since their public release in 1999 (www.livejournalinc.com/aboutus.php#ourcompany; www.blogger.com/about). All of these features would be identified as positive points of comparison for the selection of a system through the Open Source Maturity Model (OSMM) or similar approaches to selecting software candidates in the open source domain.

15.3 New eCommerce?

With over 400 Blogshops in existence by the end of 2008 the phenomena is developing rapidly and continuously adapting. Over a relatively brief development trajectory of 2–3 years Blogshops reveals a common evolution of individual experiences, including technological and design experience, from a 'simple' blog as a personal but public diary into a Blogshop to the point of either complete abandonment as a shop, development as a more conventional online shop (and in at least one case a physical shop) or to the role of wholesaler supplying other Blogshops. Blogging system preference is largely the result of self-selection as both the most popular options were already popular in Singapore with the ability to easily link images from third party services providing an additional benefit (Nardi et al. 2004). Both blogging systems offer large amounts of design flexibility enabling relatively novice users to customise and personalise their blogs with readily available tools to include mobile phone camera images and stock clipart. Further advantages include the relative small amounts of 'competing' commercial advertising added by the systems themselves and pre-built templates that offer minimal barriers to full participation as a Blogshop host. The earliest, most experienced hosts further enforce this preference for particular systems by refusing to link out to other Blogshops hosted anywhere else – effectively developing networks of Blogshops that offer, very broadly, a degree of overall navigation and structural consistency. The rationale for maintaining only intra-system links is also an unexpected type of trust formation that presumes Blogshops hosted anywhere else may be 'commercial' operations.

Just as the distinction of designer and user is problematic within Blogshops the distinction between host and buyer is not a clearly demarcated difference and individuals adopt multiple identities simulataneously. Buyers become hosts through a slow transition of practice that is not mutually exclusively.

So went around to look for their basketball shoes, and they got it at the shop with this real freaking nice uncle (: YAY! I got a surprise for John bestfriend and hell, I think he'll curse me real hard when he opens the present (: LOLS. I need to update my wants list (: Save up! It's time to really really do so (: Jarl Jiejie and his friend's (cause I don't know how to spell her name) going to keep me accompanied when we go shop again (:

I saw AiLin and Vincent there and thir gang tee is nice, and they got the MaoMao bag, like all together! OMG la. Oh well, today's really a nice day with nice bumping into each other fer like 3 times, and >.< Jarl Jiejie, I HATE TICKLES! (http://theloudestsilence. blogspot.com/2007_04_01_archive.html).

Over time buyers add offers to sell items such as jeans or t-shirts as posts between more regular diary-like messages. Th-littlepig.blogspot.com offers a series of photos of goods that are a collection of things 'seen' rather than items offered for sale, however, the form and style of the page is one of a Blogshop and all that is missing is the invitation to buy one of the items captured in the photographs. In some cases the items for sale are referred to as having appeared in a previous photo being worn by the host. While a use patina is sometimes desirable and fashionable in clothing such as jeans and some types of t-shirts as well as jewellery these self-referential observations between postings, perhaps initially unintentional, offers proof to the potential buyer that the host had at least at some point actually possessed the item they are attempting to sell and by implication have also assumed the role of buyer. But equally importantly for the primary audience of the host herself these posting document her evolving fashion sense and tastes in a photographic journal – the original intention of the blog itself.

Topshop inspired boho dress

Worn once, selling for $19 (Bought for $27)

SWAPS AT 27 (threeofbroccoli.blogspot.com)

This is not 'trust' in the consciously 'designed in' sense of existing eCommerce literature (Harrison McKnight et al. 2002) that is crafted through hallmarks of authority but is nonetheless another of the – unintentional – methods of establishing trust around an individual Blogshop and its host.

An initial indicator of the self-oriented design focus of Blogshops is the tone and style adopted by the majority of hosts. While 'true' Singaporean English can be excruciatingly obtuse or unintentionally witty to a non-native reader the majority of hosts employ a form of language that just appears quirky to those outside Singapore and reconfirms they are from more privileged backgrounds (Crystal 2004: 508 and 522). Individual usage of Singaporean English, as with elsewhere in the English-speaking world, is linked to socioeconomic status and ethnicity (Crystal 2004: 400). Newer Blogshops show increasingly complex and confusing phrasing that suggests their development has now been more widely adopted across a broader social spectrum of Singaporean teenagers. The expanding numbers of Blogshops is beneficial to all hosts in Singapore as the range of networks across which goods can be exchanged is increased and this presents greater opportunity for the disposal of unwanted second hand items at higher prices into alternate circuits where the item may still be fashionable or even emerging as fashionable. This benefit however can only be realised by the host if they can find buyers who are in more than one network or at least become buyers outside their most immediate network (Castells 1999). As this necessitates negotiations with people outside familiar networks such as friends, college or geographic proximity the language of personal accumulation is combined with phrasing more often found on formal eCommerce sites (Fig. 15.1). The 'terms and conditions' still remains focused on more local exchange circuits (of friends) and much of the quirkiness of phrasing and terms comes from the use of local references and slang.

> For those who are studying or working in Rivervale Primary School, you can collect your items in school. However, you would need to pay first. But you can pay in school :) (joycefashionshop.blogspot.com).

> Preorder on Wallets & Mp3 Players! Mix and match with up to 50 or more designs to choose from. And all preorders just cap at a small amount of 5–10! So obviously it isn't a long wait! :D Alright, so let me see, the Mp3 players are really a good buy. Its imported from Korea! iRiver leh! I think everyone knows that brand right ^^ . Andand, its unique hor! :D Go take a look okay! :D Muahahaha(: (hotand-cold.blogspot.com).

However, these authoritative statements are often combined with a sense of playfulness and ironic frustration. Comments such as "Im so so annoyed, some people just got ALL the time in the world to make others feel their fake sincerity before they totally disappear!" and "I emphathize very STRONGLY on TRUST&HONESTY. I'm really nice if you respect me, & rest assure I don't bite (: I appreciate fastdeals lots! (: To have a better idea of the sizes I usually wear; I'm a UK6–8 (mostly UK6), height 160cm, size 6 for feet by the way. I'm a VERY impulsive buyer and am a sucker for livejournal clothes, hence the need to clear out my wardrobe as some clothes don't fit/suit me nicely."

Such intimate reflections all disgress markedly from the phrasing of conventional top down eCommerce. The conventional presumption that a website designed for sales will speak (politely) to a global audience is largely absent from hosts' statements. However, immediate contradictions are revealed when hosts who are caught up with the need to break away from their safe networks that have been constructed through the security of immediate social networks deal with strangers who, if hosts' posts are to be entirely believed should never be trusted. Hosts' 'terms and conditions' blogs present their accumulated knowledge about (bad, unknown and more distant) buyers and their peculiarities with some terms referring to individual incidents that the host has no desire to experience again. This further reinforces the presence of the host herself as the primary audience and the use of the blog as a way of reminding herself of these bad experiences. This narrative of poor host experience is sometimes complemented with an additional black list of buyers and hosts with no opportunity for the accused to defend their actions.

> NOT THAT I WANT BLACKLIST THEM, 'M SICK OF MIA-ERS/BACKOUT-ERS. NO MATTER HOW SMALL THE CRIME IS, 'M STILL BLACKLISTING THEM. WHO CARES?

> Name: ####

> Hp Number: #######

School: Bendemeer Secondary

Email: Unknown

Item: "Why are all the good men either gay, married or broke" Slogan

Crime: Mia-ed. Claims that have sent out money, but didn't recv. Text, email, all didn't reply.

Blogshop: http:// #########.blogspot.com/

Name: #####

Hp Number: ########

Email: Unknown

Item: Domukun Pouch

Crime: Mia-ed. Claims that will sent out money, after negotiating with me for more than 1hour. Text, email, all didn't reply. Lucky, 've unlimited smses. Thanks for entertaining uh. (: (charmycloset-blacklisted.blogspot.com with names anonymised)

Disrupting the formal top down eCommerce design Shopblogs' "term and conditions" have become a very public knowledge management tool that informs other hosts and buyers. These common features of Blogshops constitute them as a harbinger of grassroots management and exchange that problematises the possibility for participatory commerce that is regularly claimed as democratic (Milward 1996). What is offered by Blogshops is a wide social and economic network of teenagers in Singapore that are composed of a collection of smaller more personal networks that are at the core of each host's network of friends and relatives. Iterative and polymorphic design practices enable these teenagers to take full advantage of a wider range of smaller networks to maximise their individual advantage. Irrespective of the closeness of personal connections that are drawn upon by the hosts they are driven by personal motivation (boyd and Ellison 2007) and take advantage of the small variables of fashion preference that can exist even in a small geographic region such as Singapore. By attempting to offer a parallel to conventional down-the-line trading of contemporary capitalist supply chains (Thrift 2005) while wanting the items of fashion crafted by this system the need to profit from trading is subsumed by the hosts to the more fundamental desire to possess.

15.4 Blogshop Hegemony

Blogshops enable a form of technologically mediated exchange which presents a resistance to prevalent forms of capitalist hegemony regularly experienced online and directly within Singapore. For both the hosts and buyers the Blogshop encourages commercial resistance, forms of recycling and shifts emphasis of consumption practice away from 'sites' of mainstream shopping. Blogshops also in this way alter the usual seller 'producer', buyer 'user' dichotomy so often presumed in online shopping exchange (Friedman et al. 2007). For the host their motivation is focused around acquiring fashion items that are currently popular with the host and her circle of friends and disposing of those items that have fallen out of favour within the same circle. The host in this way transcends the disassociated role of producer who conducts their activities with profit as primary motivation (Cormode and Krishnamurthy 2008). Friends are only one of the influencers that determine what items are fashionable with wider circles of fashion referenced throughout the postings. For example, "We have the latest trends and fashion imported directly from Japan, Korea and HongKong" and "30–40% OFF RETAIL PRICE!! BRAND NEW, Specially Imported (not available at local stores) from mainly JAPAN n KOREA with some DESIGNER APPAREL, only 1 pc available unless stated!" are postings from missydixie.blogspot.com and shopping-for-trend.blogspot.com respectively. On charmycloset.blogspot.com the situation is made clear. The following blog post not only reveals the cultural pressures that the shifting foibles of fashion bear upon the hosts but also the ways in which conventional notions of profit are heavily mediated and subsumed within the Blogshop environment.

> Meetups are not advised as im busy in school.
>
> Also, Im willing to sell off my items at a lower price,
>
> All prices can be lowered,
>
> We can discuss and nego is possible. :D
>
> As Im in need to clear my wardrobe! :D
>
> So, pplease do help k :D
>
> Also, do look out my for my friends' items also :D
>
> We're all in need to clear our wardrobe! :D.

Many of the Blogshops stress that their second-hand clothes have been worn 'only once' or 'lightly' by them but few references are made as to whether these items were bought new or from another Blogshop. The host at ruthneedsmoney.blogspot. com offered a dress that was subsequently sold with the price difference representing an intermediate rental cost to the host.

> Tube dress!
>
> Looks a bit weird in th pic but it's really quite nice.
>
> Worn only once for abt an hr, condition excellent.
>
> Free size, fits UK 6–8 best, tube is smocked at th back (top part)
>
> Bought for 26, seling at 23 NEGO.
>
> SOLD

The unconventional business practices of the hosts reveals a form of capitalism that is orientated around the temporary accumulation of goods and the iterative possession of specific symbols of prestige (visual, technological and spatial to name but a few). In many situations the exchange also invokes a form of ongoing obligation between the host and her buyers. Disentangling the distinctions between users and designers (Lamb and Kling 2003) does not suggest that Blogshop hosts are simply engaged in forms of gift and commercial exchange but rather that they are taking advantage of 'social networking' and even the implied cultural obligations built into these networks in order to obtain personal benefits that are measured (currently) by having skinny jeans and Cookie Monster t-shirts rather than pounds or dollars. The Blogshops are designed to enable a particular teen lifestyle for the host herself. The mash-up of personal life revelations, mirror photos, borrowed commercial images and transportation requirements reveals the technology enabled environments of a generation capable of designing the means to suit their desired lifestyle.

For the buyers the benefits of Blogshops may appear marginal such as slightly cheaper clothes, jewellery or makeup than mainstream shops or the convenience of a more local pickup for hard-to-get items. However, it is important to not overly disentangle 'being' a host from activity as a buyer as the two roles are necessarily inter-related. Buyers who are 'good' or easy to deal with will often be named in the blogroll – a common design feature of blogs turned to a different purpose – and this can often act as a passport to enable purchases from other hosts and other exchange networks. The practice of exchanging items at a college suggests that 'buying' has also become a form of schoolyard 'play' that is preparation for excursions to further flung networks and different items of desire. The various descriptions of exchanges at MRT stations can vary from a social outing to something akin to a spy mission in enemy territory making the act of buying itself as much the focus of social activity as the actual possession of any specific items. The most intangible rationale for buying is that it provides content for blog postings. This crafts the blog with dual purpose. It provides the mechanism for arranging the exchange of physical items and offers reasons to form and maintain a social network. Equally importantly the act of exchange provides textual and visual content for the blogs as well as still further items to exchange.

The general reluctance to conduct straight 'swaps' of items could be interpreted as an attempt to generate profit from exchanges – as a financial transaction is required to obtain items. But it is the influence of fashion, issues of trust and the hosts' own motivations that mitigate this as the sole rationale for the 'no swaps' policy of many Blogshops. In the relatively closed exchange networks of the Blogshops the range of items available to swap will only produce marginal benefit for the host as what is available will only fall within a narrow range of acceptable items. Exchanges outside the trusted network of a college or similar location increases the possibility that there is no recourse to compensation for a 'bad' swap and consequently emphasising the need for a social network to name and blacklist 'bad' buyers. With a host insisting on money – as a known item of recognised and consistent value rather than just a mechanism for accumulating profit – for the exchange they remain "in charge" of the exchange and minimise their own personal risk.

15.5   Designing Trust – and the Love

Blogshops increase a host's economic independence and improves their cultural standing among peers by provisioning them with the latest fashion items and desirable rare goods. While this may appear trivial motivation it is indicative of a fame obsessed culture that is, encouraged and shaped by the ready and rapid dissemination of large of volumes of gossip and imagery through the Web. This is further reinforced by the intersection of cultures represented in Singapore which in effect becomes a point of convergence for a global range of attitudes and understanding (Jones 2007: 450). Blogshops formed from conventional blogging activity (Nardi et al. 2004) with the site listing a set of desired clothing or items that were superfluous to the host's requirements. Most hosts were buyers first and continue to buy. In this environment, Blogshops are a form of eCommerce crafted without the nuances of conventional online shops that addresses the desires of teenage girls to possess fashion items. The bias of the 'terms and conditions' on Blogshops are entirely in the hosts' favour and authored to benefit their desires. Despite being a key feature of Blogshops the terms and conditions also reveal that meetups are a problematic distribution method for hosts with each offering different solutions. The majority of hosts complain about buyers wasting their time by being late or not showing up to exchange goods and money. Many insist on the buyer having a valid or pre-confirmed mobile phone but far more incorporate the right to charge late fees in generally blunt tones. Robot and Girl (duabui.blogspot.com) says "If you are late without telling me beforehand, a penalty of 50c/5 min will be charged." Cutiesweetieslovelycloset .blogspot.com demands a "$10 charge for cancellations within an hour. $1 will be charged per minute of lateless after 10 min of waiting." Xkimiirawrrs.blogspot.com takes a different approach by offering to deliver directly to the buyer's door if the buyer is prepared to pay the two-way cab fare. The onus is very much placed onto the buyer to be in the right place at the right time implicitly reflecting an underlying cultural belief in the efficiency and security of the MRT and public transport system of Singapore. Ultimately for many of the hosts as their Blogshop has developed and expanded many now refuse to do meetups of any sort and will only work on the basis of posting an item once payment has been received – in effect, a conventional eCommerce model for overcoming issues of trust or rather its lack (Essler and Whitaker 2001). The responsibility for establishing trust rests entirely with the buyer. Despite the proliferation of Blogshops few hosts have also adopted more conventional approaches for establishing trust by, for example, advertising the length of time they have been operating, instead hosts have chosen to use claims such as that used by awesomehighway.blogspot.com, "i am nice i don't bite." The necessities of crafting trust do not obliterate the central premise of Blogshops to benefit their hosts and yet a number of the better established sites are now claiming to be making a lose. The conventional balances and relationships of communicative authority and commercial power to personal consumption have become altered with Blogshops. The terminology of Blogshops reveals this sentiment with a blend of bloggers terms such as MIA-ing (missing in action) and wholesale terms such as FOC (free of charge). Hosts are imitating the tone and language of conventional commerce but remain motivated by a desire for consumption and possession without the mediating process of accumulating monetary profit in order to buy goods commercially. At an operational level this means that each additional cost associated with an exchange is directly and transparently passed onto the buyers including transport, the cost of labour (expressed through the time a host waits at an MRT station or the cost of turning raw materials into a desirable item) and loses incurred by non-payment of goods. Few Blogshops offer a single total cost for purchasing an item (as would be done in conventional commerce or eCommerce) making the exchange error-prone and offering (too) many opportunities for buyers to negotiate.

At 0reocheesecake.blogspot.com "SWAPS are acceptable, unless stated otherwise" but this generosity is moderated by the additional statement that "If you initiate the swap, it will have an additional charge of $3 on top of the stated price for the particular item." effectively making it unclear as to whether the exchange is a swap or a purchase. Similarly at crownedauctions.blogspot.com, "SWAPS ARE WELCOMED(PROVIDED THAT I AM INTERESTED IN YOUR ITEM)." and "PRICES OF ITEMS ARE INCREASED(STATED) WHEN DOING SWAPS REGARDLESS OF WHO INITIATED IT."

The language of Blogshops has shifted over time towards imitation of retail outlets such as those at cometomyshop.blogspot.com where "ALL PREORDERS !!! all clothes are 100% material guarenteed !!" and mis-matchnmix.blogspot.com where "for any enquires or orders all items are BRAND NEW otherwise stated price are NON-NEGO as they are of the lowest we can offer NO SWAP is allowed all price are EXCLUDE POSTAGE." Many Blogshops focus emphasise on goods that are currently trendy in respected but exotic destination such as Hong Kong or Japan. This trajectory differs from earlier attempts to solely divest the host of their second hand items.

These developments suggest that there is a progression through the roles of 'buyer', 'swapper' and 'spree-er' to host and onto the roles 'shopowner', 'wholesaler', 'MIA-er' or 'clearance seller'. However, this interpretation can only be applied when a single site is viewed in isolation, as an individual will be active across a network or series of networks.

This chapter shows Blogshops as a polymorphic and iterative form of eCommerce practice that is motivated by a desire for consumer goods initiated without the mediating process of accumulating profit. Organic user-oriented design found in the grassroots ecosystem management (GREM) of online shops, challenges Canas' (2009) assertion that designers work in academic or industrial environments. Examples provided in this chapter illustrate how the intersection of Web2.0 tools with self motivation result in complex technologically-enabled social exchanges. In the cases explored here Blogshops enable a capacity for direct conversation and aesthetic expression through social media to produce unexpected empowerment. The rapid development of Blogshogs has enabled a commonality and evolution of individual experience enabled by a rich assemblage of technology, culture and location that offers a first level insight into a complex environment that brings together this form of economic need, locational circumstance, and technological capacity. Grassroots participation draws upon bottom up expertise and community knowledge is clearly relied upon and presented through these technologically enabled environments. The complexity of organising sprees, meetups and the general quality of goods offered by hosts all raises issues concerning trust and interaction via technologically enable social networks. Hosts will often reveal their personal phone number, name, general location, sometimes photographs of themselves and in a few cases their banking details (for the purpose of buyers transferring funds to them). The engagement between hosts and buyers and the range of images the Blogshops employ all reflect a complex cultural relationship that extends beyond 'simple' direct commercial exchange (Riegelsberger et al. 2003) and often written out of more convention commercial design practices. Blogshops offer significant insight into a broader series of contemporary cultural experiences including the meaning and extent of eCommerce and social networking, forms of globalised youth culture, the imprecision of fashion and shifting mainstream attitudes towards self-representation. While our discussion focuses around cultural practices in Singapore, ongoing financial uncertainty in the US and in Europe offer the potential for the Blogshop to gain in popularity in a wider range of situations. Blogshops also offer the possibility for the development of the new iterative and polymorphic design practices that question and problematise assumptions already made in relation to eCommerce including the construction of trust, the distinction of the role of user from that of designer, the notion of audience and the mechanisms through which contemporary exchange is conducted.

Acknowledgements The authors thank Donna Duncan for her assistance in identifying the Blogshops examined in this chapter.

References

Beer, D. (2008). Social network(ing) sites revisiting the story so far: A response to danah boyd & Nicole Ellison. *Journal of Computer-Mediated Communication*, 13(2), 516–529.

Beer, D., & Burrows, R. (2007). Sociology and, of and in Web 2.0: Some initial considerations. *Sociological Research Online*, 12(5), http://www.socresonline.org.uk/12/5/17.html.

Boyd, d., & Ellison, N. (2007). Social networking sites: definition, history, and scholarship. *Journal of Computer-Mediated Communication*, 13(1).

Canas, J. (2009). The Future of Interaction Research: interaction is the result of top-down and bottom-up processes. In P. Saariluoma & H. Isomaki (Eds) *Future of Interaction Design II*, Springer-Verlag: London.

Castells, M. (1999). *The information age: economy, society and culture*. Oxford: Blackwell.

Cooley, M. (1987). *Architect or Bee: The Human Price of Technology*. London: The Hogarth Press.

Cormode, G., & Krishnamurthy, B. (2008). Key Differences between Web 1.0 and Web2.0, *First Monday*. 13(6), firstmonday.org/htbin/cgiwrap/bin/ojs/index.php/fm/article/view/2125.

Crang, M., Crosbie, T., & Graham, S. (2007). Technology, time-space, and the remediation of neighbourhood life, *Environment and Planning A*. 39, 2405–2422.

Crystal, D. (2004). *The Stories of English*. Allan Lane: London.

Essler, U., & Whitaker, R. (2001). Re-thinking E-commerce Business Modelling in Terms of Interactivity. *Electronic Markets*. 11(1), 10–16.

Friedman, B., Kahn, P., & Borning, A. (2007). Value Sensitive Design and Information Systems. In P. Zhang & D. Galletta (Eds), *Human-Computer Interaction in Management Information Systems: Foundations*. M.E. Sharpe: New York.

Greenbaum, J., & Kyng, M. (1991). *Design at Work: Cooperative Design of Computer Systems*. Lawrence Erlbaum: Hillsdale, NJ.

Greenhill, A., & Fletcher, G. (2009). Blog/shop: technology and grassroots management, *The 6th International Critical Management Conference*, Warwick Business School, 13–15th July.

Harrison McKnight, D., Choudhury, V., & Kacmar, C. (2002). Developing and Validating Trust Measures for e-Commerce: An Integrative Typology, Information Systems Research, *INFORMS*. 13(3), 334–359.

He, J., & King, W. (2008). The Role of User Participation in Information Systems Development: Implications from a Meta-Analysis. *Journal of Management Information Systems*. 25(1), 301–331.

Jarvenpaa, S., Knoll, K., & Leidner, D. (1998) Is anybody out there?: antecedents of trust in global virtual teams, *Journal of Management Information Systems*. 14(4), 29–64.

Jones, C. (2007). Hong Kong, Singapore, South Korea and Taiwan: Oikonomic Welfare States, *Government and Opposition*, 25(4), 446–462.

Lamb, R., & Kling R. (2003). Reconceptualising Users as Social Actors in Information Systems Research, *MIS Quarterly*. 27(2), 197–235.

Milward, H. B. (1996). The changing character of public sector. In J. Perry (Ed.) *The Handbook of Public Administration*, Jossey-Bass: San Francisco.

Muscari, M. (2009). Sexting: New Technology, Old Problem. *Medscape Public Health & Prevention*. www.medscape.com/viewarticle/702078.

Nardi, B., Schiano, D., and Gumbrecht, M. (2004). Blogging as Social Activity, or, Would You Let 900 Million People Read Your Diary? *CSCW'04*. 6(3), 222–231.

Nielsen, J. (1999). *Designing Web Usability: The Practice of Simplicity*, New Riders Publishing: Thousand Oaks, CA.

Riegelsberger, J., Sasse, M., & McCarthy, J. (2003). Shiny Happy People Building Trust? Photos on e-Commerce Websites and Consumer Trust, *CHI 2003*, April 5–10, Ft. Lauderdale.

Thrift, N. (2005). *Knowing Capitalism*, Sage: London.

Weber, E. (2003). *Bringing Society Back In: Grassroots Ecosystem Management, Accountability and Sustainable Communities. American and Comparative Environmental Policy*. MIT Press: Cambridge, MA.

Whiteley, N. (1993). *Design for Society*. Reaktion Books Ltd: London.

Chapter 16
Stakeholder Involvement and Team Working in Systems Development Practice

Hilary Berger

16.1 Introduction

It is a given that information Systems (IS) play a central role in the construction, adaptation and renewal of an organizations IS infrastructure (Beynon-Davies and Williams 2003). Hence, system development approaches are of significant importance to organizations considering or implementing IS development or business process reengineering. A considerable number of software system developments these days are large and complex in structure, and incorporate the concept of computer-supported co-operative work (CSCW). Grudin (1991) believes that CSCW has become significantly important since its introduction in 1984 by Paul Cashman and Irene Greif, and indeed, that collaborative computing is already affecting us because it changes the ways in which we work. Resultant changes reflect how people now-a-days work in team settings and supported by a range of technology. For example people may work in small teams but they form part of larger work environments within an organization where interfaces and systems have to accommodate multi-stakeholder communities despite conflicting goals (Grudin 1991). This has created formidable challenges for developers who need to fully comprehend organizational activity in order to design collaborative business processes to respond to the dynamic environments. Furthermore, the collaborative work processes relevant to the diversity of stakeholders involved are positioned in relation to an organizations structure, culture and policies together with the existing technologies. As a consequence integrated enterprise systems and collaborative computing have emerged to accommodate the current rapidly changing, distributed and global business environments (Hevner et al. 2004).

More recent research by Henderson-Sellers and Hawryszkiewycz (2008) supports this notion. The increasingly volatile nature of business environments has influenced a move to the development of collaborative systems that integrate shared

H. Berger (✉)
Cardiff School of Management, University of Wales, Cardiff, UK
e-mail: Hberger@uwic.ac.uk

H. Isomäki and S. Pekkola (eds.), *Reframing Humans in Information Systems Development*, Computer Supported Cooperative Work 201,
DOI 10.1007/978-1-84996-347-3_16, © Springer-Verlag London Limited 2011

processes and business practices. They maintain that as the complexity and diversity of distributed business settings necessarily evolve, then the team settings adopted may be separated by distance, time and cultures. Therefore, workers have to coordinate their activities whilst continuing to perform as teams towards achieving common corporate goals. They claim that collaboration in knowledge intensive environments is key to success in dynamic systems design such that business change can be accommodated. Systems need to accommodate multiple dependencies, to comply with standards and government regulations, to adapt to rapid technology innovation, to team diversity, and most importantly the dynamic requirements of current business environments (Kirova et al. 2008).

Moreover when examining user involvement it is necessary to understand what is meant by the term 'user'. *'The term 'user' is a somewhat confusing one'* (Beynon-Davies 2002: 183), different people apply different interpretations to the term. It is not possible to provide an unambiguous definition of 'user' (Carmel 1993). It has been used to define the non IS people, the non-technical people, and also the operational people of an organization who are affected by the system being developed. Additionally, the term 'stakeholder' is often used to describe those people who will be significantly affected by the system or have a material interest in it. Their involvement is considered essential for successful development (Beynon-Davies 2002; Willcocks and Mason 1987). For this research study the terms 'user' and 'stakeholder' have been use interchangeably to refer to the same community of project participants. It is also important to understand what is meant by 'Information Systems Development Methods', this is discussed below.

16.2 Information Systems Development Methods

Extant literature posits a number of meanings relevant to information systems development. Truex et al. (2000) put forward the view that an information systems development (ISD) method is considered to be *"an orderly, predictable and universally applicable process"* (p 54). Others believe that ISDs refer to prescriptive processes using appropriate techniques and computer tools supported by a set of assumptions, or normative principles pursuant to individual circumstances (Lyytinen and Hirschheim 1987; Mathiassen 1997). Fitzgerald et al. (2002) use the term formalised development methods to describe documented commercially available approaches. Regardless of interpretation empirical studies show that developers rarely adopt methods in their entirety in practice (Fitzgerald et al. 2002). Madsen et al. (2006) support this analysis *'prescriptive literature emphasizes how ISDs should be used, while empirical grounded writings focus on how they are actually used* (p 226). Others believe it is possible to tailor development processes to fit the individual contingencies of different development situations. (Avison et al. 1998; Jacobsen et al. 1999). Fitzgerald (1997) and Fitzgerald et al. (2002) introduced the method-in-action concept *to account for the relationship and tension between the formalised methods and their use in practice* (p 226) that reflects how developers might accommodate situational contexts. They conclude that a clear business vision of the project must be established around which the project work is organized rather than apply fixed project plans. In this view formalised methods are a guide and not a prescriptive basis for project planning and action.

However, success of a system development approach is tempered by the absolute nature of an organization i.e. its context, and its limitations. A methodology does not necessarily map directly onto an understanding of the organization, its rationality or the context of its users (Coughlan and Macredie 2002). Therefore where there is a cultural mismatch, the benefits of the approach chosen will be either lost or unrealized. It may be necessary for the development process to undergo a transformation and respond to the changing culture and situation exigencies of development arenas (Bayer and Highsmith 1994; Highsmith 2000, 2008). It is the ISD that controls the emergent situation and not the project management. Thus it is important to apply an ISD method that is suitable to the contingent circumstances of the organization and the developing system in situ (Fitzgerald 1997; Fitzgerald et al. 2002). We discuss next the traditional IS development approach that is generally utilized in bureaucratic arenas with the more recent agile approach that was adopted for the research case study.

16.2.1 Traditional vs. Agile Development

Traditional or 'heavyweight' development approaches such as the Waterfall Model demand a prerequisite determination of system requirements, a relatively stable business environment and a predictive linear life-cycle (Boehm 2002). Emphasis is placed on having complete, consistent, definable and accurate requirements upfront to enable developers to maintain a predictable schedule where documentation is significantly heavy. However history has shown how the associated long development times, lack of flexibility in the resulting system and little or no user involvement during the project lifecycle means there is no guarantee that the final system will actually meet the customers' needs. "One major cause of system failure is the neglect of human factors in dominant system analysis and design practices" (Willcocks and Mason 1987: 70). Indeed, Chaffey and Wood (2005) report that from a survey of 134 organizations, 56% had experienced IT project failure, with an average project loss of £8 million, the largest single loss of £133 million.

Hence, agile or 'lightweight' development approaches based upon an evolutionary and incremental life-cycle have emerged to respond to the increasingly volatile and complex nature of business environments aimed at embracing unstable and changing business needs (Agile-Alliance 2001; Boehm 2002; Highsmith 2008). Such approaches focus on providing adaptable and flexible development practices designed to mitigate the risks of unexpected and unprecedented business and environmental change. Examples are the Dynamic System Development Methodology, predecessor of agile methods (DSDM Consortium 2004); SCRUM, team based development (Schwaber and Beedle 2002); Extreme Programming, focuses on analysis, development and test phrases (Avison and Fitzgerald 2006). Indeed, the Agile Alliance, formed in 2001, puts forward a 'Manifesto for Agile Development' which promotes flexible system development practices that place a high value on human roles and relationships rather than the tools and process emphasis of the 'heavyweight' methods (Cockburn 2002; Highsmith 2008).

The outsourced developers put forward an agile development approach for the case study due to the dynamic nature of IS development project. This was agreed by senior management at project inception. Below we discuss the characteristics of agile development pertinent to the case study context.

16.2.2 Agile Development

Agile development necessitates an incremental project lifecycle, iterative development and the intensive involvement of stakeholders, particularly end-users where appropriate. Continual feedback is used to build later versions of the system so that all critical business change can be accommodated. Such elements are considered as fundamental to agile development (Agile-Alliance 2001; DSDM Consortium 2004).

The consensus is that a team working culture that engenders joint collaboration, active co-operation and the promotion of team spirit between project participants (developers, business people and other stakeholders) where responsibility is shared is not just a characteristic of agile development but it is significant to success. Adaptive teams and user centric involvement are core to agile development, that emphasizes people over process (Highsmith 2008).

Although it is the people that make the agile process happen, people are heterogeneous by nature. The literature illustrates that involving users in systems development is a complex issue, and that the lack of attention to user involvement, for example in requirements elicitation, has contributed to continued IS development failures (Beynon-Davies 1998). Pekkola et al. (2006) suggest that requirements management is considered to be one of the most challenging tasks in system development. In fact the active involvement of core stakeholders is regarded as key in the negotiation of systems requirements and crucial to successful development (Santosa et al. 2005). The degree of system success can be proportionally linked to the extent of user involvement (Beynon-Davies 1998; Luna-Reyes et al. 2005).

Through the evaluation of a case study concerning a real-world UK Government IS project we examine how the IS development project was hindered significantly by the impact of the host organizations' culture on the agile development approach adopted. Thus, this chapter aims to increase the understanding of the difficulties of user involvement within the domain of agile IS development. The premise is that the inherent social capital of the case study organization bound key stakeholders to specific working cultures that undermined a successful shift to a team working culture. We examine how organizational protocols played a significant role in the accepted working patterns and behaviour of key stakeholders that hindered a cooperative team culture being created. In particular we present practical insights into problems experienced with human issues and their management with a focus on active user involvement and team working during the project lifecycle.

The chapter has the following structure. In this section we introduce the theoretical backdrop to our case study and consider the concepts of IS development methods. Through the literature we look at the move away from traditional heavy weight development methods to lightweight agile approaches. Next we set out the research approach. In the following section we describe the context of, and background to our case study in terms of the particular structure and culture of the host organization, the context of IS project and the development approach adopted. We then consider how the characteristics of agile development were occasioned within the case study setting focusing on the agile characteristics of stakeholder involvement and team working ethos. Subsequently we look at how, in practice, some of these agile characteristics were mismatched against the hosts' organizational culture. Finally we put forward our conclusions and present a table detailing the cultural mismatches that reflects back to the literature reviewed.

16.3 Research Methodology

Peffers et al. (2007) state that *"Information Systems is an applied research discipline* (p 46). Hevner et al. (2004) put forward behavioural science and design science as paradigms that characterize IS. Behavioural science *'seeks to develop and verify theories that explain or predict human or organizational behaviour'* and *'seeks to extend the boundaries of human and organizational capabilities by creating new and innovative artifacts* (p 75). Peffers et al. (2007) argue that although the use of interpretive research paradigms are widely accepted such approaches are considered to be mostly explanatory and *'not often applicable to the solution of problems encountered in research or practice* (p 47). However, after deliberate consideration an interpretive stance was adopted for this research study, and ethnography was used as an immersive method of rich qualitative data collection in the field within the case setting.

The suitability of this approach has been demonstrated in previous work (Myers 1999; Strauss and Corbin 1990; Walsham 1997; Yin 2009). The intent of interpretative research is not to generalize but to understand the deeper structure of a phenomenon that could not be obtained by other research methods such that it can provide unique insight and be used to inform other similar settings (Orlikowski and Baroudi 1991). In terms of analysis, a grounded theory (Glaser and Strauss 1967) approach was applied as a continuous stream of activity in parallel with iterative data collection.

This combination of interpretive epistemology, ethnographic data collection and inductive data analysis was particularly suitable for understanding the practicalities of user involvement in the case study context. Thus, the researcher acquired a rich understanding of the multiple layers of perspective within the particular IS development project (Gill and Johnson 1991; Walsham 1997). Literature recognizes that rigorous and relevant interpretive case study research can make a valuable contribution to both IS theory and practice (Walsham 1997; Yin 2009).

A longitudinal study situated within the case study setting was carried out over 3 years. An initial intensive observation period of 9 months was fundamental to getting close to the participants, in understanding the organizational context and the actual substance of the system being developed. It also enabled the analysis of participants' behaviour by observing events as did, or did not occur, within their natural context (Silverman 1985 cited in Alvesson and Deetz 2000). Moreover literature emphasizes the observation of social process as the most fundamental element of qualitative research (Silverman 2005). Observation activities involved attending formal/informal, regular/ad hoc meetings, workshops, presentations and discussions between senior managers, business managers, developers and stakeholders. A project diary recorded daily field notes together with a diversity of supporting project documentation. Next key participants were shadowed for 1or 2 day periods in order to attain specific knowledge and insight relevant to individual specialisms that also enabled the identification of people as key informants to be interviewed.

Following these activities 126 informal, semi-structured interviews were conducted, audio-taped and respondent-validated for added rigour and to offset any unintentional bias by the observer (Alvesson and Deetz 2000). Therefore an ethical stance was maintained that afforded interviewees the opportunity to clarify, delete or amend inaccurate or incorrect data. These interviews were timetabled iteratively across the 3 year project in order to provide a diversity of perspectives. Importantly this approach facilitated triangulation but more significantly it ensured a richness of interpretation to emerge. The number of interviews per person was dependent upon their status within the evolving development stages, their potential contribution, availability and willingness to participate. For example key actors such as project and business managers were interviewed approximately 5 times in addition to the daily interaction throughout the project. The role of the researcher within the context of this project development was initially as a 'fly on the wall' and then as an independent observer/researcher, no action research was involved.

16.3.1   Data Analysis

The use of QSR NUD*IST Vivo, a qualitative analysis software tool, facilitated the dynamic interrogation of the data to aid audit trails important for conceptual development (Myers 1999; Yin 2009) across the diverse empirical data. Initial analysis involved methodically 'open coding' of data into themes through an iterative process of sharing, reflection and enquiry. The empirical materials were organized into conceptual structures conformant with the research focus. Axial coding then established how categories might inter-relate and link to sub-categories to uncover any relationships and links (Kelle 1998).

Data gathered from interviews were aligned to the concept of Alvesson's (2003) *'eight alternative conceptualizations of the interview'* (p 14) such that iterative reflection was undertaken from different angles to allow multiple interpretations. Accordingly it was possible to consider a range of different meanings rather than simply accepting conventional or situational dominant understandings.

Secondary research involved an in-depth and systematic analysis of published literature, project documentation and artefacts that facilitated cross-checking such that strong substantiation of analysis and conclusions drawn could be established. Triangulation occurred across the variety of empirical materials as advised by Alvesson and Deetz (2000). The aim was to enhance reflection and provide rich data from breadth, depth, plausibility and a variation of perspectives (Alvesson and Deetz 2000).

16.4 Case Study Scenario

The case study concerns an IS development project within a UK Government department (we refer to them as the 'Client Organization'). The initial project cost was estimated at about £10 m, with a timeframe of 2–3 years, and utilizing a core project team of approximately 50 people described as organizational participants [senior managers, business managers and other business/end users] and outsourced participants (developers, designers, and analysts). We refer to them collectively as stakeholders, it is this stakeholder community that participated in the research study.

The Client Organization is an EC (European Commission) Paying Agency, an independent body accountable for administering all aspects of the EC's Common Agricultural Policy (CAP) through a number of grants and subsidy schemes across the region. These are measured in terms of 100,000s of grant and subsidy applications per annum. Thus, the Client Organization is answerable directly to the EC. Fines and penalties are imposed for any failure to satisfy, or for non-compliance with CAP regulations and EC legislation. Each CAP scheme specifies the EC rules and conditions that detail the eligibility for its grants and subsidies. Historically CAP scheme administration was organized into separate, hierarchical silos i.e. independent discrete teams that dealt with the individual schemes and their requirements. Scheme management was the responsibility of scheme specific business Process Managers working individually, reporting to one of two Scheme Managers (we refer to these as business managers). It was these business managers who attended to the business needs and administration of the schemes respectively.

A previous history of late and inaccurate payments, low customer satisfaction and an increasing inability to accommodate the EC's changing needs meant that the new system was aimed at improving the administration and expenditure of the CAP schemes. However the CAP schemes are subject to yearly modifications, with new schemes being drafted as required. Thus, the development project needed to be able to respond to an evolving and dynamic business environment that experienced a high degree of change in both business requirements and the

EC legislation. For these reasons the developers believed an agile development approach was eminently suitable for such a volatile setting.

Owing to the lack of in-house expertise development of the new IS system was outsourced to a commercial company (referred to them as the developers). The developers were selected on the basis of their experience in the field of systems' transformation and of developing customized software and hardware. They adopted their own in-house agile Iterative Application Development (IAD) approach, a formalised method as defined by Fitzgerald et al. (2002).

The project arena consisted of a centrally located government building where both the Client Organization's participants and the developers were co-located together for the project duration. A predefined reporting project structure was created that involved a number of joint development teams made up of key business partici-pants (senior managers, business managers and other business related users) and developers (designers, analysts, developers) who were specialist and/or subject specific according to development need.

The outsourced developers believed that their IAD approach would promote a controlled, structured but flexible development method aimed at providing incre-mental delivery that they aligned to agile development because it encompassed the common features of agile development i.e. iterative development, Joint Application Development (JAD) workshops, time-boxing, prototyping and intensive user involvement throughout the project duration. Additionally it presented the most appropriate project delivery lifecycle, and thus, was suited to the uncertainty of, and continually changing business requirements. The initial development plan was composed of four key development stages, each of which had a number of phases involving JAD workshops, time-boxed development iterations and intensive user involvement throughout. Essentially the developers envisaged completing the initial development work during stages 1 and 2, and then revising and modifying the system and incorporating new business needs during iterations in stages 3 and 4. In this way the agile 'fit for purpose' principle is applied where core business needs are prioritized and subsequent needs are met through the iterative development cycles rather than trying to deliver 100% of requirements up front.

16.5 Organizational Culture

Literature posits that organizational culture embraces the shared beliefs, perceptions and expectations of individuals in organizations i.e. the shared mental models of particular views and opinions that some refer to as an organization's social capital (Cohen and Prusak 2002; Côté 2001; Hofstede 2003). A social world's behaviour and decision-making are influenced by the characteristics of its members and their inherent experiences, values and knowledge (Mark and Poltrock 2004). Implicit are the organizations' persistent norms and values that influence employee behaviour. It is through the habitual interactions and interrelationships that occur in daily work activities that a sense of shared trust is built up between individuals, it is the lack of such trust that is often considered to be the cause of failure of change initiatives (Boan 2006).

Therefore, it is important to understand the inherent culture of the host organization to appreciate the nature of the difficulties encountered during the development project. The Client Organization is described as bureaucratic where structure is typically hierarchy driven, and business processes are regulated and highly procedural (Hofstede 2003; Wallach 1983). In this context the social capital encompasses both the human capital in terms of individual knowledge, skills and competences, and the cultural norms cultivated over time by the nature of the organization. Thus, protocols were steeped in traditionally structured, hierarchical working practices, which characteristically were not fluid (Mark and Poltrock 2004). It is seen as a control-oriented environment where employees tend to be risk averse because they believe they are operating within a blame culture.

Below we examine how the organizations inherent culture was mismatched with the some of the aspects of agile development. We focus particularly upon the characteristics of stakeholder involvement and team working practices that presented significant difficulty and concern for the development project. Collaboration and co-operative behaviour are pertinent to both characteristics. The details and intricacies of the case study will emerge during the following sections.

16.5.1 Stakeholder Involvement

Both stakeholder involvement and team working practices are closely related as the former is intrinsic in the latter. Thus, it is difficult to extricate them entirely for independent discussion due to the recognized overlap. Additionally, they equally encompass collaboration and co-operative behaviour as integral elements. However in this section we will deal specifically with stakeholder involvement in relation to their availability, commitment and capacity to shift from former working practices and embrace the agile development approach. Then, in the following sections, we extend the discussion around problems experienced with a team working ethos, engendering of a trust environment and decision-making activities.

16.5.2 Stakeholder Availability and Commitment

We have discussed above the view that sustained active user involvement is principle to agile development. Where an IS development has a projected duration then co-ordination of stakeholders and developers from different domains is needed and can be facilitated through co-location (Fischer et al. 1992). Within the case study scenario an assumption was made by the host organization that co-location of the developers and organizational participants was the most effective way to facilitate availability, engender commitment and encourage collaborative interaction between stakeholders. Observations confirm that business stakeholders were indeed present on site, co-located with the developers for the duration of the project. Therefore, in one sense there is evidence that intensive stakeholder involvement was achieved.

However on another level the anticipated commitment to the project and assumed co-operative behaviour associated with co-location was not evidenced. Poltrock and Engelbeck (1999) suggest that co-location can prove to be both impractical and unrealistic because within large and complex projects stakeholders will have multiple responsibilities which by their nature will fluctuate according to the development stages of the project lifecycle. Thus, the necessary high levels of user involvement can be very demanding on business stakeholders. This analysis is, in part, true of the case study. However, although co-location was facilitated business managers were also responsible for their 'business as usual' activities that ran concurrently with project development. Thus levels of availability to the project were jeopardized by the pressure to maintain the day-to-day activities. As a consequence business managers found it difficult to commit fully to the project. The following statement from business manager (11) epitomizes a common view held by the business stakeholders *"To be honest with you I think we should have been taken off our day-to-day work and worked with them full time, on a scheme by scheme basis. We were basically in the situation where we were still doing our day-to-day work processing and developing the old systems and everything and trying to define the requirements ..."*. The organizational routines implicit in the expected daily work responsibilities influenced stakeholder behaviour (Mark and Poltrock 2004). Here it is the first mismatch. It is evident that there was a disparity between the level of availability and commitment of business stakeholders to the IS project that was expected by the organization, and the actual level of availability and commitment that was occasioned due to pressure to sustain routine operations. As we shall see business knowledge belonged to individuals making it difficult to back fill posts when people were allocated to the project.

16.5.3   Embracing Agile Development

This situation was further compounded by a deeper level of mismatch that was observed in the JAD design and development workshops between stakeholders' actual behaviour and the anticipated co-operative behaviour. Such workshops are characteristically used to identify, gather and drill down into the system requirements. Therefore, co-operative collaboration between stakeholders and developers was deemed essential in order for the developers to meet specific time-boxed development iterations linked to agile incremental delivery schedules. It was anticipated that those involved would behave in a collaborative and co-operative manner embracing a common vision of the project goals.

Stakeholders with key business knowledge and experiential know how (tacit knowledge, Nonaka 1991) were required to articulate, negotiate and communicate effectively in JAD workshops to provide the critical business requirements and appropriate feedback in line with agile development practices. However, the traditional working patterns operated on a 'one person, one job' basis. As a consequence knowledge was owned by individuals creating specific skills sets and domain specific knowledge that was not shared or passed on. The corollary of the inherent organizational working culture meant that business managers believed themselves to be accountable for 'their' schemes performance. Hence, they felt responsible for the prevention of fines, penalties (the disallowance of monies already paid out) which is imposed by the EC for non-conformance to regulations and legislation. This sense of accountability drove business managers to maintain individual agendas that were counter to the creation of a collaborative common vision. By prioritizing their individual business goals it can be argued that the actual behaviour and attitudes of key stakeholders was not as anticipated.

Business manager (7) explains '...*the balance* (of scheme X payments) *have to be paid on time...otherwise there are serious repercussions, and disallowance applies*. Business manager (4) confirms '*In the end if we don't get it right then we don't get the money that we are paying out*'. Business manager (7) substantiates this view '*Last year ... we faced disallowance because we didn't make out payments on time. They disallow any payments that go through late, for instance the deadline is the 30ᵗʰ June, we didn't start making our advance payments until ... they were 5–6 months late so any payments we make after the 30ᵗʰ June the EC won't fund so the Department has to foot that*'. In a later interview she explains '*That is one type of disallowance, then we get disallowance for lack of key controls and that can be anything from 2 –5% of the funds, it depends which schemes ... it could be 2% of disallowance across £170m* (£3.4m)'. As a result knowledge sharing was inhibited such that the diffusion of critical business data consequently led to inaccurate requirements, development schedule slippage and project delay. The above quotations illustrate business managers felt under pressure to prioritize timely payments of grants and subsidies which was at odds with the need for collaborative interaction. Their behaviour, embedded within the former organizational protocols and working patterns, impeded the anticipated shift towards a team ethos which we discuss later.

Thus, in agreement with Coughlan and Macredie (2002) the ability of the business stakeholders to engage in a collaborative manner was tempered by the absolute nature of the host organization. This analysis supports their view that a methodology does not necessarily map directly onto an understanding of the organization, its rationality or the context of its users. Even though the understanding was that the agile method adopted was considered suitable to the contingent circumstances of the organization (Fitzgerald 1997; Fitzgerald et al. 2002) there was a cultural mismatch. Contrary to the views that it is the ISD that controls the emergent situation (Fitzgerald 1997; Fitzgerald et al. 2002) for this case study it was the working ethos entrenched in former practices that prevailed.

Literature posits that where a cultural mismatch can be identified, the benefits of the development approach chosen will be either lost or unrealized (Bayer and Highsmith 1994; Highsmith 2000, 2008; Coughlan and Macredie 2002). This is what occurred in the case study project. Although organizational change was achieved through changing the business processes and procedures of the new information system it did not follow that people's individual or group cultures evolved along the same lines and in parallel with those changes. Culture by its very natures evolves; it cannot be changed quickly or achieved overnight.

16.6   Team Working

In this section we focus on problems experienced with creating a team working culture that is a fundamental feature of agile development. We further extend the discussion on difficulties experienced with the stakeholders' collaborative and co-operative behaviour with particular reference to the issues of trust creation and decision-making activities.

The creation of a joint development arena that emphasized a team working culture was an important and fundamental criterion of the IS project. A senior manager explains "...in the first instance it was very much a partnership of our own people and [the outsourced] developers working together as a project team. Secondly ... for us to insist that the developers actually came and worked with us in our building ... at the outset was an important element in trying to generate a real team spirit...". Nevertheless, the move towards creating such an integrated and collaborative team ethos proved challenging within the case study setting.

Literature proposes that a team is not just a group of people, not all groups are teams (Coughlan and Macredie 2002). Consequently there is a considerable difference between a real team and a group of people who merely work together. A 'jelled' team is a group of people so strongly knit that the whole is greater than the sum of its parts. However, as Coughlan and Macredie (2002) point out a team can just as easily degenerate into being less than the sum of its parts. Here we can identify one more mismatch between what was required and indeed, anticipated, and what actually occurred in the case study setting.

Agile development requires that team members work together towards a common goal in order to create a sense of unity, team spirit and identity (Balogun and Hailey 2004) towards a common vision. However, we have already established that business stakeholders did not fully commit to the common vision and continued to work independently. Observations confirm that in most cases team scenarios reflected groups of individuals rather than the integrated, collaborative collectives anticipated by the host organization, that are also necessary for agile development.

As previously discussed, the host organizations' bureaucratic protocols played a significant role in determining the working patterns, behaviour and attitudes of the stakeholders. Traditionally, individualism and individual accountability through the perception of a blame culture are emphasized. Thus, an integrated team working culture is not the normal practice. Consequently, business stakeholders found it difficult to move away from the previous working ethos inhibiting a shift to the 'new' team culture and philosophy. Senior managers considered such adherence to former practices to be a real problem, "That caused a lot of tension ... through *development. They could not align themselves to that thinking* [team working], *they tried to protect, over protect in some instances, their silo mentality*" (senior manager 3). He continued "*People had got used to the silo type systems that they had*"; "*... we've been battling against the culture of the organization ...* (senior manager 3). McConnell (1996) agrees with this analysis and puts forward the view that a lack of trust is a contributory factor, '*One reason that teams usually don't form within bureaucratic organizations is that the organizations are based on lack of trust* (p 290). For this case study the limited engagement in creating a team environment together with the subsequent lack of cohesiveness did not generate the necessary levels of trust required for successful development – we discuss this aspect next.

16.6.1   Trust, Collaboration and Co-operation

The attempts at a team working culture did not generate the trust that binds people together. Indeed, it proved to be counter productive to the expected collaborative project setting which eventually deteriorated into an 'us and them' scenario. In fact the lack of a trusting environment meant that business managers who felt that their 'individual' needs had not been met declined to sign off development work impeding project progress. Evident was the lack of collaboration or co-operative behaviour. Developers commented '*We are trying to get people to sign off ... that's very hard to do here, the Business don't want to sign off something that isn't 100% complete*' (developer 9); '*...they in many cases have said that I can't sign off*' (developer 12). Consequently developers struggled to meet planned deadlines. Business managers responded that they would not be held responsible for deadlines they had not agreed, for example '*I certainly can't be held accountable for deadlines and planned delivery dates that I've never signed up to*' (business manager 4).

   Observation and discussions with the developers and business stakeholders involved revealed that they had differing views as to system scope, and ultimately of the business requirements. The former adhering to the agile characteristic of 'fit for purpose' compared to the business stakeholders requesting development of 100% of their individual needs. Thus, rather than creating an co-operative development milieu, this mismatch of expectations contributed to perceptions of 'us and them' that eventually led to conflict between the business stakeholders and the developers, making interactive collaboration problematic.

   For example "*I think it's a shame that there is very little trust between us* (developers) *and the business managers, we are both at fault but they don't trust us to do our jobs to their satisfaction*" (developer 18). Business managers aware of the situation commented "*It's created a lot of problems, a lot of unease and a lot of distrust now, will we get what we need for our schemes to meet business and EC objectives ... we're very cynical*" (business manager 13). "*We had a lot of difficulties, there was definitely an 'us and them' attitude*" (developer 6); "*There was this divide, it was very 'them and us*" (business manager 5). Hence, business managers became defensive and distrustful of the developers. As a consequence there was no common vision and therefore no team identity, unity or spirit, there was no 'we–ness' and thus, no trust. The creation of a mutually reciprocal working ethos was not achieved.

The perceived lack of cohesion between the business stakeholders and the developers was further exacerbated by a limited unity between the business managers themselves. Observations and interview data confirm that this problem was particularly visible in development meetings where difficulty arose in the prioritizing, and the subsequent scheduling of development work. We present commentary that supports this analysis "*When we started to try and get the Business to really prioritize and they couldn't, they just couldn't ...*" (developer 1); '*I had to promote my business needs so I could do my job*' (business manager 7). Such conduct caused a lot of angst and concern for the developers that led to tension and conflict in development workshops and more generally across the project environment. In scheduled meetings those business managers present believed their own priorities to be paramount and although required to make decisions, did not feel able to do so if they felt it was counter to their own individual agendas. Thus, we move on to discuss the difficulties experienced in decision-making activities in the following section.

16.6.2   Decision-making, Collaboration and Co-operation

Decision-making is closely linked to the issues discussed above, and encapsulates the agile concept of 'fit for purpose' development principle necessary to meet core business needs. Agile development relies heavily on the ability of stakeholders to make empowered decisions in a timely fashion without having to resort to higher management for guidance or control. The JAD workshops necessitated stakeholders reaching consensus on the prioritizing and scheduling of development activities. However for this study effective decision-making proved problematic, and was often not achieved due to former cultural traditions. Historically, the inherent predefined decision-making procedures adhered to the custom of deferring decisions up the management chain where decisions were authorized. Consequently the need for speedy decision-making practices required for agile development was mismatched with the hosts' generic culture. Adherence to former decision-making protocols meant that the intrinsic cultural time-horizons did in practice influence the speed at which decisions could, or could not be made. In decision-making activities business stakeholders declined to make decisions and in some instances actually left meetings leaving situations unresolved.

As a solution key business stakeholders were specifically empowered with decision-making responsibility to facilitate the rapid decisions necessary. However, within the case study environment there is a fine distinction between being authorized and being empowered to do something. Being authorized carries an implied responsibility, an ownership of a decision taken and an expectation of culpability. Whereas, being empowered reflects the ability to make a decision without the expectation of being held responsible if the decision is wrong. Senior management explained that the former adheres to the idea of blame, whilst the latter was designed to remove the blame issue and emphasize a 'learning from mistakes' culture. Senior management understood that an important objective was the implied removal of the blame perception from the empowerment status that accompanied the former authorization status.

However, it seems that the subtle nuances behind this issue were not effectively communicated to those involved. Business managers remained reluctant to take ownership of decisions. Here are just two developers' remarks that support this view '*if decisions were wrong they* (business managers) *would get blamed for it*' (developer 15); "*Individuals, while they might be empowered to make decisions don't feel that they are empowered or feel that it is too much of a risk to make decisions*" (developer 8). Thus, the empowering of key business stakeholders with decision-making status was not successful. Developers reported that in the joint sessions the relevant manages still circumvented decision-making. Their preference was to postpone decisions, defer to line managers and, at times, leave issues unresolved, for example, "*It takes a room full of people to take a decision and then they have another meeting about it*" (developer 22); "*...the people in the room ... didn't feel really, even in reality, that the authority was delegated to them, that they could take decisions and that made it difficult*" (senior developer 4). Such behaviour had a negative impact on the iterative and incremental development cycles that in turn, reduced the ability of developers to meet time-boxed deadlines in line with development schedules effecting project delay. Empowerment is not enough, there has to be a willingness to make important critical business decisions.

This view is acknowledged in the literature, Morgan evaluates, as proved to be the case here, that empowered decision-making is inhibited by hierarchical cultures. He states, '*the limits of 'empowerment' are usually quickly felt as people run into the constraints imposed by the existing hierarchy*' (Morgan 1997: 169). Empowerment focuses on people rather than the process. The emphasis is on who makes the decision rather than the input into the decision to make the correct decision and avoid blame. The host organizations' basic culture was contrary to such collaborative behaviour as was evidenced in problems experienced when attempting to create a team working culture. Thus, further evidence of a cultural mismatch.

16.7 Conclusions

In this chapter we have examined the agile development approach utilized for the case study scenario and identified a number of mismatches between what was anticipated and what was actually occasioned in practice. From a theoretical standpoint the literature reviewed maintains that developers rarely adopt methods in their entirety in practice (Fitzgerald et al. 2002; Madsen et al. 2006); that an organizations social capital can negatively influence stakeholder behaviour (Mark and Poltrock 2004); and that collaborative stakeholder involvement is key to system development success (Beynon-Davies 1998; Highsmith 2008; Luna-Reyes et al. 2005; Santosa et al. 2005).

Table 16.1 Agile characteristics mismatched to the host's organizational culture

Agile characteristics	Cultural mismatch	Impact	Literature
Stake holder involvement	– Traditional working patterns	– Availability compromised	Fitzgerald (1997)
	– Need to maintain daily tasks	– Reduced commitment	Fitzgerald et al. (2002) Mark and Poltrock (2004)
	– Former hierarichal mindsets	– Lack of common vision	McConnell(1996)
Team working ethos	– Traditional working patterns	– Limited jointed collaboration	Balogun and hailey (2004)
	– Former ownership of business knowledge	– Little active co-operation	Coughlan and Macredie (2002) Highsmith (2008)
	– Perceived individual accountablity	– No creation of team spirit	Luna-Reyes et al. (2005)
		– Lack of trust generated conflict	Santosa et al. (2005)
Timely decision making	– Traditional working patterns	– Postponement of decisions	Beynon-Davies (1998) Mark and Poltrock (2004)
	– Former deferral to line management	– Conflict and mistrust	Morgan (1997)
	– Perceived blame culture	– Missed deadlines	
		– Delayed delivery	

From an implementation perspective we can conclude that a number of agile characteristics were put into practice by the developers who utilized an incremental project lifecycle involving iterative development using JAD workshops, and also by the host organization through the creation of a joint development arena, i.e. co-location, and intensive involvement of business stakeholders.

However there is clear evidence that the inherent culture of the host organization was mismatched with the some of the other agile characteristics. Indeed, in agreement with Fitzgerald et al. (2002); Madsen et al. (2006) we can say that for this case study that although a number of the agile characteristics were in place that the agile approach was not embraced entirely. The agile characteristics of a joint team culture composed of collaborative working practices, reciprocal trust and co-operation and consensus in decision-making were not achieved. The facilitating mechanism of the joint development arena did not of itself ensure a successful transition to an active engagement by stakeholders of a joint team culture. The social capital of the organization embedded in stakeholders' attitudes and behaviour borne from former working practices negatively influenced the practice of agile development (Mark and Poltrock 2004). Key stakeholders did not buy into a common vision and thus, did not form a collective towards achieving the common goal. Table 16.1 above sets out the areas of mismatch of the agile approach adopted to the host's organizational culture.

From Table 16.1 we can further conclude that where strong organizational cultures are dominant and where cultural control outweighs change management a methodology does not necessarily map directly onto the understanding of the organization, its rationality or the context of its users (Coughlan and Macredie 2002). Thus, for this case study where a clear business vision was established the organization of project work around the perception of a 'common' vision was not successful. It was the working ethos entrenched in former practices which prevailed that controlled the emergent situation in this case study rather than the ISD. Although this to some extent challenges Fitzgerald (1997) and Fitzgerald et al. (2002), they also emphasize that formalised methods are a guide and not a prescriptive base, that it is necessary to address the contingent circumstances of the organization and the developing system in situ, and that the current development methodologies may not suit the increasingly complex natures of development situations.

Thus, findings suggest that two key lessons emerged from the case study. First, although the literature states that active user involvement is key, as evidenced in the case study, we can say that in practice it does not of itself guarantee successful outcomes in IS development projects. Secondly, although a decision was made to adopt agile practices, assumptions made by senior management that stakeholder attitudes and behaviour would follow suit proved wrong – in practice there is no guarantee that this will happen.

References

Agile-Alliance (2001). Manifesto for Agile Software Development. http://www.agilealliance.org/. Accessed 25 January 2007.

Alvesson, M. (2003). "Beyond Neopositivists, romantics, and localists: A reflexive approach to interviews in organizational research," *Academy of Management Review* 28(1), 13–33.

Alvesson, M., & Deetz, S. (2000). *Doing Critical Management Research*. London, UK: Sage Publications.

Avison D.E., Wood-Harper, A.T., Vidgen, R.T., & Wood J.R.G. (1998). A further exploration into information systems development: The evolution of Multiview2. *Information Technology & People*, 11(2), 124–139.

Avison, D. E., & Fitzgerald, G. (2006). *Information systems development: methodologies, techniques and tools*. 4th Edn. London, UK: McGraw-Hill.

Balogun, J., & Hailey, V.H. (2004). *Exploring strategic change*, 2nd edn. Herefordshire, UK: Prentice Hall.

Bayer, S., & Highsmith, J. (1994). RADical Software Development, *American Programmer Magazine*, 6.

Beynon-Davies, P. (1998). Rapid Applications Development (RAD). Briefing Paper. *Kane Thompson Centre*, University of Glamorgan.

Beynon-Davies, P. (2002) *Information Systems An introduction to Informatics in Organisations*. *Hants*: Palgrave.

Beynon-Davies, P. & Williams, M.D. (2003). The diffusion of information systems development methods. *Journal of Strategic Information Systems*, 12, 29–46.

Boan, D.M. (2006). Cognitive-behaviour modification and organizational culture. *Consulting Psychology Journal: Practice and Research*, 58(1), 51–61.

Boehm, B. (2002). Get ready for Agile methods with care. IEEE. doi: 0018-9162/02.

Carmel, E., Whitaker R.D., & George, J.F. (1993). PD and Joint Application Design: a transatlantic comparison. *Communications of the ACM.* 36(4), 40–48.

Chaffey, D., & Wood, S. (2005). *Business information management – improving performance using information systems,* Harlow, UK: Prentice Hall.

Cohen, D., & Prusak, L. (2002). *In good company: how social capital makes organizations work.* Boston, MA: Harvard Business School Press.

Cockburn, A. (2002). *Agile software development.* Boston, USA: Addison Wesley.

Côté, S. The Contribution of Human and Social Capital, (2001). *ISUMA – Canadian Journal of Policy Research,* 2(1), 29–36.

Coughlan, J., & Macredie, R. D. (2002). Effective communications in requirements elicitation: a comparison of methodologies. *Requirements Engineering,* 7(2), 47–60.

DSDM Consortium (2004). Dynamic systems development method. http://www.dsdm.org/version4/2/public/ Accessed 25 April 2005.

Fischer, G., Grudin, J., & Lemke, A. (1992). Supporting indirect collaborative design with integrated knowledge-based design environments. *Human–Computer Interaction,* 7, 281–314.

Fitzgerald, B. (1997). An empirical investigation into the adoption of systems development methodologies . *Information & Management,* 34, 317–328.

Fitzgerald, B., Russo, N.L., & Stolterman, E. (2002). Information Systems Development: Methods in Action. London: McGraw Hill.

Gill, J., & Johnson, P. (1991). *Research Methods for Managers.* London: Paul Chapman Publishing Ltd.

Glaser, B.G., & Strauss, A. (1967). *The discovery of grounded theory: Strategies for qualitative research.* Chicago, USA: Aldine.

Grudin, J. (1991). CSCW Introduction. *Communications of the ACM,* 34(12), 30–34.

Henderson-Sellers, B., Hawryszkiewycz, I. (2008). Comparing collaborative and process semantics for cooperative information systems. *International Journal of Cooperative Information Systems,* 17(2), 155–76.

Hevner, A.R. March, S.T., Park, J., & Ram, S. (2004). Design science in information systems research. *MIS Quarterly,* 28(1), 75–105.

Highsmith, J. (2000). *Retiring Lifecycles Dinosaurs, Software Testing & Quality Engineering,* July/August, 22–28.

Highsmith, J. (2008). *Agile software development ecosystems.* London, UK: Addison Wesley.

Hofstede, G. (2003). *Cultures and organisations – software of the mind.* London, UK: Profile Books Ltd.

Jacobsen, I. Booch, G., & Rumbaugh, J. (1999). *The unified software development process.* Reading, MA: Addison-Wesley.

Kelle, U. (1998) *Computer-aided qualitative data analysis.* London, UK: Sage.

Kirova, K., Kirby, N., Kothari, D., & Childress, G. (2008). Effective requirements traceability: models, tools and practices. *Bell Labs Technical Journal,* 12(4), 143–158.

Luna-Reyes, L. F., Zhang, J., Gil-Garcia, J. R., & Cresswell, A.M. (2005). Information systems development as emergent socio-technical change: a practice approach. *European Journal of Information Systems,* 14, 93–105.

Lyytinen, K., & Hirschheim, R. (1987). Information systems failures: a survey and classification of empirical literature. *Oxford Surveys in Information Technology,* 4, 257–309.

Madsen, S., Kautz, K., & Vidgen, R. (2006). A framework for understanding how a unique and local IS development method emerges in practice. *European Journal of Information Systems,* 15, 225–238.

Mark, G., & Poltrock, S. (2004). Groupware adoption in a distributed organization: transporting and transforming technology through social worlds. *Information and Organization,* 14(4), 297–327.

Mathiassen, L. (1997). Reflective systems development. *Aalborg University,* Denmark.

McConnell, S. (1996). *Rapid development – taming wild software schedules.* Washington, DC: Microsoft Press.

Morgan, G. (1997). *Imaginization: New mindsets for seeing, organizing and managing*. San Francisco, USA: Berrett-Koehler.

Myers, M.D. (1999). Investigating Information Systems with Ethnographic Research, *Communications of the AIS*, 2(23), 1–20.

Nonaka, I. (1991). The knowledge-creating company, *Harvard Business Review*, 69, 96–104.

Orlikowski, W.J., & Baroudi, J.J. (1991). Studying Information Technology in Organisations. *The Institute of Management Sciences*, 2, 1–28.

Peffers, K. Tuunanen, T. Rothenberger, M.A., & Chatterjee, S. (2007). A design science research methodology for information systems research. *Journal of Management Information Systems*, 24(3), 45–77.

Pekkola, S., Kaarilahti. N., & Pohjola, P. (2006). Towards formalised end-user participation in IS development process: bridging the gap between participatory design and ISD methodologies. *Proceedings of Participatory Design Conference*, ACM Press, 21–30.

Poltrock, S.E., & Engelbeck, G. (1999). Requirements for a virtual collocation environment. *Information and Software Technology*, 41, 331–339.

Santosa, P. I., Wei K. K., & Chan H. C. (2005). User involvement and user satisfaction with information-seeking activity. *European Journal of Information Systems*, 14, 361–370.

Schwaber, K., & Beedle, M. (2002). *Agile software development with SCRUM*. Hemel Hempstead, UK: Prentice Hall.

Silverman, D. (2005). *Doing Qualitative Research*. London, UK: Sage Publications.

Strauss, A., & Corbin, J, (1990). *Basics of Qualitative Research – Grounded Theory, Procedures and Techniques*. London, UK: Sage Publications.

Truex, D., Baskerville, R., & Travis, J. (2000). Amethodical systems development: the deferred meaning of systems development methods. *Accounting Management & Information Technologies*, 10(1), 53–79.

Wallach, E. (1983). Individuals and organisations: the cultural match. *Training and Development Journal*, February, 29–36.

Walsham, G. (1997). *Interpreting Information Systems in Organisations*. NY: Wiley.

Willcocks, L., & Mason, D. (1987). *Computerised work: people, systems design and workplace relations*. London, UK: Paradigm Publishing.

Yin, R. (2009). *Case Study Research: Design and Methods*. 4th edn. CA: Sage Publications.

Chapter 17
Epilogue

Samuli Pekkola and Hannakaisa Isomäki

17.1   From Pluralism To?

In this book we have portrayed several perspectives on humans in information systems development. Although we have aimed at providing as comprehensive understanding as possible, these perspectives are only some small glimpses and examples on the topic. Consequently, these papers can be seen to reflect the dispersed but interdisciplinary HCI communities as identified by Grudin (2006). His communities on human computer interaction, namely human factors and ergonomics (cognitive psychology perspective), HCI in management information systems (managerial, technology acceptance perspective), and computer–human interaction (social psychology perspective), provide historically justified view to the topic. This view can still be identified in the articles of this book.

Table 17.1 illustrates our interpretation of the articles and of their historical scientific communities according to Grudin's classification. Human factors refer to papers having strong roots on cognitive psychology. From those the paper by Huang and Bias is the most obvious example. The second viewpoint HCI in MIS focuses on the "managerial view of individual behaviour" (Grudin 2006). Correspondingly the focus is not on humans as social or cognitive actors but as workers that try to accomplish certain tasks. Under the circumstances technology acceptance model is often seen dominant (Venkatesh and Davis 1989). CHI (computer–human interaction), origins itself from social psychology and sociology. While human factors papers try to understand the user as a cognitive actor, CHI pays more attention to the social settings where the use of technology takes place. Consequently these perspectives mirror, historically, different schools in psychology (c.f. Sampson 1981).

S. Pekkola (✉)
Department of Business Information Management and Logistics,
Tampere University of Technology, Finland
e-mail: samuli.pekkola@tut.fi

H. Isomäki
Department of Mathematical Information Technology, University of Jyväskylä, Finland
e-mail: hannakaisa.isomaki@jyu.fi

H. Isomäki and S. Pekkola (eds.), *Reframing Humans in Information*   283
Systems Development, Computer Supported Cooperative Work 201,
DOI 10.1007/978-1-84996-347-3_17, © Springer-Verlag London Limited 2011

Table 17.1 The articles and their division according to Grudin's (2006) framework

Article	Human factors	HCI in MIS	CHI
On the emergence of techno-religious spaces (El-Sayed et al.)			×
Towards lifeworld-oriented information systems development (Basden)		×	
A power perspective for understanding the business client – systems developer relationship (Rowlands)		×	
A semiotic analysis of interactions between end users and information systems (Huang and Bias)	×		
Information systems development as an intellectual process: Designers' perceptions of users (Isomäki)		×	
Participatory design in information systems development (Bødker et al.)			×
Reflecting, tinkering and tailoring: Implications for theories of information systems design (Hovorka and Germonprez)		×	
Evolutionary application development: Tools to make tools and boundary crossing (Mørch)			×
Design science research for user-centeredness (Iivari and Iivari)		×	
"20 years a-Growing": Revisiting from human factors to human actors (Bannon)			×
Three levels of failure: Analysing a workflow management system (Gross and Pekkola)			×
When and how do we become a "user"? (Lindblad-Gidlund)		×	
Use of mobile IS: new requirements for the IS development process (Andersson and Henningsson)	×		
Reframing online shopping through innovative and organic user-oriented design (Greenhill and Fletcher)			×
User involvement and team working in system development practice (Berger)			×

As seen, the articles published in this book reflect to some extent Grudin's historical classification. The articles have studied human-centered ISD from different viewpoints, often achieving different conclusions and making dissimilar suggestions how to solve the problem. However, sometimes this "problem" is not conceptualized, phrased, focused, studied or reported in a commonly agreed way. For example, in this book two commentary articles; the one by Iivari and Iivari and the other by

Bannon comment, criticize, crystallize, and develop three previous articles from their own viewpoints, roots. Iivari and Iivari are very critical and make concrete suggestions for improvements. Bannon adapts different viewpoints and warmly welcomes such scientific pluralism. From our point of view, both commentaries are arguably correct – within their own communities, from their own perspectives.

Instead of trying to encapsulate humans in information systems development into a statement, we argue that such unity cannot be gained. The roots of humans as technology users, and this statement already demonstrates one historical perspective, form our foundations for the future. However, we should not stay only on those premises but try to develop our understanding of the user with respect to the diversity of authentic human qualities emerging holistically as the features of a cognitive and social actor using the technology for certain purposes. This view cannot be dissected.

17.2 The Future of Human-Centered ISD

However, the situation with separated communities is not as straightforward as it seems. Despite there are several communities with different theoretical basis, questions of interest, and publication outlets, nowadays there is a tendency to move towards a unified understanding about the user as a comprehensive human being. This book is one such example. These articles have offered new views that challenge and develop traditional small-minded notions of human-centered ISD – as requested by Iivari and Iivari (2010) and Isomäki and Pekkola (2005). Under the circumstances, we will quote Liam Bannon from his article earlier in this book.

> The emerging paradigm of creative collaboration and innovation that we see in, for example, Web 2.0 and social media, requires us to re-think our conceptual frameworks concerning IT design, development and use. Foremost in this re-framing must be the (re-)emergence of human and social actors. The articles in this book are a modest beginning towards this re-conceptualization and it is time for the broader information systems community to engage with these exciting developments.

We hope this book has helped you in this endeavour.

References

Bannon, L. 2010. "20 years a-Growing": Revisiting From Human Factors to Human Actors. In *this book*, chapter 11.

Grudin, J. 2006. Human factors, CHI, and MIS. In P. Zhang & D. Galletta (eds). *Human-computer interaction and management information systems: foundations*. M.E.Sharpe. pp. 402–421.

Iivari, J. & Iivari, N. 2010. Varieties of User-Centeredness: An Analysis of Four Systems Development Methods. To appear in *Information Systems Journal*.

Isomäki, H. & Pekkola. S. 2005. Nuances of Human-Centredness in Information Systems Development. *Hawaii International Conference on Systen Sciences HICSS-38*. Big Island, Hawaii: IEEE Press.

Sampson, E. E. 1981. Cognitive psychology as ideology. *American Psychologist*. Vol 36(7), Jul 1981, 730–743.

Venkatesh, V. & Davis, F.D. 2000. A Theoretical Extension of the Technology Acceptance Model: Four Longitudinal Field Studies, *Management Science*, Vol. 46, No. 2 (Feb., 2000), pp. 186–204.

Index